# Yogi

## The LIFE
## &
## TIMES
### of an
## AMERICAN
## ORIGINAL

Carlo DeVito

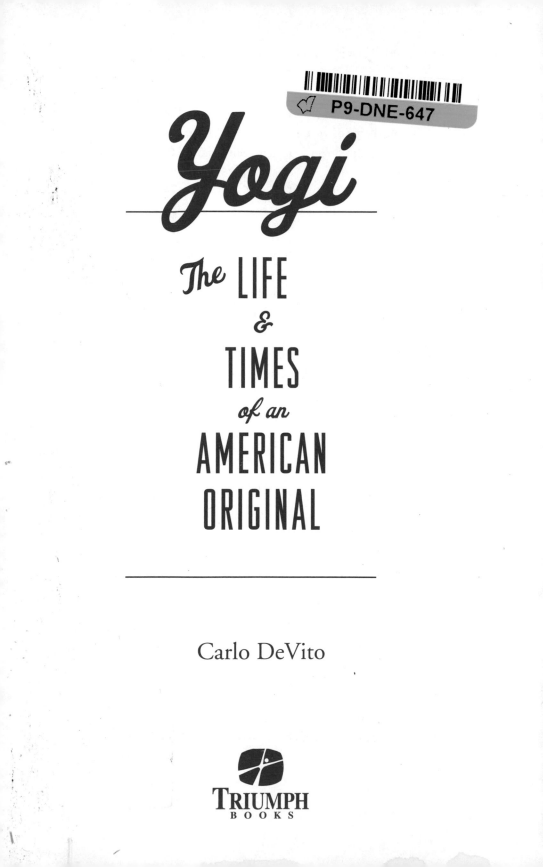

## TRIUMPH
### BOOKS

Library of Congress has catalogued the previous edition as follows:

DeVito, Carlo
    Yogi : the life and times of an American original / Carlo DeVito.
        p. cm.
    Includes bibliographical references and index.
    ISBN-13: 978-1-57243-945-0
    ISBN-10: 1-57243-945-9
    1. Berra, Yogi, 1925–  2. Baseball players—United States—Biography.
3. Baseball coaches—United States—Biography.   I. Title.
    GV865.B46D48 2008
    796.357092—dc22
    [B]

                                                    2007040526

This book is available in quantity at special discounts for your group or organization. For further information, contact:

**Triumph Books LLC**
814 North Franklin Street
Chicago, Illinois 60610
(312) 337-0747
www.triumphbooks.com

Printed in U.S.A.
ISBN: 978-1-57243-966-3
Design by Patricia Frey
All photos courtesy of Getty Images unless otherwise indicated.

*This book is dedicated to
Dawson Cordell DeVito, the All-Star catcher in our family, and to
Dylan Charles DeVito, the All-Star pitcher in our family, and to
Eugene T. Venanzi II, my brother and a huge sports aficionado.*

# CONTENTS

Preface     vii

Acknowledgments     ix

Introduction     xi

**Chapter 1:** Life on the Hill     1

**Chapter 2:** Becoming Yogi Berra     19

**Chapter 3:** Berra's Big Break     29

**Chapter 4:** In the Navy Now     39

**Chapter 5:** Newark     53

**Chapter 6:** The Yankees     65

**Chapter 7:** Love Finds Yogi Berra     83

**Chapter 8:** Becoming a Winner     89

**Chapter 9:** A Life in Baseball     101

**Chapter 10:** The Business of Baseball     125

**Chapter 11:** A New Dynasty     141

**Chapter 12:** Mr. Yoo-Hoo      169

**Chapter 13:** The Golden Age of Baseball      175

**Chapter 14:** The Heart of the Yankees      199

**Chapter 15:** The End of an Era      215

**Chapter 16:** Managing Mr. Stengel's Team      227

**Chapter 17:** The New York Metropolitans      257

**Chapter 18:** Living in the Bronx Zoo      297

**Chapter 19:** Managing Mr. Steinbrenner's Yankees      309

**Chapter 20:** Yogi Berra, Incorporated      323

**Chapter 21:** The Legacy of Yogi Berra      331

**Afterword**      349

**Sources**      355

**Index**      403

# PREFACE

Yogi Berra is one of the most famous players in the history of Major League Baseball. He has written several different versions of his own life, and there have been numerous unauthorized versions of his life. He has appeared in several hundred books as a character in someone else's story. And he is quoted as often as Sir Winston Churchill, the great British statesman, and Mark Twain.

Over the years he has often been misquoted, and stories apocryphally have been ascribed to him that never really occurred. He even wrote a book about it himself titled *The Yogi Book: "I Really Didn't Say Everything I Said,"* in an effort to set the record straight.

Regardless of his efforts, there are many instances where quotes attributed to him are told in different settings, with different people, or with different words. Some are the work of overzealous sportswriters and historians, and Berra himself has told the same stories differently over the years.

Sifting through more than 4,000 newspaper articles, magazines, interviews, books, and programs, I have tried my best to get to the real story. In certain instances, I have called out the most egregious errors. In other instances, I told the story based on the best research available.

I have done so to the best of my abilities.

# ACKNOWLEDGMENTS

The author must acknowledge and commend Ken Samelson, who offered up my name to Triumph some time ago. I thank him for his advice on this book, his researching assistance, and his diligent fact-checking. Without Ken, this book would not have happened, and I am grateful for his friendship and advice.

Any author of such an effort owes a great debt of gratitude to those who went before him. Several writers' works have proved invaluable, including Peter Golenbock's, Roger Kahn's, and Maury Allen's many works; David Halberstam's *Summer of '49* and *October 1964;* Jim Bouton's *Ball Four;* Robert Creamer's *Stengel;* Leigh Montville's *Ted Williams;* Richard Ben Cramer's *Joe DiMaggio;* Joseph R. Carrieri's two books, most recently *Searching for Heroes;* and of course the memoirs of Mickey Mantle, Whitey Ford, Don Larsen, Phil Rizzuto, Billy Martin, and many other teammates of Yogi's from throughout the years.

Also to be thanked are the numerous biographers who have gone before me, including Dave Kaplan, Edward Fitzgerald, Tom Horton, Phil Pepe, Bob Klapisch, and Gene Schoor, as well as playwright Tom Lysaght's *Nobody Don't Like Yogi.*

Of course, I poured over more than 4,000 original sources, including some 1,000 interviews with players, umpires, managers, and other assorted folks. I also examined newspaper and magazine articles from Berra's youth all the way to the present. It is hard to imagine writing this work without the dedicated and hard-working beat writers who covered the team over the years, including Arthur Daley, Joe Trimble, Red Smith, Phil Pepe, Dick Young,

John Drebinger, Leonard Koppett, Dave Anderson, Robert Lipsyte, Mike Lupica, and many others. Without their dedicated coverage and investigative reporting, the book could not have been written. My apologies to anyone whose name was inadvertently left off this list—you can probably be found in the notes at the end of this book.

As ever, I owe a debt of special thanks in all of my professional endeavors to Gilbert King for his ear, opinions, advice, general good cheer, and encouragement.

I would, of course, like to thank Tom Bast and Mitch Rogatz of Triumph Books, who helped make this book a reality. Were it not for their excitement and enthusiasm, I might have given up under the weight of this massive project. I also owe a huge debt of gratitude to editors Kelley White and Adam Motin who helped mold a rather large manuscript into readable shape.

I would also like to thank my agent and friend Edward Claflin of Edward B. Claflin Literary Agency. I thank him for his encouragement and assistance, and for his belief in me.

I would like to thank my sons, Dylan and Dawson, whom I have taken too much time away from in order to pursue not only this work, but also my other professional aspirations. I have attended almost every game of their Little League careers, but there is no replacement for a catch or an ice-cream cone, many of which were robbed by my other pursuits. I vow to them to spend more time playing and less time working.

And lastly I would like to thank my wife, Dominique, who has suffered this project and my other pursuits with a smile in the worst of moments. She is an incredible life partner—friend, confidant, counselor, confessor, secretary, and manager of our homes and lives. My successes in business, as well as in parenthood, are a direct result of her effort, love, understanding, and immense patience. She makes my failures and disappointments seem inconsequential. I thank her, as usual, most of all.

# Introduction

Recently, in New York City, two new baseball stadiums were erected and completed. One is situated in the Bronx, the other in Queens. Both are near the location of their predecessors. If you are lucky enough to live in the New York metropolitan area, there is a fitting tribute to Yogi Berra in each. They are as subtle as they are unmistakable. If you go to the new Yankee Stadium, there is a giant version of the famous picture of Berra hugging Don Larsen after the fireballer completed a perfect game in the World Series. It is one of the most iconic photos in baseball history. Now of course, if you are a baseball fan, you will also make your way over to Citi Field, the new home of the New York Mets. There, in a photo just as huge and just as famous, is the photo of Jackie Robinson stealing home on none other than the same Yogi Berra.

That Yogi Berra is featured at both ballparks may seem odd to fans today, but both franchises lay claim to the small, muscled ex-catcher. Berra played his entire career with the New York Yankees, save a few at-bats with the New York Mets. He went to 14 World Series with the Yankees during the course of his life, but he also led the Mets to their 1973 World Series appearance. In fact, he spent seven years within the Mets franchise and was one of its most popular personalities. He has been a featured old-timer in both ballparks.

"I've done it before," Berra told the press, on the day of the opening of the Stadium. He had thrown out the first pitch in a Yankees home opener seven times. "I hope I can get it there. Let's see what happens."

Berra bounced his pitch to Jose Molina on April 19, 2009. The crowd cheered anyway.

"I think they've got too much room in the clubhouse," Berra said. "It's an awfully big locker room. To me, if you want to talk to a guy, you've got to walk a half a mile."

Yogi Berra has been a fixture, a fact of life, in New York baseball since 1947. For more than 66 of his 88 years, he has been a much loved, iconic figure in a city that can be notoriously impatient as it can be harsh. They booed Joe DiMaggio—they could boo anyone. But Yogi Berra...not so much.

That is Yogi Berra. Not bad for a kid from St. Louis.

Of course, before he got to New York, he had to go to France. At the age of 18, Berra enlisted in the United States Navy, and D-day found the young baseball hopeful launching rockets at the Germans on the beaches of Normandy.

"I think his military service has been a little overlooked, because the men like him really didn't talk about it much," said Carmen Berra, Yogi's wife of 64 years. "He never talked about it. It wasn't a big thing to him, or to men like him. It was just what they had to do."

In the fall of 2013, Berra's service was recognized when he won the Bob Feller Act of Valor Award. "Feller...was a star pitcher for the Cleveland Indians. The day after Pearl Harbor, he walked away from a $100,000 contract to join the Navy and served aboard the USS *Alabama* as a gunner," reported Mark Di Ionno in the Newark-based *Star-Ledger*. After once being asked what the biggest win of his life was, Feller had reportedly answered, without hesitation, World War II.

"He didn't like me," Berra said. "One day I asked why."

"I don't respect people who didn't serve their country," Feller retorted.

"What are you talking about? I was at D-day," said Berra emphatically. "After that, we became best friends."

Indeed, Berra was on the front lines of D-day, sitting in a small 36-foot boat firing rockets and machine guns at German strong points.

When asked if he was scared, Berra replied, "I didn't even think about death. I figured if you got hit with a bullet, you wouldn't know it. So I just did what I was supposed to do...It was like the 4th of July out there. You couldn't stick your head up or it would get blown off."

How ironic, that more than 66 years later, his service record would be the thing being celebrated. But that is quintessential Berra.

\*    \*    \*

If you were born in 1965 or after, you never saw Berra pick up a baseball bat, outside of hitting a few grounders as a coach. You never saw how deadly he was with a bat in his hands. You didn't see him when he was among the most feared hitters in all of Major League Baseball. You didn't watch pitchers and managers wince when he came to the plate, knowing he was the best hitter in baseball with men on in the last three innings of a game. But they did wince.

"Mickey Mantle's a tough hitter," the famed Jackie Robinson once told Dave Anderson of *The New York Times*, "but that Yogi Berra is the guy that frightens me. You just can't pitch to him."

You never saw him argue with an umpire in his prime. You did not see him throw dirt on opposing batters' shoes while waiting for the next pitch. You did not see him gun down runners. You did not see him argue violently with Casey Stengel or handle some of the most ferocious pitchers of his era.

If you were born in 1965 or after, you know Berra as a cuddly, lovable, famous New York Yankee. He is as much a part of New York as dirty-water dogs and cheesecake. He is a punch line, a veritable fount of humor and wisdom. He is a folk hero. He is a pitchman featured with a duck for Aflac insurance, along with numerous other products. He is a funny old-timer.

In the late 1990s he was packaged as a comic figure, a towering colossus of malapropisms. Berra is now known mainly for twisting the English language and for his sage wisdom.

He is the man who signed his 20th wedding anniversary card, "Love, Yogi Berra," and he is the source of such classic lines as:

- "Nobody goes there anymore; it's too crowded!"
- "It ain't over till it's over."
- "Always go to other people's funerals; otherwise they won't come to yours."
- "Baseball is 90 percent mental, and the other half is physical."

- "How can you think and hit at the same time?"
- "I wish I had an answer to that because I'm tired of answering that question."
- "If people don't want to come out to the ballpark, nobody's gonna stop 'em."
- "When you come to a fork in the road, take it."

And many others.

Berra is a prisoner of his own fame, and his legacy is a victim of it as well.

"Lawdie Berra grew up to be a legend," Joe Garagiola wrote in his *New York Times* best-selling book *It's Anybody's Ballgame.* "And like most legends, he doesn't really exist. It's as if there are two Yogis, the one I have known all my life and, as Yogi himself once said, 'the one you read about in the papers who's a kind of comic-strip character like Li'l Abner or Joe Palooka.'"

If anyone should know, it's Garagiola. In fact, it was Garagiola who helped to create, embellish, and spread the legend of Yogi. Garagiola made a nightclub act out of stories about the famed Yankees catcher. He singlehandedly turned Berra into a punch line. But Garagiola also knew the truth—Lawrence Peter "Yogi" Berra was one of the most talented athletes ever to come out of St. Louis.

So who is the real Yogi Berra? By all accounts, he is not a comedian. He can repeat some of his funniest lines, but he is not a wise-cracking, stand-up comic. That's Garagiola.

"He never talked much, and he wasn't a slapstick kind of guy," said Mickey Mantle. "He said maybe a third of what he has been quoted as saying. Garagiola made up a third, and the writers made up the rest."

Most people who meet Berra and expect such are inevitably disappointed. Mantle once related a conversation he had with Berra about those interactions, asking what happened when he didn't start firing off a barrage of one-liners and jokes at them.

"They act surprised," responded Berra.

"Then what do you do?"

"I tell them to ask me questions. But the funny thing is, sometimes I just stand there and they start laughing."

But many fans are pleased to find out that Berra has not lost his humanity for all his fame and accomplishments. One of the best descriptions ever written about Berra is by Robert Lipsyte, who wrote in 1963, "First of all, the myth is loveable because people can never hate a man they can laugh at and admire for his skill but at the same time feel a certain superiority to. Ted Williams and Joe DiMaggio and Stan Musial were respected but never attained Berra's lovability quotient because they were above the masses.

"Yogi is not a loveable teddy bear: he is slow to respond because he is relatively inarticulate, filled with the innate suspicion of the slum kid, prone to sudden bits of crudeness when he thinks he's being put on the spot or conned.

"'How the * * * * should I know?' he will answer to a harmless question from a stranger. With a man he trusts, he will sit down and explain his answers."

"Those who liked Yogi considered him funny and loveable; those who didn't called him inarticulate and dumb, unsociable and selfish," wrote Leonard Koppett a decade later. "In reality he is not a humorist.... However, his speech and some shyness often conceal excellent judgment and a knowledge of players and game situations."

"Ballplayers must be split personalities because what I read about them and what I personally know about them are two different things," Carmen once said.

"What a rare man is this person named Lawrence Peter Berra. What a gem this guy called Yogi. What a treasure.... I have never known another like him. He is unique," wrote Phil Pepe of the *New York Daily News.*

But legendary baseball owner Bill Veeck had a different point of view. Veeck said, "Yogi is a completely manufactured product. He is a case study of this country's unlimited ability to gull itself and be gulled.... You say 'Yogi' at a banquet, and everybody automatically laughs, something that Joe Garagiola discovered to his profit many years ago."

"It's the part of the legend that always disappoints a lot of people," Garagiola wrote in *It's Anybody's Ballgame.* "They think they are going to meet Henny Youngman, and when [Yogi] doesn't rattle off one-liners, they resent him for holding back."

Garagiola also confronted the question of intelligence, asserting, "Yogi is plenty bright when he needs to be." Garagiola tells the story of how Yogi failed math throughout grade school, but play gin rummy with him or talk about money, and you've never seen anyone add any faster.

What is ultimately clear when confronted by the facts of his life is that not only is Berra one of baseball's greatest characters, but he is genuinely one of the greatest players ever to pick up a bat and ball as well. And no matter how humorous his remarks are, his accomplishments were hard-earned and fairly won.

Berra was among the fiercest and most consistent competitors of his era. He was an excellent fielder and a stupendous hitter. He is one of the greatest catchers in the entire history of baseball. And he is one of the most successful baseball men in the history of the game as well.

As a ballplayer, coach, and manager, Berra is unrivaled. The Hall of Fame inductee won three MVP awards, participated in 21 World Series (14 as a player, two as a manager, and five as a coach), and was on 13 World Series–winning teams (including during his coaching days). That's more than John McGraw, Connie Mack, Stengel, Babe Ruth, DiMaggio, or Mantle. He is one of only seven men to manage one team from each league to the World Series.

His has simply been one of the greatest careers in the history of baseball. He was the link between DiMaggio and Mantle. He was no weak link, either. He was among those who led those teams in the 1950s. Mantle and Whitey Ford have both attested to it.

As a catcher, he is in the company of Bill Dickey, Johnny Bench, and Mike Piazza—among the greats. Maybe he is foremost. His accomplishments as a manager place him near Tony La Russa, Sparky Anderson, and Miller Huggins. And his involvement in world championship play is unparalleled.

During his years as a player, Berra was a well-liked clubhouse friend and manager. He was open, honest, and funny. But on the field, Berra was a completely different person. He played up his humorous antics to distract batters from hitting and was one of the smartest catchers in baseball. Berra was ruthless between the lines, employing any trick or mind game available to get hitters out. In the batter's box, he showed incredible concentration, and in an era of greats—including Tommy Henrich, Mantle, and Roger Maris—Berra was considered the best clutch hitter during the great dynasty of Yankees championship teams between 1947 and the late 1950s.

\*    \*    \*

Lawrence Peter Berra grew up in a tough neighborhood in a gritty section of St. Louis called the Hill. There he played baseball in ballfields studded with rocks and broken glass, where other kids laughed at and made fun of his unusual appearance. But they stopped laughing when they saw him play sports. In fact, baseball was not the sport he was best known for—he was considered one of the best soccer players in St. Louis. From the rough-and-tumble streets, Berra made his way into minor league baseball, where he was ridiculed again for his unathletic looks and toothy grin. But despite remarks that he didn't even look like a ballplayer, he forced others to take notice by plying his trade obsessively. Eventually, Berra broke into the majors, where he was ridiculed yet again—until his play silenced each critic once and for all. But those experiences would always be a chip on his shoulder. They would be the driving force of his career—to prove the naysayers wrong, to prove he belonged. He was a fierce, dedicated, tough, and relentless competitor.

The tale of Yogi's life includes such baseball legends as DiMaggio, Mantle, Maris, Ford, Phil Rizzuto, Garagiola, Stengel, George Steinbrenner, Billy Martin, Gil Hodges, Ron Swoboda, Nolan Ryan, Joe Torre, and many, many more.

Yogi's life included the highs of three MVP seasons, 18 All-Star Game selections, 14 World Series matchups, and seven World Series coaching and managing stints with both the Yankees—where he served as one of the stabilizing factors in the crazy days of the Yankees' Bronx Zoo—and the Mets—where he witnessed firsthand the 1969 Miracle Mets and the Ya Gotta Believe Mets of 1973.

But through it all, from his heartbreaking youth to his difficult and desperate struggle to break into Major League Baseball, Berra came through with his integrity and his humanity intact.

From the streets and playgrounds of prewar America, Berra's life is the story of an entire era of first-generation citizens. He was one of the many children raised in non-English-speaking homes in ethnic neighborhoods packed with families, where nationalities were broken down to grunts such as "Mick" or "Kraut" or "Wop" or "Dago." For Berra, those labels were used as proud tags of ethnic heritage as often as they were indications of degradation. It was a time when Little Italy abutted the German enclave and the tough Irish and Jewish neighborhoods. It was a time and place when neighborhoods clashed on city streets, and when alleys and parking lots, for an hour or two, were turned into ballfields. It was a time when the train was king, ballplayers wore flannel uniforms, automobiles had running boards, and factory jobs were the real gold standard that backed the mighty American paper dollar.

Berra's is a tough but great American story. A story of immigration and success. Of family and dedication.

He is one of the Greatest Generation, a soft-spoken World War II veteran. A man who served on a rocket-launcher for three straight days after D-day, whose boat was eventually blown out of the water, and who survived bullet wounds suffered in the engagement.

He underwent a cruel and mean-spirited rite of initiation like few other men have had to endure in sports because of his odd physical stature. Maligned by vicious opponents and fans, the squat catcher also suffered indignities from his own teammates and even the Yankees' clubhouse manager. Sportswriters of the time were no better, recording for posterity such withering names as gorilla, Neanderthal, caveman, nature boy, Quasimodo, and other horrific monikers.

And there is another side to Yogi Berra. He was one of the most financially successful Yankees of his generation and before. He was a hard-nosed businessman who made thousands of dollars investing in a variety of businesses; as a ubiquitous pitchman who has been featured in print and on television for decades; and as an indefatigable promoter and professional celebrity. After players like Mantle and Ford had blown thousands on confidence schemes, they and others turned to the hardworking, quirky financial wizard for help with investing their monies in stocks and land speculation.

After enough time spent analyzing Berra's career and life, one begins to see a man of tremendous integrity, a man as comfortable with a gas-station attendant as he is with a captain of industry, a strong-willed man, a man to be properly respected.

# ~ Chapter 1 ~

## LIFE ON THE HILL

Ellis Island was originally a small spit of land that barely rose above the water's reach during high tide. Because of its abundant and rich oyster beds and plentiful and profitable shad runs, Ellis Island was originally called *Kioshk,* or Gull Island, by the local Indian tribes. And for generations during the Dutch and English colonial period it became known as Oyster Island, as well as Dyre, Bucking, and Anderson's Island.

During the 1770s Samuel Ellis became the island's private owner. After Ellis's demise, the island became a hangout for pirates and was later named Fort Gibson, which was an ammunition and ordinance depot. It was eventually designated as the site of the first federal immigration station by President Benjamin Harrison in 1890.

From 1855 to 1890, Castle Garden in the Battery (originally known as Castle Clinton) served as the New York State immigration station, with approximately 8 million immigrants, mostly from Northern and Western Europe, passing through its doors. These early immigrants came from nations such as England, Ireland, Germany, and the Scandinavian countries and constituted the first large wave of immigrants that settled and populated the United States. Eventually, the docks at Castle Garden proved inadequate for numerous reasons, and a new location was needed to process new immigrants.

The island measured roughly 3.3 acres, but through the years, with the addition of landfill obtained from ship ballast and possibly excess earth from the construction of the New York City subway system, the small island mushroomed to 27.5 acres. The new immigration station on Ellis Island opened its doors on January 1, 1892. According to the Statue of Liberty–Ellis Island Foundation, Inc., "Annie Moore, a 15-year-old Irish girl, accompanied by her two brothers, entered history and a new country as she was the very first immigrant to be processed at Ellis Island on January 2. Over the next 62 years, more than 12 million were to follow through this port of entry."

Certainly other American ports had similar offices, including Boston, Philadelphia, Baltimore, San Francisco, Savannah, Miami, and New Orleans. However, for major steamship companies, such as White Star, Red Star, Cunard, and Hamburg-America, the most frequent port of call was New York Harbor, making Ellis Island the main portal for immigration during that period.

"First- and second-class passengers who arrived in New York Harbor were not required to undergo the inspection process at Ellis Island. Instead, these passengers underwent a cursory inspection aboard ship; the theory being that if a person could afford to purchase a first- or second-class ticket, they were less likely to become a public charge in America due to medical or legal reasons," states the Foundation. "The Federal government felt that these more affluent passengers would not end up in institutions, hospitals, or become a burden to the state."

This was not the case, however, for steerage or third-class passengers. With few amenities and traveling in cramped quarters well below ship, these passengers were mostly poor, having either pooled their life savings, borrowed money, or spent every cent they had to cross the Atlantic to begin their new life in the New World. Few had anything but a name to point to in this strange new land, if that. Few spoke English or had a practical profession. These passengers were ferried over to Ellis Island for processing, including a health inspection and a mental examination. For those who seemed healthy and whose papers were in order, the three- to five-hour ordeal was uneventful. For those who did not seem healthy, their stay might be several weeks or longer.

\*    \*    \*

In 1912 a diminutive Italian man standing 5'3" stood on the wooden deck of *La Lorraine*, an old passenger steamer, which had sailed from Le Havre, France. Built by Compagnie Generale Transatlantique in St. Nazaire, France, in 1899, *La Lorraine* was 580 feet long and 60 feet wide, had two funnels and two masts, and ferried 1,114 passengers across the Atlantic Ocean.

On *La Lorraine*'s way to docking, the man looked up and, among a small crowd of other passengers, saw for the first time the largest and most famous statue since the Colossus of Rhodes. He saw the Statue of Liberty.

He stood, like the others, gazing at the statue and the skyline of this famous port city. The statue, with its green-copper cloaking, smooth lines, and flaming torch held aloft, was a symbol of a simpler time, when many people from around the world kicked the dust of Europe and other continents off their boots and prepared to make a new life in this new land.

It would not be easy. He did not know the language, like many of his fellow passengers of mixed extractions, but it did not matter.

Pietro Berra first saw the Statue of Liberty on September 28, 1912. Like so many other immigrants, he had come over in steerage class and was one of those who was taken by ferry to Ellis Island, where he was processed with the other poor of Europe. He was 17 years of age. The manifest says that he was on his way to see an uncle in St. Louis, Missouri.

Pietro had plans. He was coming to America to seek his fortune and eventually establish his family. He had been a tenant farmer in the small town of Malvaglio, approximately 25 minutes south of Milan. In Malvaglio, Pietro had courted a young girl named Paulina, and his goal was to make enough money to go back, marry this slight woman, and bring her to the New World.

After being processed, he left the East Coast and headed west to make his fortune. According to Yogi, "After he worked in Colorado and California, he got a job in St. Louis." In California his father worked as a farmhand. Eventually Paulina and Pietro were married, settled in St. Louis, and had a family.

\* \* \*

In St. Louis, Pietro, like a number of other Italian immigrants, had found a home on the Hill—or, as it was called then, Dago Hill—a small but tight-knit low- to middle-income neighborhood of St. Louis. This was the Little

Italy of that metropolitan area. Even up until the mid-1960s, the area was still popularly referred to as Dago Hill, but eventually this name was seen as degrading and offensive, and locals began to refer to it as simply the Hill. In fact, in 1961, in one of his numerous autobiographies, Berra pointed out that his family was referred to as "hill guineas, which is alright with me because everybody knows that's where the best Italian cooks come from."

Its streets, not unlike Little Italies in New York, Trenton, and Philadelphia, were dominated by small, brick row houses and dotted with barber shops, shoe and watch repair stores, and fresh produce and fish markets, as well as corner groceries, bars, and restaurants.

The Hill is located on high ground south of the River des Peres and Interstate 44. The neighborhood's traditional boundaries even today are Shaw Boulevard to the north, Columbia and Southwest Avenues to the south, South Kingshighway Boulevard to the east, and Hampton Avenue to the west. It was named the Hill because it was, in fact, the highest point in the city.

St. Louis historian Tim Fox wrote, "The area came to be dominated by Italian immigrants in the late 19th century, who were attracted by jobs in nearby plants established to exploit deposits of clay discovered" in the 1830s.

Pietro took turns working as a farmhand and construction gang member, and then he worked on the St. Louis Arena. Like many other new immigrants, Pietro eventually worked in one of the numerous factories. He and fellow Italian Giovanni Garagiola eventually settled in at the Laclede-Christy Clay Products Company, where they produced brick and other clay products. Pietro and Giovanni worked side by side, right near the fiery-hot kiln where the clay was baked.

On February 21, 1913, Giovanni Garagiola had arrived from Le Havre at Ellis Island. He, too, was headed for St. Louis. Giovanni and Pietro would become lifelong friends. Little did they know it, but their families would still be connected well after the turn of the next century.

In the beginning, Pietro and Paulina lived on Columbus Street. Their first child, Anthony, was born there around 1914. Three years later, Paulina was pregnant again. Homesick, she decided to return to Italy to visit family.

While there, World War I broke out. Their second child, Michael, was born in Malvaglio. Mother and son would stay several years before returning. Then they had John in 1922, and on May 12, 1925, Lawrence Peter Berra was born in St. Louis. Pietro, by that time, had been a naturalized United States citizen for two years.

Pietro and Paulina had actually named their son Lorenzo Pietro Berra. But in their family's attempt to assimilate, like many European families, the names were translated into English. Neither Pietro nor Paulina could pronounce the English version of Lorenzo, which was Lawrence. At home he was called Lawdies. That was the best either parent could manage. Outside in the neighborhood, he was known as Lawdie, whether he liked it or not.

With steady factory jobs and ruthless saving, the family could eventually afford better accommodations and moved to 5447 Elizabeth Avenue, which was one of a new series of houses being built. Lawrence was five years old when they moved to this new house in 1930. It remained in the possession of Berra family descendants for almost the rest of the century. Giovanni Garagiola, his wife, Angelina, and their family moved into 5446 Elizabeth Avenue.

All the homes in the Hill were narrow row houses, which were usually owned by their residents. Many were passed down from parents to children and remained within families for generations. The houses were usually kept in good repair, well painted, and well cared for. Lawns were usually well tended, and the small backyards were dotted with vegetable and flower gardens. The Garagiolas had a bocce court in their backyard, where Pietro and Giovanni spent many afternoons and evenings together. Statues of the saints and members of the Holy Family adorned most plots. People spent lots of time talking over back fences. Most owners were factory workers, but there were small business owners, tradesmen, and a few professionals as well. Most people who lived on the Hill were Italian.

The area became known for the 39<sup>th</sup> Street Market, a produce market, and for the numerous little Italian restaurants that dotted the small enclave. The area was known for foods like John Volpe and Co., Home of Splendor Brand Italian Salami, and Mama Foscano's Home-Style Italian Ravioli, as well as restaurants like Cassani's and Ruggeri's. Residents of the Hill were fond of their restaurants, as were people from all over the rest of St. Louis, who eagerly sought out the foods and atmosphere.

Life in the Berra household was very much like it was in many immigrant Italian American households. Everyone worked. Everyone's earnings went into a communal pot to be distributed by the husband and wife jointly. Expenses were kept low, and money was continually and steadily—if not in great quantity—saved for important purchases and the costs of surviving old age. Times were tight during the Depression, and factory workers did not have the same unions and protections of the current age. These families had to manage their money carefully.

Pietro was the center of this family. Short and lean, he was nevertheless a powerfully built man whose musculature improved from the hard factory work of the period. And his rule, in his house, was law.

"Pietro ruled his little family with an iron hand," wrote Berra biographer Gene Schoor. "He was the old-fashioned Italian father. No one could have loved his children more, but he insisted on the discipline he had learned and lived under in the old country." No one dared speak the word "no" to Pietro in his own home. And corporal punishment was the norm. According to Schorr, "Pietro enforced that law with his good, strong right hand." Paulina very rarely punished the boys herself, but would instead tell her husband about infractions of the family code, and Pietro would mete out the punishment.

Expectations were low and simple: live a good, clean life, work hard, make money, and support the family.

No one wore fancy clothes. Few women on the block ever bothered to look at ads for the stores downtown; instead, most of the women bought material from a Jewish dry-goods merchant named Gianin. He came through the neighborhood, selling his wares. Gianin was able to dicker with these women in their own dialects, be it Lombard, Sicilian, Piedmontese, or some other regional tongue.

As Mickey Garagiola, Joe's brother, remembered later, Christmas gifts the children received were usually fruit. "We didn't expect much," he said. "Maybe a new pair of pants. You wore those pants on Sundays and never to play ball." Everyone went to church together on Sunday morning—no exceptions.

Both Pietro and Giovanni went to bed around 8:00 in the evening and were generally up at dawn. Giovanni was especially fond of puttering around in his garden before boarding a truck bound for the Laclede-Christy Brick Works. Giovanni had another reason to be mindful of his garden. It turned out years later that he had been burying money in the garden, having become distrustful of banks during the depths of the Great Depression. This was a commonplace practice on the Hill in those times. When confidence was restored, many residents began digging up their savings and bringing their money to the bank. "It smelled to high heaven," Mickey said, looking back. The reason? Many used horse manure to help grow better tomatoes.

The center of activity in the Berra household was the kitchen. While breakfast and lunch might be rushed or chaotic, dinner was planned and, like church, everyone attended. Dinner was always a big event, whether during the week or on the weekend. But rules were rules. And the first rule was, no one reached for or grabbed anything until Pietro helped himself to whatever he wanted in whatever proportion he wanted. And no one was permitted to leave the table until he excused himself first.

During the week, bread and milk or coffee were the breakfast norm. Eggs were expensive and not normally served. Dinner meals consisted of meat and potato dishes, featuring liver, chicken, pork chops, or lamb chops. All these were served alongside of big bowls of piping-hot spaghetti, and lots of fresh bread.

According to Berra, Sunday dinner started early, with an antipasto loaded with luncheon meats such as salami, ham, balogna, capicola, and other Italian meats. These meats would be served with assorted slices of breads and rolls. It was not unusual for the Berras to go through five or six loaves of bread a day.

Antipasto was followed by the risotto course, which was served separately. Yellow or white rice, flavored with saffron and cheeses, was sometimes accentuated by different small pieces of meat or fish mixed in.

A salad always accompanied these meals: lettuce, cucumbers, scallions, radishes, tomatoes, and sometimes escarole. The salad was mixed with oil and vinegar and a little red wine, which Pietro made down in his basement.

"I used to like to help him with the wine," Berra said.

Pietro would load dark grapes into a barrel as Yogi cranked the press, creating a purplish froth and thick juice. They would leave it for a few days while it fermented, then drain just the juice into a galvanized tub before ladling it into small barrels. They would rest the wine for two months and then bottle it. While the whole family loved Pietro's wine, Yogi always stuck to milk.

After the salad, the two main courses were offered. There was always a chicken dish and an alternate meat dish, which varied. Sometimes it was roasted lamb, other times it was beef. And on special occasions, Paulina served her own homemade ravioli. Paulina always served side dishes of fresh vegetables, heaping bowls of steaming fresh string beans or carrots or lima beans.

Berra related that he once nibbled on bread during a meal without finishing his piece and left a large part of it on his plate. Pietro backhanded the young Berra in a flash.

"What did I do?" asked a shocked Lawdie.

"What do you think I buy bread for? To eat, not to waste!" glared the elder Berra. From then on, Yogi always ate everything he took.

Like many Italian neighborhoods, bread was a popular and important staple. It was not uncommon to hear the familiar call of *"Andiamo due pane!"* yelled out from bread trucks passing by. Fazzio's was a popular choice. Another was the Missouri Baking Company, which was owned by Stefano and Anna Gambaro. Lino Gambaro was friends with Yogi Berra and Joe Garagiola and is still known in the neighborhood as "Uncle Lino" to family, friends, and customers.

As late as 1999, Lino looked forward to visits from his old, out-of-town friends when they regularly returned to the Hill.

"You know the difference between the two?" Gambaro said. "Yogi always comes quietly by the side door to say hello. Joe will burst through the front door and announce, 'Here I am,' to everybody. But we love seeing them both."

\*   \*   \*

For youngsters, the main feature of the Hill was Sublette Park. "Probably due to the proximity of Tower Grove Park, this area did not acquire much park acreage until relatively recent times. Sublette Park, which had been the site of the old Female Hospital since the early 1870s, was created after that old institution was razed [in 1914]…and was acquired by the City through donation in 1915. Its name was changed from Manchester Park to Sublette Park in 1925," wrote Fox of the five-acre parcel. This was where many ballgames were played. This was considered the preferred venue for sports and was always filled.

Yogi and Joe usually played at the Shaw schoolyard, which was only two blocks away from their homes on Elizabeth Avenue. If not there, then they played in alleys or abandoned lots, fields, or parking lots, wherever games could be organized or played.

While Lawrence would go on to fame as a ballplayer, many who knew him did not think he was even the best player in his own family. His brother Anthony was the first to come up against their father's old-fashioned notions of what a man did for a living.

Anthony was known in St. Louis as "Lefty" Berra, and he was easily noticed. He was an excellent fielder and an exceptional hitter. His fame and accomplishments in St. Louis earned him a tryout with the Cleveland Indians. But Pietro was horrified. Pietro did not like baseball and saw it as not only an odd game, but also, like many of his generation, a schoolboy's game. It was a thing to be enjoyed on a day off, but not the profession of a real man. It was foolery, and it was not to be tolerated. Eventually, to please his father, Lefty went to work in St. Louis, working to save money for the family and to become a responsible adult who would eventually raise his own family. Respectable men did not play games for a living.

"I always claimed that Tony…was the best ballplayer in the family," recalled Yogi, "but he never had a chance to do anything with it except play semipro ball. He had to go to work."

However, it was strong tonic for John and Yogi to live with. Their brother was a local legend. And it must have been tough to watch the neighborhood pickup soccer and baseball games on weekends, as the factory workers played and hustled. Yogi himself said years later that Anthony was the best athlete in the family. The younger Berras must have marveled at their brother's feats of athleticism.

But Pietro's resistance was not seen as something out of the norm back then, especially for immigrants who had come to this country to better their lot in life. As Garagiola pointed out with his own father, "Papa saw the paper, but he never read the sports pages. He didn't know third base from a coach's box."

Yogi later remembered his brother fondly, recalling that it was Tony who took him to see his first professional hockey game when he was nine or 10 years old. Yogi loved watching the game, featuring the St. Louis Flyers of the American Hockey League. Tony then began taking Yogi often. "I would sleep for a couple of hours in the afternoon so Mom and Pop would let me go with him at night," Yogi recalled.

Among the families on the Hill, the Berras and the Garagiolas were good friends—particularly John Berra and Mickey Garagiola. One of their friends, Ben Pucci, also from the neighborhood, went on to play professional football. Mickey was an outgoing youth who went on to become a local celebrity in his own right. A longtime waiter at Ruggeri's, one of the most famous restaurants in all of St. Louis, he was also heavily involved with St. Ambrose Church and knew many of the police-department personnel by their first names. In fact, Mickey got his job when his friend John Berra told Mickey's father that the restaurant was hiring part-timers—just after their graduation from St. Ambrose's elementary school in 1936. Mickey started as a dishwasher and remained a fixture with the restaurant for 45 years.

"They were all good guys," said Adele Garagiola of the neighborhood crowd. She knew Mickey and his friends from childhood and later married Mickey. According to Adele, king of the hill was a popular game that was played on stoops up and down the block.

Michael Berra had taken in his brother's accomplishments, and he had decided he would push their father further. Michael, also an excellent baseball player, excelled in sports locally, gaining a name for himself outside of Lefty's shadow. He eventually received and attended a tryout with an American League pro team, the St. Louis Browns. He was offered a contract, but even with Anthony's lawyering, Pietro held firm. Michael would not be allowed to play professional baseball. And he, too, was sent to work, to prepare for adulthood and responsibility.

It must be remembered that these were the days of breadlines and soup kitchens, sky-high unemployment and lean living. Entertainment was at a premium. For little kids, especially in warm weather months, sandlot baseball was king. This is no longer the case for the youth of today.

"Sandlot baseball is a relic. Look for a game today, and you may as well be searching corporate offices for a Remington manual typewriter," wrote Cynthia Billhartz of the *St. Louis Post-Dispatch*.

But in his day, Yogi "never had to look far for a sandlot game when he was growing up on the Hill in St. Louis in the 1930s." Yogi could remember "when every block in St. Louis had a sandlot team. The players would get up early every day to stake out a field before others could get there," wrote Billhartz.

"Whatever field was open, we played on it," Berra said. If no field was available, they would play right there on Elizabeth Avenue.

The games were not supervised by adults in any way. Yogi and Joe formed their own team, the Stags A.C., and they played other made-up teams with names like the Royal Falcons, the Hips, the Fawns, the Hawks, and the Wildcats. Some teams had sponsored T-shirts, and a few (the lucky ones) had complete uniforms. Yogi remembered years later that those were the teams he wanted to beat the most.

Another sandlot player from the era, Walter Price, played baseball nearly every day as a teenager, mostly at Sherman Park. "You have to understand there were baseball fields all over the place, behind the large manufacturing plants like at Leschen Wire Rope Co. [on Hamilton and Maffitt Avenues], Wrought Iron Range Co. [on Natural Bridge Road], and the wheel foundry on Goodfellow near Natural Bridge," Price said. "And I was in the middle of it, and all my friends were, too. That was our life. We had no money, and there were no cars."

The boys played "with hand-me-down gloves, splintered bats, and well-worn balls," wrote Gene Schoor. It was not uncommon for a bat to be splintered, nailed back together, and taped.

"Everybody chipped in to buy a new ball once or twice a summer," said Joe Garagiola.

"We played with what we had, that's what it amounted to," Price said. "If nothing else, it occupied our time, and it gave us a great love of the game of baseball."

"I must have been 10 or 11 when I began to play ball," Berra has said. They played in the Shaw schoolyard when they were not able to play at Sublette Park. Garagiola caught and pitched, as did Berra. Berra also played second and third on occasion, and he prided himself on his ability to play almost any position.

They would bring sandwiches early in the morning. After a game of softball, they would retire under some trees to eat their sandwiches and discuss the game and any other important topics 11- and 12-year-olds discuss. Then they would get up and play hardball the rest of the afternoon, doing it all over again.

In 1936 Berra and the Stags even built their own version of a major league park when they cleared the local dump, the Clay Mines, and created a baseball field.

"Yogi made our neighborhood games possible," Garagiola recalled in later years. "He was the great organizer. He engineered the whole project of turning an abandoned clay mine, which was really the neighborhood dump, into our baseball field. Yogi was the project foreman."

"All of us Stags got out there on the dump one day and worked like crazy setting up that ballfield," Berra remembered. "We even went so far as to drag two wrecked cars up along the foul lines for dugouts. Nothing was too much work for us if it was for baseball."

The rival gang in the neighborhood was the Vikings Athletic Club. Garagiola and Berra spent many an afternoon playing games against this group. Whether it was baseball or football or soccer, this was the team they most wanted to beat. The Vikings were a similar group of boys to the Stags. They came from similar circumstances, and many of their fathers worked alongside the Stags' fathers in the numerous plants around town.

Berra recalled one year when the Vikings' star fullback showed up with a helmet. He was the only kid with any equipment because all the other boys, on both sides, were too poor to buy sporting goods that expensive. Berra was honest in his recollection that the Stags gave the young, brash boy a good razzing, teasing him for wearing the helmet. There's no doubt jealousy also played a role. But there was also no doubt that the Vikings felt that they had a new and invincible tactical advantage. But they underestimated the determination of Lawdie Berra.

Berra was the star fullback of the Stags while the helmeted opponent was playing linebacker. On one play sometime during the game, Berra burst straight up through his own line on a fullback dive, made it through the defensive line, and headed straight for his helmeted opponent. The little boy put his head down, and the two went at each other like charging rams. Berra bent his head down and charged forward into the linebacker. A great *crack* could be heard when their respective heads met.

The helmeted boy was stunned, staggered back, and sat down on the grass with a plop. He then began to cry. Eventually he got up and ran home. That was one of the childhood stories that made Lawdie Berra a legend on the Hill long before he became Yogi Berra.

When they played on Elizabeth Avenue, they usually played with a softball. They even painted base lines and bases on the blacktop. As Garagiola recalled, "Painting those bases, we ruined Papa Berra's best paint brushes and used up Papa Garagiola's brown paint. For the football season, it meant more ruined brushes and more paint to mark the 10-yard stripes, and Elizabeth Avenue could have been called Zebra Drive."

They would play in pickup football games after school. Berra was the designated punter. He punted for both teams. Not only could he kick it farthest, but he also kicked it straightest, which cut down on the chance of broken windows during games.

"Yogi was the guy who would get us out of a hole. If it was short yardage—give the ball to Yogi. If we needed a long punt—let Yogi kick it," recalled Garagiola.

Berra recalled years later that he would get chastised by his father for spending so much time playing sports, particularly baseball. He often came home dirty, and said his father "would smack me for sure if my pants were torn. I used to worry about it when I was sliding."

More often than not, Berra would tear his pants, and upon his return home, his mother would mend the pants before his father could see them, if time allowed. More often than not, though, his father would be there, and Berra would be hit. It was a different time in child rearing.

Although his mother got mad at him, she rarely struck Lawdie, if ever. But his father "never talked; he was all action," Berra said.

"The other fathers were the same way," he added. But Berra was quick to point out that this was only in cases of discipline. He was not beaten, and he was only struck for transgressions. But upon his return from the sandlot games, Berra always asked first if his father was home yet.

In those days, all games ended when the Blackmer and Post Fire Clay Products Company's 4:30 afternoon whistle screamed out across the city. This signaled the end of the work shift for many plants. Sandlot games dispersed instantly.

"When I heard that quitting whistle blow, I started for home even if the score was tied in the bottom of the ninth and I was up with two men on and a three-and-two count on me. It wasn't safe not to," Berra remembered.

Both Berra and Garagiola would race home, collect 15¢ from their mothers and a small pail, and race to Fassi's to fill the pails with beer for their fathers' homecoming. Fassi's was a saloon on the corner of Dugan and Sublette at the end of their block on Elizabeth Avenue. Russo's was another popular spot for beer.

If either Pietro or Giovanni returned home without that pail of cold beer, there would be hell to pay. This was not a joke. Every boy in the family had this chore fall to them in their turn, and failing at this was worse than showing up with torn pants.

"The kids whose pops worked at the Manchester plant would be first in line at Fassi's because those workers would be home first," Garagiola reminisced. The boys would jockey for position to get one of the beer boys, especially one named Emil who gave out the least foam, to fill their pails first before the Marnati carry-all truck arrived in the neighborhood with the returning fathers.

*    *    *

Berra loved all sports, including football, soccer, hockey, and baseball. He was known as an excellent running back, an aggressive soccer player, and a talented baseball player.

"He'd get the equipment together for street hockey—the sticks and stacks of magazines we used as shin guards. We'd show up to play, and Yogi would have everything waiting," wrote Garagiola later. Garagiola once told a story about how Berra had come up with a plan to get footballs. They would go stand outside of the fence for St. Louis University football games. On point-after attempts and field goals, the boys would race up, get the ball that had flown outside the stadium's boundaries, and throw it immediately to another boy farther down the street. That boy would in turn spin and throw to another, until in a quick succession of throws, the ball was blocks away before anyone could protest.

But baseball was king. And this was certainly cemented by a woman who lived across the street, a Miss Beltrami. She was a sponsor of the Cardinals' Knothole Gang. As a sponsor, she would accompany a large group of children to Cardinals games. On Saturday home games, the stadium dedicated a section of the upper left-field stands to children for free—first come, first served.

"I used to worship the ballplayers," Berra fondly recalled. His favorites included Spud Davis, Dizzy Dean, Leo Durocher, Frankie Frisch, Bill Hallahan, Stu Martin, Joe Medwick, and Ernie Orsatti. "Watching them play was the biggest thing in our lives."

The most popular player at first was Jack Juelich, who played for the Pittsburgh Pirates and who happened to live on the Hill. Frank "Creepy" Crespi also lived in the neighborhood for a short period. Eventually, these early legends were replaced mainly by Joe "Ducky" Medwick and Terry Moore.

However, boys on the Hill had stars who were more accessible to them, specifically through a local sporting club called the Hawks. It was a loose collection of approximately 50 neighborhood men and teenagers who played pickup games against similar clubs from other neighborhoods. Mike Berra was a Hawk and was a notable infielder for the club. The Stags A.C. shagged many a foul ball (and lifted a few each game), making the Hawks the main suppliers of broken bats and worn balls for this little band of budding baseball players.

The boys were no angels, however, and they got into plenty of trouble. For one thing, there were injuries. Berra split his tongue one time playing soccer, which was painful and took months to heal. Garagiola once broke his arm and refused to tell any adults until it was so swollen the next day that he had no choice. To Berra and his fellow band, getting hurt was as bad as coming home with torn pants, and an injury might earn you another backhand from a parent, so most injuries were dealt with as quietly as possible.

The favorite hangout of the Stags' was Riva's candy store. It had a pinball machine for those temporarily wealthy enough to play a game or two. Gently tilting the table was not out of bounds, but the store owner's son was the equalizer and was just as happy to jolt the table violently when he passed so as to cause a "tilt," thereby ending the player's game.

The Stags did their own version of the Dead End Boys in those days. Garagiola might walk into the 39th Street Market with his gang and start asking a lonesome or maybe a harried clerk a lot of questions and start up an animated conversation. While Garagiola had the young man's attention, the other boys grabbed anything they could get their hands on.

They were also industrious. They would buy a pack of Twenty Grand cigarettes, named after the famous racehorse of 1931 that won the Wood Memorial Stakes, Kentucky Derby, Belmont Stakes, Dwyer Stakes, Travers Stakes, Saratoga Cup, and the Jockey Club Gold Cup. The Stags would buy a twenty pack for a dime and sell the cigarettes for a penny a piece. They might parlay a big payday into a carton of cigarettes or a carton of candy bars that they would, in turn, sell and thereby double their money.

Every boy needed to throw in a certain amount of money each month because the Stags had a clubhouse—an old, beaten-up garage—and the rent on it was 12¢ a month. Each boy was responsible for his share. At that time, Berra's father gave him 15¢ a week for spending money. Sometimes, in weeks when Papa Berra was flush, he might give his son an extra 15¢ in the same week. While Berra's father was strict, he was not an unreasonable man for that period and for his background.

The Berra family was constantly thinking about how to make money. Everyone was responsible for kicking in. And working also provided spending money. Tony and Mike had earned several dollars per week selling the *St. Louis Post-Dispatch* and the *St. Louis Globe-Democrat* in downtown St. Louis, but money from those jobs went to their mother, Paulina. It was the same in the Garagiola house, too, and in most immigrant houses back in those days.

So to afford candy or anything else they desired, children of the period spent time scheming to make extra money. This was a pivotal part of Berra's early childhood. The idea of thinking about money and how to get it began then and continued for the rest of his life. Casey Stengel would later joke that

Berra went to bed each night thinking about money. It was the financial lessons he learned in those early years as a lower-middle-class child in Depression-era St. Louis that would eventually make him one of the richest Yankees of his generation.

It was not beneath Berra and his friends to scoop up manure from horse-drawn carts to sell to neighborhood gardeners. The boys could earn as much as a nickel or a dime for a bag of the powerful fertilizer. The boys on the block alternated chasing after the horse-drawn wagons, collecting the valuable, rich piles.

On Saturdays in the fall, Garagiola, Berra, and the boys would walk around open fields on the edge of the Hill hunting rabbits. They went with broom handles and rocks. According to Berra, some of the boys were good with broomsticks, clubbing the swift little bunnies or delivering the deathblow, but he was better with a rock. He could stand there, get a bead on a moving rabbit, and peg it from 60 to 90 feet away. Without realizing it until later, Berra was improving his accuracy and arm strength. It might seem horrifying to modern American readers, but one must remember that rabbit is a much more popular and common dish in Italy and France. At one time considered a peasant dish, it is now seen by many as a delicacy. And rabbit was a welcome prize when brought home to the Berras. But before heading home from the hunts, the boys went to the St. Louis University football games, placing their dead rabbits at their feet until the game was over.

They also followed trucks from the 39th Street Market headed for the dump. The Stags would pick out the best, most salvageable vegetables and fruits and resell them on street corners for pennies and nickels. They might also carve out the good parts of cantaloupes and watermelons and bring them home like hard-won prizes.

All these activities were a great distraction to Berra. Garagiola was a good talker and a good-looking young man, slick enough to get through school with little real trouble. Berra, on the other hand, was much more concerned with things outside of school and paid little attention to classes, frittering away even the slightest amount of time on homework in his after-school hours. Nothing got in the way of sports.

This caused no end of hassle in the Berra household, as Lawdie was always in trouble for his failing grades. Pietro, who took education seriously, was especially vexed by his son's lack of interest in his own education. Pietro always believed that these after-school distractions, especially baseball, were ruining his son's chances of getting a good job—a better job than his—and equipping himself properly for buying a home and starting a family. But try as Pietro might, his style of strict discipline, which had worked on his other sons, was useless against his youngest son's determination.

In light of his later accomplishments, it must be said that Berra's grades were a reflection of two forces. First, he was bored stiff by teachers and the formal school setting, paying little attention inside the classroom. He was not book smart, though he could read well enough to enjoy newspapers and comic books, which he read voraciously as he got older. Also, he was absolutely focused on sports. He was mesmerized by watching sports of almost any kind, and as his own prowess and skill continued to grow and improve, he became more and more obsessed with baseball and honing the skills that would make him a better player.

His older brothers, by this point in Berra's life, had all shown ability in baseball and were all offered contracts and tryouts with major league clubs. Anthony had to forego an offer from the Cleveland Indians, and both Mike and John had been offered tryouts and contracts with the local St. Louis teams. Pietro had said no. Now Tony was working at a bakery, Mike was working in a shoe factory, and John worked with Garagiola's brother at Ruggeri's. They were working good, honest, dependable jobs—jobs you could raise a family on.

"My brother Tony played semipro ball. My brother Mike played semipro ball. My brother John played semipro ball. But they only played on Sundays," Berra said in an interview years later. "And I always kidded my dad, 'See that, Pops? You let all your sons go, you'd have been a millionaire.' He said, 'Blame your mother.'"

It also must be pointed out that although he was not book smart, as formal education almost surely judges, Berra was certainly street smart and did not lack IQ. Without question, Berra seemed to have blossomed later in life outside of baseball and to a greater degree than many of his contemporaries, if money, property, and business success are any means of judgment.

Still, his dislike of school would eventually put him on a path of collision with everyone in his life.

# ~ Chapter 2 ~

# BECOMING YOGI BERRA

The local Italian American Club on the Hill promoted amateur boxing events. The club had been established in 1922 and had entertained ambassadors, royalty, generals, and 150 Olympic athletes from Italy on their way to the California 1932 Olympic games. The manager of these boxing events was Frank Mariani, a former boxer himself. Mariani knew Berra and asked him to help out. Mariani intended to use Berra as a sparring partner for his better-trained boxers.

According to Garagiola, it wasn't that Berra was so technically astute, but rather that he understood the game and had a simple rule: I get hit, I hit back.

In a few sessions, Berra went from training partner to featured fighter. Mariani tutored the young Lawdie, teaching him how to step, jab, and defend. Eventually Berra was slated on a card against a fighter from another St. Louis boxing club, and he won handily. He soon became a regular. His long arms and low center of gravity made him a hard target to hit. And his powerful arms were formidable. What made these boxing matches especially attractive to the young Berra was that he collected $5 to $10 per fight. Even though they were amateurs, the fighters were awarded small purses, depending on the draw of the gate.

Berra liked the training that boxers experienced, and it was the first sign of his love of athletics as more than a recreational adventure. He genuinely enjoyed the training, the hard work, and the camaraderie in the clubhouse atmosphere, hanging out with the guys in the locker room afterward. In the winter, boxing especially seemed like a great way to blow off steam because there were few other athletic opportunities. Berra fought nine times and lost only once. It was a loss he later avenged.

"I enjoyed it," he said of this particular victory.

The truth of this episode is undeniable. But neither Berra (in numerous autobiographies and biographies) nor Garagiola tell the story the same way twice about why Berra stopped boxing. In one version, Berra handed all the money over to his mother, like the rest of his earnings. In another story, the boxing program was disbanded. In another version, his father forbade him, and in yet another, one of his older brothers found out and insisted on Berra's leaving fighting behind. Regardless of how it ended, the experience taught Berra to defend himself and to fear no man. In fact, having been trained this way, he was more experienced than many boys his age in the art of self-defense.

Boxing may have been an enjoyable diversion, but baseball was a constant for Berra and his friends. The Stags stayed together year after year, and eventually they looked for a more official organization in which to participate.

The local secretary of the YMCA, Joe Causino, organized a baseball tournament. And the Stags wanted in. When the team took the field for the first time, Causino must have had a moment's hesitation. The boys had worn-out gloves, neither uniforms nor matching T-shirts, and they played in old hand-me-down shoes and tattered overalls.

When the Stags were finally accepted into the YMCA tournament, they were the only team not to have some kind of uniform. But the boys could play. Over the course of the long, hot summer, they finished second in the tournament to the Edmonds, despite the Stags' equipment disadvantages.

As Garagiola later told the story, every kid, whether he missed other games or not, always showed up for a game against the Edmonds. They were rivals, and everyone's heroics in a game against the Edmonds, as well as their miscues, would be remembered and recounted.

According to Garagiola, one time the Stags were down by a run in the last inning. By all accounts, Berra was a great clutch hitter even then. The manager of the Edmonds saw him preparing to bat and yelled out, "You'll never hit it over that wall. You'll never do it." He was trying to rattle the batter, make him think too much.

Berra stepped out of the batter's box and turned toward the manager. "For 10 bucks?" he asked.

Garagiola laughs now. According to him, "The whole team didn't have 10 bucks."

Berra stepped back into the batter's box, and everyone was watching. He clubbed the next pitch over the wall for the win and the $10.

\*    \*    \*

The first time the Stags ever got T-shirts was when they enrolled in a local soccer tournament. The shopkeepers on the Hill, poor Europeans in the main who had emigrated to the United States, looked down on baseball and would not sponsor the Stags for a sport they considered stupid. However, soccer was another story.

Many of the shopkeepers had played soccer in the old country. It was a game whose nuances they understood and admired. This was a game they could get behind. Young Garagiola and Berra and the other boys were able to persuade the Southwest Drugstore to buy them shirts that read Stags A.C. on the front and had the store's name on the back.

"I played a lot of soccer," Berra said later. "I love soccer. I love to watch soccer games on TV. And back there on the Hill, we played against... We had Spanish living there, the Italians and Germans and Irish. We played against each other. And I used to enjoy it. That was good. That's a good conditioning game, that soccer. It is."

One of the big events on the Hill was the annual soccer game played on Thanksgiving Day. The players were a combination of teenagers and men, and the game was played by two clubs, the Fawns and the Wildcats. These were local, neighborhood clubs. The competition was jokingly called the Urinary Bowl, but there was no question that the games got serious.

"I could tell we were all getting old," Berra admitted in 1961, "the last time I was home because nobody even knew where the bowl was." In fact, all the Berra boys were considered excellent soccer players, and many neighborhood folks considered Berra a better soccer player than he was a baseball player.

The Stags began to break up not long after the YMCA tournament, as each boy went on to another team in the Recreation Intermediate League, which was the next level up. Both Garagiola and Berra were recruited by the Edmonds team—the team that had won the YMCA tournament. The Edmonds team was part of the Recreation Intermediate League.

On one of the most exciting days in both their lives, the two boys put on their uniforms and shook hands.

"Now we look like real players," said Berra. Years later, he chuckled and said, "Joey and I were lucky because the Edmonds won the championship, and the restaurant threw a big dinner for us."

Garagiola was the everyday catcher until he caught a foul tip in the groin. In those days, other than a chest protector and mask, there was little other protective wear. Cups were nonexistent. Players sometimes even caught without a mask. Not surprisingly, Garagiola didn't play catcher for a while, and Berra took over those duties.

*    *    *

There was little doubt about where Berra's schooling was going. He was adamant that he wanted to quit school, and his father fought him at every turn. But the son was wearing the father down.

Berra was now in eighth grade, and he was tired of it. And his father was tired of fighting about it with him. As the school year came to an end and the decision about high school loomed, Berra was insistent: he wanted to quit school. This was a huge event in the Berra family household, and many outsiders were called in to mediate this major confrontation between the father and his son. Certainly Pietro pointed out that his son's friend Joey Garagiola was going to high school. But the younger Berra refused to budge.

Both the school principal and the parish priest, Father Palumbo, were called to this meeting. Tony, Mike, and John were also in attendance.

"I was a lousy student and pretty stubborn, and felt I was wasting my time," Berra wrote years later.

A heated conversation ensued, where the priest and the principal tried to impress upon Berra, with his father's urging, the importance of education and the importance of continuing that education. They all warned him that he would become a bum, which was his father's greatest fear.

Then his brothers joined the fray, also insisting that he continue his education, but even under this second, withering barrage, Berra held firm. Exasperation started to take its toll. The principal and Father Palumbo eventually softened. "It's sometimes better for a young man to go to work. Not everybody is born a scholar," they said.

His parents relented, and they came up with a truce: young Lawdie would go to work, and from now on in the house he would be known as Larry. If he was going to take on a man's job, he did not want to be called by a boy's name.

"I realize now this was a major turning point in my life, and I was fortunate," Berra concluded. He was taking the chance of a lifetime, although at the time he didn't understand that. But later in life he knew he'd been incredibly lucky.

Thus began Berra's working career. At the age of 14, he took a job working in a coal yard. He hated it. He was always dirty and he loathed the fact that on nice days after school let out, his friends were out there playing and he was working.

Berra would eventually run through a series of jobs. He went to work every day with a large sandwich and baseball glove wrapped in newspaper. At 3:00 PM, when Garagiola and all the boys got out of school, Berra would often abandon his place of employment and go play ball.

"Where were you yesterday afternoon?" asked the coal yard foreman.

"I didn't feel good," answered Berra.

"You don't feel good every afternoon."

"Not every afternoon."

"Well, you can take this afternoon off, and tomorrow morning, and the day after. We don't need you here."

Papa Pietro was furious when Berra lost his job at the coal yard, which paid a good wage in those days of $25 per week. The average annual salary in the 1940s was $1,299. Bacon cost 27¢ per pound, eggs were 33¢ per dozen, and milk was 13¢ per quart.

Pietro then got him a job working on a Pepsi truck, delivering soft drinks in St. Louis. He blew that one too. And that paid $27 per week.

Berra's relationship with his father was at an all-time low. Another family conference was called. In attendance were his three brothers, Father Koester of St. Ambrose, and Causino from the YMCA.

Pietro accused his son of becoming a bum, claiming he was irresponsible, unfocused, and bound for trouble.

"I want to be a baseball player," Berra told those assembled.

"That's a bum!" Pietro exploded.

Father Koester was more deliberate and gentle. "There is nothing wrong with playing baseball," said the priest. He reasoned that baseball was indeed fun, but Berra's parents weren't wrong to think he might turn out to be a bad boy. "You can play baseball, but there are other things in life, and you have to attend to those things, too."

The younger Berra appealed to Causino, saying, "You told us a man ought to spend his life doing what interested him."

Causino said yes, that's what he had said, never anticipating what the boy was thinking. Causino tried to impress upon the young Larry that a man ought to do what was important to him. He told Berra he had to make up his mind about that interest and give it his all.

"Well, what's it going to be, Larry?" pressed Causino.

"Baseball," answered young Berra. "That's what it's got to be. Baseball."

Pietro exploded. If it were not for the priest and the friendly advisor, Pietro would have thrown his son across the room.

"Not everyone who wants to play baseball can make a profession of it," they told him.

Berra fought them all off.

The priest came up with a compromise. Larry would attempt to make it to the pros. There would be some time limit, to be determined, but in the meantime, he would find jobs, preferably at night, that would allow him to play baseball in the afternoons.

His mother and father were disappointed, but they relented. And his brothers, who knew how hard it was to get into the big leagues—let alone make it pay—were also skeptical. But the deal was made. And Berra was thrilled.

*    *    *

Berra took his turn selling newspapers, selling the *Post-Dispatch* and the *Globe-Democrat* on Southwest and Kingshighway in St. Louis at night. It was a huge pay cut, but not to him. He had been turning over his pay to his mother from the start, living on the $2 a week she kicked back to him because he was living at home.

One of his most cherished memories of this period was selling newspapers to Ducky Medwick. The starstruck Berra often chatted with the St. Louis baseball star. Medwick always handed Berra a nickel for the 3¢ newspaper and told him to keep the change.

Medwick, Berra's favorite player, was known as a wild-swinging star. Known to his friends as Muscles, but more commonly known as Ducky because of his waddling gait, Medwick was a tough and gruff outfielder with tremendous competitive spirit who typified the rowdy Gashouse Gang Cardinals of the 1930s.

Van Mungo, a pitcher from the period, once said of Medwick, "I'd rather pitch to any other hitter in the league. He's bad news all the time. No game is ever won against the Cardinals until Medwick is out in the ninth."

Medwick was considered one of the best bad-ball hitters in baseball at that time. It is probably not a coincidence that Berra also became one of the most notorious and best bad-ball hitters in the history of the game because he admitted he patterned himself after Medwick.

Once, in the 1934 World Series against Detroit, Medwick, believing a throw was on the way, slid hard into Tigers third baseman Marv Owen. After the inning, upon taking his position in the outfield, Medwick was pelted with beer and pop bottles by Tigers fans until Commissioner Judge Landis halted the game so Medwick could be replaced for his own safety.

Medwick was also known for being belligerent to opposing players as well as his own teammates. His numerous offenses ran a mile long. He once flattened St. Louis teammate pitcher Ed Heusser, who had accused him of not hustling. He also cold-cocked another teammate, Tex Carleton, when the pitcher unwittingly strolled by Medwick one too many times during a photo session. However, Medwick was a tenacious teammate in the field and a great clutch hitter. Medwick, for better or worse, displayed passion.

"You know who one of my newspaper customers is?" Berra said to Garagiola.

"No, who?"

"Joe Medwick, that's who. He's buying the paper from me and givin' me a tip."

Garagiola told all their friends, and according to Garagiola, the entire neighborhood of boys showed up the next night to watch Medwick buy a paper from Berra. The boys were shocked the ballplayer knew Berra's name. From then on, Berra was now someone special. He knew Joe Medwick personally.

"As kids, we believed that professional athletes like Joe Medwick were good people who wanted to play sports because they loved playing, not just because they loved getting money, because they didn't make that much," Berra said years later of Medwick.

"When a guy makes the big leagues, he's usually the best player in his town, or in his high school, or at least in his neighborhood. I wasn't even the best player on my block," said Garagiola. When choosing up sides, Berra was always picked first.

*   *   *

Another childhood friend of both Garagiola and Berra was a boy named Bobby Hofman. Bobby had a real connection to baseball—his uncle was Circus Solly Hofman, who was known as a slick, colorful center fielder. A good base runner and a timely hitter, he was both player and general handyman for the four Cubs pennant winners of 1906–08 and 1910. He was nicknamed Circus Solly for his many "circus" catches in the outfield. He was also known for his clowning around on and off the field.

In a 1908 game between the Giants and Cubs, it was Hofman who retrieved Al Bridwell's single and threw to Johnny Evers at second base for a force-out on Fred Merkle. Merkle had not tagged second while rounding the bases, thus causing one of the most controversial endings in baseball history. The Cubs then beat the Giants in the makeup game to win the pennant.

Thus there is some hilarity in the fact that Circus Solly's nephew was the one who hung on Berra one of the most famous nicknames in American history.

"One day at a movie, Hofman watched a scene about an Indian yogi who made a snake curl up from a basket," Garagiola recalled. In fact, many of the boys from the Stags went to matinees together.

"We're all movie nuts, the whole gang, but Yogi is the worst," Garagiola said.

One of the features was a travelogue about India. One of the many pieces was about a Hindu fakir, a snake-charmer who sat cross legged with a turban on his head. Once his feat was accomplished, the fakir stood up to walk away from the camera. The yogi waddled, and Hofman cracked, "That yogi walks like Lawdie Berra."

Berra indeed has a distinctive walk, and according to Garagiola, Berra is the only guy he knows who scuffs the inside of his shoes as he shuffles. As Garagiola pointed out, you could see Berra from up in the stands, and no matter the number on his jersey, only one guy in the majors walked like that.

"From the moment that yogi on the movie screen started to walk, Lawdie Berra had a new name. He became Yogi to everyone, and I mean everyone," said Garagiola. Even his parents, who could never pronounce his real name, now called him Yogi.

Today it is one of the most famous nicknames in the world. And there is no question who you are referring to when you use it. As Garagiola quipped, "You don't ever hear anyone ask, 'Yogi who?' do you?"

In one of his several autobiographies, Berra recounted that it was Jack McGuire Jr. who gave him the nickname. McGuire was the son of the scout Jack McGuire, who was coach of the Stockham Post and a scout for the St. Louis Cardinals. According to Berra, Jack Jr. said to him one day while he sat cross-legged, "You look just like a yogi. I'm gonna call you Yogi." Regardless of which version is true, the facts remained the same. The boys all agreed that Lawdie looked like a yogi—and thus began a part of the legend during Berra's first step toward the majors.

# ~ Chapter 3 ~

# BERRA'S BIG BREAK

Leo Browne had made a lot of money as an oilman, and he managed the Lawrence Goudy, Fred W. Stockham Post Number 245. He had been an umpire at one time in the Eastern Baseball League. His opinions on baseball players were well respected. And playing for him was tantamount to a tryout for the major leagues.

Browne was impressed with both Garagiola and Berra. At the time, Garagiola seemed much further along and much more polished. He was a natural talker and so seemed to many people to be, if not a wisecracker, a more mature individual. He also had a full head of hair back then and cut a dashing figure. On the other hand, Berra's looks were still held against him, and he was still discovering the techniques that would make him a better player. But what made Berra seem like such a diamond in the rough was his ability to hit, which seemed unorthodox but still remarkable.

"The kid can hit," Browne told everyone. "He's a slugger, a murderer. I don't care where you pitch it, he whams it."

Berra was not as good with a glove, but he had speed and ability. He didn't look pretty like Garagiola, but Browne could watch Berra hit all day long. It was not a pretty swing—in fact, it was a brutal swing, like a caveman swinging a club, trying to kill something. And he swung at everything, no matter whether it was way far outside or down by his toes or over his head. And he tomahawked all of them into the deep outfield.

Browne believed Berra was a natural catcher and would be adequate in the outfield. Berra was well liked by his manager and his teammates. He was like a big puppy growing into who he would be. The kids constantly razzed him, but you could tell they liked him as well. He was very good-natured but became a tough, focused competitor once he stepped between the lines.

Neither Berra nor Garagiola did themselves any harm by making it to the American Legion semifinals two years in a row. Their names appeared in the local papers. And because the two brought bottles of Pietro's homemade Dago Red wine to St. Louis Cardinals clubhouse boy Butch Yatkeman, they were able to roam Sportsman's Park and even took batting practice there. However, Pietro did not know he was contributing to his son's career. The wine had been purloined.

"By the time we were teenagers, Yogi and I were pretty good ballplayers, good enough to be working out at Sportsman's Park," reminisced Garagiola. "Even then, Yogi was popping balls off the screen in right field."

At the age of 15, Garagiola got a job within the Cardinals organization as a groundskeeper and assistant clubhouse boy for the Springfield farm club. Garagiola was being hidden for a year by the Cardinals.

In the meantime, Berra was going to get a tryout. Browne had talked to everyone about him. Unbeknownst to Berra at the time, Browne had persuaded newspaper man Bob Burnes from the *Globe-Democrat* to take a look.

It was an American Legion game. Burnes was introduced to Berra, who seemed preoccupied. Berra was obviously upset about missing his turn at batting practice, and that seemed to bother him the rest of the game. He got one impressive hit, struck out swinging at one a foot over his head, and played a passable third base. Burnes told Browne he was "oversold on the kid."

Berra and Garagiola also played in a Works Progress Administration (WPA) project that took talented youngsters once a month to a baseball clinic and gave them a day with players, coaches, and scouts from the Cardinals. Dee Walsh, a Cardinals scout, made a big pitch for Garagiola. McGuire backed Berra.

Browne arranged for a real tryout with the Cardinals. The boys met on the street early in the morning to make their trek over to Sportsman's Park. Branch Rickey, the reigning baseball genius of the day, would be there personally to see the dozens of kids.

Under his arm, Berra had a big bag. Garagiola brought a little one. They were lunch bags, and Berra chided his friend that he would be hungry. "You'll ask me for some, don't worry," Berra said.

"I don't want to die young. I know what's in there," said an unimpressed Garagiola. Inside were Berra's favorite huge hero sandwiches: bananas and mustard.

When they got there, Yogi unabashedly stared at Rickey. Rickey was smoking a great big cigar.

"Stop staring, you dope," Garagiola said. "He's supposed to look at us, not us at him."

But before Berra turned away, Rickey winked at him without smiling.

"He winked at me," Yogi said.

"Everybody winks at you, Yogi," said Garagiola.

Like all tryouts, the boys were tested for speed, ability to catch, bat, and other skills. Garagiola went first. For all his awkwardness as an adult, with his shiny chrome dome, Garagiola in his youth looked every bit the ballplayer. He was tall, lean, and good-looking, with a nice swing and good speed. And he was graceful and quick. By the time Garagiola was done, Berra could see the men standing around Rickey nodding. Garagiola had cemented his contract.

Berra went next. A big, blond pitcher said to Berra, "Don't worry, kid. I'll put it in there. All you have to do is hang on to it."

Berra did well, but his arm was off. He had plenty of power in his arm, but his throws sailed over the second baseman's head.

Berra pressed in the batter's box. Garagiola whispered at the batter's cage, "Ease up, ease up. Just meet the ball." But Yogi continued to struggle.

After the tryout they were told to shower and meet Rickey. Garagiola went in first while Yogi flipped through magazines in the office. Garagiola came out with a huge smile. He had been offered a contract while he was a groundskeeper but told to keep it quiet until after he was 16 years old. This tryout was to confirm his place in the organization. He received a $500 bonus for signing the contract and told the scout he needed the money to pay off his father's house.

Berra knew about his friend's contract. When Rickey offered Berra a contract, he offered him no signing bonus. Rickey was nice, but told Berra he was not yet ready and to come back in a year. His throws were too wild, and he was too small. Berra countered he was good and deserved a place in the minors. Rickey was impressed by Berra's pluck and told him he would not send him to Springfield, but somewhere else.

"What about a bonus?" asked Berra.

Berra knew his parents would have a fit if he accepted a contract with no bonus. They knew about Garagiola's contract. And he could show up with no less. It was a matter of pride for Berra as well. His friend looked better and could talk a better game, but deep down, Berra thought he was the better athlete and deserved the respect that the bonus conveyed.

Rickey relented and offered Berra $250. He refused again.

"Mr. Berra," said Rickey with a sudden scowl, "I'm afraid this negotiation has gone far enough. It wouldn't be fair to the club and our stockholders. Frankly, and I say this for your own good, I don't think you can ever be a major league ballplayer. You're not built for this game."

"I want the same as Joey's getting," said Berra. He couldn't have cared less about the weekly salary itself, but his counteroffer was final.

Rickey balked at going any higher. Neither Berra nor McGuire, who spoke on Berra's behalf, could understand Rickey's refusal. McGuire pressed Rickey.

"The boy is too clumsy and too slow. He'll never make anything more than a Triple-A ballplayer at best, and I'm looking for boys who can go all the way," Rickey countered.

Berra was devastated. He had another tryout with the Browns, but that also ended badly. They would sign him to a farm club but without a signing bonus. Berra stuck to his guns and refused again. He had batted fourth while Garagiola had batted third on almost every team they played. Why was this so difficult?

"I couldn't understand it. It really hurt," wrote Berra years later. "Ever since I had been a little kid, I had been used to having the other guys laugh at me because of my looks and poke fun at me because I was so clumsy, but I had always been as good a ballplayer as any of them and better than most of them, so I never minded."

But now he was hurting. This hurt was made all the worse when, in the summer of 1942, Garagiola took off for Springfield. He was a professional baseball player, their childhood dream, and Berra was still a sandlot player. Berra was stung deeply.

*   *   *

Yogi went back to factory work, this time with his brother Mike at Johansen's Shoe Factory, pulling tacks from women's high-heeled shoes. The heels were attached to the sole of the shoe with wet glue and tacks. After the glue dried, Yogi pulled the tacks so the shoe could be finished. But Berra's mind rarely stayed on work.

At the factory he was making $35 per week, which he handed over to his mother, who then gave him back $3 for spending money. At one point he was identified by city inspectors as not having the proper paperwork because he was under 18 years of age. He had to go down to City Hall to file for proper paperwork.

In the meantime, he played sandlot games and such, playing for $5 and $10 per game, filling in for different clubs around St. Louis. His swing was getting better, but the better he became, the more discouraged he became. How come he couldn't catch on with a real club? A major league club?

Without Berra's knowledge, Browne sent a letter to an old acquaintance named George Weiss. Weiss had been the New Haven manager of the Yankees farm club when Browne was an umpire. Weiss was now the general manager of the New York Yankees. Brown wrote to him, "All this kid wants is $500 to sign. Whatever you give him a month, he'll take it."

In October 1942, the New York Yankees lost the World Series to the St. Louis Cardinals in five games, with the Redbirds sweeping the last four games en route to upsetting the perennial world champion Bronx Bombers.

After the Series, Weiss told bullpen coach Johnny Schulte to check Berra out and to sign up Berra if it didn't cost too much. Schulte came to the Berra household and didn't ask to see Berra try out. He'd talked to enough people. That was good enough for him. He offered Berra a $500 signing bonus and $90 per month. Berra would go to the Norfolk Tars in Virginia to compete in the Piedmont League. Berra kept his factory job until spring, when it was time to report to training camp at Excelsior Springs, Missouri.

Before Berra left for spring training, a telegram arrived from Branch Rickey, who had left the Cardinals and was now with the Brooklyn Dodgers. Rickey wanted Berra to report to their Bear Mountain, New York, camp, where the Dodgers were training and where Berra would sign a contract with a signing bonus.

It was too late. Berra was already the property of the New York Yankees, and he never responded to Rickey's offer. There has been some speculation over the years that Rickey may have known when he first met Yogi that he was leaving the Cardinals, and his refusal to sign Berra was an effort to salt him away for the Dodgers. Berra, to his credit, did not believe this.

Truly, the concept seems unlikely. Rickey had no idea when he was approached about Berra that he was headed to Brooklyn. The position in Brooklyn was held by Larry MacPhail, who was a sound and respected baseball man. It is unlikely the Dodgers ownership was in any hurry to get rid of MacPhail. But he did leave the Dodgers in October to enter the war, and Rickey took his position.

Regardless of the conjecture over this issue, it was a compliment to Berra that he obviously stuck in the memory of the Great Mahatma, as Rickey came to be known for his baseball genius.

"I've often thought if Yogi had spent his career in Ebbets Field, that short right-field fence would have made him the first player voted into the Hall of Fame while he was still playing," opined Garagiola. Of course, the same could have been said of DiMaggio and Mantle.

Just before he left for camp, on May 12, 1943, Berra got another letter. This one wasn't from a baseball team. It was from the U.S. Army. He had been drafted. Berra wrote back asking for the paperwork to be sent to him at Norfolk. The paperwork was delayed, and he was able join his team and realize a lifelong dream.

\* \* \*

Norfolk, Virginia, was the base for the Atlantic fleet of the United States Navy and the Fifth Naval District headquarters during the Second World

War. Its population was some 750,000 people in a small town that had barely recorded 180,000 people in the previous census.

Sailors were everywhere. They choked the sidewalks, the theaters, the saloons, and anywhere else people congregated. Also, because of the shipyards, there were thousands of shipyard workers and construction workers. Sailors who were bored and drunk eventually got into fights.

"Lots of noses got punched in that town every night of the week," Berra said.

Berra arrived at camp and started playing, but he never received his $500 bonus. After a few weeks, he approached club general manager Jim Dawson about it. Dawson explained that Berra would only collect the $500 signing bonus if he stuck with the club for the whole season. Berra said Schulte didn't sell it to him that way. But no matter how adamant Berra was, Dawson shook his head no. Berra would have to play the whole season to get his money.

This was possibly the worst thing the Yankees could have done, and they paid dearly for this little trick for more than a decade and a half. From then on, Berra's contract struggles with the organization, once he made the major league team, would be legendary. Weiss was notoriously cheap, but Berra was a stickler for language and money, and he would extract every dollar he could from the thrifty general manager, always remembering the lesson he learned in Norfolk. Not only did this experience teach Berra about reading the fine print, but his slim salary was tough to live on. And he would remember that the rest of his life.

"Money was a serious problem to me during my time in Norfolk," Berra admitted years later. As Berra pointed out himself, he could have made more money shining shoes. Between rent and trying to buy food, Berra had to write home to his mother to ask her for money. Once or twice a month she would write back and send him a money order for $10 or $15. And she would write a note to him in Italian, "Don't let your father know you're hungry, or he will make you come home."

To be sure, Berra was not a spendthrift, and he was not wasting his money on booze and women. First, Berra at this period in his life was afraid of women. If he saw a pretty girl walking toward him or looking at him, he crossed the street to avoid contact. He was obsessed by baseball and with making a major league club, not with finding a lady friend.

Second, Berra was and remained thrifty throughout his entire life. Growing up poor and now living poor on his own made him very aware of how money was spent. Later in life, Yankees teammates would accuse him of being cheap. He was well known as a borrower of other people's toiletries, such as deodorant, toothpaste, shaving cream, shampoo, and the like. And that was when Berra was one of the high-paid members on the team. One time Mantle became so disgusted by Berra blatantly taking advantage of his good nature that he substituted glue in his deodorant. As usual, Berra came over to borrow the canister—and right in front of the sportswriters. The prank worked perfectly, or maybe too well. His arms became instantly stuck to his sides. Whitey Ford and Mantle had to bring Berra into the trainer's room, away from the press, and literally sheer hair and skin away until Berra's arms came free. Berra never borrowed Mantle's deodorant again.

It is not a stretch to assume Berra, under such penurious circumstances in Norfolk, would pinch pennies where necessary. While he was there he shared a room with pitcher Bill Sukey. Their extravagances included a few drive-in restaurants and hot dog wagons.

"I borrowed money from anybody who would lend it to me. I was hungry all the time, and I was broke all the time," Berra said.

One time, Berra was mad, so he decided not to eat before a game. He complained to manager Shaky Kain. Kain was aggravated and felt sorry for the poor kid from St. Louis. He dug into his own pocket and handed Berra $2. Berra bought and ate four hamburgers and two sodas. He got at least two hits that night.

The only relief from weekly hunger pangs came on Sundays. One of the loyal team followers, a female fan, brought Berra food. She normally brought a loaf of Italian bread filled with cheese and luncheon meat. Needless to say, Berra looked forward to weekend home games.

Newspapers of the period called him Larry Berra. On August 1, 1943, 18-year-old Berra had six hits, many of them extra-base hits, and tallied up 13 RBIs in a game against Roanoke. The next day, Berra rang up six more hits and 10 additional RBIs, also against Roanoke. For the two games, Berra had 12 hits and 23 RBIs, with three homers, two triples, and a double. For his other 109 games, Berra had just four homers and 33 RBIs. He went on to hit .253 for the year and led the league in errors.

During the season, Berra's team played a game against the Norfolk Air Station. That team boasted major league players like Phil Rizzuto of the Yankees, Don Padgett of the Browns, Sam Chapman of the A's, Dom DiMaggio of the Red Sox, Freddie Hutchinson of the Tigers, Eddie Robinson of the Indians, and Hugh Casey of the Dodgers.

Berra struck up a conversation with Gary Bodie, the manager of the air station team and a warrant officer. Berra told him that he, like his opponents, would soon be drafted into service. Bodie told Berra that most of the big leaguers were going to be shipped out, but if he joined the navy, Bodie would try to bring him to the air station. Yogi had stars in his eyes, but they were shaken from his head soon enough.

Upon passing his military physical, for which he volunteered in Richmond after the season, Berra was asked which branch he wanted. He emphatically told them the navy.

"How much time do I have before I report?" he asked.

"A week," the officer snapped.

"How much does the army give?" asked Berra, hoping to be able to go home to visit his family before leaving for the war.

"A month," said the officer.

"I'll change my mind. I'll take the army," said Berra.

"I'm sorry, fellow," said the officer, indicating the paperwork in front of him. "You're in the navy now."

# ~ Chapter 4 ~

# In the Navy Now

Bainbridge Naval Base was a training center that was created in 1942. It was a facility of several hundred acres located above the Susquehanna River, some 40 miles northeast of Baltimore. It was established to deal with the massive training requirements necessitated by America's entry into World War II.

The base was filled with hundreds of thousands of sailors from all over the United States. It had one large theater and one large amphitheater, as well a mammoth drill hall and commissary, a dance hall named Fiddler's Green, and dozens of barracks. The welcome center for new recruits was an unassuming metal and glass door, over which hung a sign that read, Welcome Into the Navy.

This was where Seaman Second Class Berra went through basic training, and it was grueling. Like most basic training experiences, it was hours spent drilling, followed by hours of boredom between drilling. Berra was concerned with only one thing the entire time he was stateside before shipping out—a letter from Warrant Officer Bodie transferring him to Norfolk for the naval base baseball team. It never came.

What did come was bad news. His mother was sick back in St. Louis. Berra applied for emergency leave through the Red Cross. The people at the naval base were nice to him and understood. He raced back home.

His mother had to undergo a breast operation. Berra stayed at his parents' house and shuttled back and forth to the hospital where his mother lay sick and weak. He felt powerless, but the doctors told him that his visit home to see her was the kind of tonic she really needed.

This episode led to many anxious moments for the young Berra. He loved his mother deeply, and until his old age, he carried a picture of his parents in his wallet. He stayed in St. Louis until his mother was released from the hospital and returned home. He remained concerned about her health, but his obligations to the navy outweighed his right to stay home until his mother fully recuperated.

Upon returning to Bainbridge, he completed basic training, and he was sent to Little Creek, Virginia, for amphibious assault training. Little Creek was very near Norfolk, which Berra loathed because of the thousands of young, obnoxious men who crowded its streets.

*   *   *

Despite an abundance of food and movies, two of his favorite things, Berra missed the physical activity sports provided. He was bored, as he was with everything in his life that was not connected with baseball. He was bored enough that he would do almost anything to get out. During a showing of *Boom Town*, starring Spencer Tracy and Clark Gable, an announcement interrupted the show. It was a call for volunteers for training on a new kind of ship—the LCS rocket launcher. All men who were interested were supposed to report back to their barracks immediately for volunteer duty. Berra raced back to his barracks and enlisted for this exciting new service. He was tired of being bored. He wouldn't be bored anymore.

The LCSs were landing craft support vessels that would be used in up-close situations for amphibious assaults.

"Landing craft support are small, but we used to say landing craft suicide squad," joked Berra years later. "We had the nicknames for all.... An LSD [landing ship dock] we call a large stationary target."

Each boat carried one officer and five seamen and was only 36 feet long. There were 12 sites to launch rockets from and six machine guns. As Berra later recalled, "It wasn't anything except a platform to carry a whole lot of live firecrackers." The boats would be carried by larger boats and then dropped into the water like Higgins boats. The guys on board were going to be in the thick of the action.

Berra was slated to be a machine gunner. He didn't realize how serious the assignment was until he learned that the volunteers would not be allowed to write a word about what they were doing. It was a top-secret mission, and even the slightest hint of what they were training for might compromise the success of the campaign. They were not allowed to tell other navy personnel, nor were they allowed to discuss it amongst themselves in public. The fact was the navy didn't want anyone to know—especially the Germans—that they would be equipping LCSs with rocket launchers.

The intensive training lasted five weeks, and then the entire outfit was moved to Lido Beach, Long Island. This was their embarkation point. They sat there for another three or more weeks. Berra gained five pounds filling in as a soda jerk in one of the base's stores.

Eventually the sailors were packed on a boat in Bayonne, New Jersey, which made another stop in Boston. Like many other landlubbers who hailed from all over the country, seaman Berra was sick the entire way to Boston. He was not alone. The hold was where the transporting seamen were supposed to sleep in hammocks four high. Half of those men were seasick. No matter how sick they were, everyone at one time or another tried to escape the hold to escape the stench.

Then the voyage began. Their ship hooked up with a large convoy in Halifax, Nova Scotia, and went over to Glasgow, Scotland. Berra felt fine during the Atlantic crossing, but he was not fond of navy life. The hours for sleep were not long, and the loudspeakers were constantly crackling and nagging the sailors. When they weren't barking orders, they were sounding general quarters to prepare the men for battle.

"I don't think there's any feeling worse than being down in a hold of a ship when they sound general quarters. You look at the side of a ship, and you wonder how thick that iron is," Berra remembered. Inevitable thoughts of bombs hitting the deck and torpedos breaching the ship's sides and water rushing in dogged the crew. Most sailors hit the deck running when the commanders sounded general quarters because they never knew when it might just be the real thing.

After arriving in Glasgow, Berra and the others took a train to the Devonshire coast of England to stay in Plymouth, an ancient seaport. Not long after their arrival, enemy submarines began picking off ships coming out of Plymouth. Berra's crew was assigned a ship to patrol the waters off the port, but never saw any action. Now, they were to wait for D-day.

Berra and his crew would man one of the support craft selected to lend cover fire and to launch rockets at Omaha Beach. The men and their LCSs were loaded onto the USS *Bayfield*, and the ship then waited in the harbor. June 4, 1944, came and went, and the men waited still. The night of June 5, they were told they would be going in early in the morning, no matter what the weather.

Berra's LCS was lifted up on the davits and lowered into the water at exactly 4:30 AM on June 6, 1944. And off six small ships went in the early morning dark, equipped with maps, machine guns, and rockets.

There were, of course, five beaches that the Allied command attempted to open that day. They were codenamed Sword, Juno, Gold, Omaha, and Utah Beaches. None were easy. Many men died. Omaha was located along Sainte-Honorine-des-Pertes, St. Lô, and Vierville-sur-Mer in France.

The German armed forces had prepared the Atlantic Wall defenses well. A gentle downward slope provided an excellent field of fire. The German 352nd Division defending Omaha Beach was one of the better-trained units in the area. Twenty-seven of the Allies' 32 amphibious Sherman DD tanks, intended to give armored support, foundered in the rough seas before reaching shore. The Allied air bombardment of the beach defenses prior to the landings was largely ineffective, as the bombardment fell too far inland. The initial naval bombardment proved somewhat ineffective as well because of the short time allotted to the naval guns (40 minutes). As a result, the German defenses were left largely intact when the first assault waves hit the beach. Soldiers who were not immediately killed found almost no protection on the 182-meter-deep beach (at low tide), and what little cover was provided by the beach obstacles was nullified by overlapping fields of fire presighted by the Germans.

As portrayed in the movie *Saving Private Ryan*, the German machine-gun nests were set inside reinforced concrete bunkers on the bluffs. The Germans were able to shoot straight into the landing crafts the moment the ramps went down. The effects were immediate and devastating.

Lieutenant J.G. Tom Holmes piloted Berra's boat, which was one of those that went in 40 minutes before the first landing crafts opened their doors to the murderous fire. The air force and the battleships were firing at will, hoping to soften up the beachhead, as the six boats came nearer the beach.

"Being a young guy, I thought it was like the Fourth of July, to tell you the truth. I said, boy, it looks pretty, all the planes coming over. The battleship opened up on the beachhead. And I was looking out, and my officer said, 'You better get your head down in here if you want it on,'" Berra told journalist Keith Olbermann.

"I wanted to see the view, I really did. Being a young guy, I didn't think nothing of it until you got in it. And so we went off 300 yards off beach. We went in before the—what do you call the—we protect them. If they ran into any trouble, we would fire the rockets over," Berra continued.

"We had a lead boat that would fire one rocket. If it hits the beach, then everybody opens up. We could fire one rocket if we wanted to, or we could fire off 24 of them, 12 on each side. And it was pretty good. And we stretched out 50 yards apart. And that was the invasion. And nothing happened to us. That's one good thing. Our boat could go anywhere, though. We were pretty good, flat bottom, 36-footer."

Berra, his five crewmates, and Lieutenant Holmes went back and forth on that LCS for 12 days. They ran interference at Omaha and Utah Beaches for the landing crafts and other ships and transports. Berra loaded and fired his rocket launcher and fired his machine gun, and he and the others did anything they could to soften up the German defenses.

"We had orders to shoot anything that came below the clouds. And one of our own planes came down over the clouds, and we shot it down. And we were the closest to him to pick up the pilot. And you should have heard the words he was saying," recalled Berra. "He said, 'If you guys shot down as many planes before, the war would be over a long time ago.' He was really mad."

Their LCS also led the way for more troop ships, guiding them through mine-filled waters. In those two weeks there was little sleep for the six-man crew. No one shaved, and they ate K-rations as they worked.

When the battle was over and their tour done, the boys went to sleep. Many passed out in their bunks, still unshaven. Even when the general quarters alarm went off during those first few days of precious sleep, few of their six-man crew responded.

"If it hits, let it hit. I can't move," Berra remembers saying.

The crew was eventually transferred to Bizerte, Tunisia. Bizerte was of strategic importance at that time in the war. It is located on the north coast of Tunisia, approximately 50 miles north of Tunis and 10 miles away from Cap Blanc, the northernmost point in Africa. Bizerte is on the Mediterranean coast and is close to both Sardinia and Sicily. Known as the oldest and most European city in Tunisia, it was founded around 1000 BC by Phoenicians from Tyre and eventually fell under Carthage's rule. It figures in much of Mediterranean history.

"The only thing I knew about Bizerte was that song, 'Gertie from Bizerte,' which made it sound like a real live town, but it was strictly nothing. If there was anything to see there, I missed it," said Berra.

At this time, it was a giant depot, and Berra and his crew lived in tents on the beaches, moving fuel supplies from one end of the beach to the other. While there, Berra was promoted to Seaman First Class and received a $10 pay increase. He was now making $84 per month. With no rent and no costs for food or any other wants, he was sending most of the money back home. This made him feel good as he repaid his mother for all of her kindnesses when he was suffering in Norfolk. He was very proud to be sending her money, and it made him feel a whole lot better about everything he had been through.

His crew's next assignment was as dangerous as it got. Their LCS was chosen to target a large resort hotel that had been turned into an arsenal by the German command. The rooms were reinforced and outfitted with machine gun and mortar nests. Berra and the crew's job was to go in as close as they could and pepper the building with rockets and machine-gun fire.

The LCS squadron that went out was very large and was a combined force of Allied ships. Naval gunfire came from their ships, including the French battleship *Lorraine*, British battleship HMS *Ramillies*, and the

American capital ships USS *Texas*, *Nevada*, and *Arkansas*. A fleet of more than 50 cruisers and destroyers supported the landings. Seven Allied escort carriers provided air cover. There were weapons firing on all sides. The entire area was a killing field.

More than 94,000 troops and 11,000 vehicles landed on August 15, 1944. A number of German troops had been diverted to fight the Allied forces in northern France after Operation Overlord, and a major attack by French resistance fighters, coordinated by Captain Aaron Bank of the Office of Strategic Services (OSS), helped drive the remaining German forces back from the beachhead in advance of the landing. As a result, the Allied forces met little resistance as they moved inland. The quick success of this invasion, with a 20-mile penetration in 24 hours, sparked a major uprising by resistance fighters in Paris.

The arsenal they were targeting was the main target of the second day's fighting at a place codenamed Yellow Beach. The fighting during the prelanding and landing phases was fierce and closer than what Berra and his unit had experienced on D-day.

Berra and the crew began firing their rockets into the hotel, firing one after the other in a fierce barrage. They pulverized the building as smoke billowed out. And suddenly there were German troops trying to escape the entrenchment. Now the crewmen manned their machine guns and fired relentlessly, knocking down one opposing soldier after another.

Suddenly, someone yelled, "Heads down!"

Berra dropped a rocket he was holding and dove under a machine gun. As he recalls, there wasn't even enough time to say a Hail Mary. It was a rocket launched from a British warship, but it turned out that the rocket was a dud. It landed a yard shy of the stern and only created a big splash, almost swamping the boat. In the end no one was hurt, but the crew was badly jostled. It woke up the young crew about the dangers they had been facing.

After the fighting ceased, the crew went ashore, and people came out of their homes to welcome the American and British soldiers and sailors as heroes.

"One minute it was all shooting and killing," Berra recalled. "The next thing you know, there are all the Frenchmen and women and kids, too, coming out with bottles of wine and bouquets of flowers for you with kisses and with tears in their eyes."

\*    \*    \*

The LCS crew was then ordered to Naples. In Naples, they stayed at an old inn. Forty seamen and eight officers took up residence in a hotel that oversaw the Bay of Naples. While they hung around awaiting new orders, they ate and slept well. It was like a paid vacation. First they squandered days, then weeks. Berra even managed to get a pass so he could go visit the Isle of Capri. Berra didn't have to waste much money. He had packs of cigarettes and bars of chocolate, which were a currency unto themselves.

Berra could speak enough Italian to get by, though the dialect he spoke at home was not easily understood by the friendly Neapolitans.

One day, Berra ran into someone he knew from St. Louis, Bob Cocaterra. Cocaterra was headed to Milan in a jeep and asked if Berra wanted to ride shotgun. He declined, but asked if Cocaterra wouldn't mind taking him as far as Rome.

"It's all right with me if it's all right with your C.O.," said Cocaterra.

"I don't know when they're shipping us out again," shrugged the noncommittal C.O. "They don't tell me. Maybe it'll be tomorrow. Maybe we'll be hanging out down here another month. Do what you like."

Berra figured nothing serious would happen to him. According to Gene Schoor, an early Berra biographer, "He'd already been awarded a Distinguished Unit Citation, two battle stars, a European Theater of Operations (ETO) ribbon, and a Good Conduct Medal."

Upon their arrival in Rome, Cocaterra tried to persuade Berra to come up to Milan with him. But he refused. He wanted to see Rome, not Milan, and he had another reason.

"I hear there's still fighting up that way," Berra said, and shook his head.

He went to the Vatican, seeing the Sistine Chapel and the various sights. He was also quite pleased that he saw Pope Pius XII standing on the balcony while he was there.

He was even more pleased when he returned to Naples and found that the squadron had received no new orders—things were just the same as when he had left. As the war was winding down, the army's and navy's need for their services in the European theater was limited. Some of the crews were split up and sent to other wartime duties.

Toward the end of 1944, Berra and his crew were transferred to Oran, Algeria. Oran is the most important city in western Algeria. But again, no assignments were meted out to the crews, and they were left to do as they pleased.

For Berra, his most memorable moment was attending midnight mass on Christmas Eve in a church in Oran. Later, they received orders to ship out on New Year's Eve—they were being sent back to the United States. While some soldiers and sailors were redistributed to the Pacific Theater of war, Berra drew the lucky card. For all intents and purposes, the war was over for him.

*   *   *

"We came back on an LSD, same way we went over. It took us 19 or 20 days to get over, and same way going back, and went back to Little Creek. They took us in to see the doctors. You know, 'Guys, were you scared, and, you know, going overseas and all that?' I said, 'Well, it was a little bit.' I said, 'Yes, it was scary,'" Berra remembered. "Later, you do get a little scared. You see the people. And I've seen guys drown. We would pick them up and everything."

There was one thing Berra never wanted to do: go back to war. Olbermann put it best, saying, "Of that terrible place, he says, in the grimmest of tones and with the common-sense simplicity of his eloquence, 'I've seen it.'"

On his return home, Berra got a 30-day leave. He raced back to St. Louis. He'd been worried about his mother the entire time. She greeted him the best way she knew how, filling him up on spaghetti, ravioli, lasagna, and antipasto. He ate fresh Italian bread and drank his father's red wine. He saw his family and many friends. And just when it was starting to get old, he was due back to the navy. Only now he was headed to a submarine base in Groton, Connecticut.

Berra was apprehensive about this new assignment because he was afraid the navy would turn him into a submariner just when he thought his stint was over. And he did not like the idea of being cooped up in a submarine, where he could not go up top on deck for fresh air the way he often had on regular ships.

But his fears were allayed when he arrived. He'd listed sports and recreation in his enlistment papers for personal preferences. By either luck or paperwork or happenstance, Berra found himself assigned to sports and recreation at the Groton base. They had a ballclub, and it was run by Lieutenant James "Gee Gee" Gleeson, an outfielder who had played five years in the big leagues for the Indians, the Cubs, and the Reds. He had played his last game in 1942, a career .263 hitter.

However, Yogi was not assigned to the ballclub. Instead of his beloved baseball, Berra had been assigned to the theater. He was there to mop up and to keep the place generally clean. It wasn't a hard job; he saw plenty of movies and there was little to repair or fix. But this did little to shake his thirst for baseball. He pestered the personnel officer, Commander Robert H. Barnes.

Berra insisted that he was indeed a professional baseball player. And, in fact, he insisted he was a New York Yankee. Barnes was hard-pressed to believe him, but he acquiesced and sent Berra over to Gleeson, who managed the base's team, called the Groton Raiders.

"You're a ballplayer?" Gleeson asked in disbelief. "Says here you're a boxer."

"I did some boxing, but I'm Yankees property, like I told you. I'm a professional ballplayer," Berra insisted.

This back-and-forth with Gleeson went on for some time. Gleeson even brought in Ray Volpe, a former Kansas City Blues pitcher. Together they quizzed Berra over and over until they figured maybe he wasn't lying. So Gleeson relented and told Berra to show up in April for baseball practice.

When April came, Berra was so wound up he ended up clouting the ball all over the field, and Gleeson was impressed. Unfortunately, he had two top pro prospects for catchers, so Berra was forced to play the outfield. It was said that Gleeson cringed every time a fly ball went to Berra, but Berra's bat always overshadowed his mistakes.

One of the Raiders, Joe Glenn, had been a catcher for the Browns, Red Sox, and Yankees, and he was eventually shipped out. And Tony Anselmo, a

Pacific Coast League star, left after hurting his ankle. Thus, Berra played the entire second half of the season at catcher. He handled the pitchers well and was good behind the plate, but he lacked accuracy throwing to second. He played every game that season.

During this period Berra played lots of baseball. He was honing his skills, such as they were. The Raiders played semipro teams and other service teams, and on days when he had leave, he easily found other teams willing to pay him to play. In some weeks he made as much as an extra $50.

One game easily stood out that season, a game the Raiders played against the New York Giants. The famous Mel Ott was managing the Giants. Ott was mesmerized as Berra got hit after hit, violently clubbing the ball both in batting practice and in the course of the game. Berra went 3-for-4 against Giants pitcher Ace Adams.

"That was a wild pitch he hit," Ott told Gleeson.

"He'll hit anything that comes near the plate, and a lot that's off the plate," Gleeson replied. "He's awkward. He can't throw, but he's got the quickest wrist action I've ever seen."

Ott was impressed. Upon his return to New York from New London, Connecticut, Ott went right up to see Larry MacPhail, who was now president and general manager of the New York Yankees.

"You're pretty fixed for catchers, aren't you, Larry?" asked Ott. "We'd like to buy one of 'em. A kid you probably don't even know you've got."

Ott offered $50,000 for Berra on the spot.

"That kid catcher?" MacPhail replied, stalling for time. "Yeah, I know who you mean," he lied. "Fifty thousand dollars?"

"That's what I said," said Ott.

MacPhail demurred, saying he would seriously consider the offer.

"Truth be told, I'd never even heard of Berra. But I figured if he was worth 50 grand to Ottie, he must be worth 50 grand to me. That's why I turned him down," MacPhail admitted years later.

As soon as Ott was gone, MacPhail grabbed the phone and called Paul Krichell, a scout with the team. Krichell knew almost everyone in the Yankees organization. MacPhail peppered him with questions about Berra and then insisted Berra be brought to New York for MacPhail to get a closer look.

Krichell sent a wire to Berra in New London, telling him to come down to New York immediately, as MacPhail wanted to see him. Berra was thrilled and took advantage of his next possible leave to take the train down to New York.

"I'm Yogi Berra. You asked me to come see you," Berra said as he entered the room.

MacPhail did a double take. Berra didn't look like a baseball player at all. To MacPhail, Berra in his navy dress whites looked like a vaudeville comedian.

"So I waited for my first look at the prize package that was worth $50,000. The instant I saw him my heart sank, and I wondered why I had been so foolish as to refuse to sell him. He had no neck, and his muscles were virtually busting the buttons off his uniform…. The sailor suit accentuated every defect," said MacPhail of the first meeting.

Whatever it was, Berra did something to impress MacPhail. MacPhail told him that after his turn was up in the service he was to report to the Newark team in the International League, the top minor league team of the New York Yankees.

Berra was elated, but that didn't stop him from asking a solid business question: "Who's paying my expenses for this trip?"

MacPhail said later, "Maybe I didn't think much of him when he walked into my office, but when he asked me to pay for his train ticket, I didn't have to be told that I was dealing with a professional ballplayer."

Six days before his 21st birthday, on May 6, 1946, Yogi Berra was released from the hold of the navy. He went to St. Louis and celebrated his birthday with his family. He had not heard from MacPhail and wasn't sure that he would follow through on their conversation. But sure enough, a telegram came, telling him to report to the Newark team.

In the meantime, Joey Garagiola was working out with the St. Louis Cardinals. He was 6'0", 180 pounds, and he was the backup catcher. By the end of the year, he would catch 70 games, making him the person who played the position most during the year.

The St. Louis Cardinals were among the most successful teams of the era. Between 1926 and 1944, the Cardinals won eight National League pennants and five World Series. The Cards tangled with the Yankees four times on the national stage, taking two of four Series. And they had finished with records of 100 or more wins in 1931, 1942, 1943, and 1944. They were the home of the Gashouse Gang, the Dean brothers, Rogers Hornsby, Johnny Mize, Stan Musial, Frankie Frisch, Red Schoendienst, Joe Medwick, and many, many more. In effect, they were the Yankees of the National League.

And because their games were broadcast over radio powerhouse KMOX, the Cardinals were one of the biggest draws and most popular teams in the Midwest. Aside from being hometown boys on major league teams, for Berra and Garagiola—for any boy from that neighborhood—there could be no bigger dream than to play for the Cardinals.

While Berra toiled with the Newark team, still in the minors, Garagiola made his major league debut on May 26, 1946. He was a Cardinal alongside Musial, Schoendienst, Terry Moore, and Enos Slaughter, among others. He was hanging out in the clubhouse with those players. He was one of those players.

Berra was happy for Garagiola, but he was also a little bit jealous. In truth, it was to be an exciting, wild ride for the two boys from Elizabeth Avenue.

# ~ Chapter 5 ~

# NEWARK

Berra caught up with the Newark Bears in Rochester, New York. The team, as a whole, was disappointed with him when he arrived. Here they were, waiting on a pitcher named Walt Dubiel, a promising young right-hander. No one had ever heard of the odd-looking Berra. So dubious was George Selkirk, manager of the Newark Bears, that he insisted that Berra produce the telegram that had brought him to the Newark team. Berra dug into his suitcase and found the crumpled cable.

"Get him a room," growled Selkirk.

Selkirk was not in a mood to be toyed with. Newark was a good team, and they were in the middle of a long road trip that could be instrumental in their taking the International League pennant. And his bonus money was based on how his team performed.

George "Twinkletoes" Selkirk was not to be trifled with. He had played for the New York Yankees for nine seasons and retired with a lifetime batting average of .290. He had clouted 108 home runs in his day, amassed 576 RBIs, and participated in six World Series, collecting a winning share in five of them. He had been an All-Star in 1936 and 1939. Selkirk won the nickname Twinkletoes while playing for the Newark Bears—his teammates gave him the name because he ran with his weight on the balls of his feet.

Selkirk had been an important cog in Joe McCarthy's dynasty. In 1936 all three Yankees outfielders hit for .300 or better. Selkirk was known as a patient hitter. Four times in his career he drew two walks in an inning, and he walked

103 times in 1939. Selkirk hit five home runs in four consecutive games in 1939 and drove in more than 100 runs in 1936 and 1939.

Selkirk, who was born in Huntsville, Canada, would go on to accomplish great things in baseball, but even if he had stopped any involvement with baseball after his playing days ended, his mark still would have been made. First, Selkirk had been the man brought in to follow the great Babe Ruth and was given No. 3 before it was retired. So he knew about pressure. And second, in July 1935, the colorful Yankees outfielder suggested that a cinder path six feet wide be installed in the outfield so a player would know when he was nearing the wall. It was Selkirk who had contributed what is now known as the warning track to Major League Baseball.

Selkirk himself had only recently returned from the navy, where he had been an aerial gunner. Now he had one of the toughest jobs in baseball—to manage one of the top farm clubs of the most successful ballclub in Major League Baseball. Expectations for the Bears were no less than they were for the Yankees.

"During the 1930s and 1940s, the best team in the American League—the New York Yankees—kept most of their top prospects on the rosters of two top minor league teams," wrote minor league historians Bill Weiss and Marshall Wright. "One of these clubs was in Kansas City, where the American Association Blues enjoyed the Yankees' largess. The other team played closer to home, in Newark, New Jersey. In 1941 the Newark Bears enjoyed the fruits of this relationship, putting together one of the strongest teams of the era."

However, none of the New York teams liked a strong club, minor league or not, just across the river. It was thought that they would take away fans from the three competing clubs and put bad ideas in the minds of men who saw success on the Jersey side. Since the late 1800s, Newark had supported a series of teams (both successful and not) that had been either bought or sold, only to be moved or dissolved.

According to Weiss and Wright, "Following the 1931 season, the team received a shot in the arm. On November 12, Colonel Jacob Ruppert, the owner of the New York Yankees, bought the Newark franchise for a reported $600,000." For a long time, many major league owners and Ruppert himself had understood that the reason behind the success of the St. Louis Cardinals team was the leadership and innovation of Branch Rickey. "Rickey had developed a series of 'farm teams'—minor league teams where he could develop Cardinals talent. To this end, Ruppert purchased the Bears to serve as the Yankees' primary farm team. Newark's era of baseball glory was about to begin," wrote Weiss and Wright.

Ruppert's involvement with the Bears showed instant results. Packed with new Yankees prospects, the 1932 Bears roared through the league and took the International League pennant. They finished with a 109–59 record. From 1931 to 1945, the Bears won seven pennants, finished second five times, and finished third and fourth three times. The Yankees had taken one of their most successful pressure players and placed him in a tough job. Indeed, Selkirk's predecessor, Billy Meyer, had never finished less than second.

\*    \*    \*

On the morning after Berra's arrival in Newark, the Bears' condescending trainer, Jimmy Mack, who had obviously taken his cue from the disappointed and cynical Selkirk, pieced together a worn-out uniform for Berra to wear. The shirt was too small, and the pants were too large. It was obvious Mack didn't think too much of Berra. Berra accepted the uniform with grace and humility, even after he noticed the shirt had no number. However, when Mack handed him an old, used, frayed hat that was too small, Berra handed it back. To add insult to injury, Mack merely split the seam at the back of the hat so it would fit and handed it back to him.

Finally Berra lost his temper and tossed the hat and uniform back.

"Hey, I want a new uniform. I ain't tryin' out. I play for this club," shouted Berra.

Mack gave Berra a new uniform and a brand-new cap that actually fit.

"I was an old clubhouse boy myself. And I knew what the score was," Berra said. This was just another of a long line of troubles he was to have with clubhouse boys and other baseball men who didn't think he belonged. He didn't look like a baseball player.

Unfortunately, it didn't matter much what Berra wore because he didn't do anything for the first few weeks but watch. He took part in warm-ups and in throwing and running drills, but he got little to no batting practice, and Selkirk completely ignored him.

Berra's roommate, however, would turn out to be a lifelong friend. His name was Bobby Brown, and he hailed from San Francisco. An infielder by trade, he was actually studying to be a doctor, which he eventually became. Brown was a studious fellow who carted huge books around with him. He was always reading, especially the thick, cumbersome medical textbooks, as opposed to Berra's comic books. Having already attended UCLA and Stanford, Brown went to Tulane University in the off-season, where he eventually earned his degree. But he was no pushover as a player. Brown batted .344 that year for Newark and finished second for the batting title. He was one of the great bonus babies of his generation, signing for a whopping $30,000.

Where Berra was unpolished and crude (but never in a menacing manner), Brown was the epitome of sophistication and knowledge. Not only was Brown book smart (which, of course, impressed Berra and everyone else in baseball), but he knew how to enter a room, how to dress, how to order food in a fancy restaurant, and so forth. The two roommates, who got along famously, could not have been more different.

One of the most famous stories about their friendship centered on their choice of reading material. One night while on the road, Brown sighed, rubbed his eyes, and closed the big medical textbook he had been absorbed in. But Berra was still reading his comic book.

"Come on, put out the light," said the tired Brown.

"In a minute. I'm almost through," said the engrossed Berra, determined to finish the story. "I'll turn it out."

Finally, the story done, Berra closed his comic book, placed it on the nightstand, and turned off the light. Then he said to Brown, "Gee, that was a good one. How did yours turn out?"

"Yogi doesn't forget much," Brown remembered years later, noting that Berra always reminds him how he outhit Brown when they were called up to the majors at the end of the 1946 season. "I will never forget how much knowing him over the years enriched my life. The world needs more people like Yogi Berra. They don't need to look like him, just be like him. Kind, thoughtful, interesting, and humble."

\*   \*   \*

Meanwhile, MacPhail was anxious. Bill Dickey, the current Yankees catcher, was in the last year of his career. Yes, the Yankees had other catching prospects, but Berra was special. If he was really worth the $50,000 Ott offered for him, MacPhail had his next catcher. If Berra was a bust, MacPhail could sell him to Ott quickly and realize a hefty profit.

But Selkirk scowled at Berra every time he saw him and eventually had to be forced to use him. In the first game of a doubleheader on a Sunday, Selkirk finally piped up for Berra, using him as a pinch-hitter. Berra got a hit. Selkirk put him in the lineup at catcher for the second game, and Berra delivered, calling a good game and hitting 2-for-3. From then on, he was in the lineup for the Bears. He played in 77 games and hit .314 with 15 homers and 59 RBIs.

Berra was on his way to having a good season, but there were a few mishaps along the way. His erratic throwing continued to plague him. In one game he made two wild throws. One hit a base runner he was trying to throw out; the second unexpectedly walloped an umpire positioned 10 feet away from second base. In another game he actually hit his own pitcher while trying to throw to second.

\*   \*   \*

In the meantime, Garagiola was playing in the majors for the St. Louis Cardinals, who were headed for the pennant. He had played in 74 games and batted .237, with three home runs and 22 RBIs. On September 5, 1946, the people of the Hill sponsored Joe Garagiola Night at Sportsman's Park.

Folks on the Hill were so proud that one of their own had made it that one night, on his way to the park, a local vegetable peddler said to him in his best English, "Gioi, you the firsta boy what comes from the Hill with a name with a ends *A, E, I, O* getta name in the paper and no kill somebody."

Garagiola said it was the first time his parents had gone down into that section of St. Louis without going to the bureau of naturalization for citizenship processing. His brother Mickey and his parents, Angelina and Giovanni, sat in the stands, and his mother said she felt sorry for the man who had to pay for all the lights they had on. When Mickey explained that all the other 29,000 people there had paid to get in, she scoffed, saying the boss could afford it.

"It will always be a top thrill for me because that night I saw many people there like Mama and Pop—people who didn't know what baseball was, but wanted to be there because 'this is one of our boys,'" said Garagiola.

*   *   *

Berra and Garagiola had good seasons, but Selkirk's Bears did not perform as expected and finished 80–74 and in fourth place. The Bears squeaked into the playoffs on the last day of the season with a 5–4 win over Syracuse on September 8, 1946.

The Bears were down one run after the Syracuse club touched them for the go-ahead run in the top of the ninth. "The Bears came right back when Larry Berra, who was voted most popular Newark player in a fan poll, hit the first pitch over the wall for his 15th home run," reported the Associated Press.

The Bears were then slated to play the Montreal Royals. It was Newark's 14th straight year in the playoffs. Montreal had won the pennant that year and so drew the least successful of the clubs to make the playoffs. Montreal had finished 20 games better than the Bears and were led by an electric player named Jackie Robinson, who was the International League batting champion. It didn't hurt that Montreal's players also included Johnny Jorgensen, Al Campanis, Marv Rackley, Les Burge, and other solid players.

Going into the first round, the Bears were overmatched, but managed to make a decent series out of it. Montreal took the first two games, but the Bears came back. "Larry Berra hit the first home run of the series in the second," reported the Associated Press. Adding runs in the fifth and seventh on sacrifice flies by Ken Holcombe, the Bears took the third game 4–0. The Bears then took the fourth game 3–2 to even the series 2–2. Despite strong pitching by Vic Raschi, Montreal took Game 5 2–1.

The fourth game was a wild affair. A crowd of 19,953 attended the hotly contested game and got their money's worth. The Royals were down 4–3 with two outs in the ninth inning. Then up came the big first baseman, Les Burge. With a 2–2 count, Burge let the fifth pitch go by without swinging. Umpire Artie Gore called it a ball, and the Bears went wild. Selkirk had to be restrained. On the next pitch, Burge crushed a game-tying home run. The Bears were hot, screaming at Gore. Selkirk came out and started screaming. Other Bears joined him. Selkirk, pitcher Herb Karpel, Johnny Moore, and Jack Phillips were then all thrown out of the game by Gore.

Reliable old Bears fireballer Alex Mustaikis came in to pitch. Montreal's Tom Tatum greeted Mustaikis with a single. And then Herman Franks sent a double to the outfield, and Tatum raced home. The throw was right on target. Berra scooped it up and tagged Tatum.

"When Gore called Tatum safe on a close play at the plate, catcher Larry Berra of the Bears rushed at the umpire. Berra was restrained by fellow players," the Associated Press claimed.

By all accounts, Berra literally had to be pulled back as he let fly with a stream of invectives against Gore. He gesticulated violently. Berra was a tough, focused competitor. He had fought to get where he was, and he was not going to be denied. He would fight now.

"The Montreal players and the police had to assist Gore off the field to prevent angry Newark players from molesting him," continued the Associated Press article.

Later Gore explained that Berra had juggled the ball and thus did not have possession during the tag, though he also admitted that Berra had not dropped the ball.

"Either way, I thought he was dead wrong," Berra said later. Berra also admitted that if he hadn't been restrained, he would have actually struck Gore.

After the loss, International League president Frank Shaughnessy fined Berra $500. But the Yankees picked up the tab, sparing him the expense.

*   *   *

On September 20, 1946, a small article appeared in *The New York Times*, whose headline read, "Yankees Recall Four: Brown, Berra, Colman, Raschi Are to Return from Newark."

In the baseball business, players who get called up from the minors in the last weeks of the season experience a "cup of coffee." This means they get a taste of the big-league experience, no matter how brief.

Frank Colman had been a player for the Pittsburgh Pirates in the past. He was trying to find a way to stay in baseball, but his career, though he may not have known it, was almost over. As for Vic Raschi, Bobby Brown, and Berra, this little cup of coffee would be just the beginning of an amazing run for these three players.

Brown was actually owned by the Yankees, so he was truly recalled. But the Yankees had to buy the contracts of Raschi, Berra, and Colman to bring them up.

On September 22, Colman, Brown, and Berra all performed well. Louis Effrat wrote that the three "already figured in the plans for the future. Certainly their work yesterday did not hurt their chances."

"Berra, a 21-year-old ex-sailor who resembles Charlie Keller in stature and at bat, collected two hits in his four trips. The second time up, in the fourth, he hit a home run with Keller on base, which served up the victory for [Spud] Chandler," wrote Jim McCulley for the *New York Daily News*.

Reportedly, in one of his first at-bats in the big leagues, Berra let the first pitch go by for a strike.

Philadelphia A's catcher Buddy Rosar said to Berra, "This ain't Newark."

Berra stepped out of the batter's box, loosened up, took a swing, and got back in the batter's box, all the while looking at the pitcher. Then he said to Rosar, "They tell me you got a ball team in Philadelphia."

"You'll learn up here if they ever let you stay up here," Rosar was supposed to have said.

"I'm staying here all right."

Buddy signaled A's pitcher Jesse Flores for a curve. When the pitch came, Berra tattooed it for a home run.

As Berra crossed the plate after his round-tripper, McPhail, clapping in his box, reportedly said, "And Mel Ott wanted me to sell him for $50,000."

*   *   *

Berra went 2-for-4 in the top half of a doubleheader, including a two-run home run. The next day the Yankees won behind Raschi, and Berra hit another home run.

Effrat wrote, "The work of Bobby Brown at short, Berra behind the plate, and Colman in right field continued to be better than fair."

All the time they were around Yankee Stadium and the clubhouse, Berra stole looks at Joe DiMaggio, Tommy Henrich, Phil Rizzuto, and the rest of the famous players on the Yankees roster. It was like a who's who of baseball greats.

At the end of the season, the Yankees released Dickey, the All-Star catcher for the Yankees for many years. A lifetime .313 hitter, he had struggled to hit .261 in 1946, his 17th season.

In all, Berra had appeared in seven games and had batted .364 with two home runs and four RBIs. He was now a Yankee. He played on the big stage, wearing a real major league uniform in one of baseball's most famous parks. He was happy and looking forward to the next season. The club did, in fact, have a lot of catching talent, even with Dickey gone. He would have to compete to make sure he got his shot. But he was confident.

He also met another young man that year who would be influential in his life.

"I guess it was Paul Krichell who introduced us," Whitey Ford remembered years later. Ford had been signed at the end of 1946, and they brought him down to the stadium to watch a game. It turned out to be one of the seven games Berra played in.

"Larry, I want you to meet Eddie Ford, who just signed with us. Eddie, this is Larry Berra," Krichell said.

"People were still calling him Larry then, and I wouldn't become Whitey until I was in the minor leagues," Ford recalled. Ford would disappear into the minor leagues for a few years before reemerging at Yankee Stadium, but Ford never forgot the meeting.

*    *    *

Although his first games in the majors were finished, there was something just as exciting to occupy Berra. Garagiola was playing in the World Series. The Cards had faltered in the last weeks of the season, and so they ended up in a tie with the Brooklyn Dodgers, the first time since 1908 that a playoff had been forced. In the first game, Garagiola went 3-for-3 in his first three at-bats, playing catcher, and the Cards won 4–2. The Cards went on to win the second game, 8–4, to take the short playoff.

Berra raced back to St. Louis so he could watch his boyhood friend play in the park of their dreams for a world championship during a year in which they had both played in the major leagues. Garagiola was about to play for the hometown St. Louis Cardinals against the famed Boston Red Sox.

Garagiola played the best baseball of his career in that World Series. He completely rose to the occasion. Known today as a pitchman, talking head, and raconteur, Garagiola played incredibly well for the Cards in 1946. He batted .316 in the seven-game Series, getting six hits in 19 at-bats, punching two doubles, and tallying four RBIs.

His best game was Game 4 in Boston. His four hits tied the record for hits in a World Series game at the time, as the Cards destroyed the Red Sox 12–3.

Berra watched the seventh and final game at Sportsman's Park. Garagiola caught into the eighth inning, but he split his finger when he caught a foul tip off the bat of Ted Williams. Garagiola was done for the Series.

"Everybody on Elizabeth Avenue was drinking more Dago Red than usual all week," remembered Berra.

It was as perfect an ending to the year as Berra could hope. Garagiola played well, their hometown team won the World Series, and both would be playing professional baseball the next year.

Between the end of October and the beginning of spring training, both Garagiola and Berra worked at the local Sears & Roebuck store in St. Louis.

The two clowned around a lot and didn't take the job very seriously. One time a customer approached Berra and asked for specific-sized screws. Berra shrugged and pointed to the proper section, saying, "You better pick them out yourself. I don't know one from another." Berra admitted later, "I was only being honest."

## ~ Chapter 6 ~

# THE YANKEES

The Yankees were the class of Major League Baseball. They were the butt of jokes on many teams, but not because they were bad. Everyone wanted to win like them, be thought of like them. Managers killed themselves trying to emulate the Yankees' success. It became an obsession. There was one story that always made the rounds during spring training.

In 1940 the Cardinals and the Yankees were working out very much near each other. During a team meeting, Ray Blades, the Cardinals manager, asked if there were any questions. This was probably not a wise thing to do with professional baseball players.

Pepper Martin, one of the great stars of the era, said he noticed the Yankees were only working out once a day and were winning championships, and the Cardinals team was working out twice a day. Why was that?

Blades went on to say that his goal was for his team to work twice as hard, since they made twice as many mistakes. "The Yankees' record should be incentive enough!" said Blades emphatically. "Any further questions, Pepper?"

"Yeah," said Pepper. "I got a jackass back in Oklahoma, and you can work him from sunup till sundown, and he ain't never gonna win the Kentucky Derby."

A small article appeared in the papers during the preseason of 1947, when the Yankees released their figures for 14 night games. The attendance came to 683,744 for night games in 1946. That was an average of 48,838 customers per game. The night games had proven themselves to be extremely popular with fans, and the Yankees noted that they were hoping to see similar results in 1947. The team was thinking about scheduling more in the future. MacPhail, ever the baseball promoter, cooked up an unpopular but lucrative scheme for the 1947 spring-training season. MacPhail named 33 players who would report early in 1947 to play a series of exhibition games in San Juan, Puerto Rico, and Caracas, Venezuela, where the Yankees would play the Dodgers three games. Then the Yankees would move on to Havana, Cuba, for a few more games with the Dodgers before joining the rest of the team in St. Petersburg, Florida.

The team would assemble and work out on February 15, in San Juan. The entire trip would be made possible because the team would fly to each destination, which made this very exotic, especially in the age of rail travel. The first game would be played on February 22.

Manager Bucky Harris was all for the early trip, as it would give him a chance to draw a bead on the many new players he had in camp and give them a little extra time to jell. Listed among the four catchers were Berra, Ralph Houk, Sherman Lollar, and Aaron Robinson. And waiting in Florida were Charlie Silvera and Gus Niarhros. Bobby Brown and Vic Raschi were included with Berra, as were some of the more well-known names, like DiMaggio, Rizzuto, Henrich, Allie Reynolds, and Charlie Keller.

For the most part, the trip went well enough for Berra. He got to meet the many stars yet again. And he got to play, sometimes catching and sometimes playing the outfield. Harris had seen Berra in the International League the year before. Harris had just come from Buffalo to take over the team when Dickey resigned and was sure he would find a place for the young man from St. Louis.

Leo Durocher, the Dodgers manager, opined during the trip, "He can hit what he can reach. Big-league curveballs will kill him." But by the end of the games they'd played against the Brooklyn nine, Leo the Lip, as Durocher was called, admitted, "I'll be darned. I don't know how he does it. How do you pitch to a guy like that?"

According to Berra himself, his teammates were more or less friendly, and by the end of the international junket, he was popular enough with the other players. His fielding was lacking, but he was good with a bat. And the writers knew they had something when they met Berra. Things weren't going too badly yet.

Berra took some lighthearted ribbing, which was normal among the players, on the way back from Havana to Florida. None of the players were fond of flying, and joking on the flight home helped to take the edge off their nerves. At one point, the Yankees' team doctor, Marvin A. Stevens, walked over to the nervous Berra. "Don't worry, my lad," he said, with all seriousness. "There's nothing to worry about. I'm the flight surgeon, you know, and I want to reassure you." Berra cracked his crooked grin, and the players all chuckled. Rizzuto clowned around in a huge sombrero he had bought during the trip.

At one point, each of the players took turns visiting the pilot's cabin. Upon returning from his turn in the cockpit, Berra was wearing the captain's hat. He stood tall, and everyone laughed. Frank Shea, a pitcher, borrowed the hat, cupped his mouth, and feigned an announcement, saying, "Don't be alarmed, gentlemen, but Captain Berra, our pilot, has just informed me that the fuel is running low. We've only got enough for four hours more aloft. By the way, we are only 18 minutes out of Tampa." Everyone cracked up again.

Early in March, Harris had told everyone that Berra would be in right field. It seemed Harris would do what he had to do to make sure Berra saw his turns at the plate. Columnist Quinton Reynolds once said of Harris, a two-time World Series champion manager, "He studies baseball as a medical student studies anatomy. He seems to be able to get the best out of mediocre talent."

"Yogi Berra, of course, continues as a fixture in right," wrote Arthur Daley in *The New York Times* on March 20. "His play continues to astound Bucky with each succeeding day. Yogi insists he is still in a terrific hitting slump, but blows continue to fly from his bat and he has yet to make a bad play in the outfield. No manager could expect more from a converted catcher."

Berra continued an impressive spring, collecting hits and RBIs. And by March 23, he started to grab his first headlines, collecting three hits as the Yankees routed the Red Sox 13–5 in Sarasota. By late March, he had compiled a 13-game hitting streak.

Sportswriter John Drebinger took note. He wrote, "Manager Bucky Harris became a minor casualty when a stray ball during the pregame practice cracked him on the right knee. Much of the pain vanished when Berra smacked a single into right in the third, extending his hitting streak to 14 games. Bucky takes deep and pardonable pride in the chunky little Yogi who, under cover of a series of night games in Caracas, was converted from a catcher into a surprisingly fine right fielder."

In April, Berra and Garagiola caught against each other, with Berra going 1-for-4 and Garagiola going 0-for-3. In an unremarkable game for both, New York prevailed over St. Louis 7–2, but it was the first time the old friends had faced each other in major league play, albeit in spring training.

When camp broke, the Yankees did a little barnstorming on their way back to New York. They played teams like Kiki Cuyler's Atlanta Crackers and the Norfolk Tars. Berra went on a rampage, and Drebinger wrote in early April, "Looks as though something will have to be done about this Yogi Berra, and very soon this burden will rest with the seven other clubs in the American League.... Yogi alone seems totally unaware of the commotion he is stirring all around him."

*　*　*

Berra had always swung at some of the wildest pitches throughout his career and was known as a bad-ball hitter. So much so that he became known as the best bad-ball hitter of his era and possibly one of the two or three best bad-ball hitters in the history of the game.

Roommate Bobby Brown once opined, "He has the biggest strike zone in baseball. It goes from his ankles to a foot over his head, from his breastbone to as far away from the plate as his bat can reach."

Opposing managers and pitchers were also flummoxed. Steve O'Neill, the manager of the Detroit Tigers, once said, "There's no way to pitch to him. He has no weaknesses. You can't even waste a pitch on him. Throw him a bad one, and, likely as not, he'll bang it into the stands."

Decades after their retirements, former Dodgers pitchers Don Newcombe and Don Drysdale were talking about the many batters they had faced, and Yogi Berra came up. Newcombe had seen many of his games unraveled by Berra in World Series play.

Newcombe rolled his eyes. "I don't know. I couldn't get him out," he reportedly said.

Drysdale laughed. "He was easy to get out," Drysdale reportedly replied. "I just threw him strikes right down the middle. He didn't know what do to with them."

Berra's penchant for golfing low pitches and hacking at high balls drove Harris and the other coaches to distraction. Charlie Dressen, who was on the Yankees' coaching staff at the time, told Berra he could improve tremendously if he only laid off some of the bad pitches he was swinging at.

"Don't let them sucker you into swinging at the bad ones," Dressen told him.

Dressen was obsessed with getting him to lay off bad pitches. In one game, Berra hit a home run, and as he rounded third base, Dressen was standing in the coach's box, shaking his head.

"It was a bad pitch!" he yelled to Berra.

"Nah! It was a good pitch," waved Yogi. "Right where I wanted it."

"Good hitters usually subscribe to the theory that you 'hit the ball where it's pitched.' Yogi's philosophy was to hit the ball *if* it was pitched. In his words, 'A bad pitch ain't a bad pitch anymore when you hit it into the seats,'" said Joe Garagiola.

According to Arthur Daley, in the earliest version of the story that can be found, Bucky Harris was in need of a pinch-hitter in June 1947 and chose Berra.

He said to Berra, "I know you are in a slump, but you aren't thinking enough at the plate. Think before you pick out a ball. Make sure it's good before you swing. Think!"

Berra went up to the plate with a scowl on his face and swung inelegantly. He struck out, flailing at a ball, and then stomped off to the corner of the dugout, muttering to himself. According to Daley, Harris wandered down to the far end only to hear Berra saying to himself, "How can a guy hit and think at the same time?"

*    *    *

Despite Berra's prowess at the plate, his fielding mistakes caused cringes among players, coaches, writers, and fans alike. What he lacked in skill, though, he tried to make up for with zeal.

The concerned Yankees executive and coaching staff brought in Joe "Ducky" Medwick, Berra's childhood hero, to coach the rookie outfielder. The former St. Louis legend signed with the Yankees as a free agent on December 11, 1946. He was hired to tutor Berra, showing him how to judge a fly ball, how to break on it, and how to set himself. Berra was thrilled to see his old newspaper customer helping him out, but Medwick couldn't make Berra steady and confident in such a short period. And while Berra's arm was strong, his aim was suspect. Eventually, Medwick was given his release by the Yankees on April 29, 1947.

Berra's adjustment to right field also affected center fielder Joe DiMaggio, who at one point had told Berra, "If I hear your voice, the ball is yours."

Years later, Berra would say about DiMaggio, "You had to play offa him." Put more succinctly, if DiMaggio had made up his mind the ball was his, it wasn't going to drop.

At one point, out in right field, Berra dove for a ball and crashed into the ailing DiMaggio. Fans and writers alike were aghast.

"I called for the ball, all right," DiMaggio explained to his teammates and the press, "but Yogi was too anxious to help me. He knows all about that bad heel of mine, and he figured he was doing something to save me…. He thought I was telling him to make the play. And he did try and pull away at the last minute."

But DiMaggio could sometimes be caustic. One time the young Berra approached DiMaggio seeking advice on how to approach a certain pitcher. DiMaggio snapped, "Just walk up to the plate and *hit* the ball. There's no talent involved."

Despite this, Berra has said on several occasions, "DiMaggio was the best player I ever saw."

Years later he said that DiMaggio, while portrayed as aloof in Richard Ben Cramer's book *Joe DiMaggio: The Hero's Life,* regularly played cards on the train with the other fellows. But Berra was the first to admit, "He'd get off the train in another city, and a car would be there to take him to the hotel while the rest of the guys waited for the team bus." But whenever Berra went out with "the Big Dago," as DiMaggio liked to be called, Berra never picked up a check. Of course, close friends would chuckle at a statement like this, as Berra was known to be very frugal. Berra has always displayed a reverence and empathy for DiMaggio over the years. He would always tell people that he remembered DiMaggio, legs crossed in the locker room, sipping a cup of coffee and enjoying a cigarette, as the best player he ever played with.

\*     \*     \*

While Berra continued to gain popularity with his teammates and garner favor with his manager for his play, he also became a target of much ribbing. As in other places, players began to make fun of his looks. Always a good-natured man, he put up with much of it, trying to smile through it as he dealt with jibe after jibe.

It must be said that bench-jockeying has taken place in baseball since they started throwing a ball to a batter. It can get pretty hairy in the world of professional baseball. It is a rite of initiation, and it is part of the game. The idea is to harass, distract, change the mood, and cloud the focus of the man at the plate, thus decreasing his chance of getting a hit.

But for Berra, the rite of passage became a hazing.

"The many jokes, remarks, and cruel comparisons made about Yogi's looks was part of baseball's nastiness. Opposing players would tease an opponent to upset and annoy him," wrote Berra biographer Gene Schoor. "It was all the cruelest kind of hazing, and it might have destroyed the confidence of any other youngster, killed any chance of making the baseball big-time."

"Sometimes the writers and his own teammates went too far," confessed baseball writer Milton Shapiro. "They made cruel sport of his looks and his lack of education, his penchant for reading comic books, and the things he said."

Berra was first tormented by his own team, then later by other teams, and then by the press. There is no question that Yogi Berra was about to go through a ring of fire he had not expected. He always greeted teasing with a shrug and that crooked smile of his, but deep down, whether he admitted it or not, it had to hurt, and it had to hurt bad.

In his first few years he was called ugly, Neanderthal, caveman, gorilla, ape, nature boy, freak, Quasimodo, and many other names. Worse yet was his own manager calling him "the ape." In the beginning, Harris didn't even call him by his name—he would just address Berra as "Ape."

Joe Trimble of the *New York Daily News* once relayed a story of how he and Harris were having a drink after one of the games. Harris said to him, "Did you see the ape hit that ball today?"

Later in the season, when DiMaggio's heel was hurting and he might miss a few games, Trimble asked Harris who he would bat fourth. "Maybe the ape could do it," Harris said after some thought.

Charlie Keller had a photo of himself and Berra. He told his teammates that he brought the photo home to his wife and said to her, "Any time you get to thinking I'm not so good-looking, just take another look at Yogi."

Berra always read, even if the materials weren't quite adult. At one time, he had a children's book of animals. As a joke, the players took turns writing each other's names under each of the photos. Under a raccoon was Jim Coates. Under a moose was Moose Skowron. Under the picture of the gorilla, someone had simply written, "Guess who?"

Opposing players weren't any nicer. Berra told the story that Mike Ryba, a Red Sox pitcher, once started in with him when they were still down in spring training in Florida. Ryba had a fun little hobby; each year he would put together his All-America Ugly Team. The first time Berra showed up in Sarasota, Ryba said to him, "Kid, I'll have to see you again tomorrow. You must be sick today. Nobody could look that bad unless he was sick."

The next day in St. Petersburg Ryba said to him, "Yogi, I hereby appoint you the captain of the All-Time All-America Ugly Team. You are the ugliest man I ever saw in my whole life."

Red Sox and Yankees players spread the story. The joke running around Florida that spring training—and around the league that year—was that

Berra was the only catcher whose looks were improved by putting on the catcher's mask.

Washington pitcher Ray Scarborough would scream at Berra, and as soon as Scarborough had his attention, he would hang by one arm from the dugout roof, and scratch his underarm with the other, pretending to be a gorilla or monkey, making the appropriate noises.

From the dugout, someone once said, "Yogi, you're ugly."

"So? I don't hit with my face," responded the stoic Berra.

The writers were no better.

"The sportswriters recognized him as wonderfully human and colorful copy, a character with everything an editor could want to enliven his pages," wrote earlier Berra biographer Gene Roswell. "The kid was droll, a clown with muscles, unbelievably naïve, skirting between pathos and humor, always bobbing up with the right word or the right hit."

Rud Rennie from the *New York Herald-Tribune* once said to Harris, "You're not really thinking of keeping him, are you? He doesn't even look like a Yankee."

Daley, the dean of sportswriters in New York, regularly called his articles about Berra "Nature Boy," making jibes about Berra's apish looks. Daley's moniker was an inside joke, a nod to Harris's nickname "the ape." In another reference, Daley compared Berra to a noble savage, pulling out the rubric, "one of nature's true noblemen—the honest heart that beats beneath the rough exterior," and referring to Berra's "homely grin." Alternately, he once jokingly wrote, "Yogi Berra is barred from baseball for life because he isn't photogenic enough."

Years later, Daley wrote in *The New York Times* that "Berra is a pure throwback to the *You Know Me Al* Lardner era," referring to famed baseball writer Ring Lardner's caricatures of players as idiot savants, rubes, or guileless, naïve country bumpkins. "The writers go around from day to day, asking each other, 'Did you hear the latest Berraism?'" For his part, these literary references and jokes went right over Berra's head.

"To the sportswriters, Yogi is a made-to-order buffoon, an uncomplaining peg to hang wild anecdotes on and only incidentally a highly polished performer of his art," *Reader's Digest* once reported.

"Everyone calls him Yogi—as well as less kindly names," Daley wrote somewhat sympathetically. "No ballplayer is ridden more cruelly, or as unmercifully, as he."

"Once before a game, [Berra's teammate] Johnny Lindell and a particularly opinionated newspaperman got into a friendly but heated clubhouse argument," wrote Roswell. Berra was listening to their conversation with rapt attention. Berra agreed with Lindell and stuck his nose into the conversation. He mimicked Lindell's argument, basically adding nothing new, but repeating it word for word. The aggravated newspaperman snapped, saying, "Stop acting like a busher and imitating grown men."

Harris eventually found out about the insult, confronted the writer in a friendly but direct way, and diffused the situation.

*  *  *

Berra was bewildered and confided some of his ongoing anger and hurt feelings to Garagiola, whose team trained not far from the Yankees.

"Yogi, you just keep hitting," Garagiola told him. "That's all you have to do. Let 'em build you up as a character or anything else. It'll mean more money someday."

Still, Berra found it hard to let some of the criticisms slide.

"Yogi was very good at pretending he didn't hear or at least didn't care about comments made about him, both in the clubhouse and from the stands. He was not simply good, he was a master," Rizzuto said.

The truth is, as late as the 1960s, writers were still following Daley's lead. In 1963, the highly acclaimed and erudite writer Robert Lipsyte called Berra "a cuddly noble savage who lusts after comic books, innocently scratches himself in public, loves children and dogs, exudes natural humor, and swings down from his tree house to excel in a game he would happily play for nothing."

And in 1973, Leonard Koppett pointed out that at the time Berra joined the team, Charlie Keller was called King Kong as a measure of respect. "They dubbed Yogi Little King Kong right away, and although the nickname was soon forgotten, the attitude toward him persisted," he said.

In the end, Yogi turned out to be one of the most popular Yankees of all time and one of the most popular players in the history of the game. But that fame is a tribute to Berra's ability to withstand insult after insult, smile through it, and let his bat do the talking.

And the curious thing about Berra was his charisma, for there is no other word for it. No matter where he was—St. Louis, New London, Newark, New York—he always ended up becoming one of the most popular players. The odd-looking little man had an innate charm that was hard to describe but unmistakable.

\* \* \*

One of Berra's fondest memories was of Babe Ruth. On April 27, 1947, they celebrated Babe Ruth Day at Yankee Stadium. Ruth was dying of cancer and had just undergone throat surgery, and in order to ascend to the microphone, Ruth had to be helped up the steps of the dugout. In attendance were Commissioner Happy Chandler and Francis Cardinal Spellman. Berra remembered how Ruth was cringing with pain, pale and emaciated. But Ruth stood straighter and squared up his shoulders as he stood in front of the microphone, ready to address the assembled thousands.

After his address, the Babe looked a little unsteady, and one of the Yankees asked if they should go out and help him. Another teammate spoke up, saying, "Leave him alone. He knows where the dugout is." Ruth struggled back to the dugout under his own steam.

Ruth would appear at Yankee Stadium twice more. On June 13, 1948, he appeared in uniform for the last time when the Yankees retired his number forever. Ruth died on August 16, 1948, at the age of 53. His body lay in repose inside the main gate at Yankee Stadium. His funeral was two days later at St. Patrick's Cathedral in New York.

Back on the field, Berra remained a defensive liability. The Yankees moved him back to catcher and then tried him in left field. Berra played where they told him and never complained or dragged his feet. He tried to give each position they assigned him his best effort, happy they were working to keep him in the lineup. Eventually, he ended up playing catcher more and more. It was the safest place to put him and keep his bat. And there were times he showed sheer brilliance. He was one of only 14 catchers in history (at the time) to execute an unassisted double play.

It happened during a home game at Yankee Stadium on June 16 against the St. Louis Browns. The Yankees were up 2–1 in the top of the ninth inning. The Browns were attempting a suicide squeeze play—with the pitch, the runner on third base, Jeff Heath, tore for home as the batter, Johnny Berardino, laid down a bunt. Berra pounced on the ball and shoved Berardino out of the way while tagging him, then blocked the plate and tagged out Heath in a collision.

"I just got the ball and tagged everyone I could see," Berra told the writers.

"Including the umps?" asked one of the writers.

"Yeah, including the umps."

On June 23 Berra hit his first grand-slam home run, accounting for four of the team's five runs in the first inning to take a 6–5 ballgame from the Detroit Tigers. The next day, Berra clouted another home run, and in a two-day run had tallied six RBIs for "Bucky's Brigadiers."

One of the biggest moments in Berra's first year was Yogi Berra Night, sponsored by the same folks on the Hill who had sponsored Joe Garagiola's night. At the time, Berra was plagued by what he thought was a sore throat. It turned out to be a strep infection. During a road trip, he was hospitalized in Cleveland, but got out of his sick bed to attend the event on his behalf in St. Louis. Berra was proud of the moment, and he was even more proud for his parents, who had their pictures taken and appeared in the newspaper.

Before the game, he asked Bobby Brown to help him prepare a two-sentence speech. Berra stayed in the dugout as long as possible, trying to memorize the short speech and afraid of facing the crowd. Playing in front of them was one thing, but addressing them was another. Eventually his teammates had to push him out of the dugout onto the field.

On that night he received a television set, some patio furniture, and a new Nash sedan. He was as nervous as could be. Wrote Daley in *The New York Times*, "The embarrassed Yogi grabbed the microphone, shuffled uneasily for a moment, and blurted, 'I wanna thank everyone for making this night necessary.'"

There was a pause from the crowd and then a loud cheer. More than anything, Berra sighed. He was done. He was relieved. But his speech was not the only thing to go awry that night.

After the game, Berra and a group went out and ended the evening at Grassi's, a neighborhood bar on the Hill. Grassi's was an old, dusty, neighborhood saloon, and everyone there had known Yogi since he was a kid. While they were proud of him, they weren't impressed by his fame, and they treated him like he was working in the factory. He felt like one of the regular folks there.

With a full complement of passengers, Berra backed his brand-new Nash out of its parking space and hit a fire hydrant.

"What happened?" asked Berra

"I don't know, but there's a hell of a lot of water coming out of the thing. We better get out of here," replied one of the passengers.

And so Berra hit the gas and took off, but he was turned in by a neighbor and had to pay $300 in fines and repairs for the fire hydrant.

\*   \*   \*

The Yankees that year had an awesome team, loaded with talent, and took the pennant. That placed them in the World Series against the Brooklyn Dodgers. In 1947 another rookie had put up with even more abuse than Berra—his name was Jackie Robinson. While Berra was a character with an eighth-grade education, Robinson was blazing a new path in Major League Baseball as the first player to break the color barrier, which had been in place for more than half a century. Berra was a raw talent armed with a massive bat and inconsistent fielding, plus an ability to murder the English language. Robinson was a polished diamond, eloquent, educated (he had graduated from prestigious UCLA), and multitalented. The two rookies could not have been more different or more competitive. While Berra had a good year, Robinson had electrified baseball in a myriad of ways and helped lead the Dodgers to the promised land. While both had undergone a crucible of sorts, both were destined to become loved and remembered fondly by generations of fans. But 1947, and the importance of that season, will always belong to Robinson and his heroics in breaking an unjust, unspoken rule with class and dignity enough for any man of any race, creed, or color.

The 1947 Series was an exciting one. In addition to Robinson, the "Bums from Brooklyn" had a slew of stars that included Pee Wee Reese, Pete Reiser, Carl Furillo, Dixie Walker, Ralph Branca, Joe Hatten, and Hugh Casey. The Dodgers had turned back the defending champion St. Louis Cardinals to take the pennant and were battle-tested.

The Bronx Bombers' mystique of power-hitting had deserted them in 1947, with no player reaching the 100 RBI plateau. DiMaggio still led the team in hitting, and other players filled in with solid performances, including Berra, Rizzuto, Henrich, and Billy Johnson. However, their pitching was strong, including hurlers Allie Reynolds, Spud Chandler, Spec Shea, Joe Page, Bobo Newsom, and Vic Raschi. The Yankees had won the league with a strong run that had started in June, and they took the pennant by 12½ games.

In his first full year in the majors, Berra played in 83 games, hit .280, had 11 homers, and drove in 54 runs. Twenty-nine of his 82 hits were extra-base hits, and he scored 41 times.

The 1947 World Series was historic for a number of reasons. It was the first to feature an African American player, Robinson. It was the first televised World Series in baseball history, although coverage was limited to New York, Philadelphia, and Washington, D.C. It was the first World Series to produce total receipts exceeding $2 million. (Gate receipts totaled $1,781,348.92, radio rights brought in $175,000, and television rights netted another $65,000.)

As late as early September, Berra was still facing throat trouble and battling an infection. There was concern that the penicillin he was taking might affect him, but the Yankees were desperate for a big bat—especially in the World Series. However, his defensive lapses were seen as a shortcoming, and the newspapers generally agreed that while the Yankees had the better pitching staff, the Dodgers held the edge at catcher.

Yet Harris announced that Berra would catch Game 1.

"Yogi Berra, the freshman Yankee catcher, has about as much sensitivity as a fire hydrant," wrote Daley, as he previewed the Series. "He's a phlegmatic, unemotional chap who will be no more awed by a World Series game as by a sandlot engagement."

The newspapers played up the fact that Berra and Robinson had faced off against one another the previous year in the minors. When asked before the Series if he was worried about Robinson stealing bases, Berra countered that he had experienced no problems during his series with Robinson the year before. But Brooklyn made it known that they would challenge the less-than-stellar Yankees receiving corps. And Brooklyn had one of the best groups of base stealers the Series had seen in years.

Sure enough, Robinson drew a walk in the opener and hopped, faked, and danced Berra to distraction. When Robinson finally raced toward second, a roar erupted from the crowd, and Berra dumped his throw into the dirt. However, the threat was eliminated on the next at-bat when Robinson was caught in a rundown between second and third base. Reese also stole a base on Berra, but the Yankees prevailed 5–3.

In the second game, Reese got to first twice. He stole second the first time, but Berra got him on his second attempt. However, Berra was in a batting slump, going 0-for-7 in the first two games. Nevertheless, the Yankees won the second game at Yankee Stadium and took a 2–0 Series lead.

Harris sat Berra in Game 3 at Ebbets Field but then called upon him in the seventh inning to bat for Sherman Lollar. Harris's faith in Berra was rewarded when he hit a pinch-hit home run. It was the first pinch-hit home run in the history of the World Series. But the Yankees lost, 9–8.

Game 4 was a game Berra would rather have forgotten. This game became forever known as the Cookie Game. Yankees pitcher Bill Bevens was pitching a brilliant, if sometimes erratic, game. By the ninth inning the Yankees had spotted him a 2–1 lead, and he had not yet allowed a hit despite giving up many walks and creating dangerous scenarios that the Yankees escaped each time. In the ninth, Al Gionfriddo was on first and attempted to steal second. Berra threw the ball wildly, and Rizzuto needed to leap high in the air, which caused him to miss the tag. A solid throw would have ended the game.

"The suspicion is growing that catcher Yogi Berra will have to take out burglary insurance," opined one newspaper. "The Brooks have stolen five bases on him in only three games."

"I should have got him," Berra said later.

Manager Bucky Harris decided to intentionally walk the next batter, Eddie Miksis. Cookie Lavagetto then entered the game, pinch-hitting for Eddie Stanky.

Calling Lavagetto's hit, Red Barber, the Dodgers' radio announcer, said, "Two men out, last of the ninth...the pitch...swung on, there's a drive hit out toward the right-field corner. Henrich is going back. He can't get it! It's off the wall for a base hit! Here comes the tying run, and here comes the winning run!"

The play ended the no-hitter as Gionfriddo and Miksis scored the winning runs for the Dodgers. The Dodgers had pulled off the unthinkable and tied the Series. Berra was embarrassed by his gaffe, and insult was added to injury as he again went hitless, making him 1-for-12 in the Series so far.

As one wit in the press box said to his fellow scribes, "Don't bother writing about it because no one will believe you anyway."

"Now We're Cooking," screamed the headline of the *Brooklyn Eagle*. The early edition of the next day's *Eagle* had a headline that ran, "More Miracles Today."

For Berra, Game 5 was blur, as he sat on the bench with no reprieve. The Yankees won without him, 2–1.

In Game 6, Berra went in to right field for Johnny Lindell in the fourth inning. Berra redeemed himself somewhat by going 2-for-3, with an RBI in a losing effort as the Dodgers staved off death with an 8–6 victory.

Game 6 also featured a memorable baseball moment. In the sixth inning, George Stirnweiss walked. Then Berra hit a two-out single, setting the stage for DiMaggio to notch the potential tying run. DiMaggio smashed a tremendous shot to the outfield.

Dodgers broadcaster Red Barber shouted, "Swung on, belted. It's a long on. Deep into left-center. Back goes Gionfriddo. Back, back, back, back, back, back. He makes a one-handed catch against the bullpen. Whoaaahhhh, doctor." Gionfriddo had caught the ball just to the left of the 415-foot marker.

Shocked and frustrated, DiMaggio shook his head and kicked at the dirt. It was the only time in memory that he had ever shown real anger on the ball field.

Before the final games, Harris told reporters, "They were mighty lucky we didn't beat them four straight, and it wouldn't surprise me any if we got licked."

In Game 7, big outfielder Gene Hermanski tripled to the right-field corner in the top of the second inning. Trimble wrote, "Yogi Berra, playing out there, wobbled like a drunk in a hurricane as the ball caromed crazily off the low fence. It went one way and he went the other, and he fell down. By the time he got up, the batter was safely on third. Yogi looked funnier than most of the comic book characters he enjoys."

Berra went 0-for-3 and was pulled in the sixth inning.

Despite Yogi's lack of production, the Yankees won 5–2 and were world champions. Harris became the first manager to win the World Series with two different teams. He had won before with the Washington Senators in his freshman and sophomore years as their manager in 1924 and 1925.

While his teammates were ecstatic, Berra himself did not feel like celebrating. He had not played well, and his usually consistent bat had deserted him, producing a 3-for-19 effort resulting in an uncharacteristic .158 batting average.

"The Dodgers stole everything from him except his chest protector," wrote Daley.

"Never in a World Series have I seen worse catchin'," said the grand old man of baseball, Connie Mack.

"Berra got a number of bad breaks in that World Series," Harris later told the press. "For one, I don't think he had fully recovered from the illness that knocked him out in early September, although he assured me he felt all right. For another, the strain on a first-year catcher working in the World Series is terrific, and to make matters worse, the laxity of our pitchers holding runners just about sank him."

"A guy doesn't get into the World Series every day. After all, I'm human, ain't I?" said Berra to reporters after the Series.

Regardless of his erratic play, Berra finished 15th in the voting for Most Valuable Player of 1947, with DiMaggio taking the honors.

# ~ Chapter 7 ~

# LOVE FINDS YOGI BERRA

In 1947 Garagiola had hit 20 points higher than his first full year in the majors, finishing with a .257 batting average. He had only 17 extra-base hits and played in three more games than he had the year before.

Still, the two childhood friends were heroes in the old neighborhood. Wherever they went, they were cheered and generally celebrated.

"Later on, when Joey and I were in the big leagues, Papa John and my pop had to walk over to Fassi's for their beer," Berra said. But this had its own compensation—half the time they didn't have to pay because they had become local celebrities themselves, and the two proud fathers were treated to many a draft.

The two always did especially well if a beer salesman came through and inquired about the boys. Berra's father would say right out, "Buy the beer," and the two fathers would toast their sons, "Let them go with God."

"Neither of them cared a hell of a lot about baseball, but they knew how to make it pay," Berra said.

Because of the strep-throat problem that plagued Berra the entire second half of the season, Weiss insisted that Berra have his tonsils removed, which he did. Weiss also insisted that DiMaggio have an operation in November 1947 to repair his ailing elbow. In the meantime, Berra and Garagiola still worked at Sears in the off-season.

*    *    *

The winter between 1947 and 1948 was magical for Berra. He and Garagiola loved going to St. Louis Flyers hockey games. And after the games, they often went to Julius "Biggie" Garagnani's restaurant (which was co-owned by Stan Musial).

"We used to go in every night and sit in the corner. We couldn't afford to eat," said Garagiola. "One day I asked Yogi why we kept going in there, and he said it was because he liked to look at Carmen. I told him to ask her out for a date so I could get something to eat someplace else."

"As Carmen remembers it, he walked into the restaurant from a round of golf, or so she surmised, as he was still wearing his spikes. He wasn't exactly a Gary Cooper look-alike—5'8" with floppy ears, an overdeveloped snout, and a gap-toothed smile," wrote journalist Christopher Hahn after an interview with Berra and Carmen years later.

Even as a well-known Yankees slugger, at the age of 22, Berra was still bashful around women.

"She was the prettiest girl I ever saw in my life," wrote Berra.

Berra had confided to DiMaggio in 1947, "The girls won't bother with me. I guess I'm just too ugly for dates."

"Probably the most mistaken notion about the legendary Yogi is that he is not sensitive," wrote Garagiola. "His sensitivity might not be very obvious, but it's there, and it's deep. He has always been sensitive in his own quiet, sometimes funny way."

For her part, Carmen was intrigued by Berra. "Carmen Short didn't know the ballplayer's name, but she liked what she saw. A waitress at Biggie's in St. Louis, she wanted that dark-haired guy with the winning smile to ask her out. Only she wanted him to think it was his idea," wrote Maureen Houston after an interview with Carmen years later.

Biggie was nice enough to introduce the love-struck slugger to his beautiful waitress. At first, Carmen was taken aback. Biggie had convinced her Berra was Cardinals outfielder Terry Moore, who was married. She was appalled. But it was all a gag by Biggie and Garagiola. The attraction between the two proved mutual, and Berra and Carmen became an item almost immediately. All winter the two were inseparable, and they often double-dated with Garagiola and his then-girlfriend, Audrie Rose. They went to movies, basketball games, hockey games, or for dinner and drinks.

"I was working in a restaurant and served him his lunch," said Carmen, sitting across from her husband of 52 years. "I knew he was a baseball player. I liked baseball. We used to go on Ladies Day. I wanted to marry a famous person, and I knew he was going to be famous," she said.

How did she know?

"I heard he had driven in 23 runs one day in the minor leagues. I figured any boy who could drive in 23 runs in one day was going to be famous."

"It was a doubleheader," said Berra, with a smile.

The romance blossomed, and after a six-month whirlwind courtship, Berra and Carmen got engaged, albeit in an unusual way.

Berra invited her over to dinner with his family. As it happened, she was seated next to Berra's brother Tony. When Carmen was distracted in conversation with Tony, Berra quietly slipped a small jewelry box onto her plate without saying a word. He had bought a diamond ring in Washington with Bobby Brown, from a jeweler friend of Brown's. There was no mistaking what was in the box, and Carmen excitedly and happily opened the small box and pulled out the ring. She then placed it on her finger and displayed her hand. She was laughing and smiling.

"Yogi never did actually ask her to marry him, and Carmen never did actually say she would," wrote biographer Gene Schoor. "For once, Yogi's difficulties with the English language didn't get in the way. Nor did his shyness."

It got around St. Louis and the sports world fast that Yogi Berra had a girlfriend. During the off-season, both Berra and Garagiola did a lot of speaking engagements and dinners. At one sports banquet, the famed announcer Harry Caray interviewed Berra and asked him about Carmen and their relationship.

"This girl, Yogi, is she Italian?" asked Caray. Berra answered she was not. And Garagiola, in his version of this story, always interjected that it was almost a crime in their old neighborhood not to marry another Italian.

"Well, Yogi, what will the girls in the neighborhood think?" asked Caray.

"I dunno," Berra said, shaking and bowing his head. "They all had their chance."

In a surely made-up story, Berra was supposed to have responded to a similar question by answering, "She wasn't the first girl I went out with. She was the third."

In another made-up tale, the supposed inquirer asked Berra why an attractive woman like Carmen would marry a mug like Berra. He supposedly replied, "I ain't sure because all of our dates have been at night. She ain't seen me in the daylight yet."

True story or not, that was just the type of exchange that would set Carmen off. A sure way for an acquaintance to earn her instant ire was to make jokes at her husband's expense in front of her. And most people got that point fast when she was around.

She was not above rolling her eyes herself at some of the things he said, and after they were married, they apparently had as many disagreements as any other married couple—if you are to believe some of the stories Berra has told, anyway.

He was a tough man who could take care of himself, but while Carmen and their family could make fun of him, he was not to be the butt of jokes by outsiders. She remains fiercely proud of him to this day.

They were married on January 26, 1949, at St. Ambrose Church. Pete Rieser of the Dodgers, Joe "Ducky" Medwick, Lonny Frey, and many other players were in attendance. Garagiola was his best man.

"There were about a hundred people in the church," Garagiola told the press later, "and Yogi was scared to death. I had to laugh in his face. Crowds of 75,000 at Yankee Stadium had never made him nervous, but a hundred close friends had him terrified.

"He's quite a guy," he continued, with real appreciation for his friend. "Yogi married a beautiful and wonderful girl. But she couldn't have married a nicer, more gentle, or finer man in this world than Yogi Berra."

The groom and his best man made quite a splash walking through the neighborhood in morning suits, which Carmen and Audrie both insisted on. After the wedding and reception, the new couple took off in Yogi's Nash sedan and drove to New Orleans. They had a month between their wedding and the date Berra was supposed to report for spring training in 1949. From New Orleans they went to Daytona Beach and then up the Florida coast, enjoying their new status and each other's company.

As Berra famously uttered, "We have a good time together even when we're not together."

"Yogi and Carmen Berra—you don't find better souls anywhere," said Brown.

"Anybody who knew Yogi knew how lucky he was to have Carmen as his wife. She had a huge measure of charm. Most of all, he knew it," said teammate Bobby Richardson.

"Unlike most baseball wives, she refuses to go through a batting slump or to talk shop after a bad day," reported *Reader's Digest.* If he came home in a snit after a bad day, she would stop him with a cold look, saying, "Look, it was you who played today. Don't take it out on me."

Carmen also came in handy when it came to sporting equipment. It was well known that Berra, who broke almost every finger in his hand during his career, had sensitive fingers. One of his secrets during his career was stuffing his catcher's mitt with a woman's falsie—usually used to pad a brassiere—to protect his hand.

"I used to stick a falsie in the glove. It was perfect," Berra said.

"I had to go buy them for him," said Carmen. "He was too shy."

There was an apocryphal story about Carmen at Yankee Stadium during a game against Cleveland, when she summoned an usher.

"Please get Frank Scott for me immediately," said Carmen, referring to the Yankees' traveling secretary. "It's an emergency. I must get a message to Yogi."

When Scott rushed to her side, fearing something wrong, she asked somewhat sheepishly, "Oh, Frank, can you ask Yogi whether he wants pork chops or lamp chops for dinner tonight? I forgot to ask."

# ~ Chapter 8 ~

# BECOMING A WINNER

In January 1948, Weiss brought in Gus Niarhos to shore up the catcher position. With Berra's shaky fielding, it was important to have other choices. In the previous year Berra had caught 51 games and played in the outfield 24 times.

In February 1948, the first of 19 rounds of difficult contract negotiations with Weiss began. Berra was upset by his contract, valued at $8,500, which he thought was well below the market average. Weiss told Berra he was impertinent and that the bigger contracts came to those who proved themselves over the years. After some ugly back-and-forth, Berra gave in, but he stored in his memory the words Wiess had said to him, and he would pull them out in later years.

When it was announced that Berra had signed, sportswriter Roscoe McGowen wrote, "Berra, a rugged individualist, chose to announce his own signing from St. Louis, where he lives, and stated that his contract…was en route to New York."

Negotiations completed, Harris was now able to put his plans into place. He would concentrate on Berra and turn him into a proper catcher. He would be their dependable backstop. However, Weiss kept touting Niarhos in the papers.

Berra remained a favorite of the press and the fans. During this period, "Berra was the Yankees' one flash of color on an otherwise drab canvas," wrote Milton Shapiro. "Often accused of being coldly efficient, winning world championships with dispassionate ease, the Yankees were glad to have Yogi aboard." And so were the sportswriters.

"Baseball writers are forever searching for 'characters.' They enliven their existence, enrich their copy, add spice to their often humdrum daily reportage," Shapiro explained. "On their part, most ballclubs do not discourage the search and often lend a hand in the cultivation of such colorful players, knowing full well the dollar value of the ensuing publicity."

The writers continued to report (or make up) stories about Berra, no matter how banal. And now comfortable with his colleagues, Berra could do more needling in self-defense.

"You know, Marshall, you're going to be a much better pitcher this year," Berra was supposed to have said to Clarence Marshall.

"Thank you, Yogi, why do you say that?"

"Because you're not as good-looking as you used to be," Berra replied, believing his pitcher looked more intimidating this year but, as usual, having his thoughts come out wrong.

Around the batting cage was always a favorite place to pick up Berraisms or any tidbit from the stocky backstop.

"Whose bat are you using?" Henrich asked Rizzuto.

"One of Berra's," answered the Yankees shortstop. "Everyone uses Yogi's bats. He's the only guy with a bat left. The rest of them are split."

And at the batting cage, while watching Yogi take batting practice before a series with the Red Sox early in the season, Henrich was supposed to have said, "Poor Yogi, he thinks this game was planned improperly. He believes it should be split into two kinds: one for fellows who hit for a living and another one only for those who field."

It was a surprise in the spring of 1948, as spring training evolved, that the Yankees' pitching and receiving corps were in a state of flux. The pitchers all seemed off at the same time for different and sundry reasons. There was serious attention being paid to "the rehabilitation of Yogi Berra as the sort of catcher he was, or that he was before last October's World Series scared the wits out of him," wrote *The New York Times*.

However, Harris thought his pitchers were just as much to blame as Berra was by not holding runners on base. The opposition had rattled Berra, and the pitchers had been happy to let him take the fall. But Harris was having none of it. They would get better. They had been too lax. "That laxity is going to be corrected," he told the press.

Again, as camp broke, they barnstormed north, stopping in Montgomery, New Orleans, Birmingham, Memphis, and Indianapolis before arriving home for their yearly spring tussle with the Dodgers.

Berra seemed to do reasonably well that spring, and there seemed to be reason for optimism. However, the Yankees would be in a difficult race, as the Indians and the Red Sox were prepared to fight for the pennant right down to the last day.

In a controversial series in June, Berra was ejected from a game against the Indians as the two teams battled for first place. After the series, the Yankees would fall to third place.

In the fourth inning of the final game of the series, umpire Cal Hubbard, who was calling the game behind Berra, stopped play and threw him out.

"Yogi made quite a scene until manager Bucky Harris told his player to leave," Hubbard said.

Berra was a notorious second-guesser and chatterer at the plate. Hubbard had finally had enough.

Garagiola had once refered to Berra as "the last of the playing umpires."

Berra claims that he had complained about a couple of calls. But on one, Hubbard was blatantly wrong, and Berra swung around quickly and started arguing with him. "I stepped out in front of the plate, mad, and threw the ball back hard to Tommy [Byrne, the fourth Yankee pitcher of that night's contest]," Berra said. "When I turned around, I almost bumped into [Hubbard]. I didn't know Hubbard had come out after me, and when I turned around I almost bumped into him."

It would be hard not to laugh at such a sight, with the short, stocky Berra bumping into the towering Hubbard, a former professional football player. Hubbard pulled his mask off and started screaming at Berra.

"One more word from you, and your ass is out of here," Hubbard said to Berra.

"Say you missed it, and I'll shut up," an angry Berra fired back.

Hubbard tossed him right there, and Harris came running out to home plate.

Anarchy followed. With Berra gone, the fans at the stadium got loud and rowdy. "Then came the hoots and the catcalls, paper, bottles, and cans. The fan who reached the field and aimed a can directly at Hubbard missed and was ejected forcibly," wrote Louis Effrat.

Hubbard had a famous saying, which was oft repeated among players: "Boys, I'm one of those umpires that can make a mistake on the close ones. So if it's close, you better hit it."

Berra knew what he was doing. He liked to needle umpires, and he and Hubbard worked together a lot. "I said sometimes, 'That ball was pretty close, wasn't it?' and all that. Yeah. You talk to the umpires. They don't like for you to turn around. That's the only thing. You look straight ahead, don't do nothing. There's one story I could tell you about Cal Hubbard. We were playing a game in Boston. We were way ahead. And I wanted to get out of the game. It was hot. And I said, 'Well, you missed that damn ball. You missed that, Cal. What's the matter with you? You having a bad day back there?' and everything. You know. And he said, 'Yogi, you could call me anything you want. If I'm going to suffer, you're going to suffer with me.'"

In another game, Berra once snapped at Hubbard, "I think you got hit in the head once too much," referring to Hubbard's football days.

And to another football-playing umpire, Hank Soar, formerly of the New York Football Giants, Berra once barked, "You shoulda worn your helmet when you played ball."

Berra was a tough competitor, and this was not his first nor his last run-in with an umpire. Alternately, few umpires relished the idea of sitting behind him for an afternoon. Many loathed his tenacity and jabber. Bill McKinley was one of the old-time umpires in the league who had broken into the American League in 1946, at the age of 36.

"My most difficult game was working the plate in the longest game, time-wise, in American League history," McKinley recalled years later. On June 24, 1962, the Yankees played the Tigers in Detroit. The game began at 1:30 PM and ended at 8:30. McKinely recalled that he was tired and ached. He never left the field the entire game. A bat boy had only brought him a cup of water once.

"Toward the end of the game, Yogi Berra asked me to brush off the plate," McKinley said.

"Brush it off yourself, you Dago. I know where it is," shot back McKinley. "I wasn't about to bend over at that point. I should have gotten extra pay for going 22 innings behind Berra," he confided.

"Yogi Berra wasn't a bad guy, but he was a pest," McKinley added. "He would get the crowd and the bench on you with his actions. He was always turning around, saying something. That's the worst thing a catcher can do because it gets everybody on you. You could never change him."

In 1959 umpire  Bill Summers threw Berra out in much the same way Hubbard had. Summers was fed up with Berra's calling of the game, and Berra complained more than a few times on calls.

Ryne Duren was pitching in relief. "[He] quickly became the most feared reliever in the league. 'Blind Ryne,' who had uncorrected vision of 20/70 and 20/200, would frighten hitters when he entered the game, squinting toward home through bottle-thick glasses. He enhanced the effect by intentionally throwing his first warm-up pitch back to the screen. Initially, it may not have always been planned; while in the minors his control was so erratic that he once hit the on-deck batter," wrote baseball historian George D. Wolf. Because of his glasses, Duren's Yankees teammates jokingly called him Mr. Magoo.

"He's got four pairs of glasses, and he can't see out of any of them," Berra jokingly told the press.

Duren went into his windup and let loose a fastball right down the middle.

"Ball!" called Summers.

"Where was it?" asked an incredulous Berra. He knew he was dancing close to the edge with Summers, as he later wrote, "He was ready to throw me out for the least little thing."

"It was off," said an irritated Summers.

"Horseshit!" shot back Berra.

Summers immediately gave Berra the heave. Duren came racing in, and before the manager could reach home plate, Duren was thrown out, too.

Bill Kinnamon was another famous American League umpire. He umpired between 1960 and 1969. He was 41 years old when he broke into the majors.

"Yogi Berra was as good a receiver as I ever worked behind. He had as good an arm as I have ever seen, and an innate ability to catch the ball.… I never saw a ball hit the dirt and get by him to the backstop. If the ball was close, he would get it. He was so quick back there—not fast, but quick."

"Bert Campaneris was on first base in Kansas City one day," Kinnamon said. "Campy could fly, and he got a jump on a pitch like you couldn't believe. The batter foul-tipped the pitch, and I'm telling you, before it ever got to Yogi's glove, he opened that glove. The ball hit right in that glove and fell to the ground. I'll swear it on a stack of Bibles that if Campy hadn't been running, Yogi would have caught that ball. Catching a foul tip is pure reflex; you can't control it. Now Yogi didn't *drop* the ball because if he had, I would have left Campaneris at second base. He didn't *catch* the ball, and I swear he did it on purpose."

Regarding Berra's mannerisms, Kinnamon said, "Yogi was not the most delightful guy to be behind because he chattered all the time. Every time his pitcher threw the ball it was a strike, and when he was hitting, every pitch was a ball. I mean every pitch…. One time a pitch bounced up there, and he said, "Wasn't too bad, was it?"

He continued, "Fortunately, when he was batting, he swung at an awful lot of bad pitches. He was such a good hitter he could pick them out of the dirt and double them off the wall."

\*    \*    \*

The 1948 season was a bust for the New York Yankees. They finished 94–60, third in the American League. Berra did well enough as a batsman; he hit .305, with 14 home runs, 24 doubles, 10 triples, and 98 RBIs. By the end of the season he was considered one of the best hitters in baseball. He finished in the top six for at-bats/RBI ratio. He was also in the top 10 that season for slugging percentage. And he finished sixth in triples.

Despite playing in 125 games, 71 of them behind the plate, his fielding continued to be a problem. Niarhos caught 82 games that year, Ralph Houk worked 14, Sherm Lollar 10, and Charlie Silvera caught four.

Also unchanged was the ribbing Berra received from opponents. In early July the players were overheard talking at the batting cage just before a Red Sox–Yankees game.

"Why don't you give it up, Henrich, and let a young guy play?" taunted Red Sox player Joe Dobson.

"While you're at it," added Mickey Harris, "why don't you do Yogi's thinking for him?"

"Nature Boy gave forth with what would have been an elfin smile on anyone else," wrote Daley.

"You're not nearly as good looking as Rizzuto, and he's no bargain," chided Earle Combs.

"Don't feel hurt, Yogi, you're a much handsomer guy than Keller," yelled someone from the stands.

"What tree did you sleep in last night, Yogi?" joined in Earl Johnson.

"If everyone didn't like him so immensely, he'd have been ignored," Daley assured his readers. But it was slugger Ted Williams who came to Berra's rescue. Williams, certainly one of the most noted authorities on the art of hitting, told the press that day, "The ball just flies off his bat. They can kid him all they like, but he's a real strong hitter." A real compliment, considering the source.

"Berra could move the runner, and move him late in a game like no one else I ever saw play the game," Williams said of Berra's abilities with a bat. "A lot of people said their shortstop Rizzuto was too small, but, damn, those two guys knew how to beat you. Makes me sick."

Berra and Williams would have a long love-hate relationship over the years. The two were linked in 1946, when Tom Yawkey, the flamboyant owner of the Boston Red Sox, had talked out loud about trading Williams for DiMaggio and Berra for Mel Allen. "Can I do this? Naw, the fans in Boston would hand me my scalp," he said.

In 1991, Williams biographer Michael Seidel wrote, "Berra to this day has no idea he was ever trade bait for Williams, though he and Williams chatted incessantly over the course of their careers. Berra always begged Williams to take him fishing."

Williams loved to tell the fictitious tale about riding a train with Berra along the Hudson River Valley after the war. Both saw a ship emblazoned with a red cross. Berra supposedly remarked to Williams, "Must be an iodine ship," mistaking the insignia he'd seen in the navy sick bay with the symbol of the Red Cross.

But Berra also had his fun with Williams. At one point in his career, the Yankees developed a shift for Williams. In an effort to draw Williams's attention away from the field as he approached the batter's box, Berra once asked him. "Are you a better bone fisherman or fly fisherman?" knowing Williams's intense love of fishing.

"When you going fishing this year, Ted?" Berra would consistently ask.

"You old Dago, you're twisted up," Williams said on more than one occasion to Berra.

"Have a good dinner last night?" Berra sometimes asked Williams.

"Didn't eat. Wanted to stay quick for today's game," replied Williams. On other occasions Williams replied, "Maybe just shut up, you ugly bastard."

"If you leave a tip, the food gets better," Berra would reply, ignoring Williams's response.

"As our catcher, he was great at talking," Rizzuto remembered. "I somehow think he thought it was part of his job, like putting on the shin guards."

Berra was famous for throwing dirt on batters' shoes to distract them. At least once in an important series with the Red Sox, Berra tossed dirt onto Williams's shoes to distract the powerful hitter. Williams once threatened to beat him with his bat.

"I liked to talk to the hitters. I just liked to talk to the hitters. But not when the ball was on the way. I'd just say, like, 'Where you going tonight?' 'What are you doing in the wintertime?' Just to keep a conversation going," Berra said years later.

Red Sox catcher Birdie Tebbetts once told Williams, "Watch out for Yogi Berra and the other catchers, Ted. Don't let them talk you out of anything."

"[Ted] didn't like to talk. He'd talk to you after. But he was a nice guy, too. We did a lot of things with him," Berra said years later.

Yankees pitcher Tommy Byrne loved to taunt Williams, trying to distract him, saying things like, "Ted, how's the Boston press these days? Still screwing you? That's a shame. I think you deserve better from them. By the way, what are you hitting? You don't know? Goddamn, Ted, the last time I looked it up, it was .360 or something, not bad for someone your age."

"Yogi," Williams would complain, "can you get that crazy left-handed son of a bitch to shut up and throw the ball?"

Bobby Doerr once told Rizzuto, "When we played you guys, it was always a big game with a big crowd, and Yogi's banter always relaxed me. I know if [Eddie] Lopat made me look bad on a pitch and I could feel my neck getting hot, and Yogi would tell me to step in to the ball, make the fans think you know what you're doing—you just had to smile to yourself. He was trying to make you madder."

Unfortunately, it didn't always work against Doerr, which Doerr relished to the end of his days. Once Doerr remarked to Berra that his chatter didn't bother him. Berra smiled and shrugged slyly, "It didn't work with everybody. Nothing does."

\*     \*     \*

"In 1948 Yogi Berra did not yet seem to understand that baseball as played on this team was a deadly serious matter," wrote David Halberstam. In this season, Berra finally came to an understanding about what it took to play championship ball, and he learned a lesson that would be pivotal for a number of reasons.

In a game against Detroit, "Berra had not run out a pop-up; he had made it only to first. That cost the Yankees a run, and as it turned out, almost cost them the ballgame," reported Halberstam.

As he was strapping on his catcher's gear to take the field, Keller asked him, "You feeling all right, Yogi?"

"Yeah, I'm fine."

"Then why the hell didn't you run it out?" Keller shot back.

Lindell also joined in on Berra for his lackadaisical effort.

"Berra looked over to DiMaggio as if to ask for help, particularly because he was a fellow Italian American. DiMaggio gave him a withering look. Eddie

Lopat, who had watched the entire scene unfold, thought to himself, 'Now I know why this team is special,'" wrote Halberstam.

The moment said a lot about the generation in which he was playing and what it expected. Here, the Yankees policed themselves. Harris and Casey Stengel could be caustic, but suffering the same fate from your teammates was even worse. These were the members of the Greatest Generation, steeled by the Great Depression and a major world war. Excuses, showboating, and lazy play on this team—in this era—were not tolerated. It was the hint of things to come. It was what had made and what would make the Yankees the best team in baseball for more than three decades. The lack of these kinds of moments, later in his career, would also be Berra's undoing when he was a manager.

As Halberstam pointed out in *Summer of '49,* "When Henrich had first joined the Yankees, the older players were the enforcers. Then, in the late '40s, he, Keller, Lindell, and Billy Johnson took over. DiMaggio was above it; it was out of his character to push others, although he could on occasion cast a cold glance on a malingerer."

Berra had learned his lesson. But later, in his career as manager, there would be no mature Yankees to carry on this policing.

Later in the 1948 season, the Yankees were making a run toward the pennant. The Yankees were facing a doubleheader in August. Despite unbearable pain, DiMaggio himself insisted he play both games of the doubleheader. He practically had to be carried off the field by Lopat and Reynolds.

Berra, who always hated doubleheaders, begged out of the second game. Niarhos, playing in Berra's place, had come up with men on base several times and come away empty.

When DiMaggio saw Berra, still fresh from sitting out the second game, he exploded, "Whatsa matter, you *tired*?"

Disgusted, DiMaggio yelled loud enough in the locker room for everyone to hear, "Jesus Christ, a 20-year-old kid and he can't play both ends of a doubleheader when we're fighting down the stretch. What kind of bullshit is this?"

No one uttered a word while DiMaggio raged on. DiMaggio, usually quiet, lambasted Berra for a full 10 minutes in front of the entire clubhouse.

There was no question that Berra's attention to detail improved after these instances.

*   *   *

One of the most exciting moments for Berra was his selection to the 1948 All-Star team. It would be the first of his 18 consecutive selections to one of baseball's premier events. The special part for him was that it was played at Sportsman's Park on July 13, 1948, although he did not get off the bench.

In his evaluation of the American League catchers before the game, Daley wrote, "The most valuable catcher? Don't snicker, please. It's Nature Boy, the quaint Yogi Berra of the Yankees."

In August, the night Babe Ruth died, the Yankees were playing the Giants for the Mayor's Trophy. This interleague game was played for charity and was considered a bit of barnstorming during the season. But the hometown fans loved such matchups.

Before the game was a home-run derby. Berra sent three deep versus Keller's two, while the Giants' Bobby Thomson, Walker Cooper, Willard Marshall, and Johnny Mize sank one each. Berra won $150 for his little demonstration of power.

But the ribbing in the press continued. According to sportswriters, Berra still had to endure jibes.

"Does Berra ever autograph a ball?" George Stirnweiess said someone asked him.

"Yogi looked at him suspiciously for a moment and then swallowed the bait in one gulp, 'Why?'"

"Well, I just didn't think you ever learned to write."

"I had a guy ask me if it was true that Yogi didn't have any neck," Rizzuto said.

"Whenever he gets a hit and you ask him if it was high or low, he just mumbles, 'I dunno. It was a good one,'" said Shea.

"Nuts," joined in Lindell. "Yogi never hit a good pitch in his life. He just hits the bad ones. The good ones he just fouls off."

On September 1, Berra's power made the difference in a 5–4 ninth-inning win against the St. Louis Browns at Yankee Stadium, which put the late-surging Yankees only a game out of first place. The 22,000 fans in attendance mobbed the field, and Berra had to push his way through the throngs to score the winning run. However, the Yankees eventually finished third.

At the end of the 1948 season, Dan Daniel, the man who had helped to make Babe Ruth famous by convincing him to re-sign with the Yankees in the 1930s and by writing one of the many famous biographies of Ruth in that period, wrote a column in the *New York World Telegram*. In it, he discussed the many changes that would be taking place on the Yankees team, including the departure of Harris, the retirement of George McQuinn (opening the door for Henrich), and that the Yankees were definitely in the market for still another catcher:

"Yogi Berra has quit catching, and that's a big break for the lad from the Hill in St. Louis. His short arms and stubby fingers made him a woeful receiver. He handled the pitchers well, but those curves he threw to second base were plain murder."

# ~ Chapter 9 ~

# A Life in Baseball

Charles Dillon Stengel was born on July 30, 1890, in Kansas City, Missouri. The nickname "Casey" came from the abbreviation "K.C.," which stood for Kansas City. In his youth, he was also known as "Dutch," which was a common nickname for Americans of German ancestry. It was in his later years, as the manager of the New York Yankees and New York Mets, that he eventually earned his famous nickname, "the Old Professor," for his sharp wit and sarcastic comments.

Stengel had made a name for himself as a tempestuous player for the Brooklyn Dodgers (1912–17), the Pittsburgh Pirates (1918–19), the Philadelphia Phillies (1920–21), the New York Giants (1921–23), and the Boston Braves (1924–25). Stengel played in three World Series, with appearances in 1916 for the Dodgers and in 1922 and 1923 for the Giants. In the 1923 Series, he hit two game-winning home runs for John McGraw's team in a losing effort, for which he was rewarded by being traded. In 14 major league seasons he accumulated a .284 batting average.

He once said of his career, "I had many years that I was not so successful as a ballplayer, as it is a game of skill."

He also joked, "I was such a dangerous hitter I even got intentional walks during batting practice."

Even though Stengel eventually became better known as a manager, it was not his first few stints for which he was remembered. He led the Brooklyn Dodgers from 1934 to 1936 and the Boston Braves from 1938 to 1943. All those years were fairly disastrous for his teams, with none of them ever finishing better than fifth in an eight-team league.

While Stengel learned his craft in the majors, it was not until he was demoted to the minors that he found the formulas that would lead to his success.

In 1944, Stengel, over the strong objections of owner Bill Veeck (away serving in the war), was named the manager of the Milwaukee Brewers, then a minor league team. He led the Brewers to the American Association pennant that year. In 1948 Stengel managed the Oakland Oaks to the Pacific Coast League championship. Then the Yankees were in the market for a new manager, and Stengel was in the right place at the right time.

Newspaper reporters were a little skeptical, given his colorful language and character and his earlier losing records. "Ole Case had better win the pennant or else be awfully funny," cracked one.

Thus Stengel and George Weiss became the brain trust running the New York Yankees, and both dedicated themselves to turning Berra, always a good hitter, into a dedicated backstop for his second season—all the while keeping Gus Niarhos, Ralph Houk, and Charlie Silvera on the roster just in case.

But just getting Berra to report to camp was a more grueling chore than making him a catcher. After the year he had enjoyed at the plate and coming into his own as a batter, he believed it was time for Weiss to deliver on the promises he had made regarding performance and restitution, and they entered into an uncomfortable contract dispute.

Weiss offered Berra $9,000, but Berra believed he deserved $15,000. This was in the days before agents. Berra staged a mini holdout.

According to writer David Halberstam, what none of the Yankees knew at the time about the notoriously cheap Weiss was that owners Dan Topping and Del Webb based Weiss's bonus on how much money he saved out of the payroll budget. For every dollar Weiss saved them, he made money. However, years later, Joe Causin, a longtime Yankees accountant, disputed that view, stating simply that Weiss was very well paid despite his cheapness with the players. Either way, few players of the era enjoyed their contract negotiations with the penurious Weiss. In the meantime, Berra was not going to budge.

"We're ready to pay you what you're worth," Weiss reportedly told Berra. "Prove to us you're worth $15,000, and you'll get it. We're prepared to pay a man what he earns." Eventually they came to an agreement, making Berra the 34th Yankee to sign that spring.

"Yogi's holdout collapsed under the enticing influence of a $12,000 contract and the persuasive conversational tone of Mr. Weiss," reported the press.

"Berra's value to the club is unquestioned," reported *The New York Times*, noting that Berra ranked behind only DiMaggio and Henrich as the best batsman on the club. "The outlook for Berra this season is of uninterrupted catching—if Casey Stengel's plans materialize."

Early performances in spring training seemed to show that Niarhos would be the catcher and that Berra would find himself in the outfield again. "But Casey liked the way Berra did things on the field," wrote Stengel biographer and baseball writer Robert Creamer.

"Fortunately for Berra, Stengel fell in love with his talents and realized he had to protect him before the locker room baiting, which had a cruel edge, got out of hand. This was remarkable, for Stengel had a quick and sometimes cruel tongue himself," wrote Halberstam.

"It might be said, in hindsight, that the Yankees' failure in 1948 was a key factor in the success of Yogi Berra. Failure meant that Bucky Harris was fired," wrote sportswriter and baseball historian Milton Shapiro. Casey's arrival, Shapiro wrote, "made all the difference in the world to Berra's future as a catcher."

Stengel took to referring to Berra as, "Mr. Berra, which is my assistant manager," which the sportswriters and the fans eagerly ate up. And there was never meant to be any sting to it. According to Creamer, the sportswriters eagerly reported the latest Berraism to Stengel, and he thoroughly enjoyed them. But one time they scoffed and laughed at one of Berra's offerings too eagerly. That Berraism reportedly was, "I wish I had gone to college because then I could have been a bonus player."

According to Creamer, "Normally Stengel encouraged banter of this kind. This time he cut it off. 'He talks okay up there with a bat in his hands. A college degree don't do you no good up there.'"

"Frank Graham said that Casey had a tremendous influence on Berra's development," Creamer said about the famed New York sportswriter of the 1930s and 1940s. "Aware, as no one before him had been, that there was truly a sensitive young man who was hurt by many of the quips made about him yet had the guts to smile through them, Casey acted as the buffer between Berra and those on his own club who poked fun at him. It wasn't long before the slower thinkers among the Yankees gained a realization of what Yogi meant to them."

For his part, Berra returned Stengel's affection. "I liked him. I respected him and owed a lot to his confidence in me. I could also understand why some people, like Phil Rizzuto and even Joe D., did not feel the same way. You would never hear anybody say Casey was not interested in himself," he said.

"Billy [Martin] loved Casey. I didn't. But I miss him," Berra said years later.

While Stengel always felt affection for Berra and was responsible for his ascendancy as a great ballplayer, it did not mean that Berra did not occasionally find himself in Stengel's crosshairs. Mickey Mantle recalled much later that after an uncharacteristic ninth-inning collapse in the regular season, Stengel mercilessly rode Berra for calling the wrong pitches and giving away the game.

The normally docile Berra became enraged and fired back at his manager, and the two engaged in a heated argument.

"That's it! You call the pitches from now on. I ain't gonna call 'em," Berra said.

"Oh! *You're* not gonna call the signals. *Bullshit!* You'll do whatever the hell I tell you to do!"

\*   \*   \*

Stengel and Weiss decided that Berra would have a tutor, a personal teacher. That teacher would be none other than the famed Bill Dickey.

Dickey broke into the majors in 1928 and played his first full season in 1929. With teammates such as Yankees greats Babe Ruth, Lou Gehrig, and Joe DiMaggio, Dickey's name has sometimes been lost. But in the late 1930s and early '40s, he was one of the premier receivers in the league. He was known as a smart handler of pitchers (especially the zany and unpredictable

Lefty Gomez). Dickey was also the first Yankees teammate to discover the truth of Gehrig's illness.

Although Dickey was quiet off the field, on the field he could be fiery. In a game against the Washington Senators on July 4, 1932, Carl Reynolds raced for home and collided with Dickey while trying to score. Dickey was incensed. Furious, he turned and, with one punch, broke Reynolds's jaw. Dickey was suspended for 30 days and fined $1,000 for his swing.

For his first six seasons, Dickey never batted under .300. And he could hit for power. In the second game of the 1936 World Series versus their hometown nemesis Giants, he hit a three-run homer and knocked in five runs for the Yankees. In the 1939 World Series Dickey smacked two homers and drove in five runs. He won Game 1 with a run-scoring single in the bottom of the ninth. For his career, Dickey posted 202 home runs, 1,209 RBIs, and a .313 batting average. Dickey also caught 38 World Series games, more than any other catcher at that time. At the age of 36, Dickey left baseball and enlisted in the navy.

"Bill Dickey was the heart of the team defensively and commanded tremendous respect from the Yankees pitchers. Once the game started, he ran the show," said infielder Bill Werber.

On March 1, 1949, Dickey was brought in with one job charged to him: to turn Yogi Berra into a serviceable, dependable catcher. It was a decision the newspapers followed with fascination and skepticism. *The New York Times* had called Berra "a problem."

While Stengel insisted that the Yankees, with lots of new, raw talent, be drilled in the basics and fundamentals, Dickey spent time with Berra exclusively. No one had ever made the effort to teach him his position in such a way. In the first week, Dickey taught Berra the technique of flashing signals to the pitcher so that the shortstop and second baseman could see them, but opposing base runners and coaches could not.

Dickey arrived on the third day of camp and watched Berra during batting practice. He confronted Berra right off. His general impression of Berra was that he loved batting and didn't really care about the rest. Dickey questioned Berra's dedication to the game and to the position of catcher. He was tough on the young backstop.

Berra said of the experience, "When I told Dickey I did want to be a good catcher, he helped me to be the catcher nobody thought I could be."

Berra was happier than he had ever been. He soaked up every bit of information Dickey turned over. The two were seen working on everything from Berra's footwork to his throwing. "He worked me hour after hour in that hot Florida sun," Berra said.

"He's learning me all his experience," Berra told the press. It was one of those quotes that got reprinted everywhere.

Stengel put pressure on Berra through the sportswriters, saying, "If Yogi Berra plays, it will have to be behind the plate." Surely, Stengel would have had to find a place for the .300 hitter if the experiment had failed. Fortunately, they never had to find out.

"Get up close to the batter," Dickey told Berra. "You've got two feet there you can close up. Don't be afraid of tipping the bat. You've got plenty of room."

Berra followed his advice and found that he didn't get hit by as many foul tips as before.

Dickey also told him, "Get that close to the batter, and you can step right over home plate and whip the ball to second base. That split second will cut the runner down for you."

He also worked on Berra's throwing motion, eventually keeping Berra's throws from sailing.

Dickey worked with Berra on foul-tips and pop-ups. He taught him about taking a throw from the outfield, how to judge it and how to figure out what to do with it, how to think in advance of where the play would be, based on the trajectory of the throw. Berra had to know where the runners were at all times.

"Converting Berra from a liability behind the plate to a first-class backstop was a monotonous, wearying task," wrote Gene Roswell. "Dickey worked, taught, coaxed, demonstrated—all with patience and forebearance."

"We all knew that George Weiss brought Bill Dickey back to teach Yogi, but we didn't know that Dickey would push Berra so hard. Dickey worked him harder after the game than Yogi had to work during the game," teammate Gene Woodling said years later. "Boy, did it pay off. As Spud Chandler said, 'He got good, and he got good fast.'"

Dickey was under as much pressure as Berra was, and he found it hard to judge his pupil, never sure if Berra was telling him what he wanted to hear or if Berra was speaking in earnest, knowing their jobs might possibly be on the line. Dickey had come back to baseball, and he was not going to stake his reputation on Berra if he was not sure of him. Weiss and Stengel were constantly asking Dickey if any progress was being made. The big, lanky Arkansan waffled, afraid to make any proclamation about Berra while he was still tutoring him. Dickey's personal standards of play and dedication to the position were high, and he drilled Berra, holding him up to those standards.

One difference between them, among many, was that Dickey had always wanted to be a catcher. He had dreamed of being a big-league catcher. Berra had only dreamed of being a big-league player, and he was happy to play no matter where they put him. Dickey opened Berra's eyes to the importance, the intricacies, and the beauty of playing the catcher's position—the quarterback, so to speak, of the baseball diamond.

Eventually Weiss demanded an answer. If Dickey could not convert Berra, then Weiss would have to engineer a major trade, swapping Berra for another catcher, if the Yankees were to have a shot at the 1949 pennant.

"Can he do it, Bill?" Weiss pressed.

Finally, Dickey, sure of Berra's intent and improvement, told Weiss and Stengel, "Yes, he'll make it, and he'll be a pretty good catcher."

"Give him two years, and he'll be the greatest catcher in the American League by a long shot," Dickey told the press.

"He taught me everything," Berra wrote, more than half a century later. "How to handle different pitches, how to study hitters, how to field bunts, judge foul pops, block pitches, shift my feet for throws—everything.... I always say I owe everything I did in baseball to Dickey. He was a great man."

And by midseason Stengel told the press, "Berra is why our pitchers have been doing so good. The kid's been great in the close ones and the way he's been handling those pitchers. There's nobody that has the pitcher's confidence like Mr. Berra. Nobody's running on him, and they better not. The way he's throwing, even Ty Cobb couldn't steal on him now."

But there was still another battle brewing that season, one in which Berra would be caught between his encouraging manager and his pitching staff.

\*   \*   \*

On March 11, 1949, Berra crashed his Nash sedan, wrapping it around a palm tree. The car was a total wreck, and Berra walked away with a deep scratch on one knee and some torn trousers. He had reached for a bottle of shampoo that had rolled off the seat, and the next thing he knew, he was veering off the road. Art Houtteman of the Detroit Tigers also crashed his car around the same time, prompting Cleveland Indians manager Lou Boudreau to ban his players from driving outside the city limits of Tucson, Arizona.

The accident gave the players something else to rib Berra about. "Hey, Yogi, I understand you looked into your glove compartment and found a palm tree in there," laughed Red Munger.

Asked if he had gotten it fixed, Berra explained that the car was a wreck and that he would get a check and buy himself a new car.

"When you buy that new car, Yogi, better buy yourself an armored one," said Ted Wilks.

"Or a rubber one that bounces back," said Joe Garagiola. "What did your wife say about it?"

"When I phoned to tell her about the smashup, she was more worried about me than the car. Can you beat that?" Berra replied.

Garagiola was coming back from a tough year. Despite being a huge hero in the 1946 World Series, the following years had not gone well. In 1947 he had struggled, and the 1948 season had been even worse. He had played in only 24 games, batting a dismal .107. But 1949 would be a better year for Garagiola. He would bat .261, play in 81 games, and tally 26 RBIs. Perhaps more hurtful to Garagiola than his slipping numbers were the hometown fans beginning to lose faith in him. He had been booed off the field, and many fans felt that he had never lived up to the potential they saw in his magical first year.

Spring training in 1949 went well for Berra. He had learned his position and batted well.

It is also interesting to note that Bobby Hofman, who had given Lawdie the nickname "Yogi," broke into the big leagues on April 19, 1949, playing for the New York Giants. Another boy from the Hill had made it to the big leagues.

\*    \*    \*

The bigger news of the 1949 spring-training season was Joe DiMaggio's signing of a contract for a reported sum of $100,000. DiMaggio's was the first six-figure contract in the history of Major League Baseball.

In ceremonies before the season home opener at Yankee Stadium, a monument to Babe Ruth was unveiled in center field, along with two plaques honoring Gehrig and Miller Huggins. All three would become centerpieces in the famous Monument Park that now adorns the outfield area at Yankee Stadium.

But when the season opened, Berra was sick with the flu and missed the festivities. Gus Niarhos got the start. No matter—Berra would play in 116 games, most of them as catcher.

The Yankees were seen as underdogs. Almost as soon as the Yankees had hired Stengel, the running joke in Boston before the season started was that with the addition of the Old Professor, the Yankees had been officially eliminated. But the Yankees opened hot, going 10–2 in April and 15–10 in May, finishing the first two months with a .675 winning percentage. They ended June with a three-game sweep of the Red Sox with the return of DiMaggio from injury (he had been out since April), and went 19–12 for the month, finishing out the first three months of the season 44–24, with a .647 winning percentage.

In May, at Briggs Stadium, Berra was standing around during batting practice. A scuffle broke out, and he was distracted. Just then, he was struck in the head by an errant throw by backup first baseman Jack Phillips. Berra was knocked unconscious and was eventually taken to the hospital for X-rays, prompting one of the cruelest headlines of his career: "X-Rays of Berra's Head Show Nothing."

\*    \*    \*

Berra was vital to the New York offense and achieved a number of headlines for the talking he did with his bat. One headline proclaimed, "Berra Is Big Star." Another said, "Berra's Long Hits Pace 5–4 Triumph."

At one point in the season, Berra put together a 16-game hitting streak. And as the season wore on, both he and Birdie Tebbetts, the catcher from Boston, were leading the American League in votes for the All-Star Game.

A true New Englander, Tebbetts was born on November 10, 1912, in Burlington, Vermont, and raised in Nashua, New Hampshire. As a youth, Tebbetts's high-pitched voice was notable, and it was said he "chirped like a bird."

He graduated from Providence College in 1934 and played with the Detroit Tigers between 1936 and 1947 (taking three years out for service during the war). He then joined the Boston Red Sox in 1947. He would go on to play for the Red Sox until 1950, and then went to the Indians, where he played until 1952. He was a career .270 hitter with 38 home runs and 469 RBIs in 1,162 games, and he made four All-Star teams.

Many considered Tebbetts the best catcher in the American League. During Berra's early years, despite his success with a bat, he always compared poorly with Tebbetts.

Like Berra, Tebbetts was also a tireless bench jockey, needling many of the players he faced, including his Yankees counterpart. And his insults could be quite ugly. During spring training one year, Tebbetts yelled at Berra as he approached the batter's box, "How's your wife like living in a tree, Yogi?"

Tebbetts was a Boston fan favorite because he was one of them, a New Englander, but he was also a consummate professional, with excellent defensive skills. He was one of the two catchers Berra would always be compared with. The other was a young, baby-faced catcher named Roy Campanella from the metropolitan rival Brooklyn Dodgers.

*　*　*

As the season wore on, it became apparent that Berra was going to be the everyday catcher. The pitchers were never particularly comfortable with Berra, as he was still truly learning his craft, but his bat was too valuable on the scoreboard. Vic Raschi and Allie Reynolds were particularly tough. Both thought that Berra's lack of skills cost them strikes. He smothered curveballs, as he found them hard to handle. His stabbing motion at the pitches, they thought, emphasized to the umpire that the ball might be out of the strike zone even if it truly wasn't. He would catch the ball as his hand was moving away from his body.

"Don't stab at it, Yogi," Reynolds explained to Berra. "Reach out and bring it in."

The pitchers were also suspicious that Berra, afraid a base runner might steal, was not calling the pitch that was right for that moment in the count against the batter, but the pitch that would be easiest to haul in and throw to second to cut a runner down.

According to author David Halberstam, Berra often called "a high outside fastball against a right-handed hitter. Since opposing players were very much aware of this, it was like a death warrant to his own pitchers."

But the real issue for Berra was that he got caught in the struggle between Stengel and the pitching staff. Normally, the catcher calls the game, signaling to the pitcher which pitch to throw next. Sometimes a pitcher will shake off the sign and wait for the one he wants. But neither the pitching staff nor Stengel trusted Berra just yet. In tight situations, Berra would turn to the dugout to receive a sign from Stengel, who told him which pitch should be thrown. It was what Stengel wanted, but Raschi and Reynolds hated this. Both of them were hard-throwing, brooding, high-strung competitors.

The pitchers distrusted this system. Casey hadn't been a pitcher, and he hadn't been a particularly good hitter in his day. They didn't trust his judgment to call pitches in a count. According to Halberstam in the *Summer of '49*, the pitchers held a small get-together and decided to claim Berra for themselves.

"They tipped off Yogi in different ways: Reynolds, for example, would go to his glove or his belt or his hat—changing signs regularly in a game. Yogi seemed agreeable," wrote Halberstam.

But it was hard to stop Berra from looking over at Stengel. "[The pitchers] wanted Yogi to see the game through their eyes and to learn their reason for each pitch," continued Halberstam.

Reynolds took it upon himself to break Berra of this habit. In an early-season game against Philadelphia, there were two men on. Reynolds saw Stengel wanting to give Berra a sign, waving wildly at Berra.

"Yogi," hollered Reynolds, "if you look over to the bench I'm going to cross you up."

This was not an idle threat. If Berra thought a curve was coming and Reynolds threw a fastball, Reynolds would bean Yogi for sure. Reynolds pressed, warning him, "You listen to me, Yogi. I'm dead serious."

Meanwhile, Stengel yelled louder, trying to get the young catcher's attention.

"Don't listen to him," Reynolds warned Berra.

According to Halberstam, Eddie Lopat and Raschi were beside themselves with laughter as they watched Stengel gyrating, vying for Berra's attention. "Yogi was paralyzed. It was as if he could give no sign, caught between these two powerful pulls. Everyone in the park, Reynolds thought, understood the test of wills going on," he wrote.

"Look at me, Yogi!" Reynolds shouted from the mound.

"Yogi, if you don't look over here I'm going to fine your ass!" shouted Stengel from the dugout.

Desperate, and knowing Berra's unquenchable thirst for money, Stengel was now waving a fistfull of dollar bills. But Berra didn't see them. He never turned his head.

"Don't turn, Yogi. Just keep looking at me," Reynolds told the bewildered catcher.

Pale as a ghost and sweating, Berra squatted behind the plate, ignored Stengel, and nodded to Reynolds. Reynolds hummed a fastball, struck out the batter, and ended the inning. It was a great victory for the pitchers and, ultimately, for Berra.

From then on, the pitchers could call their own games, and from then on, Berra would have their trust. It was something Berra had to do for himself. It was nothing Dickey could have taught him. But it was a giant step in the maturation of Yogi Berra. While Stengel had been his greatest supporter, almost a father figure, Berra had taken a step toward being a confident and experienced receiver, like a son claiming something of his own.

However, this story was disputed in 1994 by Phil Rizzuto, the Yankees shortstop, longtime Yankees announcer, and Berra's lifelong friend. Especially referring to Reynolds's mound comments, Rizzuto said, "I played right behind Allie at short and never heard Allie say it."

It seems unlikely that Halberstam made up the story, and it should be noted that the men concerned may have forgotten or put behind them arguments of the past, especially those more than half a century old.

In later years Berra would become one of the best signal-callers in the game, calling unexpected pitches here and there. Sometimes he would come back with the same pitch two and three times on a hitter who would be looking for something else. Eventually, many of the pitchers followed his lead and found that the odd little man behind the plate truly knew something of the game. Between Dickey and the pitching staff, Yogi Berra was nudged toward greatness.

In the end, though, the pitchers created a monster. Berra still had the immense confidence of Stengel. And in serious run-ins with Raschi and Reynolds, they found Berra could give as good as he got.

Raschi once told Berra in a mound conversation, "Just catch. I'll pitch."

Another time he said, "Yogi, you just get your Dago ass the hell back behind the plate."

And another time he told the catcher, "Yogi, get the hell out of here with your goddamn sixth-grade education."

But Berra could get Raschi's goat as well.

"Raschi pitched better when I got him mad," Berra once said. Berra would approach the mound, which Raschi hated.

Berra recalled one incident, saying to Raschi, "'You're supposed to be a pitcher. You been pitchin' for 15 years, and you can't even get the ball over.' And he would get mad at me." But Raschi would turn his fury into a winning fastball. Berra knew what he was doing.

"I think you're losing it, Vic," Berra would say, walking toward the mound.

"Yogi, you'll lose your sorry ass right here if you don't get behind that plate," Raschi would respond.

But their arguments would blow over after the game, and they became longtime friends.

Reynolds was also headstrong and intimidating, though he was not as difficult as Raschi. Once while playing bocce at Berra's home, Henrich asked Reynolds how he thought he would do in an upcoming game, and when Reynolds replied that he would do well, Henrich asked him why he thought so.

Reynolds answered, without a hint of affectation, "Because I am good at all sports."

"After the season I said I was going back to the reservation, and I told him to go back to Dago Hill in St. Louis," Reynolds said years later.

Berra's relationship with Lopat was different. Lopat was known as a junk-baller who relied on throwing slow curves.

"When Lopat was pitching, I didn't need my catcher's mitt. A Kleenex did fine. Some days, if he was throwing well, I would need more than one," Berra said later.

Lopat's favorite game was against Cleveland. It was hot and humid, and in an attempt to get out of their hotel rooms, the players went down to the stadium in Cleveland to take some cool showers and hang around the locker room. But the Indians were taking early batting practice when no one was around, having their pitching staff throw them slow curves and change-ups. They were knocking the ball over the second baseman's head.

What the Cleveland players didn't know was that Lopat had seen the whole thing. When Berra came to the park, Lopat rushed to him, saying, "No slow balls today, Yogi. Don't even call for 'em. Fastballs and sliders only."

Lopat and Berra blew through the lineup the first time through and then reverted to the usual routine when Cleveland started looking for fastballs. Lopat won 5–3.

"Counting the screwball and the curve and my fastball, and the speeds I used with each, I figured I had 11 pitches," Lopat said years later. "Yogi only counted nine. As long as he was calling the pitches and catching them, that was fine with me."

The one thing Berra held over all their heads was his ability to have them pulled out of games. Stengel had taught Berra a signal—Berra would pick up a small handful of dirt behind the plate, and with that, Stengel would walk out to the mound and the pitcher would eventually be pulled.

When Reynolds and Raschi found out, they went ballistic. Reynolds once threatened Berra, saying, "Yogi, if I ever see you give that sign again—ever, even once—I'll kill you. I mean it, Yogi. I'll fight you in the clubhouse."

However, neither could deny that Berra's opinion counted when it mattered most, and he was often kind to them, which is undoubtedly one of the toughest spots a catcher is put in.

Early in the season, Stengel slowly shuffled to the mound after Raschi had given up two hits and a walk. "What about him?" Stengel said to Berra, motioning to Raschi.

"He's still got some stuff," said Berra, "but he's getting too cautious."

Stengel lifted Raschi and called in Tom Ferrick to close out the win for Raschi.

"I'd have let him stay in if Yogi told me to. The kid knows what the game is about," Stengel told the press after the game.

Many years later, Stengel said, "When he had to go out to the pitcher and tell him what he was doing wrong, he wasn't bashful and he wasn't embarrassed and he wasn't afraid, even if it was those big, famous fellows like Allie Reynolds and Vic Raschi. He went out and he told them, and he usually didn't have to wait for me or anybody to tell him to do it."

It's been alleged that Yogi Berra once said, "All pitchers are liars and crybabies." But the Hall of Fame catcher caught some of the greatest pitchers of his era. When he was asked to choose the best pitcher he caught in his 18 years with the Yankees, he responded, "It's impossible to pick the best. You take your pick: Vic Raschi, Allie Reynolds, Eddie Lopat, and Whitey Ford. I wouldn't be afraid to call on either of them."

"First and foremost, Yogi Berra was a fierce competitor. It wasn't smart to get him riled," Yankees pitcher Don Larsen wrote years later about Berra in his prime. "Opponents were the enemy, and we pitchers certainly weren't immune. He would chastise all of us on occasion, trying to rev us up when we were pitching poorly."

In the end, whatever their differences and disagreements on the field, Berra became close with many of the great pitchers of his career. And in the end, they all spoke very kindly of him.

Reynolds called him Dago because of his ethnicity, and Berra, for his part, called Reynolds, a Native American from Oklahoma, Chief. Years later, asked why he and Raschi didn't shake Berra off more often, Reynolds replied, "It is just not good to shake your catcher off too many times. It makes the infielders lose the spring in their legs and the outfielders lose their confidence in the two of you, their pitcher and catcher. A lot of baseball and life is confidence, and shaking off is not what you want to foster."

\*    \*    \*

There was one play on July 4, against the Red Sox, that, more than any other incident, began to solidify Berra's reputation as an excellent baseball mind. And he was not lauded by his own teammates, but by the Red Sox players.

With the bases loaded and one out in the ninth inning, Boston was down 3–2. Johnny Pesky was on third, Ted Williams on second, and Junior Stephens on first. Al Zarilla came up to bat against Raschi. Bobby Doerr was on deck.

Zarilla hit a clean, safe single, and Cliff Mapes charged the ball. The question was not whether Pesky would score, but whether Williams would cross the plate. But there was some confusion on the base path—the third-base coach had told Pesky to tag up, thinking Mapes might catch the ball, and it caused a traffic jam on the base paths. Williams was screaming, knowing it was a base hit, shouting for Pesky to run.

Mapes threw a strike from the outfield toward home plate. David Halberstam wrote, "There was only one person who seemed to understand the entire play, Doerr later realized, and that was Yogi Berra."

Berra was not crouching, preparing to turn around and block the plate. He was standing there like a first baseman, extending himself to take the throw. Many wondered why he was not blocking the plate as Pesky charged home on a single. Why was he letting Pesky score? Berra caught the ball on the first bounce.

Pesky slid in, and umpire Joe Paparella called, "Safe!"

"He's out!" screamed Berra.

"You never tagged him!" yelled Paparella back.

"Look a third base—it's a force play!" Berra shot back.

It was only then that Doerr, Pesky, and the thousands in attendance realized why the husky little catcher had not blocked the plate. Now Paparella realized Berra was right.

"No—you're out!" yelled the umpire.

"Doerr stood there in disbelief," wrote Halberstam. A deep fly ball ended the game for a 3–2 Yankee victory.

*   *   *

At the end of June, DiMaggio rejoined the Yankees for an exhibition game with the New York Giants. DiMaggio did well in the pregame home-run contest, but Berra won it. When Johnny Mize got up before Berra to take his cuts and hit a towering home run, Berra mumbled, "If I was as big as him, I could hit one there, too."

Berra then proceeded, during his turn, to hit a single and two homers. When he let one pitch go by, Stengel chuckled, "That's the first one Yogi's taken all year."

By the All-Star break, the Yankees were leading the league by six games. Jackie Robinson, Roy Campanella, Don Newcombe, and Larry Doby all debuted in the 1949 All-Star Game at Ebbets Field. It marked the first appearance of African American players in the midsummer classic.

The wisdom of Berra again became apparent at a pregame meeting for pitchers and catchers on how to get Stan Musial out. After listening for about 10 minutes, Yogi simply stated, "You guys are trying to stop Musial in 15 minutes while the National League ain't stopped him in 15 years."

Despite the fact that Berra did little with his bat during that game, he caught well, and there were no steals. The American League capitalized on five National League errors for an 11–7 triumph.

*   *   *

The only detraction from his love of baseball was Berra's hatred of playing doubleheaders. It was tough on his knees and extremely tiring. But his bat was so essential that Stengel, especially when Berra was young, penciled in the catcher's name for receiving duties for both games. Berra complained bitterly to Stengel, to no avail.

Many of Berra's teammates did not like this about him. Once Lopat, tired of hearing Berra's complaints, retorted, "Hey, Yogi, what do you think Birdie Tebbetts is going to do today? Catch one game or two?" The insult had no effect.

One Sunday in mid-July, Berra came to the park and sought out Charlie Silvera. "Silvera, you're catching the second game today," he said.

"No, I'm not," shot back Silvera incredulously. "The only way I catch is if you're home sick."

A few weeks later, during a doubleheader, Berra called in sick. The Old Professor wasn't having any of it.

"You call Mr. Berra right back," Stengel told trainer Gus Mauch, "and tell him to come to the ballpark anyway—I might want him as a pinch-hitter."

Berra had sustained a number of playing injuries that season. His first serious incident came at Cleveland. With the bases loaded, Doby came charging down the line, trying to steal home. He hit Berra head on, hoping to bowl over the stout catcher and jar the ball loose. Berra injured his elbow in the collision, but despite the severe blow, he held on to the ball and Doby was out. Doby was fined by manager Lou Boudreau because he had made the attempt on his own without the go-ahead from the dugout.

"Sure, he surprised me. Who'd think a guy would try a stunt like that?" Berra told reporters after the game.

On July 15 at St. Louis, Berra homered twice, and in August the Yankees beat up on the Browns again as Berra hit a two-run homer in a 20–2 shellacking. In retaliation, Dick Starr tried to bean Berra and hit him on the hands, breaking Berra's already sensitive thumb. Berra would be out all of August, but Silvera filled in admirably.

Stengel was never one to baby his stars. A player was a professional and was expected to play through pain. Berra asked for a few weeks off because of his fractured digit, but his manager refused. Berra was forced to wear a uniform every day and suit up for each game until he worked his way back into the lineup, which took some time.

Uncharacteristically for Stengel, he even took a few shots at his favorite backstop, saying to the team just before one game, "Now, fellas, I'd like you to meet a stranger. This is Mr. Berra. Says he's got an ache of some kind."

But Berra was as hardheaded as anyone and refused to go back into the lineup until he felt he was ready. Stengel was mercilessly trying to goad the stubborn catcher back onto the field.

On August 25, team physician Dr. Sydney Gaynor removed Berra's cast. Stengel was eager to get his dawdling star back into the lineup during what had become a heated pennant race. It was just then that the team was headed to St. Louis to play the Browns, and Berra took advantage of the opportunity to visit his family.

His mother took one look at his hand, sliced a lemon in half, and stuck it on the end of the healing thumb. She insisted that this was an old family remedy and that Berra must not remove it for a certain number of days. When Stengel argued with Berra that the team doctor had cleared him to play, Berra refused, citing Mama Berra's instructions. An aggravated Stengel told the press, "My catcher, Mr. Berra, is wearing a lemon instead of a mitt."

"By the time Berra came back in September, the Yankees badly needed him," wrote Halberstam. Berra finally returned to the lineup on September 7 at Boston. He went hitless, as the Yankees beat back the Red Sox 5–2. But the Bronx Bombers continued to slide while Boston charged on. Another important series with the Red Sox later that month saw the team drop three games at Fenway.

The Yankees rebounded and took their last two games at home against the Red Sox, 5–4 and 5–3, and won a ticket to the World Series. There in 1949, they faced the Brooklyn Dodgers, stocked with such famous players as Jackie Robinson, Duke Snider, Pee Wee Reese, Don Newcombe, and Roy Campanella, among many other greats.

Heading into the Series, Berra's thumb was still bothering him, and he grumbled to the press, "Six weeks and the danged thing ain't healed yet. I was talkin' to Steve O'Neill and Jim Hegan when Cleveland was here, 'n' they told me it'd still be botherin' me next spring."

In addition, Gene Woodling, a fellow teammate, once remarked that many of the Yankees players always had someone behind them, pushing them for their jobs. Woodling said, "Yogi knew [Charlie] Silvera was ready."

"In 1949, my rookie year, I batted .315," Silvera said decades later. "Yogi broke his thumb and missed six weeks. I took his place.... We ended up winning the pennant by one game. I haven't been given much credit for the role I played in 1949. I'm going to blow my own horn a little here. I didn't hang around all those years because I was Casey's illegitimate son. I don't know whether the Yankees would have taken that '49 pennant [without me]."

This was also the first time Berra and Roy Campanella played against each other in a World Series. Campanella was born on November 19, 1921, in Philadelphia, Pennsylvania. His father was of Italian descent; his mother was African American. Because of his mother's ethnicity, he was barred from Major League Baseball.

Campanella began playing professional baseball in 1937 at the age of 15 in the Negro Leagues for the Washington Elite Giants. He became a star with that team and also played some baseball in the Mexican League.

In 1946, Campanella moved into the Brooklyn Dodgers' minor league system, along with pitcher Don Newcombe, who went to the Nashua Dodgers of the New England League.

Among sportswriters, Campanella was usually considered one of the better athletes behind the plate. "More than one observer has likened Campanella's quickness behind the plate to that of a cat. He can pounce on bunts placed far out in front of the plate, and he gets his throws away with no wasted motion. He had not only a rifle arm but an accurate one," wrote Tom Meany in the *New York World Telegram*.

In an article titled "The Man behind the Iron Mask," Arthur Daley lamented the modern catcher, who seemed to be lacking when compared to the likes of Mickey Cochrane, Bill Dickey, Al Lopez, and a few others. "Ironically, the Dodgers not only have the best in Campanella, but they have the second best in Bruce Edwards," he wrote. "Nor can the American League offer too much more.... Berra has three—count 'em—catchers back of him, none of them a hitter." Daley said of Campanella, "Of the moderns, only Campanella rates being mentioned in the same breath" as the immortals. However, by the spring of 1951, Daley would claim that Campanella was the best in the game and that Berra ran a strong second.

In Campy's best years, he and Berra were neck and neck in offensive categories, and both eventually won three MVP Awards. Many sports historians wonder what Campy's career statistics would've been if his arrival in the major leagues had not been delayed by the color barrier, and had his playing days not been cut short by a tragic car accident.

There was no question that between 1949 and 1957, two of the best catchers in baseball played in New York City. While Berra was a unique character on the New York scene, Campanella was no less colorful. Both were massively talented and relatively uneducated. Berra had quit school in eighth grade; Campy had quit during his junior year of high school. But while Berra was portrayed as a rube or a gorilla, Campanella was portrayed as boyish or a man-child. Neither were considered eloquent, but both were eminently lovable and huge crowd favorites in their own parks. The two were more alike than most people knew. But for the next eight years they would be compared and contrasted *ad infinitum.* One of the favorite barroom arguments in Gotham and Brooklyn remained unchanged for years—who was better, Yogi or Campy?

Berra fell flat in the Series against Campanella and the Dodgers, going 1-for-16 in the four of five games he played, finishing the Series with an ignominious batting average of .063. The Yankees won, and after the last out in a victorious Game 5, Berra took the last pitch by Joe Page and handed the ball to Stengel. It was Stengel's first win as a manager in the World Series.

Someone asked the skipper for it, and Stengel responded, "Not this, no, no, no. I'm keeping this one myself!"

"I know he appreciated the souvenir for his first World Series championship," said Berra in 2003. "He always said that 1949 season was the biggest thrill of his career."

The winning share for each of the Yankees was $5,626.74. For the season, Berra had batted .277, with 20 home runs and 91 RBIs, and he had finished 15th in voting for the MVP award. Despite his World Series struggle, there was no denying that Berra now merited being mentioned in the same breath as Henrich and DiMaggio.

After a big celebration party at the Biltmore Hotel that featured William Frawley (Fred Mertz from *I Love Lucy*), Bob Hope, and Ray Bolger, Berra and his wife didn't get home until the next morning.

\*    \*    \*

Several weeks after his return from New York, Joe Garagiola and Audrie Rose were married. Stan Musial was in attendance, and Berra was the best man. Joe and Audrie, like Yogi and Carmen, would be married the rest of their lives. Joe brags about Audrie to this day, "I always say that Audrie is the best catch I ever made."

On December 8, 1949, Yogi's son Lawrence Allen Berra was born in St. Louis, Missouri. He weighed eight pounds, nine ounces. Phil Rizzuto would eventually be the boy's godfather. Berra and Carmen were living with his parents and kid sister in their house on Elizabeth Avenue. Berra had paid for some renovations to the eight-room house and had the basement converted into a family room with a play area for little Larry.

During the season, Carmen found baseball life filled with ups and downs. When the team was away, she could be very lonely and spent time visiting with other baseball wives. When the team was in town, the Berras spent time with Rizzuto, Frank Shea, George Stirnweiss, and their wives.

She proved to be an excellent partner for her famous husband. She was not intimidated by his sudden fame. Knowing her husband's penchant for eating, she was more than up to the task of reminding him when they went out to dinner, "Don't make a pig out of yourself. Lay off after you have seconds." He loved her cooking, especially her cabbage stuffed with beef and rice. And his most dangerous time for weight gain was in the off-season, when a lack of exercise would coincide with more opportunities to eat.

Berra occasionally played golf with Stan Musial at the Sunset Country Club, but he spent most of his days on the Hill. Unlike his schedule during the season, he stayed up late and arose even later. He liked reading all the newspapers. His brother John and Mickey Garagiola got him a job at Ruggeri's Restaurant as a greeter. Patrons entering the restaurant were welcomed by a tuxedoed and smiling Berra. The restaurant proudly bore a sign that read: "Your Genial Host Lawrence (Yogi) Berra, World Champion Yankee Catcher, Greets You from Ruggeri's." However, Ruggeri's was not an inexpensive establishment, and Berra himself would only occasionally eat there out of financial considerations. He also seemed uncomfortable in such a formal setting.

More often than not, the famous, 25-year-old Berra hung around with old Hill friends in small-time bars and restaurants, keeping a low profile and living a life not unlike many folks in the neighborhood. He went bowling and golfing.

# ~ Chapter 10 ~

# THE BUSINESS OF BASEBALL

In 1950 George Weiss received a large envelope from Berra, and he opened it with curiosity. But he was disappointed almost immediately—Berra had returned Weiss's contract for $16,000 unsigned without even opening it.

He wanted $22,000. Carmen was astonished, and Berra admitted that he would settle for $18,000. "Weiss said they'd pay me what I was worth," he said. "I swear to the Lord I won't take less than…$18,000."

In later years, Carmen said Berra rarely broke a vow he made to the Lord.

Weiss was furious. He was insulted by Berra's $22,000 request. And the sportswriters jumped on it, as they did with most incidents of Berra's career.

"You sent back your contract?" asked a local sportswriter. "What did they offer you?"

"I don't know," Berra replied.

"How come you don't know? Didn't you read it?"

"Nope. I didn't read it."

This story circulated quickly on the wires and got back to Weiss, who was more determined than ever to hold a hard line with Berra.

Sportswriter James P. Dawson wrote on January 24, 1950, "Only the unpredictable Yogi Berra, of the players who have seen their contracts, is unsigned. He was in…last week and took his document with him to study. For all anybody knows to the contrary, Yogi still has the parchment with him."

Weiss was determined not to give Yogi his money, but he realized Berra's value to the team. For his part, Berra attended a pre-spring-training camp meeting in Phoenix, Arizona, to show good faith. But when the team assembled in St. Petersburg, he held out.

On February 17, sportswriter Roscoe McGowen wrote, "Yogi apparently is still giving weighty consideration of picking up a pen and affixing his signature, although there is no sign he is a holdout."

"You're not doing yourself or the club any good in St. Louis," Weiss told Berra over the phone. "Take a plane down here and let's talk it over."

"Who'll pay for my plane fare if I don't sign?" asked Berra.

Weiss paid for the ticket, and he and Berra met on March 7. But if Weiss sounded conciliatory over the phone, when the two met, it went badly. Weiss thought that behind closed doors he could bend Berra. But Berra was like an anvil with a temper.

The two hard bargainers stuck to their positions and went back and forth in the most uncordial manner. Time wore on. One hour passed. And as the second hour of these closed-door discussions passed, tempers started to flare. Eventually Berra bellowed, "Let me see Dan Topping or Del Webb! I can't talk to you anymore! You'd think I was a flop last year. I had a very good year, in case nobody told you!" He stormed out of the meeting, and it made headlines all over the country.

"They're not kidding me!" the irate catcher told the press. He admitted he had been offered a slight raise. But when he was asked if Weiss had gotten angry, Berra snapped, "Sure he got mad, but I got pretty mad, too."

It is interesting to note that Raschi was also a holdout at this time, which tells you something about how similar Raschi and Berra actually were in temperament. While the papers noted that Raschi was shacked up in a bungalow down the coast, Berra was reported to be staying in the same hotel as the team and hanging out with his teammates.

Also, Charlie DeWitt of the St. Louis Browns told the press that he'd be willing to offer Berra a lot higher salary than the Yankees. With the Browns' short porch and him being a hometown boy, DeWitt figured Berra could acquit himself spectacularly at Sportsman's Park. This was

*Lawrence Peter "Yogi" Berra began his Hall of Fame career with the New York Yankees in 1946.*

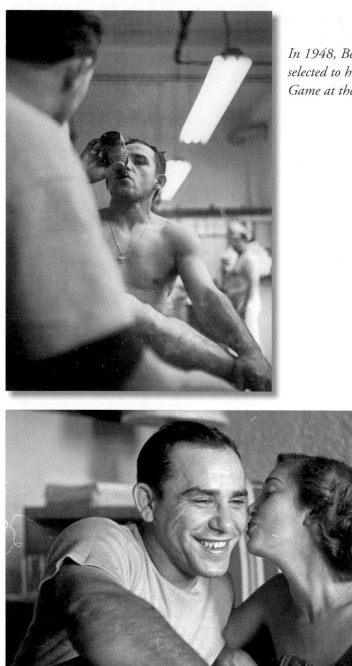

*In 1948, Berra was selected to his first All-Star Game at the age of 23.*

*Berra and his wife, Carmen, were married in 1949. They recently celebrated their 65th wedding anniversary.*

*By 1950, Berra had already become a fixture behind the plate for the Yankees.*

*Three of the greatest players in the history of Major League Baseball: Ted Williams, Yogi Berra, and Mickey Mantle.*

*Phil Rizzuto and Berra celebrate the Yankees' American League pennant victory in 1951. Berra and Rizzuto would remain friends the rest of their lives.* (Photo courtesy of AP/Wide World Photos)

*The consummate businessman, Berra's relationship with Yoo-hoo helped make him one of the most successful pitchmen of all time.*

*Never shy about expressing his opinions to the men in blue, Berra jaws with an ump during a game against Cleveland.*

*In 1955, Berra earned his third MVP award, one of only seven players in baseball history to be so honored.*

*Jackie Robinson's stealing of home plate during Game 1 of the 1955 World Series may be remembered as one of the most exciting plays of all time…*

*…but Berra was positive that Robinson was out.*

*The heart of the Yankees lineup, out of uniform: Roger Maris (left), Mickey Mantle (center), and Berra.* (Photo courtesy of AP/Wide World Photos)

*Perfection! Still the only perfect game in World Series history, Don Larsen and Berra celebrate their 1956 masterpiece.* (Photo courtesy of AP/Wide World Photos)

great ammunition for Berra, but he never really considered the offer as anything more than a negotiating tool. Berra liked being a New York Yankee.

"However, [Berra] made it clear that the next move in salary negotiations would have to come from Weiss," wrote sports scribe John Drebinger.

"He knows what I want, and when he's ready to pay me, I'll sign," Berra told Drebinger.

Weiss was set to play hardball, but Stengel, with spring training progressing without his star pitcher and catcher, had had enough. The next day's *Daily News* headline told the story: "Casey Goes to Bat—Gets Raises for Raschi, Yogi."

Stengel had talked Weiss into compromising. He got Raschi $30,000, which was a boost of $10,000, and he got Berra almost $19,000, which was an increase of $5,000.

"Weiss admitted that it was Stengel who effected the compromises," wrote Joe Trimble.

"General manager George M. Weiss, aided by the club president and manager, bagged a gullible Yogi Berra...determined to hold out to Christmas. Seemingly, Christmas came earlier than Yogi suspected," wrote Drebinger. "The gnome-like backstop never has, and likely never will, look like a ballplayer. But that singular characteristic doesn't by any means prevent him from being the number one catcher of the world champions and one of the most feared batters in the American league."

Trimble reported, "The manager actually talked Berra into signing—after getting Weiss to raise his initial offer [from] $16,000. Berra has much more faith in Casey than Weiss, who once paid him $90 a month as a rookie with Norfolk."

Stengel proudly told the press, "Sure, his feet stick out wrong, and he doesn't seem to do anything right. But he murders the ball, and when he's behind the plate, [we] win. What else can any manager expect of a catcher?"

"Yes sir," continued Stengel, "there's the man which caught two World Series in three years. They laughed at him, but they're not laughing any more.... They said he'd murder us, but he murdered them. He looks funny. He wears his shinguards wrong, but he does a job for you."

*    *    *

Most of the sportswriters that winter picked the Red Sox to take the division. The Yankees didn't mind this. They referred to their Red Sox brethren as "the Fenway millionaires" because Tom Yawkey, the Boston owner, paid his players more on average than the Yankees paid. The Yankees respected their rivals, but they thought that the Red Sox were pampered.

Not surprisingly, Stengel's message was simple: last year is over; you've got to do it all over again. For anyone who thought the Old Professor was going to bask in the extended glory of the 1949 world championship, they had another thing coming.

Stengel's caustic wit rang shrilly throughout spring training. That year, more than ever, Stengel motivated people with the threat of taking their jobs. He said at the beginning of the season that the only four everyday players on the team were Berra, DiMaggio, Henrich, and Rizzuto. But even DiMaggio found himself, gloomily, at first base. Nothing was safe, as the Old Professor tinkered throughout the season.

The Yankees would struggle most of the season while Stengel tried as many moves as he possibly could. Stengel had once told Whitey Herzog, "There are three ways to do anything: the right way, the wrong way, and my way. If my way turns out to be the wrong way, nobody's ever gonna know because my way is the only way we're ever gonna do it anyway."

Billy Martin joined the Yankees that year and made his major league debut on April 18, 1950. Born Alfred Manuel Martin in Berkeley, California, Martin was raised almost solely by his Italian mother after she separated from his Portuguese father. He had arrived at the name Billy because his mother always called him *bello*, (which means "beautiful" in Italian), which on the streets of Northern California became Billy. The wiry, confrontational, hard-partying second baseman would become a stalwart of the Yankees lineup, but his troubled life would lead him into direct confrontation with Weiss.

Martin already had a roommate, but as was the custom, the newest kid eventually wound up with Berra, who always had a tough time keeping roommates.

Berra normally roomed alone. "I could understand why," roommate Whitey Ford said. "Yogi was a royal pain in the ass."

"We were the original odd couple. Yogi used to like to go to bed early and wake up early. I liked to go to bed late and slept late.... There were problems," Ford admitted frankly. "He got up every morning at 6:00 and made sure he made enough noise in the room to wake me up. He'd want to have a conversation when he got dressed, and I wanted to sleep."

Berra would then go downstairs, buy a newspaper, have breakfast, and then return to the room about an hour or so later, making more noise while Ford was trying to sleep. Berra would then go back to bed.

Many a night Ford came back to the room late, with the lights off. He would assume Berra was asleep and would get undressed in the dark so as not to wake up his slumbering friend. Sometimes tripping or stubbing his toes, Ford always tried to be considerate. "I'd go to the bathroom, then I'd come back and crawl into bed. As soon as I got into bed, Yogi would turn on the light and want to start talking. The pain in the ass was awake all the time," he said.

*    *    *

In 1950 Berra was feeling fine, and he told Rizzuto that if he could just stay healthy for the year and avoid injury, he thought he could have a breakout season.

Several other kids from the Hill were also looking to do something special. Garagiola was back with the Cardinals and looking to get back to his World Series form. He got off to a decent start in 1950, playing in 34 games and batting .318. But he suffered a shoulder separation when he collided with Jackie Robinson of the Brooklyn Dodgers. Garagiola needed surgery, and his shoulder had to be pinned together. That kept him out the rest of the season. While he was convalescing, his interest in broadcasting was piqued when he tuned in to listen to his team's radio broadcasts.

Another Hill kid was Jack Maguire, who also had allegedly helped to make the moniker Yogi stick on his neighbor. Maguire was 25 years old when he broke into the big leagues on April 18, 1950, with the New York Giants.

\*    \*    \*

April was not kind to the Yankees, as they started out 6–4—hardly a strong showing for a team that wanted to confirm its world championship status. But May was much better, and the team notched 20 wins against just six losses. But June saw the Yankees slide backward, notching a 15–17 record. By the end of June the Yankees were 41–27. But it was a tough year, and the competition was stiff. Detroit was 43–21.

On July 1, 1950, Edward Charles "Whitey" Ford made his debut with the New York Yankees. He was born and raised in Queens, New York, and had received his memorable nickname in the minors on account of his white-blonde hair.

"When I got there, I was expecting an older club because the guys were already heroes to me. Joe DiMaggio, Phil Rizzuto, Billy Johnson, Tommy Henrich, Yogi Berra—I always used to picture them so much older than me. But when I got there, I found out they weren't. Yogi was only three or four years older than me," said Ford.

"We'd have been dead without him," Stengel admitted of Ford.

Ford loved to tell of the time he was rooming with Berra while in Chicago. Berra was getting up to go for breakfast, and Ford told him, "Wake me up before you go to the park."

But Yogi went downstairs, ate, and left, forgetting to call Ford. Ford woke up at noon, thinking the game was at 2:00 PM. Red Patterson, the Yankees' publicity man, asked what Ford was still doing in the hotel lobby when he was starting a 1:00 game. Ford took a cab and found Stengel as sharp as a buzz saw when he entered. Ford raced out and started warming up, then Hank Bauer came over to him, angry, and said, "Don't fool around with my money."

The point was made.

\*    \*    \*

By July 1950, Berra had put together two 10-game hitting streaks and was batting a blistering-hot .319. And he was cutting down runners with rifle-shot regularity. However, when Stengel spoke with the writers, they still made fun of Berra. Stengel continued to sell Berra to them, but most scoffed, which only spurred the Old Professor on.

"He's the boss out there. Yogi knows what he's doing all the time. He says a man's still got it, I go with him," Stengel said, stumping for Berra. "He says the pitcher is weakening, I signal the bullpen and get someone heating up." Stengel dared the writers to present an incident when he had shown up his catcher. But none could. And most had to admit that they had seen Berra tell Stengel it was time for a reliever and then saw Stengel pull Raschi, Reynolds, or Lopat with confidence.

Stengel was not happy with his club's overall hitting, though, and told Scripps-Howard News Service columnist Joe Williams, "We don't hit enough. We got to scramble for runs even against the weak clubs. After the pitchers get past Berra and DiMaggio, they can stop bleeding."

Berra was also swinging at fewer bad pitches, stymieing many teams' attempts to blunt his aggressive hitting. As he matured as a player, he was no longer bothered by southpaw or side-armed pitchers. In 1950, in a game against the Red Sox, Berra got up for the second time in the same inning when Joe McCarthy, the old Yankees skipper who was now piloting the Red Sox, called in Earl Johnson.

"Let's see you turn around, Ugly Man," yelled the Beantown bench jockeys, anticipating Berra's fear of side-arm pitchers. "Fall back, fall back. Don't get that pretty face ruined!"

But Johnson made an exaggerated motion, sweeping his arm around, and Berra stepped into the pitch, confidently lining it for a base hit.

In 1950 Berra was voted into the All-Star Game as the number one catcher, ahead of Birdie Tebbetts. Again, though, Berra did not perform well, but there was no denying that Berra was someone now to be reckoned with.

"Casey had Berra behind the plate, and Yogi would catch 148 games in 1950, coming into his own as one of the best players in the game," wrote baseball historian Robert Creamer.

Berra was hot. In one game in August against Detroit during the race for the pennant, Berra knocked in six runs with a homer, a triple, and two singles. Sportswriter John Drebinger called Berra "the pudgy receiver of the Stengeleers...the mightiest gunner of all."

Fewer than 10 days later, Berra hit a two-run home run in a win against the Washington Senators, as the Yankees jealously guarded their hard-won spot atop the American League. That year Berra batted .322, hit 28 home runs, and put up 124 RBIs. It would be the highest batting average of his career, a mark he would chase the rest of his playing days, and he would be one of the more productive members of the team thereafter.

The Yankees won eight of their last 11 games and finished three games ahead of the Detroit Tigers, with whom they had battled all summer. This placed them in the World Series against the exciting "Whiz Kids" from Philadelphia, who had finished two games ahead of the Brooklyn Dodgers to take the National League pennant.

In the first game of the Series, Raschi posted a two-hitter, blanking the Phillies in a nail-biter, 1–0, against stout pitching from reliever-turned-starter Jim Konstanty.

"I never shook him off once," Raschi told the press about Berra.

During the course of the fourth and last game of the Series, Johnny Mize swallowed up a grounder by Andy Seminick, turned, and wheeled toward Berra at home. "But first of all—and few noticed it—he'd jammed one large brogan on the bag to retire Seminick. Then he wheeled to the Yogi man, who tagged [Del] Ennis and rolled the ball toward the mound. He was the only person in the joint smart enough to realize it was a double play," wrote Arthur Daley.

Months later, still reveling in the play, Daley wrote, "There was the truly amazing spectacle of Johnny Mize completing a double play that was so unusual the only person in the ballpark smart enough to realize it was Yogi Berra."

Daley coyly noted, "The greatly maligned Yogi is a pretty smart cookie.... Even the umpires didn't realize for a moment what had happened. But Yogi grasped the situation perfectly." While Yogi went out to the pitcher's mound yelling that the inning was over, "everyone else was running around like crazy and wondering what had happened." Daley said movies of the 1950 World Series showed the brilliance of Berra.

The press celebrated the mighty Yankees and how they had demolished the Phillies in an anticlimactic Series. But the win was deceptive. "Take a look at the box scores. We didn't exactly kick the hell out of them," Berra said years later about the Yankees' victory. Of course, he was right—the first three games were all tight affairs that went down to the last out, and all were decided by one run.

Berra played in all four games. Despite the victory, he batted just .200 in the World Series, but he did hit one homer and scored two runs.

\*    \*    \*

In the clubhouse during the World Series celebration, regular-season MVP Phil Rizzuto asked Berra if he was going to stay in the East for the winter. Berra's mother had fallen and hurt her hip, and she was not doing well, and Carmen's mother was also ill in Salem, Missouri. The Berras would spend the winter in St. Louis on the Hill.

Rizzuto gritted his teeth. He had been wheeling and dealing, looking to line up things for the off-season. In those days, players still had to think of business outside of baseball.

Philip Francis Rizzuto was actually born Fiero Francesco Rizzuto back on September 25, 1917, in Brooklyn. Listed at 5'6" and weighing almost 160 pounds, he was often thought to be too small for sports. But despite his diminutive size, he played both baseball and football at Richmond Hill High School in Queens.

On April 14, 1941, Rizzuto played his first major league game for the New York Yankees, the team he played for his entire 13-year career, almost exclusively as a shortstop. His playing career was interrupted, like many other players of the era, by World War II. From 1943 to 1945, he served in the U.S. Navy, where he played on the navy baseball team.

Savvy and popular, Rizzuto was nicknamed the Scooter for his ability to get after a ball swiftly and deftly. John "Lollipop" Corriden once said of Rizzuto, "I have been in baseball for over, well, for 30 or 40 years at least, and I'll be darned if I ever knew a ballplayer anywhere with the priceless, perfect disposition of Rizzuto."

Rizzuto and Berra were movie fanatics, and they loved double features, especially when they were on the road. There is a famous and true story of Berra and Rizzuto getting to their hotel in Boston during a road trip. They were so concerned about the showtimes for the next Western double feature that they bought a newspaper to check and both forgot to check in.

In another amusing anecdote reported by ESPN.com, "In 1950, Phil Rizzuto received a death threat in Boston and was told he'd be shot if he showed up in uniform. So Stengel did what any right-thinking man would do—he gave Rizzuto's uniform to Billy Martin to wear."

Berra found in Rizzuto someone in whom he could confide. Rizzuto, who could be just as funny as the other players when needling them, never conveyed the menace or nastiness some of the other players had toward Berra. Rizzuto was friendly. If he chided or joked with Berra, he did not ridicule or haze him. They were becoming good friends, and that friendship was growing more and more.

*    *    *

Berra soon encountered another man who would play a major role in his career. Frank Scott was born October 17, 1917, in Pittsburgh, Pennsylvania. He attended the University of Pittsburgh, where he was the student manager of the football team that won the Rose Bowl in 1937. Jock Sutherland, the Pittsburgh coach, was eventually hired by Dan Topping to coach the Brooklyn Dodgers football team. With Sutherland's urging, Topping hired Scott as traveling secretary for the team from 1940 to 1942.

During World War II, Scott served in the navy. Topping, by then part owner of the Yankees, rehired him to become the traveling secretary for the New York Yankees in 1947. "Part of his job was to check on the availability of players being sought as banquet speakers, television guests, or product endorsers," wrote journalist Gay Talese.

In 1948 Scott and his wife-to-be eloped in DiMaggio's car. However, Yankees general manager Weiss decided Scott was becoming too close and chummy with the players. Weiss often asked for personal information on the players. As was his custom, Weiss routinely had his baseball players trailed by private detectives. Scott was uncomfortable trading on the details and secrets of their personal lives. Weiss insisted that Scott divulge certain information, and Scott refused. Weiss was furious and forced Scott out of his job in 1950.

According to sportswriter Frank Litsky, "Scott's career as an agent started almost by accident. He and his wife, the former Bette Sheppard, were visiting Berra and his wife, Carmen, when Carmen noticed that Scott was not wearing a watch."

Frank had asked what time it was. His watch had stopped.

"She excused herself," Scott recalled, "and reappeared with a whole tray of wristwatches—at least 20—and told me to take my pick."

"Where did this come from?" Scott asked Berra.

"That's what they give me when I make speeches," Berra explained.

"That's how those scoundrels had been paying off Yogi for personal appearances. He didn't know any better. We didn't know any better. It's different now," Scott said years later.

"Scott understood immediately that there was room for a new role here, that if he represented a player like Berra and negotiated his appearances, Berra might do better than getting a watch. He made an offer to Berra on the spot. Thus did Yogi Berra, by Scott's and his teammates' reckoning, become the first player in baseball to have an agent," wrote David Halberstam.

"There had been sports agents before Scott," wrote Litsky, "notably C.C. (Cash-and-Carry) Pyle, who masterminded Red Grange's professional football debut in the 1920s. But no one had concentrated on athletes' off-the-field earnings."

Instead of watches, Berra was immediately garnering up to $2,500 per engagement and thus stopped adding to his watch collection. This was all courtesy of Frank Scott Associates.

This was exactly the kind of help Berra had always wanted. Even more than food and baseball, Berra was obsessed by money. He was not greedy, but he was smart, in a way that he himself could not express.

Stengel said one time, "Money is the last thing Yogi thinks about at night before he goes to sleep."

In fact, Berra would go on to develop an incredible reputation among his teammates and friends as a bit of a financial wizard. Whereas Mantle and Ford were making great contracts, they were usually investing their hard-won Yankees money in hair-brained schemes and turning it over to optimistic speculators and con men. Among his Yankees contemporaries,

Berra, in the end, would retire as the most successful and most financially secure.

Berra was always humble, saying he was lucky. But that's part of his "aw shucks, Yogi" persona. The real Berra was obsessed with financial security for himself and his family. And step by step—either by luck, hard negotiation, or hard work—Berra was building a war chest unlike any other player from the period.

Although Berra was a fan favorite, he had yet to turn his accomplishments and his celebrity into cash. He had certainly entertained folks on the rubber-chicken circuit, speaking at banquets, but he had not fully capitalized on the opportunity.

Scott became one of the people who helped turn Berra from a local hero and baseball favorite into a national icon. Scott took the persona the writers had created and found a way to make money from it.

Berra always credited Scott "with getting him out of the kitchen, literally, by booking television commercials and appearances on programs like *The Phil Silvers Show* and *The Ed Sullivan Show*. Mr. Berra recalled that he worked with Mr. Scott for years without a contract. Business was conducted on a handshake," wrote Patricia Winters Lauro, an advertising journalist.

After Berra made the deal with Scott, teammates and various sports stars saw the success he was having and signed up with Scott themselves. Scott's first clients included Berra, Mantle, and Roger Maris. "Later baseball clients included Joe DiMaggio, Willie Mays, Henry Aaron, Whitey Ford, Duke Snider, Gil Hodges, Larry Doby, Walter Alston, Ralph Branca, Bob Feller, and Roy Campanella. He also represented Vince Lombardi, Frank Gifford, and Y.A. Tittle from football, and Oscar Robertson and Bob Cousy from basketball," reported *The New York Times*.

"Hey, Scotty, where's my loot?" was often the clubhouse refrain.

"It's on the way," Scott would say, or alternately, according to journalist Gay Talese, he would pull out a wad of checks and cash, distributing it throughout the room. By 1956 Mantle alone was making $70,000 a year from endorsements outside of baseball in an era when the average take-home pay was $3,600 a year.

In the *Saturday Evening Post* in 1957, Shirley Povich wrote, "Scott knew an agent's place. He was too smart to meddle in the players' salary debates with the ballclub. He knew, too, that there had to be rigid respect for the rule that the players' first obligation was to the ballclub."

"I never guarantee them a dime. I tell them only that I will represent their interest in negotiating off-field deals and that they must sell themselves on the playing field if we're going to make any money off of it. I tell them, 'If you don't win, you get nothing, and I get 10 percent of nothing,'" Scott said.

Talese has told the story of how Mantle was once photographed in center field blowing bubbles with bubble gum. Photographers snapped away, and the pictures were in all the papers the next day. Mantle was embarrassed by this baseball faux pas, but Scott saw it as a great opportunity. In the following days Mantle found himself significantly richer, as he was now a spokesman for Bowman Gum Company.

\*   \*   \*

The 1951 season started off with some challenges for Berra. Again he had contract difficulties with Weiss. In late January, Berra took his case to the press, telling a reporter from the Associated Press that he and the Yankees were "far apart.... I'm staying here [in St. Louis] until I get what I want," said the 25-year-old catcher.

For Berra's tremendous season, Weiss was offering a $3,000 increase. Berra had been one of the top three or four in total hits, total bases, and RBIs, and he finished first in fewest strikeouts per at-bats. His numbers had been gaudy.

Berra wanted more money. Lots more. Some insiders said he asked for as much as $40,000, which was high for the times. But a $3,000 increase seemed like a silly slap in the face.

"I think my chances of getting it are pretty good. But if I don't have a good contract by spring training time, I'm sitting right here," Berra said from his home in St. Louis on February 1, 1951.

For a month, few communiqués from either camp made a dent. But there was no denying that Berra's popularity was rising. The young, rough catcher had earned a certain kind of celebrity when, on February 28, at the tender age of 25, he was a clue in a *New York Times* crossword puzzle edited by Margaret Farrar: 29 Across was "Yogi Berra's glove."

A sign of the affection people within baseball felt for Berra was encapsulated in a game played by the sportswriters. Red Smith, one of the preeminent columnists of his generation, "invented a game he called L. Peter B., which he played over and over during the long annual auto trips to and from spring training. The idea was to supply a ballplayer's first and last initials and full middle name and ask the other participants to identify the athlete," wrote legendary baseball chronicler Roger Kahn. "Smith's favorite entry was L. (Lawrence) Peter B. (Berra). Yogi, of course, is a nickname." Other offerings might have been H. Louis G. (Gehrig) and W. Howard M. (Mays), among others.

On that same day Berra made it into the crossword, a headline blared across *The New York Times*, "Berra and Yanks Remain Adamant in Dispute over Terms." Both sides told the press there was no room for negotiation, as the Yankees were now offering $25,000 to the young backstop.

The negotiations had broken down so completely that the Yankees had issued a statement to the press that said, "Berra refuses to budge from a figure which is so far out of line there is no basis for negotiations. He wants a figure that is approximately double what any catcher in baseball is getting today. That is the situation, and it will remain so until someone or something gives." Weiss was hot.

But Berra had sound reasoning behind him. Rizzuto had been paid $40,000 in 1950, and Joe DiMaggio was paid $100,000. And Berra had had a breakout year. It was the right time to press. During the negotiations, *The Sporting News* announced their All-Star team of the year, and Berra made first team with 163 votes to Campanella's 55. Berra reasoned he would never be in a better position.

Meanwhile Berra had resumed his position as the greeter/head waiter at Ruggeri's. During a cross-country trip, Roy Hamey, Weiss's number two man, stopped in St. Louis and dropped by the restaurant to discuss the contract with Berra.

"I can give you a good seat alone," Berra joked with Hamey.

"I don't want to eat. I just want to sit down and talk with you and talk about your contract for a while."

Confident, Berra tried to get Hamey to order one of the most expensive items on the menu, pitching him the lobster, the steak, and even the spaghetti. When Hamey asked about the contract, Berra replied that Carmen was still reading the fine print.

Then things got serious. Berra made it clear he was standing pat. Berra admitted years later that every contract negotiation, in some sense, was retribution for the minor league disgraces and summers of hunger.

"They always told me I would get the money if I did the job. Well, I did the job, and now I want to get the money," said Berra, getting a little hotter.

"I'm sorry, Yogi. It looks like we've reached an impasse," Hamey said.

"What the hell is that?"

That winter Berra slept a lot, especially because Carmen was spending so much time with her ailing mother on the farm in Salem. He worked and spent lots of time at little bars on the Hill like Grassi's and Bob's Place. And he spent time bowling and playing cards in basements throughout the Hill. He and Carmen, when she was home, ate out a little more, and he even went on a guys' weekend in Chicago, taking in a Bears–Lions football game and a hockey game as well.

Berra lamented that the hardest part of the winter was sometimes saying no to the invitations on the dinner circuit. He was receiving 10 to 12 invitations per week, many from people he had known a long time. The toughest was when they approached him in person, especially at work or on the street. More than anything, Berra did not like standing in front of a room of strangers.

After the World Series, Ed Sullivan had asked Berra to stay in town a couple of days so he could appear on the television show. Berra didn't want to do it, but Sullivan talked to Carmen and offered $1,000.

"You said a thousand dollars?" Carmen asked.

"That's right," replied Sullivan.

"Don't worry about it, Mr. Sullivan. Yogi will be there."

That same weekend, Berra was included in a roundup of the "10 most interesting faces in America." He called Garagiola to find out what the word *Neanderthal* meant.

"It means primitive man," Garagiola said to Berra. "You know, back to the caveman."

Then Berra asked what *virile* meant. When his friend told him it was a word that meant he appeared attractive to women, Berra supposedly replied, "Oh my God, I hope Carm doesn't hear about this."

By late February, Berra still was not signed to return to the Yankees. And Weiss issued more statements, disclosing all the facts and figures of the negotiations between them. It was an all-out media blitz by Weiss to try to embarrass Berra into submission. It only made Berra more determined.

Players were now assembling for spring training, and Berra was missing it. Weiss called a few days later. He offered $28,000, and Berra countered with $35,000. They debated for a few minutes, and settled on $30,000, which was the base number Berra had wanted all along. Berra left St. Louis. He had missed a week of training.

But he had made his point. By his own admission, it was the last gruesome contract negotiation he ever had with the New York Yankees organization. Afterward, he always considered his salary fair market value. And Weiss stopped trying to low-ball the stubborn, stocky catcher. Instead, Berra dealt directly with Topping regarding salary, and the two always had friendly conversations, more or less.

Once at a New York sportswriters dinner, Topping was joking with Berra. "How much do you figure on taking us for next year?" he asked.

"I'll settle for $40,000."

"Okay," replied Topping, and it was done.

Berra was now the highest-paid catcher in professional baseball. He earned more than Campanella. More than Dickey. More than Tebbetts. Berra and DiMaggio both flew into Phoenix on the same day, both sluggers fashionably late for spring training.

Asked if he had interfered on Berra's behalf again, Stengel chided the press, saying, "That is exclusively the business of the front office."

When asked about his contract number, Berra replied, "I got responsibilities. I got to support my mom and dad. I have a wife and son. I have to dress like a Yankee, live like a Yankee, act like a Yankee. That takes dough."

# ~ Chapter 11 ~

# A New Dynasty

In 1951, Yankees owner Del Webb moved spring training to Phoenix, Arizona, and bought the entire team cowboy hats. Sportswriter Dan Daniel wrote of Berra, "Hopalong Berra looks especially funny, as his hat happens to be too small for him."

Berra said of the writers, "Sometimes it is tough to tell what these guys write about me. My wife, she don't like the stories which make me out a dope," wrote sports historian Kerry Keene.

"I noted that Yogi didn't respond to the laughter," batboy Joe Carrieri recalled years later. "He wasn't hurt by it, and he didn't seem to get angry about it either." Carrieri believed that Berra was always true to himself, being the same person no matter whom he was with.

Carrieri once asked Berra about a conversation Berra had with Billy Martin about hitting. "I really don't have a philosophy of hitting. It's either you have it, or you don't. Either you are a natural, or you will struggle. There are two kinds of baseball hitters: those that hit good and those that are good hitters," Berra said.

"What exactly do you mean by that?" asked Carrieri.

"Let me put it to you like this. Those that hit good are players who have worked at it very hard and have improved their skills until they're very good at playing. On the other hand, the natural, the good hitter, starts above average and just improves his skills until he becomes excellent at what he does.... Players who hit good will bat .275, .289. Good hitters will bat .310 or .320."

That spring, Arthur Daley of *The New York Times* did a series of articles that established the Garagiola and Berra legacy. Because Berra was away in Phoenix, Daley grabbed the next best prize—Berra's best friend. He interviewed the ever-loquacious Cardinals backstop, and it was then that Garagiola began to hone his stories of childhood, which he would repeat for the next 50-some-odd years, never failing to get a laugh or chuckle. Then Daley followed up with the stories of Garagiola and the Mahatma, when Branch Rickey was with St. Louis.

In a handicapping piece talking about the American League, Daley wrote, "Don't forget that Yogi is in a spot as a catcher where he is inviting injury, and he is the *must* man on the team."

Berra finished his stint in Phoenix with a .409 batting average and what seemed like a reinvigorated zeal for playing baseball. He was the number one hitter for the Yankees coming out of spring training, topping even the great DiMaggio. The only downside was that the rest of the league was now well aware of his talent. While he still might be a character, no one was laughing at him now.

"We pitch to him with psychology, but Yogi doesn't know what psychology is. But give him a bat, and Yogi smartens up," Detroit Tigers pitcher Dizzy Trout said of Berra that year.

\*    \*    \*

This was an important season for the New York Yankees. It was the introduction of a new star, Mantle, and the farewell of an old one, DiMaggio.

The season started off well for Berra and the Yankees. By May 10, Berra had a 10-game hitting streak, and the Yankees were 15–6.

Away from the field, Berra and Carmen bought a seven-room, ranch-style house in Woodcliff Lake, New Jersey, at Woodcliff Rock Estates, in tony Bergen County. The Berras put their money down on the property in June of that year, and the newly constructed home would be finished later that summer. Berra and Carmen were moving east.

This was a watershed moment in Berra's life. With the settling of his family in Bergen County, the Berras would forever change the course of their lives. For the rest of his life Berra would be a well-known, well-respected resident and neighbor of many other ballplayers and commuting executives of New York City. And he would remain, without question, one of its most notable residents for the rest of his life.

This move would also open up friendships and business opportunities he would not have been able to pursue had he not settled his family on the East Coast. Coming from a lower-middle-class Italian neighborhood, Berra now lived in a posh middle- to upper-middle-class neighborhood. And he was now in close proximity to country clubs and well-connected executives who wanted nothing better than to be able to say they hobnobbed with a New York Yankee—and a famous one at that.

And the one friendship the move would truly help cement was the lifelong bond between Berra and Rizzuto. In the next few years, the two would be seen everywhere together.

For Berra, 1951 was also a year when his fame began to skyrocket as his play garnered more accolades and applause. He also remained a popular player among the writers and was constantly in the public eye, popping up in everything from Farrar's crossword puzzles to popular television and radio shows.

Although he was enjoying celebrity, he was also focused and intense between the lines. During a series with St. Louis, Berra did the unthinkable during a hotly contested game. With the bases full, umpire Ed Hurley called a fourth ball on Raschi that Berra to this day insists was right over the plate. Berra spun and grabbed Hurley's arm—a double infringement of the code between catchers and umpires. But the angered Berra was hot, and the confrontation might have gotten physical if Stengel had not intervened. After the game, Stengel insisted Berra approach Hurley to apologize. Years later Berra admitted this small gesture with Hurley was probably the difference in saving him from a sure 10-game suspension.

By July Berra was voted overwhelmingly to the American League All-Star team, which was piloted by Stengel. However, there was speculation that Berra might be dropped because of an ailing back, which he had hurt against Philadelphia in the week before the midsummer classic.

Berra made it to the All-Star Game, but the injury reared its head again in late July, when Berra collided with Cleveland's Bobby Avila at home plate.

Avila came barreling down from third base on a bunt by Ray Boone. Berra tried to tag Avila but failed to apply the tag in time. Berra was splayed across home plate for some time but recovered. It was a scary moment for the team, but the Yankees prevailed 3–2 behind Raschi's pitching.

On August 11, Berra hit a three-run single in the eleventh inning to beat the Philadelphia A's. The Yankees finished the month of August going 21–12 and were closing in on Cleveland in the chase for the pennant. On September 14, Berra won another game for New York, hitting a grand slam to beat the Tigers.

In July 1951, Reynolds pitched a no-hitter. And Berra caught it. Now, on September 29, 1951, the Yankees were playing the Boston Red Sox, and Reynolds was once again toying with a no-hitter. If he did it, he would be only the second big leaguer to pitch two no-hitters in one season. Not only was there a no-hitter on the line, but the free-for-all that was the hotly contested pennant race between the Red Sox, the Yankees, and the Indians was coming down to its final moments. This game could decide the 1951 pennant.

Berra was catching. Ted Williams came up to the plate with two outs in the ninth inning. Berra signaled for a high fastball inside. Strike one. Berra then signaled for another high fastball inside. Strike two. This was indeed the mad genius of Berra.

As Whitey Ford told it, "Yogi called for a high fastball across the letters and tight. Allie gave it to him, and Williams hit it a mile high, but a foul over toward the dugout, and Yogi goes chasing it and loses it at the last minute and falls down and everything, and Williams gets another swing."

At that time, Carmen was in the hospital, where she was waiting to deliver their next child. She had the radio on and screamed when Berra dropped the ball. It was so loud, a nurse came running down to her room. Should she call a doctor? the nurse asked.

"My husband dropped the ball," responded the excited Carmen.

"All I could think was, 'Poor Yogi. What if he hits the next one out?'" remembered Rizzuto.

The crowd let out a mighty groan. Berra, on his knees, felt sick. He struggled up.

"I'm sorry, Wahoo," Berra mumbled.

"The pitcher, who could have been pardoned for slugging Yogi, carefully picked the squat man up, patted him on the fanny, and threw an arm around his shoulders—like a father comforting a small, unhappy boy," wrote Trimble in the *Daily News*.

"Don't worry, Yogi, we'll get him again," said Reynolds.

"When I got behind the plate, Williams started cussing me, telling me I blew the chance for the no-hitter and he'd bear down even more," Berra said years later.

"Yogi told me later that he just went back and squatted down and signaled for the same pitch all over again. He's got to be the luckiest bastard in the world. Williams was one guy who might've hit it out of sight if you gave him another swing," said Ford.

Reynolds nodded and gave Berra the pitch he wanted. Williams took a huge cut, and it popped up again in almost the exact same way.

Berra dashed over to the ball. Reynolds followed him. "Easy, Yogi, plenty of room," assured the nervous Reynolds.

"But this time, Yogi makes goddamned sure he squeezes it, and Allie gets his second no-hitter," Ford said.

"For a moment, it looked as if Berra, not Reynolds, was the hero of the occasion," wrote Drebinger.

With the ball in Berra's hand, Reynolds was the first pitcher to throw two no-hitters in the same year, and after winning the second game of the doubleheader 11–3, the Yankees claimed the 1951 pennant.

Owner Webb told Berra after the game, "When I die, I hope I get another chance like you."

But the biggest news story in New York baseball that fall was the tremendous run of the New York Giants, who, after being out of first by 13 games on August 11, had forced a three-game playoff with their metropolitan rivals the Brooklyn Dodgers. In the final game, the names Bobby Thomson and Ralph Branca became forever linked in the history of baseball. The Yankees had their work cut out for them.

In Game 1 of the World Series, things started off badly for Berra and the Yankees. Monte Irvin, the electrifying Giants outfielder, got to third and stole home in the first inning. The Giants went on to win 5–1.

Dave Koslo, the winning pitcher for the Giants, told the United Press the next day, "That Yogi Berra looked like the most dangerous hitter to me. I tried to keep the ball on the outside to him, but I got a little careless in the eighth, and he hit an inside pitch for a single."

This was the famous Series where the young rookie sensation Mantle, attempting to avoid a collision with DiMaggio in the outfield, accidentally stepped on a drain, wrenching his knee. Berra went on to bat .261 and scored four runs as the Yankees came back to take the Series 4–2.

Berra hit an important double in the last game to keep a rally alive. Hank Bauer was the hero of Game 6, leading with both his bat and glove, and Rizzuto was awarded the Series MVP. In the clubhouse, DiMaggio praised Berra and rubbed his head, smiling. The winners' share was $6,446 apiece. The Yankees held an extravagant bash at the Biltmore Hotel on October 10 before the team separated for the off-season.

Berra had a good year in 1951, but it was below the watermark he had set for himself in 1950. He played in 141 games that year, the second most of any Yankee, batted .294, knocked in 88 RBIs, and hit 27 home runs. He had been the Yankees' offensive heart and had led them in almost every category. He was now a feared hitter, and he was a confident clutch hitter, slamming timely hits in rallies and consistently knocking in game-winning runs. Unfortunately, Berra tired toward the end of the season, and his hitting started to slow down, taking 20 points off his average in September. He did not lead the league in any category.

However, Berra was finally getting credit as a good catcher. His handling of the Yankees' pitching staff helped to lead the league with 24 shutouts for the season. It was a testament to the pitching rotation—and to Berra. It was the second-highest number of shutouts in a season since the turn of the century. And there was no denying that many of the sportswriters of the time now saw Berra as one of the mainstays of the team, playing almost every day and delivering both offensively and defensively.

As a catcher, Berra had matured well beyond his years. Now, he was handling the pitchers, and they rarely shook him off. And he now knew how to manage them, whether they liked to admit it or not. Berra became a friend, confidant, and psychologist as he tried to manage them on the field.

"You've got lots of stuff on the ball. You're going real good now, Chief," Berra would tell Reynolds. "Now just slow down your pitching speed. You're working too fast," he would say to his friend. "You've got to baby Reynolds," he would say later.

Ford was different. Berra tried humor and insult to get the best out of him. "You're supposed to be a big-league pitcher! Get the ball over the plate! That's what you're paid for!" he would holler. Berra would say later, "Ford yells right back at me, and then we're in business."

Another time, later in their careers, Berra approached the mound while Ford was losing control. "Okay, Slick, the main feature at the movies starts at 6:00. It's 4:00 now, and I want to be there on time. Let's get this thing over with," Berra said. Berra would comment later, "That's all you had to do for Whitey."

Milton Gross, a popular Gotham sports scribe, wrote in a column devoted to Berra, "This squat little man has developed into one of the outstanding receivers of all time. He is a walking encyclopedia of the strong points of the opposing hitters and the weak points of his pitchers. He is different off the field, but he is a strong, demanding, take-charge catcher on it. He is death on bunts and would-be base stealers."

Still, it was a bit of a surprise when Berra won the American League MVP award on November 8, 1951. Campanella would be named the 1951 National League MVP for 1951, further fueling their ongoing comparison. Campanella made significantly less money than Berra did, which was a product of both the team he played for and his race in that era. When asked about the discrepancy between his salary and Berra's and Jackie Robinson's by the press, Campy cheerfully replied, "More power to them." And many reporters believed he meant it.

Berra was coaching at Rizzuto's American Baseball Academy at the 212th AAA Armory when he got news of the MVP award.

"Yogi Berra, the squat character who was labeled a 'clown' when he became a Yankee regular in 1947, yesterday became the most valuable player in the American League in 1951," trumpeted Trimble of the *New York Daily News*.

It was one of the closest votes in the history of the award, with Berra besting Ned Garver, the St. Louis Browns' star pitcher, and his own teammate and battery mate, Allie Reynolds. DiMaggio's name did not get submitted on any of the MVP ballots.

"I was afraid I had blown it with a bad finish," the 26-year-old Berra told Trimble. "I was pretty sure Reynolds would be picked, especially after the no-hitters."

That night Berra, ever the hockey fan, and Carmen had a date to see the Rangers. When they met for dinner, he told Carmen, "Have I got a surprise for you." Carmen thought he was talking about some home furnishing they had just purchased for their new house.

"I didn't realize what a big thing it is until the other people came over and talked with us," Carmen said. "Then I caught on, and we ordered some champagne to celebrate."

"The award means an additional talking point in Yogi's annual salary battle with George Weiss, the Yankee general manager," jabbed Trimble.

"Knowing Weiss, I'll be lucky if he doesn't try to cut my salary," Berra shot back with a laugh.

"I thought Allie deserved it, not me," Berra told Daley. Daley wrote a glowing review of Berra's short but meteoric rise to the league's top receiver but could not restrain himself from including a backhanded compliment, writing, "More extraordinary still, he is one of the smartest catchers in the business."

Daley then recounted the time when Red Patterson invited Berra on his quiz show, and Berra apocryphally replied, "Didn'tcha forget, Red? I'm supposed to be dumb."

"He ain't, though. He knows what goes on," wrote Daley. "Yogi will probably win the MVP again. By that time he'll undoubtedly deserve it."

To his credit, as late as his 2003 hit book *Ten Rings*, Berra still insisted that Reynolds was the more deserving recipient of the 1951 MVP.

Suddenly, Berra was everywhere. Now, when he attended a New York Giants football game or a Rangers game, his name was mentioned as one of the celebrities in the crowd.

\*    \*    \*

That was a busy off-season for Berra. By his own admission, "Every day was busy. I was always getting calls for appearances, speeches, even endorsements." And while Berra started to get more comfortable in front of crowds, he never went alone and was often accompanied by Rizzuto or Jackie Farrell of the Yankees' PR staff.

According to veteran sportswriter Phil Pepe, Farrell was responsible for exaggerating many of Berra's miscues. Berra would humbly and good naturedly mumble through an appearance, dinner, or banquet, and the next day one of Farrell's invented Berraisms would appear in the papers, supposedly coming from the lips of Yogi himself.

In January 1952, Berra appeared on the NBC television show *We, the People*, along with Rizzuto, Hodges, Gil McDougald, and several others. McDougald was the young Yankees phenom who'd won Rookie of the Year that year. Later in 1952, just before the midsummer classic, Berra also appeared on the *All-Star Summer Review*, starring Dave Garroway. Berra was considered the headliner on the NBC special program that evening.

Berra had gotten a new job in the off-season, working alongside Rizzuto in a men's clothing store in Newark—Berra was now a proud employee of the All-American Shop. This little men's boutique soon became a very popular place to get fitted for a suit because two of the salesmen were the last two American League MVPs.

In fact, Berra received quite a shock on his first day at work, when he looked up to see huge banners emblazoned with his name and face hung above the storefront. His first day in the store, he was mobbed by gawkers and well-wishers. Rizzuto himself was smiling ear to ear, proud he had been able to help his friend and to help the store's owner by bringing in such a local hero.

"This is just the beginning," Rizzuto said. "Wait'll you see what's lined up for you on TV and endorsements…man, oh, man."

At one point a young customer piped up while Berra was fitting him for a suit, saying, "Be careful, Yogi. Don't misjudge this like you did that foul ball on Ted Williams."

Berra glared at him and shot back, "But I caught the next one, didn't I?" And the kid backed off.

That year Berra's contract negotiations went smoothly, and he agreed quite easily to a salary of $37,500. Weiss was slightly freer with money this year because the Yankees were no longer carrying the $100,000 services of DiMaggio.

At a press conference announcing the signing, the earliest in a long time for Berra, he and Weiss were asked how the negotiations went this year. Both men shrugged and laughed.

"I just tell him the facts," Berra chuckled.

"What he considers the facts," Weiss chortled back.

Berra told the papers that he thought the number was fair, that he expected to be back in form in 1952, was hoping to bring his numbers back up to his 1950 season totals, and announced, when asked for his prognostication, that the Yankees would repeat but that the Tigers would give them a run for their money.

In 1952 Rizzuto was now Berra's roommate. And even more than the classy Bobby Brown, the savvy, older Rizzuto became Berra's friend and mentor.

Sports historian Keene wrote, "Berra said his roommate Phil Rizzuto taught him many things, such as how to act in hotel dining rooms, how to handle the press and the fans, how to conduct himself socially. He even convinced Yogi—though apparently not with complete success—to stop reading comic books and start reading novels and detective stories."

In fact, it was Rizzuto who had convinced Berra to move East and settle down, both for family reasons and for business reasons. Now the two would begin working in earnest to set up financial security, which was immensely important to both of them, while they played baseball nearby. Rizzuto was smart, and he knew that the two of them together were a good team and a good draw for businessmen.

In May 1952, Columbia Records released a series of six-inch, 78 rpm disks called *Children's Playtime*. The stars of the series were Rizzuto, Berra, Ralph Kiner, and Bob Feller. Each gave five-minute lectures on certain niceties of the great national pastime. The record jackets came with full-color portraits of the diamond stars.

And by June, Berra was endorsing Doodle Oil Bait of Chicago, a new liquid bait guaranteed to attract fish. "Baseball isn't the only sport where I've had success in making a good catch," rang Berra's testimonial. "Now I find myself getting a better catch every time. I'm out fishing with Doodle Oil. With Doodle Oil it's easy to catch the limit, and believe me, Doodle Oil Bait Perfume is the best fish attractor I've ever seen!"

But Berra's biggest pitch was the one he made for Rheingold beer. Rheingold took out full-page ads in all of the major newspapers in the metropolitan area in September 1952. The ads featured a dapper, suavely dressed Berra handing his coat and hat to a Betty Grable–esque blonde coat-check girl, and another photo of him seated at a smartly set table entertaining well-groomed guests with cold Rheingold beer.

"Who's going to win the pennant this year?" Berra asked in the ad. "What a question to ask me! That's like asking the name of the beer most people around town are going to ask for this year…"

"Berra and the Scooter got along very well as roomies except for one thing: Yogi never liked being alone, and he didn't like to sleep," wrote Rizzuto biographer Gene Schoor. "He wanted to talk to Phil all night and would get angry when the Scooter shut off the lights. Whenever Phil went to bed early, Yogi, coming into the room, would turn on the lights and wake him up."

But when it was the other way around and Berra was ready for sleep, he had a favor to ask of his friend and roommate. "He insisted on hearing a bedtime story. In self-defense, just so he could get some sleep, the Scooter would calm the savage beast in Yogi by telling him the story of the three little pigs, Snow White, or Little Red Riding Hood," Schoor wrote.

Many players knew that Rizzuto hated insects. The tradition in those days was that players used to leave their gloves on the field in between play. It was a tradition among players to fill Rizzuto's glove with any kind of insect. The only thing Rizzuto said he knew for sure was that, "Mr. Berra had nothing to do with the worms in my gloves."

"Yogi could be in a room with you for an hour and feel no need to say anything. He is happy with himself. He is sure you are happy with him, and if you are not, it is your problem. Yogi Berra is one of the most secure individuals I have ever known," Rizzuto said.

The two were known to be movie buffs who would watch almost anything, but whose favorite cinematic fare was rousing cowboy-and-Indian shoot-'em-ups. Baseball biographer Gene Roswell wrote, "There was a feeling of kinship which went even deeper than the fact that both were of Italian extraction. They understood each other without uttering a word. A true bond existed between these two poor boys who had struggled upward on their baseball talents."

The two became inseparable.

*    *    *

With DiMaggio gone and Mantle still unproven, the dependable Berra was now securely ensconced in the cleanup spot of the batting order. As many sportswriters of the time concluded, this was the right place for him, for he had indeed been the most dependable power hitter in the lineup for the past several years.

According to pitcher Don Larsen years later, Berra's importance was especially evident during the Mantle years. Larsen said, "Casey always batted him in the number-four slot behind Mantle, giving the opposing pitcher no chance to pitch around Mickey." He also said, "I loved to watch Yogi hit. He was a pitcher's nightmare."

However, this did not sit well with Berra. With Henrich and DiMaggio retired, he was now looked at as the mainstay of the Yankees attack. And the fact that he had not performed as well in the past year as he had the year before worried him immensely, no matter the bravado he displayed for the press.

"I used to be a first-ball hitter. That was the one I was hitting when I had my .322 year. Next year, I'm not laying off the first pitch," Berra worriedly told Rizzuto. "Everybody kept after me to get walks, walks, walks.... So I got 50 walks, and what was my average? A measly .294.... My RBIs dropped, too!"

But the truth was, back when they were laughing at him, the opposing pitchers sometimes got careless about pitching to the rube from New York. Berra was now a feared hitter in one of the most successful lineups in baseball. Pitchers were getting much more careful about pitching to him and purposely throwing off the plate, hoping to induce the game's best bad-ball hitter to go chase pitches well out of the strike zone. The walks were a sign of respect now being shown to one of the game's fiercest competitors.

Berra was quite the literary character that year. First, he appeared in Tom Meany's *The Magnificent Yankees*. Then, in that same spring, the publisher A.S. Barnes published *Yogi Berra*, by *Daily News* sportswriter Joe Trimble in their Most Valuable Player series. Dick Young wrote the *Roy Campanella* tome.

"I didn't like to hit fourth, but maybe I was being a little superstitious," Berra told Campanella during a spring-training game against the Dodgers in Miami.

"You over it now?" asked Campanella.

"Sure, it's malarkey. Casey's been telling me about the money I can get batting fourth," replied Berra.

And indeed, he had a tremendous spring and seemed poised to regain his old form. Through the first seven games of the Grapefruit League, as the Yankees were now back in Florida, Berra batted .317 with seven RBIs, and the Yankees went 6–1.

Berra beat out what could have been a double play against the Dodgers. In turning around to head back to first, he twisted his ankle. It was a freak occurrence. Berra did not return to action for 10 days, and in that time, without him, they lost five of their next eight games.

Stengel seemed grumpy and bitter as he told the press, "The other guys I've tried haven't delivered. It's no secret. I think Yogi can sock 'em like DiMaggio did—and if he does, we'll start moving…. It's up to him now." And Stengel walked away from the press. He had placed the pressure squarely on Berra's broad back.

By March 30, Berra was back at it, going 2-for-2, hitting a three-run homer and an RBI single to pace the Yankees to an 8–6 victory over the Boston Braves. But on April 4, in a game in Atlanta, he hurt his thumb; unable to grip the bat properly, the injury sidelined him until April 30. And without Berra in the lineup, Stengel's weak offense reared its ugly head, with the top six players on the team having a composite .279 batting average, which resulted in a lackluster 4–5 start. The Yankees stranded 81 runners in that period.

Still, even with Berra out of commission, stories of his odd behavior filled the sports pages.

"Didja ever ask Yogi to hand you a bat?" Rizzuto asked Jerry Coleman. "He does this." And with that, the Scooter dropped the bat to the ground at Coleman's feet. "He does the same thing with the batboy. He never hands it to him. He just drops the extra bat."

Coleman laughed. He did the same thing as Berra.

The Yankees roster was being decimated by the war. Mantle had been rejected as 4-F by the army board, a circumstance that many chided Mantle for. Coleman was sent to the Marine Air Force and Bobby Brown to the army. The Yankees were getting desperate.

By June, Berra was back in the swing of things, clouting two game-winning homers in that month. By June 20, he had 12 home runs, and his onslaught continued through mid-August, where he hit yet another game-winning home run against the Boston Red Sox on August 16, the Yankees' first win that season at Fenway Park. On August 27, he hit two home runs and collected three RBIs as the Yankees beat the Browns 12–7. And a few days later, on August 31, he belted his 28th home run of the season as the Yankees beat the Senators.

On September 28, 1952, the Yankees lost the last game of the regular season on the way to the World Series. The game they played, a 9–4 beating at the hands of the Philadelphia Athletics, served only as the backdrop to something more important. Berra homered during the game and finished the year with 30 home runs, besting the American League record for catchers of 29, set by Bill Dickey in 1937.

Berra ended the year playing in 142 games, finishing with a somewhat-disappointing .273 average. But he clouted 30 home runs and notched 98 RBIs, and he finished in the top five of the American League in some very impressive categories: home runs, RBIs, runs scored, at-bats per home run, and at-bats per strikeout.

Unfortunately, the 1952 World Series, like many others for Berra, was disheartening. He caught well, but his hitting was lacking, even though the Yankees took the Series 4–3. Berra belted a home run in a losing effort in Game 3. And he hit a home run in Game 6, a tight 3–2 Yankees victory.

While Mantle hit the winner in Game 6, he gave all the credit to Berra. "Yogi Berra's homer tied the game, and I think his was much more important than mine," said Mantle.

Before Game 7, Jackie Robinson encountered Berra beneath the stands.

"Tell me the truth," Robinson said to Berra. "Was that second strike I took yesterday in there?"

"It sure was," Berra confirmed. "I never saw you take so many good strikes before."

While Martin, Bauer, Rizzuto, and McDougald all batted poorly, Berra bemoaned his .214 Series average, as he garnered six hits for the Series. "It was a bad Series for me," he said later. In truth, only Mantle, Gene Woodling, and Mize batted well. The rest of the team did not perform at the plate.

After all the celebrating was finished, Berra and Rizzuto went back to the little shop in Newark and selling suits. Berra was also doing appearances and television interviews, including *Sports Varieties* and *Ring Interviews*, both on Channel 5, WABD. A football Giants fan for years, he was forever bemoaning the Giants' tendency to win big games and drop others to inferior teams, and he was always talking Giants and Rangers with anyone who was so inclined.

\* \* \*

By the end of January, Berra signed for a small pay increase and happily went to Florida. When the Yankees broke camp they were picked as the team to beat. A crew of young turks, including Ford, Mantle, and Martin, had truly come of age. The Yankees won the American League by 8½ games over Cleveland, salting away the season in mid-September. And Berra made the All-Star team again.

The biggest news, though, was the return of Captain William "Ted" Williams of the United States Marine Air Corps. According to *Baseball Almanac,* the Red Sox slugger who became a combat ace "safely crash-landed his damaged Panther fighter plane after being hit by enemy fire while flying a combat mission in Korea on February 19. He later returned home from active duty in August and finished the season with 13 home runs and an incredible .407 batting average."

Williams made a brief appearance at the midsummer classic as a spectator. He drew a warm cheer from the crowd.

"Hey, muscles," Berra shouted to Williams.

"Yogi! Now I know I'm home," laughed the jubilant Williams.

"Did you see our second baseman in Korea?" asked Berra.

"Jerry Coleman? Nope. I never saw him, but I heard he's doing a great job. Last I heard he was down in the boondocks somewhere."

The two were genuinely happy to see one another and renew their friendship. And Coleman, too, would be back in a baseball uniform by mid-September.

The 1953 World Series saw the Yankees and Dodgers at it again. But this year the World Series would be a stage for Berra. In Game 1 he belted a homer and ended a seventh-inning rally by throwing two runners out at third base.

After a 9–5 win, Berra was a guest star on one of the top-rated shows in the country, *The Perry Como Show*, on CBS's Channel 2. Earlier in the year, Berra and the family had appeared on *Person to Person*, Edward R. Murrow's celebrity interview show, also on CBS.

After the Yankees took Game 2, Birdie Tebbetts was in the National League box for Game 3, as he was now the manager of the Cincinnati Reds. During Berra's at-bat, the fourth ball against Berra was a wild pitch. Tebbetts later said, "I'm hip deep in National League executives and club owners when the ball shoots past Roy Campanella to the screen.

"Run, Yogi, run!" hollered Tebbetts.

"Just as Yogi rounds first base and heads toward second, I realize I'm rooting for the wrong side. No one ever made a more violent about-face than I did," Tebbetts said later.

"Throw the bum out, Campy!" Tebbetts shouted in front of his new compadres. Tebbetts told the press after the game, "My old friend, Yogi...I'm a National Leaguer now."

With the Yankees up three games to two against the Dodgers, the two teams battled to the finish in Game 6. Going into the ninth, the Yankees had a 3–1 lead. Gil Hodges flied out for the first out. And then Berra got a little testy and almost lost his cool. Reynolds worked a count to 2–2 against

Dodgers great Duke Snider. The next pitch was a fastball "that seemed to go right over the plate," Trimble wrote in the *Daily News*. "Snider froze as he took the pitch, then he cut a sigh of relief as umpire Bill Stewart called a ball. Catcher Yogi Berra, Reynolds, and half the Yankee benchwarmers leaped high in disgust."

"No, no," screamed Berra. "Ya missed it, Bill, ya missed it!"

Stewart stood his ground. Berra finally calmed down, and Snider eventually drew a walk.

Carl Furillo came up next and, after a long at-bat, laced one into the stands to tie the game. Reynolds fanned the next two.

Hank Bauer led off the ninth with a walk, but Berra was retired on a liner to right. Mantle followed with a single, moving Bauer along to second base. And then Martin hit a shot into center field, and Bauer scored. The Yankees had won the Series again.

The Yankees had just established a new dynasty, a new high-water mark in the national pastime. Stengel's Yankees had won five World Series in a row. No other team has even come close since.

Silvera said years later, "There were eight of us who were on the team for the entire five straight years of championship from '49 to '53—Yogi, Bauer, Reynolds, Raschi, Lopat, Rizzuto, Woodling, and me. I'm the one they always forget."

\*     \*     \*

As part of a 14-game barnstorming visit, the Lopat All-Stars arrived in Tokyo, Japan, on October 23, 1953. Thousands of cheering fans turned out to welcome Eddie Lopat and his team, which included Berra. Other players on Lopat's squad included Robin Roberts, Curt Simmons, Bob Lemon, Mike Garcia, Gus Niarhos, Nellie Fox, Enos Slaughter, and Jackie Jensen.

"These people are more excited than we were when we won the World Series," Billy Martin told the press about their reception in Japan.

In their first game, the Americans fell 5–4 to the Mainichi team. Before the game, Berra came in second in a home-run-hitting contest won by Jensen, who hit five into the stands. The next day the Lopat All-Stars redeemed themselves by trouncing one of Japan's All-Star teams 13–7, with Hank Sauer of the Cubs hitting three home runs and Berra adding two.

By October 31, 1953, Lopat's team won six of seven games. And in a 15–1 romp by the Americans, Berra was thrown out of the game in the fifth inning by American umpire Johnny Stevens. Berra had challenged his calls on successive pitches, showing up the ump in front of the Osaka faithful.

Berra acquitted himself well in the next game against the Central League All-Stars in Nagoya. He belted a homer in the fifth inning into the right-field stands. On November 3, in Tokyo, Berra again belted a homer, as the Lopat All-Stars beat the Pacific League All-Stars 10–0.

The Lopats won their final game in Tokyo the next day versus the All-Japan team, 16–2, and Berra led off the eighth inning with a home run.

*    *    *

In January 1954, Berra was honored by the Newark Athletic Club as New Jersey's outstanding athletic professional of 1953, along with Bob Clotworthy, the Amateur Athletic Union national springboard champion.

In mid-January, Campanella was voted Player of the Year by the New York chapter of the Baseball Writers Association of America. He won it with 208 votes to Berra's eight votes. Berra attended the pre-dinner party to Campy's award at Toots Shor's to honor Drebinger of *The New York Times*, who was feted by the New York chapter as the outstanding baseball writer of the year.

Also in January, Berra signed a deal for $42,000 for the 1954 season.

"There was about a thousand difference.... They surprised me by agreeing so quick. Maybe I made a mistake. I shoulda asked for more," Berra told the press.

Reportedly, Buzzie Buvasi, the new general manager of the Dodgers, called the Yankees office to complain about the new market value for catchers, saying, "Why did you do this to me? Now I've got to sign Campanella."

Meanwhile, Berra and the Yankees looked forward to another drive for a pennant. Berra headed to St. Petersburg with Carmen and the kids in tow for spring training. At the Annual Baseball Player's Golf Tournament in 1954,

Berra shot a 93 in the first round. In those years, he admitted later, he had a 22 handicap.

But a big blow to the Yankees that spring training was the trading of Vic Raschi to St. Louis. Raschi had been a hard negotiator and had rankled the Yankees brass during previous negotiations. Despite the separation, Berra and Raschi would remain friends for years to come.

The Yankees compiled an 8–16 record that spring training, but Berra put together a .385 batting average and was their one shining light. In May, Berra's hot bat belted three last-inning, game-winning hits in two weeks, beating Cleveland, Detroit, and Chicago in order. Berra marked the end of May with a game-winning grand slam in Boston against the Red Sox. And June 4 saw him hit another game-winning home run against the Indians at the Stadium.

In April, at the new stadium in Baltimore, Berra hit a line drive onto the canvas above the scoreboard. Second-base umpire Bill Summers called home run. When the ball rolled back onto the field, Vic Wertz relayed the ball to home, where Berra was called out by home-plate umpire Hank Soar. Though the two argued well after the game in the umpire's dressing room, the decision was never reversed, and Berra was robbed of a home run.

During a batting practice in June, Joe Collins hit a line drive that just missed Berra's head by about an inch. "If anything happened to Yogi we'd have to tear up the franchise and rip down the grandstands," hammed up the Old Professor for the writers.

"Naturally," said the unconcerned Berra.

Several times that year Mantle and Berra held their own home-run derby during batting practice, betting a Coke for the longest distance. After hitting one that was especially long, Berra chortled, "Match that, Mantle."

Mantle couldn't.

Berra was once again voted to start at catcher in the All-Star Game. Campanella was the starting catcher for the National League. Berra, Bauer, and Mantle were among the biggest vote-getters.

While Berra enjoyed one of his best All-Star Games, batting well and catching the whole game, it was his exchange with Musial that was classic Yogi. Snider was on first in the bottom of the ninth with nobody out when

Stan the Man approached the plate. As usual, Berra had his verbal patter down pat.

"Stan, where'll we meet for dinner tonight?" asked the usually chatty Berra.

"At Cavioli's, 8:00," said Musial, who then grounded to first for the first out.

That summer Stengel told the press, in one of his comical moments, that the reason Berra had experienced problems was that he was an excellent soccer player. "In soccer, you kick the ball and never touch it with your hands, which was Yogi's trouble, like I say, 'cause he always stopped the ball with his shin guards and forgot to use his glove," he joked.

While Stengel joked with the press, the Yankees amassed a record of 103–51, usually good enough to win the pennant, but the Cleveland Indians held on with an unbelievable record of 111–43. For the first time in six years, the Yankees would not be in the Fall Classic. However, five Yankees—Mantle, Berra, Moose Skowron, Irv Noren, and Andy Carey—all batted .300 or above.

On the last day of the season, Stengel, thinking of the next year, experimented with Mantle and Berra. Mantle, who had come up as a shortstop before being shifted to the outfield, played the last game against the Philadelphia Athletics at short. Berra was moved to third base. While he made no mistakes on the field, Berra went 0-for-5 at the plate and lost the RBI title to Doby of the Indians.

\*　　\*　　\*

In 1951, Garagiola had been traded from the Cardinals to the Pittsburgh Pirates. In 1952 he batted .273, with eight home runs and 54 RBIs. After playing in 27 games during in the 1953 season, he was then traded to the Chicago Cubs; he batted .262 with three home runs and 35 RBIs between the two teams.

While negotiating for Garagiola's 1954 contract, Cubs general manager Wid Matthews told him that he'd have to take a pay cut.

Garagiola countered, threatening instead to go to the broadcasting booth and gain a pay increase.

"You can't do that. You're our only catcher!" was Matthews's reply.

Garagiola got the salary he wanted.

But Garagiola was at a crossroads in his career. After playing 63 games for the Cubs, he was traded to the New York Giants. While the Giants had been in the 1954 World Series, Garagiola was not eligible to play because he had been picked up off waivers late in the season. He had been very popular with the Giants players and had been voted a quarter of the winners' share, worth $3,000. But he was faced with a tough choice. The Giants were interested in offering him a contract for 1955. It was something he needed to think about because he could then play in the same city with Berra, but he had other options to consider.

Giants general manager Chub Feeney offered him a contract, but on October 19, Garagiola confirmed from his home in St. Louis that he was voluntarily retiring from Major League Baseball to pursue a radio and television broadcasting career. While he would not have been Giants skipper Leo Durocher's mainstay, he would have been able to hang on for another year in the big leagues. But the smart and affable Garagiola was ready to blaze a new trail to the announcer's booth, a path that would pave the way for many former athletes for years to come.

In 1954, Berra hit .307, slammed 22 home runs, and compiled 125 RBIs, 28 doubles, and six triples. In November, the shrewd Yankees front office, afraid he might garner more awards and then use them during salary negotiations, rewarded the 29-year-old Berra with a contract estimated at $48,000, which made him not only the highest-paid catcher in baseball history but also the highest-paid Yankee in 1955.

"We were at the Grantland Rice dinner last Sunday night, and Weiss asked me what I wanted next year. I told him I didn't want to name a figure. I said, 'You name one, and maybe I'll like it.' He named one, and I said, 'Okay.' That's all there was to it," Berra said.

On December 9, 1954, Yogi Berra was awarded his second American League MVP award. He was at the golf course in Woodcliff Lake, waiting for some rain to pass. Berra was thrilled, and the fellow golfers treated him to two bottles of champagne to toast him.

"Berra's powerful and consistent play throughout the season was responsible, almost exclusively, for his team's strong bid for the sixth straight AL flag," wrote

Dick Young in the *New York Daily News*. However, Berra could not shake off his own history, and Young ended his column with a reminder of unhappier days, writing, "He has come a long way in eight seasons, this 29-year-old lovable character who laughs off barbs about his anthropoidal appearance."

Daley ran a column titled, "Our Boy, Yogi." In it he wrote, "Stengel leans heavily on his smart little catcher. Yogi is as deserving of it as any of his rivals.... Everyone in baseball likes Yogi immensely. They kid him dreadfully and tease him mercilessly. With bland good nature, he just grins and lets the shafts carom harmlessly away."

Berra had just squeaked through because Minnie Minoso of Chicago and three Cleveland Indians—Doby, Avila, and Lemon—had split the votes for the award. It was one of the closest votes in MVP history.

When asked by the press if he had signed with the Yankees too early, Berra responded, "Some people told me I should have waited just for this reason, but I'm satisfied. They treated me real good."

In December, Berra and Willie Mays were considered the two best players in the metropolitan area, according to the Associated Press All-Star voting at end of year.

On January 24, 1955, B'nai Brith also named him the Professional Athlete of the New York metropolitan area, along with five others, including Mays and Durocher. All were honored at a dinner sponsored by the organization, where each was awarded a silver tray.

Berra, Carmen, and the family drove down to Florida the first week of February that year. They met up with Garagiola, now a St. Louis broadcaster, who was as popular as ever among the players. One newspaper ran a line, saying, "He now gets paid for talking."

That year several players pitched in and bought some racing dogs that raced at the nearby track. They named one after Irv Noren and one after Berra. In an apocryphal story, Garagiola chided his friend.

"Hey, Yog, you know that greyhound they named after you?" asked Garagiola.

"I hope you didn't bet on him, he's a dog. He can't run," said Berra.

"I had to Yog. Sentiment, you know. The chances are you won't believe me, but I won money on him."

Regardless of this story's veracity, Garagiola was still in baseball, and his career would only skyrocket from these humble radio beginnings.

The most notable event of spring training in 1955 was the addition to the Yankees roster of Elston Howard, the first African American to make the Yankees.

Howard was a friendly and talented player. Unfortunately, he was also a catcher. He would be yet another wonderful catcher that would sit behind Berra, who was obviously in the prime of his career. Stengel was unsure what to do with Howard, whom he once unfortunately mocked by saying, "I finally get a black guy, and they give me the only who can't run." Stengel also called Howard "eight-ball" to his face.

However, the gracious and well-loved Howard later said, "No one in the Yankee organization made me conscious of my color."

Despite his comments, Stengel used Howard where he could to gain the value of his bat, playing him at first base, outfield, and sometimes catcher to spell Berra. However, it must also be pointed out that Stengel eventually became one of Howard's biggest admirers, and Howard became one of his favorite players. "You can say that Howard is our most valuable utility player," Stengel told the press several years after Howard came up.

Like other injustices experienced by pioneering black players, Howard was sometimes not allowed to stay in the same hotels or eat in the same restaurants as his Yankees teammates.

During some barnstorming before the 1955 season, "the Yankees played an exhibition game in New Orleans, where 'colored people' could only sit in left field. Stengel decided to play Howard in right field and put Bauer in left," wrote New York sports scribe Ralph Wimbish.

"First inning, you wouldn't believe what [the white fans] called me," Howard said that day. "So Bauer suggested we be switched. And so the next inning, Stengel put me over in left field with my people."

Bauer recalled, "Later that season, when the Yankees were in Chicago, a group of Yankees were eating breakfast at a big, round table. Elston came in the room, and there was an empty seat right next to me. He saw the seat and hedged a bit. I motioned for him to come sit with us. When he sat down I told him, 'You play with us, you eat with us. You're one of us.'"

Berra and Howard became friends for many years.

In 1955 Berra picked up where he had left off in 1954. He won several games by midseason, and on occasion he teamed with Howard to power the Yankees past their opponents. In one July game, Berra supplied all the runs the Yankees scored in a 4–0 victory over the Washington Senators.

In the 1955 All-Star Game, the game went 12 innings in a very exciting contest. With the score tied 5–5, Musial approached the plate. Berra was catching and warming up Frank Sullivan of the Red Sox as Musial dusted off his hands at the plate.

"How ya doing, Yog?" asked his good friend.

"My feet are killing me," complained the usually chatty backstop.

"Don't worry. I'll get us outta here in a hurry," replied the sympathetic Musial. Musial then parked the first pitch in the right-field bleachers for a game-winning home run.

The Yankees bounced back in 1955 and found themselves pennant winners. This Series placed them in the Fall Classic versus their old rivals, the Brooklyn Dodgers. The Yankees took the first two games 6–5 and 4–2, respectively, at the Stadium.

In Game 1, in another moment that linked Jackie Robinson and Berra forever, Robinson stole home. Or he didn't, depending on who you believe.

"The most famous and hotly debated theft of home was Jackie Robinson's against the Yankees in Game 1 of the 1955 World Series. Almost 50 years later, Yogi Berra still claims he got the tag down in time," wrote Paul Post and Ed Lucas in *Baseball Digest*.

"I knew he was going to steal home," Ford, the pitcher at the time, said. "I almost dared him by taking a long windup as he danced off the bag. Sure enough, he took off for the plate, and I threw the ball to Yogi and it got there in plenty of time. The pitch was low, right where I wanted it, and Yogi just caught it and put his mitt down on the ground in front of the plate, and Robinson slid right into the tag. Robinson was out, there was no question about it."

"He was out," Berra said. "No question."

So important was the play that the editorial page of the *New York Daily News* chimed in on the controversy, "Umpire Bill Summers called Jackie safe, and Yogi called Summers lots of other things, most of them unprintable."

Berra "went wild," said Ford. "He started jumping up and down, yelling at Summers…. To this day, I still believe Jackie was out."

Luckily, the Yankees won the game. "We kidded Yogi that he didn't have his glove down on the ground," the Scooter said.

Berra has insisted through the years that Robinson was out. He has even signed photos of that indelible moment, writing, "He was out—Yogi Berra."

"Yogi gets very upset when I bring that up," says current New York Mets manager and former Yankees great Willie Randolph with a grin. "He says, 'Oh, he was out.'"

Post and Lucas wrote, "Newsreels have replayed it thousands of times, still igniting arguments whenever they're shown."

"Sure I saw the play," said Johnny Podres, Brooklyn's World Series hero. "The umpire didn't say he was out, so he was safe. I've seen Jackie steal home a lot of times. He made it easy."

Batter Frank Kellert got out of the way for the big play at the plate but had a great view, and he later told the press he believed Robinson was out. This caused a controversy in the press, as umpire Bill Summers had been involved in questionable calls before. Robinson defended the umpire in the press, confirming the umpire's decision and believing himself that he had scored safely.

Rizzuto, years later, admitted he thought Robinson was in fact safe. "Yeah, I really do. That's from the pictures, you know. From shortstop I couldn't tell," he said.

After the call Berra swung around violently, screaming at the umpire Summers. It is still one of the most exciting moments in baseball history, as Robinson gracefully slid in and Berra immediately turned, screaming at Summers.

Even with a 2–0 lead, the Yankees' usual luck abandoned them when the Series switched to Ebbets Field, where they dropped Games 3, 4, and 5, giving the Dodgers a 3–2 lead in the Series. The Yankees rose to the occasion when they won Game 6, 5–1, and many thought the Yankees would win it again.

In the sixth inning of Game 7, with two men on, Berra came up to bat. A safe single might tie the game. The tension was high. Berra rifled a shot to the left-field corner. There was no question that everyone in the stadium thought it would be a sure double. The Dodgers outfield had played a shift on Berra to the right. But Sandy Amoros, a late defensive substitute playing in left-center field, made a miraculous catch against Berra. He then swung around and completed a double play, as McDougald was caught off base.

"Martin and McDougald, not believing a catch was possible, were on their horses," wrote Trimble.

McDougald later recollected, "[Amoros] put his brakes on just before the wall, and I took off [for] third, and he found the Easter egg in his glove. I was a dead duck."

The play killed the potential rally.

"'I run and run and run,' was how Amoros characterized one of the most dramatic moments in baseball history," wrote baseball historian Harvey Frommer. "After all these years Jerry Coleman is not as impressed with what happened as others: 'It wasn't so much that Amoros made a great catch. It was the way he went after it in the sun. A better fielder would have made it easier.... The circumstance was that we may have had a tie ballgame.... As it turned out, that was our last chance.'"

"He said the incoming wind held the ball just long enough for him to catch it," wrote Dana Mozley for the *New York Daily News*.

Berra wrote, "If he wasn't left-handed, he would have never caught it."

Podres recorded a 2–0 victory at Yankee Stadium to give Brooklyn its first Series victory over the dreaded Bronx Bombers. At the end of the 1955 season, playing in 147 games, Berra had compiled another impressive pile of stats. He batted .272, with 27 homers, 20 doubles, three triples, and 108 RBIs. It was a good year, but far from his best.

The end of 1955 also saw Campanella and Berra each win his third MVP award. At the time, Berra joined some pretty exclusive company: only three players had ever won the MVP three times—DiMaggio, Musial, and Jimmie Foxx. Of course, Campanella duplicated the feat as well. Though his average was decidedly lower than many of his nearest competitors (Al Kaline and Al Smith, for example), Kaline's and Smith's teams failed to achieve much, while many writers reasoned that Berra had helped to power the Yankees to a pennant. Still, few writers thought him the best player in the business.

Young wrote an entire column questioning the voting. He eventually reasoned, "Maybe it's because Yogi is such a helluva guy."

Daley's insightful comment was along a similar vein (a remarkable moment when Young and Daley agreed on anything). Daley reasoned that every American League city had the same number of votes (three), so it was not a matter of New York stuffing the ballot box. Indeed, New York writers had not awarded Berra with first-place votes unanimously at all. "But Yogi was named on every ballot, which may also indicate that he wasn't hurt by the fact that he is the most popular player in the business," Daley wrote.

## ~ Chapter 12 ~

# MR. YOO-HOO

Berra was now one of the most popular players in the league. He was popular with other players, popular with coaches and managers, popular with sportswriters, and extremely popular with fans. The character created by the sportswriters—the funny, affable, wisecracking backstop always armed with an amusing malaprop—was one of the most in-demand Yankees on the team.

Indeed, in 1954 and 1955 Berra was the main pitchman for Mennen Menthol-Iced foam shave. The ad trumpeted: "Yogi Berra says—Quicker than brushless, closer than lather, coolest pressure shave of all." The ads appeared in many of the sports sections of the metropolitan newspapers and magazines.

Grossinger's Catskill Resort Hotel ran numerous advertisements using Berra's name. He visited the resort in October 1954, with Charlie Silvera and Joe Collins. And on January 15, 1955, he and Jackie Robinson, Robin Roberts of the Philadelphia Phillies, and heavyweight champion Rocky Marciano were honorary ice-skating judges of the Eastern Olympic speed-skating trials that were held there.

Berra's personal appearances didn't stop there. He appeared at numerous charity events. He was featured on the cover of *Sports Illustrated* on May 16, 1955, and he appeared on numerous radio and television shows, including the *Top Sports Stories of 1954* broadcast on WABC radio in December 1954, after having appeared in November on NBC's *Greatest Moments in Sports* with Walter Kiernan.

In April 1955, *New York Times* theater critic Arthur Gelb reported the story of Berra's visit to the musical comedy *Damn Yankees,* a comical farce in which the devil makes a deal with the perennial doormat Washington Senators to beat the Yankees for the pennant. After the play, Berra was taken backstage, where he was introduced to director George Abbott.

According to Gelb, Berra had some feedback for Abbott. "He was particularly concerned about a scene in which the actors sing in a baseball locker room," reported Gelb.

"The ballplayers only sing when they're in the shower," Berra told Abbott firmly.

"They say Yogi Berra is funny. Well, he has a lovely wife and family, a beautiful home, money in the bank, and he plays golf with millionaires. What's funny about that?" Casey Stengel once said.

Berra was becoming big business, and this was only the beginning. During the mid-1950s, he took more advantage of his popularity than any Yankee ever had before. While Mantle could sit back and just count on endorsements rolling in, Berra would not wait. He had plans beyond baseball. He had been schooled by people like Dr. Bobby Brown and Phil Rizzuto, people who had plans after baseball. He was now in a position to take advantage of his celebrity, and he would make his own luck.

In February and March 1955, Berra began running ads every week in the classified section of the metropolitan newspapers soliciting soft-serve ice cream franchises. The idea was to establish a national chain of ice cream franchises licensed by the Yogi Berra Agency Stores. Kraham Realty of Kew Gardens, Queens, was named as the rental agent and was charged with selecting sites for the drive-ins and home-delivery stores. The ads read:

> YOGI BERRA ICE CREAM Snack Bar franchise stores now available to qualified persons with minimum $6,000 cash. Mgrs provided for absentee ownership. No exp nec. We train you. Brker X2467 Times

In April 1955 Berra came into the clubhouse in the middle of a downpour, hoping the game would be called. Stengel disappointed the young catcher, telling him they would indeed try to get the game in.

"You won't be selling any of your ice-cream cones today, Yog," Rizzuto piped up.

Berra was jokingly referred to as the "ice cream entrepreneur."

\*   \*   \*

More than any other business venture, there was one that would define him for generations. His acumen and his understanding of business would improve dramatically as a result.

Jackie Olivieri Tucci remembered, "My dad, Albert Olivieri, met Yogi Berra on the golf course of White Beaches Country Club in Haworth, New Jersey. They became fast friends. My parents were the godparents of Dale Berra, Yogi and Carmen's youngest son."

In the 1920s, Natale Olivieri, formerly of Rome, Italy, was watching his wife can tomato sauce in their New Jersey home. He had a small fruit-soda beverage business. As he was watching his wife finish her canning, he got the idea that it might be the way to sell some kind of milk-chocolate beverage. He took several of the bottles, filled them with chocolate milk, and asked her to finish the process with them. Experimenting with them later, it turned out some of them did not spoil. Olivieri thought he was on to something. Once Olivieri perfected his Yoo-hoo processing secret, he started selling the drink with moderate success.

"When I was a little girl, I was never allowed to go into the Yoo-hoo plant because Yoo-hoo would come out of the retort pressure cooker very hot. If one bottle fell and hit another one, it would start a chain reaction, and bottles of hot Yoo-hoo would fly all over the plant," remembered Olivieri Tucci, Natale's granddaughter. "In 1957 my dad bought a sterilizer from England.... The Webster Sterilizer was a continuous sterilizer as opposed to a retort, and the bottles would come out cool. This finally eliminated the problem of having the hot bottles flying all over the plant."

Berra had been approached as a spokesman, but he countered with a different idea. Why take a fee when they could see tremendous growth if he were more involved? Berra turned the proposition around from a simple endorsement into one of the most famous product launches in American advertising and snack-food history.

Berra would get high-roller investors, as well as some of his own money, for Olivieri's business. He would promote Yoo-hoo and, most importantly, would in later years convince his Yankees teammates to be Yoo-hoo pitchmen. For these considerable services, he wanted a piece of the company. The Olivieris went for it.

"I had pictures of my grandfather standing outside of the first Yoo-hoo plant in Garfield, New Jersey, and pictures of Yogi Berra signing the Yoo-hoo contract with my dad and my uncle—his brother—but I gave them to my son and daughter," recalled Olivieri Tucci.

And, of course, there was yet another apocryphal story about Berra. Supposedly, a woman once asked him, "Is Yoo-hoo hyphenated?"

"No, ma'am, it's not even carbonated," responded Berra.

Berra's contract with the Yoo-hoo company was slated for approximately 15 years. The impact of Berra's involvement was almost instant. Within a few years, it became one of the fastest-growing soft-drink brands in America. So great was the growth that Berra was now being mentioned in *The New York Times* business and advertising section and *The Wall Street Journal*. He was among a new breed of baseball players who were raking in more money off the field than they were on the field. Madison Avenue now knew the name Yogi Berra.

And Berra was ever vigilant about his business interests. Once, during a rainout in 1959, Berra asked Detroit Tigers pitcher Jim Bunning, "They selling any Yoo-hoo in your clubhouse?"

"No," replied Bunning. "They give it away."

"I ain't gonna make no money that way," Berra growled.

"Yogi and Yoo-hoo just seemed to make sense," said Jim Bouton, the former Yankees pitcher. "We used to keep it in a cooler in the clubhouse. I once went out to the Yoo-hoo plant with Yogi. He was like a god there."

In 1961 Olivieri sold the business, but Berra's (and his friends') relationship with Yoo-hoo didn't change, and they continued to promote the drink after the Olivieris' departure. Olivieri Tucci's husband, Anthony, became a part owner of Yoo-hoo with the new owners and remained with the company until 1985, surviving the selling of the firm to Iroquois Brands, Ltd. in the 1970s.

In 1961 Berra would renegotiate his deal with the new ownership of the Yoo-hoo company. But by now the real fact was that Lawrence Peter "Yogi" Berra had crossed the line from baseball star into the world of celebrity. He was now known worldwide by people who were—and, more importantly, people who were *not*—baseball fans. The persona that the writers had created for him, and that he had backed up with tremendous play, would now serve him the rest of his life. He would only become more famous as the years progressed. Berra, and those who surrounded him, would make sure to groom that public image and to perfect it into the next century.

# ~ Chapter 13 ~

# THE GOLDEN AGE OF BASEBALL

After the 1955 season, Berra went to Japan yet again. That October it was the New York Yankees who went barnstorming, not a small band of professional players. First the Yankees stopped in Hawaii and played an exhibition game, where Berra homered. When they arrived in Tokyo, they were treated to a ticker-tape parade. Berra rode in an American Jeep through the parade. When they got to the hotel, Berra complained to the press, "Man, are my legs stiff!"

When the Yankees went to work out at Kawasaki Stadium in the Japanese capitol, the team was swarmed by thousands of Japanese youngsters, Yankees fans all. Jerry Coleman introduced his teammates to the crowd. "The biggest ovation, complete with screams from bobby-soxers, went to Yogi Berra," reported the Associated Press.

\*   \*   \*

In November Berra was the top vote-getter in United Press International's All-Star team voting, ahead of Mickey Mantle and Nellie Fox. For his position, Berra was voted in on 55 of 56 of the available ballots.

On his seventh wedding anniversary, in late January 1956, Berra and the Yankees announced his signing for the 1956 season. Berra was signed for a record $50,000, the highest salary on the team, and the highest-paid catcher in major league history.

Asked about his average, he admitted he had tired some during the season, and he complained about catching doubleheaders. Casey Stengel, with Elston

Howard on the bench as a reserve with almost equal power, would indeed give Berra's weary legs a rest. Howard would spell Berra numerous times in 1956, and the two would trade places in the outfield.

Berra had a solid spring training, hitting several home runs and generally clouting the ball all over the field. He was also featured in a major NBC special on television on April 15, 1955, when that network aired a 90-minute color program, *Salute to Baseball*. He also appeared midseason on NBC on a program called *Meet the Champions* in prime time.

That spring Berra, Campanella, and the Giants' Alvin Dark were asked to be part of an anti-delinquency drive by New York City mayor Robert Wagner. The players would do speaking engagements for youth groups and be featured in ads in all the New York newspapers.

Berra was also cementing his role as one of the unquestioned leaders of the team. As pitcher Tom Sturdivant observed, "Everybody says a lot of things about Yogi. But Yogi had a lot of dry wit, and he joked a lot with people that he knew, and you could tell when he liked you because he would kind of tap you around and punch you and kid with you. He watched the hitters, and he watched the way they moved around the plate, and Yogi would call you a tremendous ballgame. But if you started shaking Yogi off a lot, then he would sit back there and let you throw anything you wanted to, making it twice as hard for yourself, and he just let you know he was a pretty fair country catcher. He was a helluva lot smarter behind the plate than a lot of people thought he was."

By early June, Berra already had eight home runs, but he then entered a dreadful slump the rest of the month that stretched into early July. He also missed some time in July because of some nicked-up fingers, the occupational hazard of the average catcher. But by mid-August he and the team were back in form, and he walloped his 21st home run of the season and had an RBI single to help lead the team in a victory over Boston.

*    *    *

In late August, George Weiss called Rizzuto up to his office. Stengel was there when Rizzuto entered.

"We're going over the roster. [Norm] Siebern and [Irv] Noren are hurt, and we needed another left-handed outfielder for the World Series…. We want to go over this list with you. We'll have to let somebody go to get the outfielder we want. We want your help to decide who it is we can most logically release," Weiss said.

Rizzuto nodded. He felt good that they were asking his opinion on such an important topic. He read off a list of names, and each time Weiss shook his head no.

After Rizzuto tried in vain to suggest other names, Weiss eventually interrupted him, "Phil, I'm afraid we'll have to let you go."

Rizzuto knew he was near the end of his career, but he thought he would actually finish the season as a Yankee. He raced to his car and went home.

Years later, Berra was still upset by how Weiss had released his friend. "He dropped Phil for Enos Slaughter, who was even older than him. It was stunning and harsh," he said. "It just seemed real strange without him in the clubhouse, especially going into a World Series. It felt almost illegal."

But this was just the beginning of the story. The sponsor of the Yankees broadcasts was Ballantine Beer. Mel Allen would bellow, "There goes another Ballantine blast!" on the radio broadcast every time a Yankee hit a home run. Carl Badenhausen was the president of the brewery, and he was a good friend of Rizzuto's. The two played golf religiously together, and Rizzuto was among his best friends.

That fall, the Yankees' play-by-play announcer, Red Barber, walked into Toots Shor's restaurant when his broadcast partner Jim Woods approached him, saying, "Red, I'm all shook up. George Weiss called me this morning and asked me to drop by his office this afternoon. I thought it was the routine renewal of my contract for next year with you and Mel [Allen]. When I went in, George was fussing around at his desk looking unhappy, uncertain, which, as you know, isn't like him."

"Jim, sit down," Weiss told Woods. "You've done nothing but good work for the Yankees." He then offered a litany of Woods's successes on behalf of the organization. Finally, Weiss just blurted out, "Jim, Ballantine has ordered Rizzuto into the broadcast. You are out."

"Rizzuto had never done an inning of play-by-play," wrote an embittered Barber. "He has a sparkling charm when he wishes to turn it on, and no matter the jam he gets in, he gets out of it by assuming a childlike innocence he can call upon instantly."

However, Scooter had indeed visited the broadcast booth often, especially in games from which he had been pulled or didn't play in, particularly during the 1956 season. Rizzuto donned his street clothes in a flash and dashed for the booth with Barber and Allen.

"I loved it. Maybe it's the ham in me, but the more I did it, the more I loved it," Scooter said later. Rizzuto went on to become one of the true legends in the broadcast booth, broadcasting Yankees games from the 1950s to the 1990s. Despite his notorious lack of preparation and his odd verbal meanderings—especially thanking various fans for free cannoli or mentioning restaurants he frequented—he became one of the most recognizable voices in radio history.

*    *    *

On September 11, 1956, in a 9–5 win over Kansas City, Berra hit his 28th homer of the season, bringing his career mark to 236 and tying the all-time record for home runs by a catcher. The previous mark had been held by Gabby Hartnett, a former Cub and Giant. Three days later, on September 14, Berra hit his 29th of the season, against Bucky Harris's Detroit Tigers, to claim the record outright.

The Yankees sewed up the pennant in Chicago on September 18 after beating the White Sox 3–2 in 11 innings. On September 24 they beat the Red Sox 7–4 on a special day for Berra, who passed the 1,000 career RBI mark. The Yankees posted a final record of 97–57, nine games ahead of Cleveland, and would again face the Brooklyn Dodgers in the World Series. Berra finished the regular season with a .298 average, 30 home runs, and 105 RBIs.

Walter Alston started Sal Maglie for the Dodgers, with Dem Bums taking the first game at Ebbets Field 6–3. In Game 2, Berra hit a homer in a losing cause as the Bronx Bombers fell by a score of 13–8. But with the scene changing to Yankee Stadium, the Yankees hoped to regain some of their swagger. And so they did, taking Games 3 and 4 and setting the stage for Game 5.

Don Larsen, who was knocked out of Game 2 in the second inning after failing to hold a 6–0 lead, was slated to start Game 5. Stan Issacs had written about the 27-year-old, beer-guzzling, comic-book-reading right-hander in *Newsday*, "The fact is, Larsen doesn't give a damn."

"Nothing could have been further form the truth," Mantle wrote in *My Favorite Summer 1956*. "While it's true he liked his booze and he enjoyed his good times, he was all business when he was on the mound; one of the best competitors I've ever known."

Even to this day, no one other than Larsen really knew how much or how little sleep he got before the game. But there was no doubt he was seen out past midnight the night before his pivotal start.

Among his teammates, Larsen's drinking exploits were legendary. Mantle and Ford were in awe of Larsen's ability to hold his liquor. What Mantle found particularly impressive was Larsen's ability to stay on a fairly even keel despite his mixing drinks during the course of an evening. Larsen might start with a beer and then switch to rye or bourbon and then switch to yet another liquor, all in the course of a single night out.

Bob Turley, a Yankees teammate, said that Larsen was asleep in the trainers' room until noon, napping before his 1:00 PM start in Game 5.

As a pitcher, Larsen was impressed by Berra's preparation and his knowledge of each of the Dodgers hitters. "Yogi had sized up [Jim] Gilliam pretty well for me.... He told me that Gilliam had the keenest eye for the strike zone," Larsen wrote years later.

Berra had told Larsen, "He's very selective; he'll make you pitch to him." Gilliam was dangerous because he was followed by Pee Wee Reese, Duke Snider, Jackie Robinson, and Gil Hodges, and his getting on base could often lead to a big inning for the Dodgers.

"We can't throw anything soft to Jackie. Never let up. Anything tight and up is in his wheelhouse, so we gotta be careful," said the confident Berra.

"In my opinion, Yogi Berra possessed three important traits that set him apart as the greatest catcher I ever saw play," Larsen wrote later. Larsen first listed Berra's abilities as a power hitter and a great bad-ball hitter. Second, he rated Berra's ability to call a ballgame. "Contrary to published reports, never once during the fifth game did I ever shake him off or change the pitch he asked me to throw. I trusted his judgment too much," Larsen said. He went so far as to say that if a pitcher stuck with Berra's calls, he'd be a 20-game winner every year. Last but not least, Larsen pegged Berra as a winner, one who could beat you with his arm by cutting down base runners, by calling a great game, or by winning it with his bat.

"I think he was the smartest player I ever knew," Jerry Coleman once said of Berra. "He was smart enough to know how to play.... Yogi got better, and Ralph Houk and Charlie Silvera just couldn't keep up. Everybody thought they were smarter than Yogi, but they were wrong."

Of Larsen, Dana Mozley of the *New York Daily News* wrote, "He looked cool and pitched cool, but Don Larsen was numbed by the jitters in the best game he ever pitched."

"Yogi had to do my thinking for me," Larsen said. "He masterminded it."

"The score was only 2–0," Berra told Maureen Houston of Knight-Ridder newspapers. "If it was 9–0, I wouldn't think about it. I had a lot of pitchers go to the seventh, and then they got hit. We didn't talk to him after the seventh. We left him to himself."

"The crowd gave Larsen a tremendous hand when he came up to bat in the eighth, standing up to applaud," wrote Joe Trimble.

Of the top of the ninth, with Larsen pitching, Trimble wrote, "For the first time, Larsen was visibly affected. There he stood, one strike away from the most amazing feat in Series history.... Don, who pitches without a windup, then made his next throw, a fastball, letter high, and as [umpire Babe] Pinelli's right hand went up, the whole baseball world exploded."

Larsen had just completed the first perfect game in the history of the World Series. He had retired the minimum 27 batsmen.

As Trimble reported it, "A grin broke across his face as Yogi Berra dashed up to him. Berra jumped wildly into Don's arms, the pitcher grabbing and carrying the catcher like a baby for a few strides."

Photos of this moment in baseball are some of the most identifiable in all of baseball history. The image of Berra clinging to Larsen like a little child shows the joy of both men and is, without a doubt, one of the national pastime's most iconic photos.

Wrote Mike Lupica years later, "Larsen threw the perfect game. Yogi became the perfect picture."

"Except for the day I was inducted into the Hall of Fame, there is no greater thrill I've had in baseball than catching Don Larsen's perfect game in the 1956 World Series," Berra wrote years later. "Very seldom does a day go by that I don't think about Don's perfect game. It was a magical time for the Yankees and for me."

The next game was just as tense, as the Yankees lost a close 1–0 ballgame at Ebbets Field. This set up yet another Game 7 between the Yankees and Dodgers. But the seventh game was anticlimactic—the Yankees jumped out to a 2–0 lead on Berra's home run in the first inning and ran away with a 9–0 win.

In the third inning, Berra came up against Don Newcombe, with Billy Martin on base.

Dick Young wrote, "Again Newk got ahead of Berra, one and two. Again he tried a fastball—this time low. Yogi, who doesn't know high from low, and cares less, golfed it over the scoreboard in right center. This gave Yogi 10 RBIs for the Series—which is a record banged by Lou Gehrig in '28. It also gave Yogi three homers for this set, and nine in his World Series life."

"Man, that Berra is a killer," Campanella told the press. "All Newcombe has to do is get a third strike past him, and he's probably pitching yet."

"I warned him," Pee Wee Reese said of the first homer, "that if he threw a change-up to make sure it was outside the plate. Instead, he throws a fastball, high and inside, and Yogi parks it."

Berra was such a good sport and felt so badly for Newcombe that as he circled the bases, he hollered to the big pitcher, "That was a good pitch I hit, Newk!"

The Yankees were champions again. After the final game, Jackie Robinson, always a classy athlete, came to the winners' clubhouse to congratulate his opponents. At one point, he put his arm around Berra, telling reporters that he was one of the best clutch hitters he had ever seen. Little did anyone know, it was the last game Robinson would ever play.

Back in St. Louis, Pietro Berra had watched his son with pride. "He was thrilled, but he didn't say anything much," Josie Sadowski, Berra's sister, told the press. "He expected his son to do that."

Two days later Berra appeared on *The Perry Como Show,* which was one of the top television shows of the period.

On October 19, Berra was honored on the Hill by the Professional Businessman's Club as "one of the three best-known Italians in the world—Columbus, Marconi, and Yogi Berra."

Berra had told the press that the final two homers he hit were dedicated to Paulina, his mother. She was diagnosed with severe diabetes and had been hospitalized.

"The doctors said they had to amputate her leg to save her life," Berra remembered. Berra had considered going to St. Louis during the course of the Series, foregoing playing to be near his mother's side. His father had insisted that Berra play on. "Because that would make her happiest," Berra said.

"When I saw Paul O'Neill struggle to play [in the 1999 World Series] when his dad died, those memories came back to me," Berra wrote in *Ten Rings.*

Mickey Mantle was named MVP in 1956. He was the unanimous choice with 24 first-place votes. Berra finished second.

That December, Dale Anthony Berra was born at Valley Hospital in Ridgewood, New Jersey. Born on December 13, he was Carmen and Berra's third child.

Then, just before Christmas, Berra and the Yankees came to an easy arrangement. After Berra signed his contract on December 20, 1956, he would be making $58,000. Not only was he still the highest-paid catcher in the league and the highest-paid player on the Yankees, but he was now the highest-paid player in the American League. Only Stan Musial, who made $75,000 that year, made more. Campanella made $35,000 for 1957.

Just a few days earlier, the Yankees had traded Berra's backstop mate Charlie Silvera to the Cubs. Silvera had once been unkindly called "Yogi Berra's caddie," but that was nonsense. Silvera had batted .315 in 58 games in 1949. He simply lacked the power and skills Berra possessed. Most people who played on that team knew the Yankees had three starting catchers in Howard, Silvera, and

Berra. During the course of his career, there were numerous capable receivers who rode the pine behind the strong hands and bat of Lawrence Peter Berra. But Silvera and Howard were the two best.

"I get bigger tips in caddying for Yogi than most of you guys earn in a year," Silvera once joked.

*    *    *

By January, Berra was back promoting, doing an appearance at a grocery store opening.

"Mr. Berra stood at a point between margarine and mineral water and amiably autographed anything handed him," reported *The New York Times*.

And he was on hand for the screening of the annual World Series movie.

"I always enjoy the World Series movies," Berra said at Toots Shor's.

"Why not?" exclaimed the Scooter. "You're always the star of the production. Holy smokes! I'm not even in this one!"

The two were hamming it up for the press.

"Mr. Berra, sir," Rizzuto said, now officially a part of the Yankees broadcast booth, for which he was taking a razzing by his ex-teammates. "What name do I call you—Yogi or Lawrence?"

"You'll probably call me names that will get you barred from the air," cracked Berra. "Hey, Phil, how about you sneaking a mention of the chocolate drink Yoo-hoo, that I'm vice-president of?"

"Don't be so crass and commercial. Perhaps I could mention that you'd like to see all listeners at your bowling alley after it's completed," yukked Rizzuto. This was yet another instance of Rizzuto and Berra being much more sly than either of their Lardner-esque images.

Indeed, Berra and the Scooter were the proud owners of a bowling alley. Both men were avid bowlers, and there is a wonderful story about one of their outings. During a layover in St. Louis, the Scooter, Berra, Billy Martin, and Eddie Lopat decided to go bowling.

"Let's go to some out-of-the way place, Yog," the group implored. It was supposed to be a place where no one would know them.

Berra assented. He took them to some small set of lanes on the Hill.

"We walk in," related the Scooter. "'Hello, Yog,' says the proprietor. 'I got your shoes, and I've saved your regular alley for you.'"

"The nice part about it," chimed in Martin, "was that I was high man. I bowled 212. The low man? Yogi Berra. He had to pay for everything."

Berra only paid half the money for the new alley that was being constructed. Rizzuto picked up the other half. Together, they chose the site—a new, state-of-the-art shopping center called Styertowne Center near Clifton, New Jersey. Styertowne is sometimes referred to as the first suburban shopping center in America. Rizzuto-Berra Lanes was a sleek, 40-lane bowling alley that opened in May 1956.

It was not the only bowling alley Berra would own. He had another, Bowlomat, in Paramus, New Jersey, that was run by his brother John. John would be the manager of the lanes, looking out for Berra's interests. However, Bowlomat never got the publicity that Rizzuto-Berra Lanes did.

Both Berra and Rizzuto were photographed by local newspapers as they threw the first shovels full of dirt on the new construction, even though they were not the owners of the building. Each had invested approximately $50,000 and, using credit, had bought nearly $500,000 worth of equipment and supplies. Each alley floor cost $3,500, and each pinsetter cost approximately $7,700. While they had bought the pieces, they were bought on time payments. And they were given a grace period of four months.

"We start making payments in September," Berra told the press. "Even on the weekends, you gotta wait for an alley a lot of times."

A glass showcase featured each of their MVP awards and their baseball gloves.

"That's the one I caught two no-hit games with," Berra pointed out.

The bowling alley's cocktail lounge was shaped like the Yankee Stadium infield. "We call it the Stadium Lounge," Berra beamed. The snack bar was named the Dugout.

When asked how many cars the parking lot could handle, Berra shrugged, "I dunno."

But sportswriter Dick Young commented, "But he'll know how much dough comes in at the end of the month. Your children should be so dumb."

\*   \*   \*

The 1957 spring-training season started off like many before. Garagiola showed up in St. Petersburg, talking up a storm and joshing Musial and Berra mercilessly. He chided Musial about his bank account ("I've gotten a lot of thrills out of baseball, but the big one will be when you invite me to open a joint bank account," he told Stan the Man) and joked with Berra (Yogi: "You getting bald?" Joe: "Naw, I'm just getting too tall for my hair.") Everyone was getting in on the act. But no one was clown prince like Stengel.

Hank Bauer begged Stengel, "Listen, Casey, before I finish my career, I gotta catch again…. Can I catch again?"

"You'll hafta ask Mr. Berra. He helps me manage," Stengel joked.

Of course, the writers liked this one because with Stengel managing, few people would ever get to catch behind Berra. He had held back an army of well-known catching prospects. And the names would continue to pile up like a car wreck on a highway behind him.

Berra continued his onslaught against opposing pitching in 1957, crushing the Dodgers on March 24, batting in five runs in one game, and then beating them with a homer a few days later. In the meantime, Martin and Mantle also got their share of headlines.

The writers continued to use Berra as a punch line in every other article, still making fun of his twisted English, his clothing, anything to get a laugh. But Berra continued to hit well.

One of Berra's teammates did not share in his good fortune. On May 7, 1957, the Yankees were playing the Indians when Gil McDougald smashed a rocket of a line drive right back at pitcher Herb Score. Score, caught off guard, was struck in his eye. Blood was everywhere. For the young, successful power pitcher, it was essentially the end of his career. Even with a comeback, he was never the same.

"I've been around the game a long time," Berra said. "You always know something like that can happen, but you really don't believe it until it does. It was the most sickening thing I ever saw, and I saw a lot of injuries in baseball."

The Yankees exploded in May with a 10–3 run by the evening of May 16.

However, that night would be a memorable one for entirely different reasons.

The Copacabana, also known as the Copa, was a famous New York City nightclub originally located at 10 East 60th Street. Danny Thomas and the comedy team of Martin and Lewis made their debuts at the Copacabana, along with many other acts. Countless famous entertainers, including Buddy Hackett, headlined there throughout the 1950s and 1960s.

But on May 16, 1957, the nightclub achieved a degree of notoriety heretofore unknown to it. Sammy Davis Jr. was the headliner. Unfortunately, the incident involved members of the New York Yankees. On that evening, Martin, Mantle, Ford, Bauer, Berra, and Johnny Kucks, along with some of their wives, arrived at the nightclub to celebrate Martin's birthday. The excursion was testament to the scrappy Martin's popularity with his fellow players, and it goes without saying that Berra was part of the "in" crowd in the Yankees clubhouse.

The group had first met for dinner at Danny's Hideaway. Berra and Carmen had driven in to the city from New Jersey with Kucks and his wife. During dinner, Carmen suggested they all go to the Waldorf-Astoria Hotel to see Johnny Ray. Ray's big hits included "Walkin' in the Rain" and "Cry."

After the show at the Waldorf, the group went to the swanky Copacabana to see Davis, who had scored the number one album on the Billboard charts with *Starring Sammy Davis Jr.* in 1955. Two years earlier, at the invitation of Frank Sinatra, Davis had broken the color barrier at the Copa.

That night Davis, always popular with the Copa crowds, was at his usual, high-energy best—singing, dancing, telling jokes, and doing impersonations.

Next to the Yankees and their wives was a group of bowlers out on the town. They were loud, obnoxious, and many were drunk. At one point, one of the louts screamed at Davis while he was on stage, "You jungle bunny!"

Davis told the band to stop and said to the inebriated man, "I want to thank you very much for that remark. I'll remember that." But the drunkards continued their racial epithets.

Martin and Bauer were particularly incensed by the classless remarks. Both were close friends of Elston Howard (Martin was his roommate), and so they were doubly upset knowing the kind of treatment Howard had suffered at the hands of men like these.

Shouts between the two groups began, then escalated. The bowlers went from heckling Davis to heckling the Yankees, basically taunting them in front of the crowd. Eventually Martin had had enough, saying, "We're here to enjoy ourselves. You've been spouting off all night. If you want to talk about this somewhere else, we can get away from the table and settle this outside."

A heavyset man, delicatessen owner Edwin Jones, stood up and shouted back at Martin, "Let's go!"

Martin and Mantle got up. Jones and a friend also rose. Just then, Bauer got up.

"It's none of your business," Charlene Bauer told her husband. He ignored her. A third group of tuxedo-clad men rushed to break up the group, and it seemed cooler heads would prevail.

"Martin and the brother of the obnoxious, fat drunk agreed to keep the other guy away from the other Yankees," according to author Peter Golenbock, "but when they entered the spacious men's room to break up any forthcoming slugfests, they found Yogi Berra and Whitey Ford restraining Hank Bauer by the arms and the fat drunk out cold on the floor with a broken nose and other head injuries."

Ford denied seeing anyone hit Jones. According to Whitey, "I know Bauer didn't hit him, or Billy, either, because they never left our sight. They were just 40 or 50 feet in front of us all the time. The guy was stretched out on the floor when we got there. He looked like he'd been hit 15 times."

Martin had yet another version—he and Jones's brother were discussing a truce, trying to calm things down. "Just then," Martin said, "I heard a boom over in the coatroom, heard a crash on the floor, and when I went in to see what it was, here was the guy who had been bothering Bauer out cold on the floor."

As Martin said years later, "We never did find out who hit the guy. Hank didn't hit him, never touched him, and I certainly didn't. I was talking to his brother. We think that a bouncer must have followed him back and decked him."

Berra, Bauer, Mantle, Martin, Ford, and Kucks were each fined $1,000. It was a big bite for some of the players who didn't make as much as Berra. At one point later in the season, UPI reported that in Hatfield, Massachusetts, a collection box had been set up at an American Legion post to help the beleaguered Yanks pay their fines.

The Yankees reported that when Yogi Berra opened the box it contained two paper clips, an American Legion button, a small drill, two erasers, three screws, a key, a match, and 48¢ in pennies and nickels.

The players first had to meet with Dan Topping, and later with the Yankees' team lawyer.

Bauer cracked to the press, "Hit him? Why, I haven't hit anybody all year!" The joking right fielder had been mired in an early season slump, with a batting average of .205.

"Berra and Ford Benched after AM Brawl at Copa," screamed the back page of the *New York Daily News.* "Yankee Is Linked to Fight in Café," ran the headline in the sports section of *The New York Times.*

Addressing the problem, Stengel told the press, "I won't pitch Ford because the whole world knows he was out until 2:00 in the morning. He knew days in advance that he was supposed to pitch this game. He had no right to be out after hours.... Berra has been around long enough to know better. The way he's been hitting, he could use a rest instead of being out late."

"I love Bauer, Martin, and all of the Yankees. I've been a Yankees fan for years, and this incident has disappointed me," said the now-sheepish Jones. Jones lamented that he didn't want to "make a federal case out of it."

At which point his lawyer interrupted, saying, "Don't let your love run away with you."

Shortly afterward, each of the players was called in front of a grand jury. When Berra was asked what happened, he responded, "Nobody never hit nobody no how," according to *The New York Times* and *Time* magazine. However, over the years, the most-often quoted version of that testimony has been, "Nobody did nothin' to nobody." Either way, the story is true, and both quotes have been repeated to the point of exhaustion.

Many fans and sportswriters laughed at the line, but suspected that Bauer or Martin had, in fact, decked the loud and obnoxious Jones, and they regarded Berra's laughable English as a ploy for a Yankees wall of silence. But even years later, Ford, Mantle, Berra, and the others all agreed that neither

Bauer nor Martin had hit the lout and that an unidentified Copa employee was the real culprit.

"I think a Copa bouncer got him first," Berra said later, echoing Martin.

The "Bronx delicatessen owner [Jones] sued Bauer for $250,000, claiming that Hank had punched him and broken his jaw. That was silly; a Bauer punch would have broken him into little pieces," reported *Time* magazine in 1964. "But Hank was still hauled off to a police station, photographed, fingerprinted, and booked—'just like a criminal.' Partly on the strength of Yogi Berra's now-classic testimony...a Manhattan grand jury cleared Bauer of the charge."

As the team arrived in Cleveland a few days after the brouhaha cleared, Berra turned to one of the sportswriters after a breakfast and asked, with an elfish grin, "Do you know if there's a good nightclub in this town?"

On June 6 in a game against the Indians, Berra was performing his normal catching duties. In the third inning, Cleveland's Larry Raines swung hard at a pitch. The foul tip was so violent that it broke the lower part of Berra's catcher's mask. The ball struck the backstop hard, breaking his nose and causing it to bleed from both nostrils. To compound the injury, the bent wire of his face mask punctured the bridge of Berra's nose. As a testament to his popularity around the league, the Municipal Stadium faithful cheered the receiver when he walked into the dugout aided by the training staff.

When Berra got home to Carmen, the first thing she asked was, "Did you lose any teeth?"

"No! But what do you mean, teeth? Ain't you worried about my nose? It's broke," he replied.

"Honey," Carmen responded, "we can always get your nose fixed. I just don't want you to have false teeth."

"All my good looks are gone now, Ted," Berra told Ted Lepcio, the second baseman for the Red Sox later that year.

"I don't agree," replied the friendly Lepcio. "That smashed schnozzola is an improvement."

A few days later, *New York Times* columnist Louis Effrat stopped Berra. "Does your face hurt?" asked Effrat, feigning serious concern.

"No, it's all right," responded Berra, touched by the inquiry.

"Well, it hurts me," laughed Effrat, scampering away.

On June 22, in the thirteenth inning in a game against the Chicago White Sox, Berra, who had been hitless in five previous trips to the plate, blasted a home run to win the game and propelled the Yankees into first place. Although Berra was still getting game-winning hits, his batting average was lower than ever.

But another off-the-field event would soon take center stage. Billy Martin's involvement in the Copacabana incident, coupled with his later fight with Larry Doby of the Cleveland Indians, gave Weiss all the ammunition he needed to trade Martin, whom he disliked, to the Kansas City A's.

Martin, Mantle, Ford, and Berra were devastated. Stengel, also powerless to stop Weiss, was angered by the move. Martin blamed Stengel for years, but eventually the two reconciled. Despite the trade, Martin's friendship with his Yankees teammates would last for decades.

It was during this period that one of Mantle's favorite stories about Berra occurred. Berra was asked to speak at a father-and-son church banquet. Every son got a bat and a ball and was allowed to come up to the dais to get it signed. Berra noticed there was a whole group of kids who didn't get a bat and ball, and he asked one of the organizers why those children weren't getting anything.

The organizer said that they were orphans and that their baseballs had been sent to the orphanage instead. They would not be getting in line. Their treat was that they were there for free.

Berra left the dais, went over to the orphans, pulled up a chair, and started signing anything they could produce. He sat with them the rest of the evening. When he was asked to come back to the dais, he responded, "Go on with the program. I'm busy. I'm talking to some of my friends."

Mantle and Berra were the two biggest vote-getters for the All-Star Game. Stengel managed their team. Before the game at Busch Stadium, Berra saw his two old St. Louis chums, Musial and Garagiola.

"I hope you'll be kind to me, Yog," Musial told Berra. "I'm getting old and not going good. Since we're such old friends, I expect you to tell me what pitches to expect."

"I'd be glad to, Stash," said Berra, using the nickname only Musial's inner circle called him.

"I'm not sure I can trust you," retorted Musial.

"I saw your mother last night," boomed the friendly Garagiola, "and she can't understand why you're only hitting .230."

"Neither can I," said the befuddled Berra.

Whatever batting woes Berra was suffering did not seem to affect an incredible All-Star Game for the stout catcher. Paired with Detroit Tigers pitcher Jim Bunning, the American League battery silenced the National League bats for three solid innings. Bunning never shook Berra off the entire time, and he was rewarded with the first perfect service in All-Star play—three innings, nine batters, no hits, and no walks.

The game also held special meaning for Berra because he recorded his first RBI in All-Star play when he knocked in Moose Skowron in the sixth inning with a single.

Bunning felt his fastball and slider were unhittable. But Berra told the press, "If he says so. I suppose Jim ought to know. Oh, his slider and his fastball were all right, but I am sure he can throw them better than he did today."

Always the competitor, Berra would spoil Bunning's no-hit bid against the Yanks later in the month with a seventh-inning triple in a Yankees 3–2 loss to Detroit. And on July 7, Berra hit a double with the bases loaded to beat the Senators. But he was having problems seeing the ball.

It was then discovered that Berra needed glasses. Doctors had diagnosed him as having "tired eyes." He played his first game with glasses on July 13, 1957. With his perpetual 5 o'clock shadow and his aviator spectacles, Berra made quite the impression. With his improved vision, he went 1-for-4, and the lone hit was a homer he smashed over the fence to notch his 14th of the season.

Berra seemed to be fidgeting with his new eyewear the entire day. He kept adjusting them, appearing uncomfortable at best. The press later peppered him with questions. He told them he would wear them for batting and television watching. One sports scribe reported, "Berra, trying hard to get used to his new eyeglasses, seemed to have more fingerprints on the specs this morning than there are on file with the FBI."

"Yogi Learns Specs Prolong His Career," ran the headline for Joe Trimble's coverage of Berra's eyeglass episode. Sam White of the Red Sox and Bobby

Avila of the Indians were also wearing glasses. In truth, Berra did not wear the glasses very long—maybe a week or two at most. Neither he nor Carmen felt he needed them. He told the press in 1958, "All I need is a few hits, and that'll take care of my troubles."

"I was having an off year, and Weiss and Casey were still convinced my eyes were the problem," Berra wrote years later. "What really happened, I think, was that I was getting too banged up; I'd never gotten that many injuries before."

Soon Berra began to return to form, going 4-for-5 with a home run against the A's in a 10–4 July victory. In August he went 4-for-5, belting a three-run homer and totaling six RBIs, in a game against the White Sox. That had been his 20th home run of the season and had marked the ninth season he had hit 20 or more home runs.

His hitting prowess had returned (with and without the glasses), so much so that in early September, *New York Times* sportswriter Arthur Daley ran a little story about it. Per Daley, Berra was at the batting cage, chumming it up with some Red Sox players during batting practice. Berra ripped a rocket over first.

"I'd have caught that," needled Dick Gernert.

"That was a hit," said Berra proudly. And then Berra hit the next ball, a towering shot, into the right-field seats.

"I'd have caught that, too," Gernert responded.

"Not unless you bought a reserved seat," quipped Berra.

On September 19, the Yankees beat the Tigers 4–3, with newly acquired Sal Maglie pitching. Berra went 2-for-4, hitting two home runs and tallying four RBIs, winning the game by himself with his bat. And a few days later, versus the Red Sox, he hit the game-winning homer, his 23rd of the year.

The Yankees finished 98–56 in 1957 and prepared to face the Milwaukee Braves in the World Series. To celebrate, several Yankees were asked to appear on CBS's hit program, *The Phil Silvers Show*. Berra, McDougald, Ford, and the Scooter appeared on the same bill as Dick Van Dyke.

But this Series was no place for slapstick. Frank Torre and Henry Aaron powered the Milwaukee Braves into a deciding seventh game against the suddenly struggling Yankees.

With the Series tied at three games apiece, the New York press was anxious to find out the starting lineup for the final game. The first man to emerge from the clubhouse was Bauer. Several reporters pounced: "What's the lineup?"

"Me know the lineup?" laughed Bauer. "Yogi Berra will catch. That's all I know."

Despite Berra's spot in the lineup, the Yankees lost the decisive game. Berra had a good Series, hitting .320, with one home run and one double. It was only the second time in his career Berra had to accept the loser's share, which came to $5,606. By playing in this World Series, he had established four new records. He had played in more World Series games than any other player, surpassing his friend Rizzuto at the 52-game mark. He also notched another record as the catcher who had caught in the most World Series (nine). He had collected 55 World Series hits, passing DiMaggio's record, and had caught the most Series games (52), extending his own record.

But for the year, Berra had fallen off dramatically. His season batting average was 47 points lower than it had been the year before. He had 23 fewer RBIs and six fewer home runs in 41 fewer at-bats. Still, the UPI writers voted him to the sportswriters' All-Star team.

In November, Berra went to the Mayo Clinic to have his eyes checked again.

\*     \*     \*

On January 9, 1958, Berra was the first Yankee to re-sign with the organization. He agreed to the first salary cut of his career, taking a $3,000 reduction in his $58,000 salary of the previous year. The negotiations were neither difficult nor acrimonious. He agreed with the front office in its assessment of his production. Berra even joked about the cut with the press by posing for them cutting a slice of cheesecake and smiling.

"Sure, I had a bad year. Every player has a bad season once in a while, so I guess it was just one of those things. Anyway, I can't afford two bad years in a row, and I'm looking forward to a good one," he told the press.

However, it was apparent that time was catching up with Berra. Stengel and Weiss, afraid their star was wearing down, worked Howard hard that spring training, hoping that he might take on more duties behind the plate to let Berra play a little more outfield.

But Stengel insisted that Berra would play. "Do I ever take Berra out of the lineup unless he is hurt?" Stengel asked the press. "No!"

However, during their three-game match with the Dodgers in St. Petersburg, Berra hurt his hand and was looking at starting the season at less than 100 percent. He was out of action for two weeks, but returned with a homer in his first game back.

He opened the season with a 2-for-4 performance at Boston, as the Yanks downed the Red Sox 3–0. In the seventh inning of a scoreless game, Berra poled a two-run home run, and closed out the opening series with a double and an RBI in another win.

The Yankees won seven of their first eight games, but after dropping two in a row, Stengel blew up at Mantle and Berra in a closed-door team meeting, accusing the two of not focusing. In one game, the two stars had left a combined seven men stranded.

By midseason, Bobby Bragan, the Cleveland Indians manager, left Berra, Mantle, and Ted Williams off his All-Star ballot for the midsummer classic. Berra had slipped to third place in the American League as rated by his peers, falling behind Gus Triandos and Sherman Lollar. But Stengel made sure Berra suited up, as he was the manager against the National League.

On July 3, Mantle belted two homers and Berra hit another in a bludgeoning of the Washington Senators. But the real story that summer was Berra's adventures in the outfield. A hand injury kept him from catching, so Stengel played him some in Bauer's spot. By mid-July, it appeared that Berra would set an unofficial record for most near collisions by an outfielder. And ever the conversationalist, an Associated Press article titled "Outfield No Lonely Post to Yogi" joked, "Even that remote spot finds Berra in social whirl."

After a doubleheader McDougald told the press, "You think he didn't find people to talk to out there? He talked to me. He talked to the bullpen. He talked to the fans."

"Aw, I just kept asking the fella where to play. And when somebody called me, I looked around to see who it was," said Berra.

"One time I'm looking out there and he's pointing to the ground," McDougald continued. "I couldn't figure out what was wrong. Was there a hole in the outfield? Or maybe a four-leaf clover? You know what he meant? He was trying to tell me he was playing shallow."

Berra had begged off a near collision when McDougald chased a ball into shallow right. And Berra bowled over Norm Siebern in dead center going for a ball. When Berra regained the use of his hand, he was returned directly to his backstop position.

However, Berra's play in the outfield was not the biggest story of the 1958 Major League Baseball season.

That was the year Jimmy Piersall hit .272 as a fixture in the Red Sox outfield, and most importantly wrote his famous and groundbreaking autobiography with Al Hirshberg titled *Fear Strikes Out,* which detailed his 1952 nervous breakdown.

"I knew I couldn't go around looking for sympathy," Piersall said about his return to baseball. In a game against Boston, the Yankees pitchers had knocked down the two previous batters. As he dug in, he said to Berra, "If this guy throws at me, I'll wrap this bat around your neck. I can get away with it. I can plead temporary insanity."

Berra shot back, "Look, boy, on this club we don't knock down no .250 hitters."

The 1958 season also turned out this gem about Berra.

Hall of Fame pitcher and future U.S. Senator Jim Bunning said, "One day when I was with the Detroit Tigers, I was pitching against the Yankees. Bob Turley was coaching first base for the Yankees. The Yankees liked to use Turley because he was real good at stealing the catcher's signals to the pitcher, and Turley had our signs that day right from the beginning of the game. Turley would whistle on the curve.

"Hank Bauer was up first. Turley whistled at him, and Bauer lined a hit into right field. Tony Kubek batted next. Turley whistled again, and Kubek hit a line drive right to the second baseman.

"Mickey Mantle was batting third, and I'd about had enough of Turley's shenanigans. I walked over to the first-base coaching box and said to Turley, 'If you whistle to Mantle, I'm going to drill him with the next pitch.'"

Bunning then walked halfway to home and repeated the threat to Mantle's face. Sure enough, Turley whistled on the next pitch, which was another curve. Bunning let loose a fastball, and Mantle took. Bunning had enough, and he drilled Mantle with the next pitch.

Mantle was not happy and started for the mound, but the Tigers' catcher and the umpire grabbed Mantle and steered him down to first. Tempers were getting hot.

Into the batter's box stepped Berra.

"I started him off with a fastball, too, and Turley whistled again," said Bunning. "Berra stepped out of the box, cupped his hands around his mouth, and shouted, 'Jim, he's whistling, but I ain't listening.'"

*　　*　　*

But Berra always talked best with his bat in his hands. In early August he beat the White Sox with six RBIs in a 6–1 victory in Chicago. And in September, in a game against the Red Sox, Berra was picked off third in the eighth inning, only to hit the game-winning three-run homer in the bottom of the ninth. When the Yankees won the pennant that year, Stengel tied Connie Mack for most pennants won by a manager.

Berra ended the year batting .266, with 22 home runs and 90 RBIs. He and Enos "Country" Slaughter were the two oldest players on the team, and there had been a few laughs at Berra's expense as his 1947 World Series teammates played on Old-Timers Day at Yankee Stadium—minus their rookie catcher of that year, of course. Still, he was among Stengel's favorites.

In August, Berra appeared on Campanella's new radio show, *Campy's Corner*. Campanella had been paralyzed from the chest down in an auto accident, and the baseball world was deeply shaken by the tragedy. Campanella tape-recorded his five-minute interviews, which were conducted over the phone, then broadcast by New York station WINS at the New York University

Bellevue Medical Center. Jackie Robinson and Pee Wee Reese also appeared on the program, which was sponsored by Ballantine and R.J.R. Nabisco.

Stengel drove the team as hard as ever that season. By mid-August, he held another closed-door meeting, bawled out the whole team, and praised only Mantle and Berra.

The Yankees faced the Braves again in the World Series. The Yankees were determined, but so were their opponents from Milwaukee.

In Game 2, Howard's throw home for a play at the plate resulted in a run, but also in one of the most spectacular plays of Berra's career. With Wes Covington racing home, Howard threw the ball high from left field. Berra, awaiting a throw low enough to tag out the hard-charging Covington, leapt and—barehanded—caught the ball with his throwing hand, surely saving at least one run.

One of the most famous Berra stories of the '58 Series involved the red-hot slugger Henry Aaron.

With a focused, menacing look, Aaron approached the batter's box. He knew of Berra's intent to be friendly and to distract.

Berra kept telling Aaron, "You want to hit with the label up on the bat."

Annoyed, the usually affable Aaron shot back, "Yogi, I came up here to hit, not to read."

Again the Series came down to Game 7. On October 9, 1958, at County Stadium, the game was tied 2–2. In the eighth inning, Berra came up with two outs. He hit the ball, "which came within three feet of clearing the right corner of the grandstand for a homer," according to Dick Young of the *New York Daily News*. The hit resulted in a double, which started a four-run, two-out rally, giving the Yankees the game, 6–2, and another Series title.

Berra extended four of the records he already held and tied three more, including put-outs by a catcher in World Series play, and total World Series bases with 101.

"Yogi Berra sets a record almost every time he turns around," reported the Associated Press.

# ~ Chapter 14 ~

# THE HEART OF THE YANKEES

By the end of January 1959, Berra had regained the lost part of his salary and was very well satisfied. It was his 13th year in Major League Baseball.

John Drebinger of *The New York Times* wrote a piece about the number of roles Berra would play this year, including first base and outfield, as well as catcher. "Yogi's days as the number one receiver may be numbered, but not because the passing years have caught up with him. The assembly line, however, has," wrote Drebinger, who noted the maturing Howard and Johnny Blanchard behind Howard.

But Berra was not interested in first base, and Stengel made light in the papers of how Berra was catching more batting practice than in many previous years. "Funny thing, every time I look around to see if I can have a quiet talk with Yogi, I find him squatting down in that batting cage," said the amused Old Professor.

Berra refused to play first and refused to get a first-baseman's glove. He insisted that if they wanted him to play first base, they could buy him a glove. Why should he buy a glove he wasn't going to use?

One time Berra brought his son Larry to the ballpark. Larry commented, "Daddy, you've got two kinds of gloves in your locker now. Why don't you get a first-baseman's mitt?"

"You mind your own business, or I won't bring you to the games no more," Berra shot back to his curious son.

Incidentally, it was in 1959 that Berra issued one of his most famous lines, "Nobody goes there anymore. It's too crowded." Those words were spoken on a visit home to St. Louis. Over the years, many writers have pointed to numerous restaurants when invoking Berra's quote, but it was in fact uttered about Ruggeri's in St. Louis, his former employer. Berra said it to Musial and Garagiola when they were trying to choose a place to dine.

\* \* \*

At the time, Berra's mother was still quite ill. "When Mom had to go into the hospital the first week in May, we were all afraid she might never come out," Berra said later. Her strength was ebbing. Berra called every day to find out how his mother was.

Garagiola was living in St. Louis while he was broadcasting Cardinals games. "Yogi knew whenever I'd visit my mother, I'd go across the street to see his mother," Garagiola remembered.

"How's my mother, Joey?" Berra would ask.

"She's better, Yogi," Garagiola would respond.

"And I'd see the same look he'd get as a kid, the one that gave away what he was feeling, and I'm sure my look gave me away, too. His eyes would well up," Garagiola remembered.

"She ain't doin' so good, is she?" Berra would lament. For her part, she thought as often about her son in New York from her porch in St. Louis as Berra did about her.

During a break between a series in Detroit and an upcoming series in Kansas City, Berra got Stengel's permission to go home to see her. Before Berra could leave, the hospital called him at 6:00 AM and told him he better get there right away—his mother was dying.

Berra jumped on a plane as fast as he could, catching a flight at 7:00 AM for St. Louis. "I was in St. John's hospital at 11:00. Josie was there, and Pop, and my brothers. Mom was still alive," he said. But she had lapsed into a coma.

"Mom, it's Lawdie. It's me, Mom, Lawdie," said the stricken baseball star. Paulina moved slightly but was unable to speak. A priest arrived for last rites. And a few hours later she was gone. She was 64 years old.

Josie and the nurses assured Berra that his mother should, by all rights, have passed on earlier, but were convinced she held on for Berra's arrival.

"I hoped she heard me and knew I was there. I loved her very much," he said.

Gone was the secret conspirator who had helped him countless times to escape his father's heavy hand. Gone was the doting mother who had snuck him money when he was starving in Norfolk. The softest voice of his youth was now gone. Berra was heartbroken. He took her rosary beads and kept them with him for years.

\*   \*   \*

Back on the field, Berra and his former teammate Phil Rizzuto found themselves at the center of a small maelstrom when, during a Red Sox series, WPIX featured a special 80-inch camera lens that made it possible to see the catcher's signals. Rizzuto was announcing for WPIX, and he joked that an umpire was hardly necessary as Berra's signals were broadcast live over the airwaves. Eventually, Commissioner Ford Frick stepped in to shutter the intrusive lens.

Berra found himself at the center of the media again in August when *The Sporting News* reported trade talks between the Yankees and the St. Louis Cardinals about a rumored blockbuster swap of Berra for Musial. Both sides denied the reports vehemently.

From 1959 to 1963, the league experimented with having two All-Star Games. In the second game, staged in Los Angeles, Berra hit a two-run homer off Don Drysdale and won MVP honors.

On August 9, in the ninth inning against Kansas City, Berra joined the 300 Club when he clouted his 300th homer to tie the game (Ellie Howard won it with a home run in the eleventh).

On September 19, 1959, at Yankee Stadium, they held Yogi Berra Day. Carmen and the kids attended.

"I just hope I don't freeze," said the frightened Berra about the upcoming festivities. "But I'm liable to be so scared that I'll forget the words. I'd rather go to the electric chair."

The event caused every newspaper in the metropolitan area to recall Berra's previous attempt to speak during a ceremony to honor him earlier in his career.

But almost all the sportswriters lauded the stocky backstop, from the *News*, to the *Post*, to the *Times*. Arthur Daley put it best when he wrote, "Yogi may fluff his speech of thanks on the morrow. He may even lapse into a Berraism. But the sincerity of this noble little guy will shine forth anyway. After all, he was correct the first time. This occasion really is necessary."

On the day of the ceremony, Berra received 58 separate gifts from friends and family, and a $4,000 scholarship at Columbia University was donated in his honor. Among his presents were a swimming pool, patio furniture, dance lessons, a brand-new station wagon (from the Yankees), a television, and many other items. Joe DiMaggio and Ted Williams were in attendance. Carmen, Pietro, Larry (who was nine years old), and Timmy (who was seven years old) were also there.

Berra was only the sixth Yankee in history to be feted with his own day at Yankee Stadium.

Berra addressed the crowd. "Everything up until now has been fine," he said, choking up. "I was enjoying myself, and I hope you are, too. On behalf of myself and my family, I want to thank you…not for the gifts, but for showing up." Choking up further, Berra concluded, "I'm grateful to the wonderful organization, the Yankees, and to my many friends. God bless you all."

Years later, Berra said, "It's too bad Mom couldn't have been sitting there with Pop." While Pietro was proud of his boy, eventually he lost interest during the course of the ceremonies. As the size of the pile of gifts increased, Pietro grumbled.

"What's the matter?" Berra's brother John asked his father.

"Everything's for him! What's for me?" cracked an incredulous Pietro.

"I'll take you up to the Stadium Club and buy you a drink," John offered his disconsolate father. "Come on, that's better than nothing." His father acquiesced but did not stop grumbling about the booty Berra received from friends, family, and fans.

Stengel also spoke, saying to the crowd, "In my 10 years, outside of DiMaggio, the man at the plate, Berra, is the greatest player I ever had to manage, which is a great thing to enhance my career."

After finishing the game hitless, Berra treated his father to a drink in Yankees owner Dan Topping's private lounge.

"You the man who gives my boy all that money?" Pietro asked Weiss when Berra introduced his father to the Yankees' general manager. Berra made sure to move his father along lest he talk Weiss into cutting his salary. Pietro stayed East for a few weeks, spending lots of time at the bowling alley.

For the season, Berra batted .284, with 19 home runs, 69 RBIs, and 25 doubles. He also was rated the number one fielding catcher in the American League with a fielding percentage of .997. He had set a new league record for most consecutive chances without an error by a catcher, 950, and the most consecutive games without an error by a catcher, 148.

But the Yankees finished in third place with a record of 79–75, and things were unraveling quickly. Topping, Stengel, and Weiss, long the triumvirate that had made the Yankees what they were, were coming unglued as egos inflated and sharp words were used.

At the end of the season, a fan sent in the following poem:

**To an Ex-American League Pennant Winner**
*Although you were defeated, Yanks,*
*You shouldn't feel too blue;*
*Just think of all your bars and banks*
*And bowling alleys, too.*
*As businessmen you guys are tops,*
*It really seems a shame*
*That you should have to leave your shops*
*Just for a lousy game.*

\* \* \*

On November 26, 1959, Berra and Carmen took off for Rome from New York International Airport on an Alitalia plane. Berra was to distribute $1,000 worth of baseball equipment to youngsters in that city as an emissary for Baseball for Italy, Inc., a nonprofit organization.

Baseball for Europe was an organization created by major league owners as an attempt to spread baseball into other markets. They were the first league to make in-roads in this way. Today the organization still exists and is called

Major League Baseball Europe, Middle East, and Africa. So being chosen by the lords of baseball for such a venture was an impressive assignment for Berra. And it was also an instance of baseball as a business capitalizing on Berra's fame, which reached far beyond the game itself.

This was Berra's first time back in Rome since his visit during the war. Things had changed since he was there last. His first trip was an aimless amble, gawking at the sites and glory of Rome. He was a seaman and aspiring baseball player. Now here he was an ambassador for Major League Baseball in Europe.

In the interim, now age 34, he'd played in 10 World Series, married a wonderful woman, and fathered three children. While soccer was still king in Italy, baseball had caught on somewhat, with a league of its own sponsored by some soft drink companies. Alitalia contributed the tickets to Baseball for Italy for free.

The distribution of the goods was delayed when the mitts, balls, and equipment were held up by Italian customs officials. The Romans had no idea who Berra was. So he and Carmen, with a private car and tour guide provided for them, toured the city. They broke for lunch, with Berra eating a plate of spaghetti, two helpings of tripe, a salad, and some ice cream, all accompanied by a bottle of wine. It was a slightly different experience from his 1944 visit, when even the restaurants didn't have a lot of food to offer in the midst of war.

Berra refused to try to speak his father's dialect in Rome for fear of embarrassing himself. However, Ugo Antonucci, Berra's business manager, and Ugo's brother Eugene, who accompanied them on the trip, spoke Italian properly and made many inroads for them. Berra was relieved that no one knew who he was, and he could walk the streets unmolested. But at lunch, an American tourist recognized him and asked to shake his hand. Berra was polite and accommodating.

On the following Monday, Berra distributed the loot to local children. They were able to distribute the equipment to the 150 or more orphans at the Boys Town of Italy and to another organization.

While in Rome, Berra was granted an audience with the pope. When he and Carmen were introduced, Pope John XXIII said, "Hello, Yogi."

"Hello, Pope," responded the baseball star.

From then on, he was a tourist. Carmen and Berra stayed in Europe for three weeks, visiting Paris, Madrid, Naples, and Milan.

While in Milan they made the short trip to Malvaglio. He met five of his mother's sisters, one of her brothers, and countless nieces, nephews, and grandchildren. According to Berra himself, one woman was the spitting image of his mother.

"For the first time since we had arrived in Italy, I could communicate easily with the people. This was the dialect I had been brought up on, and I knew it through and through," Berra said, and he felt right at home, as if he were talking to his own mother and father.

Upon his return on December 20, Berra told the press that a lack of fields and coaches, as well as the three-hour Italian lunch hour, were stumbling blocks to establishing baseball in Italy. "In Italy, they go to sleep between 1:00 PM and 4:00 PM, so that baseball games that begin at 2:00 PM won't have much of a draw. They are thinking of putting up lights for night games, and that might help," said Berra. He pointed out that soccer was still king in Italy. "What they really need is instructors. They need a lot of practice," he added.

While Berra was away, Weiss had traded Larsen and Bauer to Kansas City for slugger Roger Maris. With the trading of Bauer, Berra was the lone player to have played on all nine of Stengel's teams.

That January Berra was honored at a dinner by Branch Rickey at the Waldorf-Astoria Hotel. Rickey was now the president of the new Continental Baseball League. Berra also appeared on WPIX for the televised version of *Campy's Corner*. And in March he appeared on CBS's *Sports Spectacular* television show.

Also, Berra and Carmen moved into a palatial home in Montclair, New Jersey. When asked how he liked his new home, Berra responded, "Great! It's fulla rooms. And the ground all around the place is fulla trees."

"I was in his home several times, and I don't think I saw all the rooms," said teammate Bobby Richardson.

Berra signed his contract at the end of January 1960, first signing three blank contracts for the newspaper photographers before signing the real one. He signed for the same amount he had the year before, with Weiss and Stengel in attendance.

When asked about the Yankees' chances, he responded, "I think we got a good chance to win this year. Much depends on our two young pitchers, the right-handed Jim Coates and the left-handed Bill Short. If they come through, we could make it."

That spring training, Stengel was determined to give Howard more opportunities behind the plate, which meant that Berra would play more in the outfield, first base, and wherever. One of the experiments that spring was trying Berra at third base. This was most notably one of Berra's most humbling experiences on a baseball diamond.

"Yogi, you play third like a crapshooter making his point the hard way. A point of 14, for instance, and the dice don't even add up to 14," Garagiola told the press in spring training. "You should have played third with your catcher's mitt."

"There is one play when he covers so much ground that I see him down near second base," Stengel told the press. "I look up and think the shortstop looks larger. But it's only Yogi helping him out."

At one point, Stengel said, "Betcha the reason he didn't back up the pitcher that time was because he was talking to the new umpire behind third. I'll stake my life on it."

Of course, the most famous line about Berra playing third came from by Red Smith, who wrote, "Watching Yogi Berra play third base is like watching a Cub Scout trying to put up a pup tent in a wind storm."

Some were kinder, saying merely that he failed to distinguish himself at third. There was no mistaking it—he was not a third baseman. By late March he was back behind the plate, the experiment at third a mere memory. And his bat was starting to warm up, as he hit a three-run home run against the Cincinnati Reds.

Before a game that spring, as Berra was emerging from the dugout, Ted Williams nodded to Berra, "You playing today?"

"Naw, I can't make the team," Berra said.

It was a joke, but it referred to the inevitable slide in both their careers. The 1960 season would be Williams's last year. He played in only 113 games that year, but batted a healthy .316. Berra would play in only 120 games in 1960, the fewest in his career since 1947. Age had caught up with both of them. But Berra was still a productive member of the team—he hit 15 home runs, tapped 14 doubles, and knocked in 62 runs.

Berra could feel his age catching up to him. He felt he could still hold his weight on the ballclub, though, and he still enjoyed playing the game.

"If all the games were home games, I would want to play forever. It's only the traveling that gets harder as you get older," Berra lamented. Traveling wears on an older player, the cities blending one into another. As Berra described it, "You don't see much of the cities anyway, just the railroad station or the airport, the hotel, the ballpark, and maybe a couple of restaurants and a couple of movies. One city pretty much looks like another."

The scribes hovered around him, as usual, for his preseason picks. He responded, "Where are the soft touches that we used to have when we first broke in?" He lamented the days when he was a rookie and they could push around clubs like Washington and St. Louis. Berra recounted the strong batters and pitchers from each of the American clubs.

"All the clubs are more evenly balanced. There are no pushovers," he said.

Berra got off to a late start in 1960 as he was sidelined with the flu for the season's first five games. When healthy, he started off with a hot bat and rotated with Howard at catcher and in the outfield.

"Now, it's Yogi Berra who is going to occupy Yankee Stadium's left field, otherwise known as Hell's Half Acre. That sounds like a helluva way to treat an old and faithful retainer, but Casey Stengel has to solve the problem," wrote John Drebinger.

"What would you do now that Maris is ready to play?" Stengel asked the press.

It was in left field where Berra did indeed utter the words, "It gets late early out there," trying to explain the difficulties of playing in New York's left field, where the shadows played tricks on many a fielder's eyes, both Yankees and opponents alike.

While age may have started to catch up with him, he was as feisty as ever. In a May 4, 1960, game, Berra had a difference of opinion with home-plate umpire John Flaherty. Playing at Tiger Stadium in Detroit, Berra turned around and squared off with the imposing older man. He once again got the heave-ho.

"I just wanna good seat," Berra told the reporters before a doubleheader at the end of May. "I'm a spectator today. Howie is gonna do all the catchin'. Ain'tcha, Howie?"

"I hope not," replied Howard. "Gosh, you getting lazy."

One Sunday, the Yankees were playing the Baltimore Orioles, and Gene Woodling shouted to Berra, "Hey, Yog, what's up? They only let you play on Sundays?"

"I gotta play. All the regulars are hurt!" joked Berra.

When the Dodgers came to town in late June for an exhibition game, Berra was hitting .297. "Usually at this time of the season, I'm hitting .220," he told Gil Hodges and Duke Snider.

In mid-July, Berra hit a grand slam and knocked in another run for five RBIs in a game against Detroit. And in September, he again was part of a come-from-behind winning rally.

Despite his on-the-field heroics, Berra was still more of a sidekick than a clubhouse leader. He had tagged along with DiMaggio, Bobby Brown, Stengel, and Rizzuto, and later with Mantle and Ford. According to Robert Lipsyte, who covered the Yankees briefly in the early 1960s, Berra was "rugged; he was muscular and strong; he was largely silent; and he wasn't going to steal your girl." He was never the leader, but he was popular and always included in the pack.

"If you could get Berra one-on-one, and ask him an intelligent question, he would try to explain it to you, he would talk with you," explained Lipsyte. "But if he was within the pack, he was not going to be seen making nice with the reporters."

An example of this came early in Lipsyte's career. Mantle had been accosted by a fan while on the road, and upon his return to Yankee Stadium, the young reporter had been dispatched to get the story. When Lipsyte arrived, Mantle and Berra were playing catch in front of the Yankee dugout, well before the game. Dressed in a shirt and tie, the young writer asked Mantle what really happened. Mantle crudely dismissed Lipsyte with a casual obscenity. Lipsyte, who was not used to Mantle's boorish behavior with reporters, worked up the nerve to ask again. At that point Mantle threw the ball "right through my hair," Lipsyte recalls. Mantle grinned. Then Berra threw the ball back to

Mantle, also through Lipsyte's hair. Both were grinning, as they continued their game of one-upsmanship.

"I marveled at their skill, their ability, to throw the ball like that. But it didn't occur to me until [later] that Berra didn't have to go along. He was the muscle-bound sidekick," said Lipsyte.

Mantle loved to ride Berra and joke that catching was easy and that handling of pitchers was overrated.

"Okay, I'll let you run the show," said a fed-up Berra. He was serious— Berra was going to let Mantle call the game. So the two huddled separately and came up with a strategy.

"When I stand straight up, it's a fastball. When I bend over and put my hands on my knees, you'll know it's a curve," Mantle said.

So along came a Whitey Ford game, who was in on it, and Mantle was calling the game.

"Going into the eighth inning, there's no score and I'm getting nervous, actually afraid I might call the wrong pitch," Mantle related. "Geez, what if I call a fastball and the hitter knocks it right out of the park?" Mantle thought to himself. "Suddenly I realize what Yogi has to go through." With the score still tied going into the ninth inning, Mantle admitted that a player he might not have normally worried about suddenly loomed like Babe Ruth.

Berra was still waiting for the signal.

"He gets off his haunches and stares at me. I turned my back. Enough of this nonsense," admitted Mantle.

Just then Berra walked up to the mound and discussed things with Ford. Ford took off his cap, a signal that Mantle was off the hook. Asked later what they were talking about, Ford cracked, "We figured that if he hit one you'd have had a heart attack. We didn't want the responsibility."

Berra was as popular as ever in this period. A constant promoter of Yoo-hoo and Camel cigarettes (along with Maris, Ford, and Skowron), he was also in the toy business. Gimbels advertised a 48" x 60" Yogi Berra Pitch Back toy. The promotional copy read, "Old Yogi Berra in a life-size picture is in there stopping and pitching back the hot ones for little or big leaguers. Yogi and regulation strike zone are both outlined on drop cloth behind the net."

And he and Mantle appeared on *Candid Camera* with guest star Jonathan Winters and star hosts Allen Funt and Dorothy Collins.

The Yankees won the pennant with a record of 97–57. The Yankees were facing the Pittsburgh Pirates in the 1960 World Series, and of all their opponents, Pittsburgh was most worried about Berra.

"Yogi Berra is the most dangerous Yankee," said manager Danny Murtaugh. "Like [Orioles manager] Paul Richards said, 'In the last three innings, Yogi is the toughest man in baseball.'"

Batting .276, Berra "was the one mentioned most in the strategy meeting held behind locked doors in their clubhouse," wrote sportswriter Louis Effrat.

"Berra, it was learned after the highly classified meeting, is the name circled, asterisked, and underlined on the scoring reports submitted by" the Pirates staff, reported Dick Young for the *Daily News*. "He is the most feared Yankee."

The Series opened in Pittsburgh, with the Bucs' colorful fans attired in all manner of Pirate garb, their bodies and faces painted, screaming loudly. The Pirates took the first game 6–4 before their thrilled fans. Berra was one of several Yankees to wear the goat horns when he was caught off second on Bobby Richardson's liner to left field in the second inning.

This Series was billed as featuring the two chattiest backstops in league history when Berra was matched up against Smoky Burgess. The first time the two met at the plate, Berra said, "Hiya, Smoky."

"Hiya, Yogi," responded the talkative Burgess. While the sportswriters waited for the bons mots to fall, they went away from the Series severely disappointed. The two chatty, friendly backstops didn't exchange any more pleasantries than that the rest of the Series.

For the second game, with the Pirates starting Bob Friend, Berra and Stengel discussed with reporters who would start in left field, as Howard and his hot bat would be the starting catcher.

"If I were the manager, I'd start [Bob] Cerv in left field tomorrow," Berra volunteered. "I'm not the manager, mind you, and I'm not looking for anyone's job, but if I were Casey, Cerv would be my man—and I'll tell you why," explained the loquacious catcher while Stengel looked on. "First of all, I haven't played much against left-handers this season, and when I did, I didn't do much good against them. Cerv murders left-handers, and besides, Bob deserves the chance. But Casey hasn't asked my opinion, and I don't think he will. Furthermore, I'm not the manager, and I'll play whenever and wherever he tells me to."

Stengel then told the press Berra was the second-best player he ever coached, the first being DiMaggio. Berra started in left in the next game, hitting 1-for-4 and knocking in two runs before a late-game substitution. The Yankees won 16–3 to tie the Series 1–1.

On October 7, Toots Shor held a groundbreaking ceremony on 52$^{nd}$ Street to announce a new restaurant he was opening to replace the one that had been demolished to make way for a skyscraper. In attendance were Jackie Gleason, U.S. Supreme Court Chief Justice Earl Warren, Don Ameche, and many others. Of course, Berra was another of the celebs to show up.

"Yogi, why don't you take your mask off?" bellowed the giant saloon keeper.

When introduced to Warren, Berra said simply, "Howaya?"

"Gleason told the crowd, 'I was very good at baseball.' Someone in the crowd shot back, 'Well, Yogi is good at comedy, too!'" reported *The New York Times*.

Before Game 3, which proved to be a 10–0 Yankees victory, Garagiola remarked, "You amaze me, Yog. You've become such a world figure that you drew more applause yesterday then either Prime Minister Nehru or Herbert Hoover. Can you explain it?"

"Certainly, I'm a better hitter," responded Berra.

However, those words rang hollow as Yogi went 0-for-4 in a 3–2 loss. In Game 5, he hit a weak dribbler as a pinch-hitter in the eighth inning of the Yankees' 5–2 loss, after Stengel pulled Howard hoping for a home run from the usually reliable Berra.

The Yankees pummeled the Pirates again 12–0 in Game 6 to even the Series at three games apiece. Berra had gone 3-for-4 with two RBIs. Johnny Blanchard went 3-for-4 while receiving behind the plate after Howard was injured early in the contest.

October 17, 1960, was the night of one of the Kennedy–Nixon debates. That same day, in Game 7, Berra brought his bat and rediscovered his stroke.

He hit a three-run home run in the sixth inning, leading a four-run rally to give the Yankees a 5–4 lead. The home run placed Berra at number three for World Series home runs behind Ruth and Mantle. Berra added another RBI and scored twice.

The Pirates had drawn first blood, scoring four runs in the first two innings, but by the bottom of the eighth, the Yankees had gained the lead at 7–4. Then the Pirates scored five runs, making it 9–7. Not to be denied, the Yankees scored two in the top of the ninth inning to tie the game—and it was Berra who knocked in the tying run.

The first Pittsburgh batter in the bottom of the ninth inning was Bill Mazeroski, a light-hitting second baseman. Yankees pitcher Ralph Terry's second pitch was lifted high to left field—Mazeroski thought it might be a double. Berra turned his back to home plate and ran toward the wall. Then, realizing what was happening, he stopped.

"It flew high and far, over the brick wall in left-center, with left fielder Berra watching it, hopelessly, helplessly," wrote Dick Young. The Pirates had won 10–9.

"When did I know we had it?" Pirates manager Danny Murtaugh said. "When I saw Yogi giving up chasing Mazeroski's homer in the ninth."

"I don't know what the pitch was," Terry later said. "All I know is it was the wrong one."

Berra had batted .318 in the Series, knocking in eight runs. And in this Series, he set or extended 14 World Series records, eight for batting and six for fielding. The records included most Series played; most games played; most runs, hits, total bases, and singles; most Series, games, chances, and putouts for a catcher; most assists; and most double plays.

After the Series, as reporters surrounded Berra, the usually cheerful backstop was upset, saying, "We made too many wrong mistakes." Berra always thought that the loss to the Pirates was one of the toughest to take. "We outplayed the Pirates badly," he lamented.

The night before Game 7, Arthur Daley, the noted *New York Times* sportswriter, ran into Berra, Carmen, Garagiola, and Frank Slocum coming back from a late dinner around 11:00 PM in front of the Yankees' hotel.

"Why aint'cha in bed? Don'tcha know you have to work tomorrow?" Berra said to Daley, poking him with a finger. Then the small catcher smiled and laughed. "I was just beatin' you to the punch." Daley noted that Berra was as pleased with himself as a small boy.

On October 18, 1960, the Yankees cold-bloodedly fired Stengel at a news conference. He had been the Yankees manager from 1949 to 1960, and the Yankees had won the pennant a record 10 times. And they had made the greatest run in baseball history under his hand. But at the age of 70, Topping and others felt Stengel was too far removed from the ages of his players. Only one player had remained with the organization throughout that entire run—Yogi Berra.

On October 20, the Yankees announced that Ralph Houk would be the new manager. Houk had managed the team for two weeks during the 1960 season while Stengel was ill with the flu.

Berra remained a committed sports fan. He was part of the original New York Rangers Fan Club, along with a number of other New York celebs, and continued to be a devoted hockey and soccer fan. He attended Knicks games as well, and attended many college and even high school sporting events. Most notably that off-season, Berra was at the infamous New York Giants–Philadelphia Eagles game where Chuck Bednarik flattened Frank Gifford, giving him a serious concussion and causing Gifford to miss an entire year. Berra attended the game with Musial.

In January Berra signed his 16th Yankees contract. It reflected a small salary increase, but Berra was happy.

New manager Houk told the press, "Yogi gives me maneuverability. He's a willing worker for whom I'm sure I'll be able to find work, whether it is as a catcher or an outfielder."

Berra would turn 36 years old during the course of the season. His sons were growing. Larry was now 11 years old, Timmy was nine, and Dale was four.

# ~ Chapter 15 ~

# THE END OF AN ERA

In 1960 Berra signed a contract to tell his life story. This would be his first foray into what would prove to be a best-selling literary career. The much-loved backstop teamed up with Ed Fitzgerald to write his life story, *Yogi: The Autobiography of a Professional Baseball Player.*

The book was excerpted in *Sports Illustrated* in February 1961 and reviewed heavily. Ads were taken out in all the major metropolitan newspapers and magazines by both *Sports Illustrated* and his publisher, Doubleday. The ads ran lines such as, "A grand-slam homer of a book," and "Yogi blasts another one into the stands!"

Arthur Daley wrote a glowing article about the book for the *Times* sports section, writing, "The enveloping warmth of his personality shines through the pages." Daley highlighted the qualities that made the real Yogi Berra so lovable, shining a light on Berra's worries: his fears about getting around on a fastball, about an injury prematurely ending his career, about the bowling alley he and Rizzuto owned, about keeping Carmen happy "so she won't be sorry she married me," about his children growing up well, and about keeping out of trouble with God.

According to Daley, "Yogi belted this one out of the park."

The book was then covered in *The New York Times Book Review* and was reviewed by pitcher Jim Brosnan, who called the book "fascinating" and "major-league."

Berra showed up at Macy's Herald Square to do a signing, where he sold 45 copies. Many were awed. One woman insisted he use his whole name and was told it was too formal. "I don't believe in last names for autographs. That way it's too formal. Anyway, I'm a lousy speller," Berra said.

Another man, however, was not as pleased. John Modowar, a Brooklynite, heckled Berra, questioning moves Stengel had made in the Series. "He should have brought in [Ryne] Duren. They wouldn't have taken a toehold on him. You should know that last game cost me," he complained.

"Look what it cost us," Berra shot back.

"Yeah, but I don't make your money," responded the loud Brooklynite.

Many other bookstores ran ads for the book as well, including Brentano's on Fifth Avenue. The book did well, but it was not the first book about Berra. Julian Messner, Inc. had published an unauthorized book in 1958 called *The Yogi Berra Story,* written by Gene Roswell. The book was a sketchy history of Berra's life, but it proved popular. By now, he had appeared in a dozen or so books as everything from a character to the subject of full-blown personality sketches.

Berra also appeared in the Catskills several times. Once, he and Skowron were celebrity judges at the World Barrel-Jumping Championships.

Berra and Rizzuto were also chosen as the cochairmen of the bowling committee of the Lighthouse Dinner Dance at the Waldorf-Astoria. The dance raised money for campgrounds for the blind men, women, and children of New York. Ed Sullivan was also involved.

And Berra was a spokesman for Savoy clothing, which ran an ad with a little boy in a cast, with the headline, "Mom! I got Yogi Berra's autograph!" The ad copy began, "Can't blame him for the smug smile—with Yogi Berra's signature on the cast! He'll want to wear it always, like his handsome Savoy togs."

In December 1960, BBC Industries of New York City acquired all the outstanding stock of the Yoo-hoo Beverage Company—Yoo-hoo had been sold for $1 million. As a means of comparison, the New York Football Giants were the first NFL team valued at $1 million that same year, and the average salary in the United States in 1960 was $4,743. BBC had also acquired a chain of discount variety stores and the Nedicks New York Bottling Company. Dr. Max A. Geller, the president and chairman of BBC, made the announcement. Albert Olivieri, the former president of Yoo-hoo, continued on in an executive capacity. Berra renegotiated his deal with the new management. He made sure his 15-year contract had remained intact and continued on as executive vice president and special sales representative of Yoo-hoo.

Geller needed Berra, as the Yankee remained a popular draw. Berra continued to show up at store openings, bottling conventions, and other events. At a single store opening or event, Berra, in a day's time, could move up to 400 cases of the chocolate drink. Berra's star power was part of what Geller had bought.

"He's becoming more and more relaxed with people now," Geller told the press. "I let him listen in on board meetings and make suggestions sometimes. He really feels like part of the team." When the plant upgraded to state-of-the-art bottling equipment, Berra and a few Yankees invited the business press to inspect the facilities. Media coverage ensued—Berra knew his value to the company. And Berra consistently joked with the press that it was Skowron who was the happiest of all because he relied on the free T-shirts and cases of Yoo-hoo. With the renegotiation of his contract, Berra would be linked to the company until the early 1980s.

\* \* \*

With the expansion of baseball into the far West and the addition of the airplane as a more consistent and safe way to travel, the teams crisscrossed the country more often than in the past. Once, after leaving Washington late and arriving in Minnesota, Berra grumbled, "Look, it may be 11:00 PM here, but it's in the morning where I was a few hours ago, and I'm tired." Some players, like Mantle, took the travel in stride. Mantle was notorious for falling asleep as soon as he got in a plane seat, while Berra was wide-awake the whole time. This was the new, modern era of baseball. Thus began the 1961 season.

Berra started off fine that season, and on May 28, 1961, he was one of 24 players who combined to hit 27 homers in a single day to help set a new American League record.

On June 11 it was decided that barring emergency, the move to the outfield was final. Berra was happy—the grind of being a catcher would have hastened the end of his career. And Berra felt like he could still contribute.

"I'm going to try and keep him out there," Houk told the press. "The crouching up and down that a catcher has to do tires a man of his age [36]. He keeps his pep longer in the outfield and seems to be a better hitter."

"A comparison of statistics confirms the opinion," wrote Joe Trimble in the *New York Daily News*. While catching, Berra's batting average was .255 with two home runs; his batting average while playing the outfield was .296 with eight home runs.

"I told you I would hit better if I played the outfield—and last longer, too," said Berra.

"Amiable Yogi worked hand in glove with Houk. And even if the skipper did change the glove from a catcher's to a fielder's mitt, that was still all right with Yogi," wrote John Drebinger. As a still highly potent pinch-hitter, Berra continued to give the Yankees invaluable service. And again Berra was voted to the All-Star Game, this time as an outfielder.

On June 28, 1961, Berra collected his 2,000[th] hit in Los Angeles. Even in a reduced role, playing in only 119 games, he hit 22 home runs, several of them game winners.

In the meantime, Mantle and Maris were chasing Babe Ruth's single-season home-run record. And Berra was the first to raise a peculiar question: "What happens if one of these two breaks the Ruth record inside 154 games, but the other winds up on top when we finish our 162-game schedule?" Indeed, Commissioner Frick was faced with a dilemma. It was Berra who brought this up in the press, and it would be Frick who made the ultimate decision.

It was after Mantle and Maris hit back-to-back homers, "for the umpteenth time," according to Berra, that Berra uttered his famous, "It's like déjà vu all over again."

In August, Mantle, Maris, and Berra, while out West, were paid to appear in a movie, titled *That Touch of Mink*. Movie crews blasé about filming Hollywood stars crowded the set, asking for autographs. The three were surrounded on the Hollywood set at every break in the shooting. This was such an event that nonworking children of lot workers, usually banned from the sets, were allowed in for the day. The three players were featured in a scene with the movie's two big stars, Cary Grant and Doris Day.

They were released after their 90 minutes of work, and Berra told the press, "This is like stealing money, ain't it?"

Berra made an awesome play that drew lots of attention on September 1, when he threw Detroit Tiger Al Kaline out at second from left field.

"This is my last year. I'm quitting. My legs must be shot when I get thrown out by the likes of you," Kaline mugged with Berra the next day.

"Pretty good throw, eh?" said Berra.

"That was ridiculous," chimed in Pee Wee Reese, now a network broadcaster. "If you ever threw to second on me in my prime, I would have scored."

It was during this period that Mantle had a pivotal night out with Berra and their wives.

"Merlyn and I were having dinner with Yogi Berra and his wife, Carmen. Now, Yogi always drank straight vodka on the rocks. He'd have a limit, maybe three or four, and that was it. Me, I'd just be starting," recounted Mantle.

Mantle had drank too much, and as they were leaving the restaurant, Berra yelled to them, in earnest, "Merlyn, I wouldn't ride with him!"

Mantle waved Berra off, and he and Merlyn drove away. Mantle proceeded to drive his car straight into a telephone pole, and Merlyn was thrown through the windshield. She required stitches, but Mantle returned to the Yankees for a doubleheader the next day. It was around this period in his life that Mantle realized he might have a drinking problem. But the cops and press kept the story quiet, and he was charged only with a small fine for replacement of the pole.

On September 20, Houk's Yankees won the pennant, and Houk was lauded for his deft handling of Yankees personnel, including the move of Berra to the outfield, when there might have been the opportunity to trade the fading catcher for younger players.

With the Yankees in the World Series yet again, this time against the Cincinnati Reds, it was remarked that with every flex or twitch of muscle, Berra was seting new marks in the World Series record books.

Berra went 0-for-2 with two walks in the first game at the Stadium, a Yankees victory, but in the second game, he hit a two-run homer before the teams headed back to Cincinnati tied at one game apiece.

The Yankees swept the Reds in Cincinnati, celebrating the World Series victory in the visitor's clubhouse after Game 5. Berra batted .273 for the Series, but the cold winds of November brought sad news from St. Louis. Pietro Berra died at St. Mary's Hospital in St. Louis on November 7, 1961. He was 76 years old.

*　*　*

The most exciting part of spring training in 1962 was meeting up with Stengel, who was the manager of the National League's new entry in baseball in New York City—the New York Metropolitans, or Mets, as they were affectionately known.

Houk, Mantle, Berra, and many of the other players and coaches came over to see the Old Professor.

"Why, Mr. Berra, you're slimmed down. Get that way from running to the dog races?" asked Stengel.

"I ain't been once this year!" scoffed Berra.

However, Berra had a tough spring, starting with a strain in his leg that dogged his early months. At 36, Berra was an elder statesman. When recalling his first season opener, Berra admitted he could not remember the name of the president who threw out the first pitch.

"William McKinley, no doubt," chimed in Jerry Coleman.

On April 10, 1962, the Yankees played the Baltimore Orioles on Opening Day at Yankee Stadium. Unbeknownst to Berra, Whitey Ford had been concocting a magic elixir that would give him better control on pitches. As pitchers age, they often find themselves looking for an edge, scuffing balls, wearing Vaseline, and so forth. In an effort to gain an edge, Ford emptied out a deodorant can and refilled it with his magic stickum.

"The thing was that Yogi was always borrowing everybody's stuff, their after-shave lotion or shaving cream or hair tonic," Ford related. "He'd be on his way to the shower room, and he'd just reach into your locker and just help himself to a dash of whatever he needed. Nobody minded too much, even though the guys would pretend to run him off."

After a game in Detroit, the mischievous Mantle swiped the deodorant can filled with glue and put it on the shelf of Ford's locker while Ford was in the shower, in such a way that Berra would be sure to see it.

"Sure enough, Yogi came out of his locker and saw this deodorant can on my shelf and helped himself," said Ford.

A few minutes later, all hell broke lose, with Berra shouting, "Son of a bitch, what the hell is this stuff?" Berra was cursing and writhing in pain.

Mantle and Ford had to artfully maneuver Berra into the trainers' room so as not to arouse suspicion with the writers. If Ford's glue was let out of the bag, so to speak, it would have been doomsday for the Bronx Bombers pitcher.

The trainer had to dissolve the glue with lots of rubbing alcohol and eventually had to cut the hair from Berra's underarms to release him fully.

"Boy, was he boiling," laughed Ford. "Look, they didn't call me slick for nothing."

That year Berra played in 84 games and batted .224. Although he still had power in his bat and clubbed several game-winning hits, he could not navigate the bases the way he once had.

From a career high of 597 at-bats in 1950, Berra dropped to 232 in 1962, with 10 home runs and 35 RBIs. Many of his appearances were as a pinch-hitter, but he continued to be a draw with fans and sportswriters alike.

"This was the first year I played under a hundred games. That was a new experience, which I didn't necessarily like. I didn't grouse to anybody, it just wasn't in my control," Berra said years later.

Berra published yet another book that year: *Behind the Plate*, with Til Ferdenzi. It was a small book of baseball stories and instruction on how to catch for youngsters.

Rizzuto and Berra announced on May 22, 1962, that they had decided to sell their bowling alley. The operation was sold to Lence, Inc., of New York. The purchase price was not released. Lence owned and operated 23 bowling alleys in New York and New Jersey.

On June 9, Berra played in his 2,000th major league game and pinch hit a three-run home run to give the Yankees a 7–3 victory over the Orioles.

Two weeks later he hit a grand slam in the first inning to pace the team to an 8–4 win over the Tigers. The next day Berra caught 22 innings in a pinch as the Yanks outlasted Detroit 9–7. He said he felt fine. His bat was still proving to be a potent weapon, as many of Berra's homers that year were game winners.

In that year, Mantle told a great story about one particularly frustrating day. "Once, I struck out three times in a game, and when I got back to the clubhouse, I put my head in my hands like I was going to start crying," Mantle recalled. Just then, he heard someone approach, and he turned around to find little Timmy Berra standing next to him.

"He tapped me on my knee, nice and soft, and I figured he was going to say something nice to me, you know, like, 'You keep hanging in there,' or something like that," said the Yankees star. "But all he did was look at me, and then he said in his little kid's voice, 'You stink.'" Just like his famous father, the young Berra had a way with words.

The Yankees played the San Francisco Giants in the 1962 World Series and took a tough 4–3 victory for yet another championship. Berra went 0-for-2 with two walks, and was almost thrown out of Game 4 when he argued balls and strikes while up at bat with umpire Jim Honochick. Still, just by participating, he broke and extended 11 World Series records.

"Personally, the year was embarrassing. I was kind of an afterthought," Berra lamented later.

Berra told the press he wanted to come back if the Yankees wanted him. Fortunately, they did.

In 1963 Berra returned, this time as a player/coach. He would bat .293, hit eight home runs, and knock in 28 RBIs. It was the first time he had hit single-digit home runs since his short major league stint back in 1946.

Berra had received several inquiries about coaching elsewhere, but the Yankees made sure to hold onto their stocky coach/catcher. Berra would be 38 years old that May.

Berra was not particularly excited about his coaching duties. "It's a little tougher than I thought. The first thing I learned was that a coach never sits down," groused Berra. "Every time I headed for the bench Old Crow [Frank Crosetti] or Johnny Sain or Houk would start snapping at my heels and tell me to keep hustling. Now what does a coach need to be hustling for? I thought the coach was supposed to keep the players hustling."

Berra as a first-base coach was a curiosity. The press had a field day as he jawed with players (both Yankees and opponents), as well as umpires. The chatty new coach talked to anyone and everyone.

Of course, he was also a target for ribbing. On one of the first days of spring training, Berra approached Ford and Mantle.

"Hey, Whitey, let's you and me go out to dinner tonight," said Berra.

"Nothing doing," said Ford with a smile. "You can't eat with the fellers anymore. You're a coach now." Ford always liked a chance to needle fellow players, and Berra was among his favorite targets and closest friends.

"Officers don't eat with enlisted men," smiled Mantle.

"Aw, come on, fellas," jawed Berra.

Several times, Crosetti would pull rank and direct Berra to the third-base coach's box in front of the opponents' hostile dugout. The resentful Berra would waddle over, his brow furrowed. But the other players had a ball. "What do I see out there?" asked Baltimore Orioles coach Harry Brecheen. "Is it real?"

"You never saw nothing like it before. That's the Yogi Bear!" shouted back Hank Bauer, another Orioles coach.

Bauer was referring to a new television character created just a few years earlier, one that would help cement Berra's place in American history. In 1958 Hanna-Barbera Productions, producers of multiple cartoon characters, melded Art Carney and Yogi Berra into a new cartoon character, Yogi Bear. Many of the mannerisms were taken from Carney, but malaprops were generally a part of the character's repertoire. Yogi Bear made his debut on the *Huckleberry Hound Show*, and by 1961 he was so popular the character got his own show.

The original Yogi was still pressed into service when necessary. He had a half-dozen game-winning hits during the course of the season. He played mostly as a catcher, but he played the outfield some, too. In one game he came off the coaching line to catch, went 3-for-4, and hit a two-run homer to pace the Yankees attack.

But that July marked the first time that Yogi Berra was not selected to the All-Star Game after 14 consecutive appearances. However, a week or so later, he once again was behind the plate, went 2-for-3, and hit a three-run home run to help the Yankees triumph 4–3 over the Los Angeles Angels. He also hit a two-run home run against the Orioles in August to help win a game.

In one game against the Kansas City Athletics, he singled, stole second, and then scored from second on a single. He singled home another run in the fifth to help the team win 5–2.

Many sportswriters joked that Berra was the highest-paid traffic cop in the major leagues, pointing out that his salary was much higher than those of other coaches. But all also remarked that he filled in like the Berra of old when given the chance, providing solid catching and skillful, clutch hitting. He was one of the veteran cogs that saved the Yankees when younger, livelier bats were sidelined. Houk again was credited with deft use of his secret weapon.

The Yankees again won the American League pennant. The Los Angeles Dodgers won the 1963 National League pennant, thanks in part to the dominance displayed by Sandy Koufax throughout the year. Koufax finished with a 1.88 earned-run average, 25 wins, and two World Series wins in a four-game sweep over the New York Yankees. Berra commented, "I can see how he won 25 games. What I don't understand is how he lost five!"

Skowron played first base for the Dodgers now, having been traded by the Yankees that winter. Berra chewed Skowron's ear off the entire Series. What did he and Berra talk about?

"Aw, he just kept telling me about the shadows," said Skowron.

"What shadows?" asked a sportswriter.

"How the hell should I know?"

The Los Angeles pitching corps was much too strong for the Yankees' bats, and the Dodgers swept the World Series. Berra played in only one game. His last at-bat was during Game 3 on Saturday, October 5, 1963, at Dodger Stadium, as a pinch-hitter. He lined out to right.

*   *   *

By the time he played his last game, Berra had ceded to Mantle a few World Series records. As Mantle mounted his attack, Berra's career was in decline. Still, Berra had played in 14 World Series and held numerous World Series records—most games by a catcher (63), most games by a player (75), hits (71), at-bats (259), and doubles (10)—as well as being second in RBIs, third in home runs, and third in walks. Berra also hit the first pinch-hit home run in World Series history in 1947, and he owned 10 World Series rings—the most any player had ever earned.

For his career, he led the league in chances for a catcher eight times, a record he shares with Gary Carter and Ray Schalk. He led the league six times in double plays by a catcher, and he caught three no-hitters, one of which was Don Larsen's perfect game. And he had a career fielding percentage of .988.

He had been an All-Star 15 times. He had been among the league leaders (top 10) in runs four times, hits three times, total bases seven times, home runs nine times, RBIs nine times, extra-base hits seven times, at-bats per strikeout ten times, and at-bats per home run nine times.

Berra won three MVPs and had finished as one of the top four vote-getters for seven years in a row, a feat not equaled by any other player in history. He had a .285 batting average, with 358 home runs (his 306 as a catcher was the most among catchers for a career at the time he retired), 2,150 hits, 1,480 RBIs, 321 doubles, 49 triples, and a slugging percentage of .482.

In comparison with Bill Dickey, the two shared the exact same fielding percentage. Dickey outhit Berra for batting average by 28 points, batting .313, and he hit more doubles (343) and triples (72). Berra, on the other hand, had more home runs, hits, and RBIs than Dickey (202; 1,969; 1,209).

Rizzuto pointed out that during the course of Berra's career, the Yankees had attempted to bring up 22 different catchers to either spell the hulking Berra or replace him. Even Howard, who eventually replaced Berra, sat behind him for years. Other catchers included Charlie Silvera, Aaron Robinson, Sherm Lollar, Ralph Houk, and Johnny Blanchard. Few players, at any position, blocked so many other capable replacements.

ESPN's Jayson Stark hunted down the following statistics on Berra's true value: between 1950 and 1956, Berra's average with the bases empty was .258, but he batted an incredible .318 with runners on and .314 with runners in scoring position. And in the last three innings of a close game, his average was .327, bearing out the Pirates' worries about the indomitable Berra years earlier.

Stark also pointed out that Berra was the only catcher in history to drive in more than 80 runs in 11 straight seasons. Berra only struck out 414 times in his entire career and amassed 13 seasons in which he had at least as many walks as strikeouts. In 1950 alone, he hit 28 homers and struck out only 12 times.

"Yogi Berra was not just another Yankee. Nowadays, in revisionist history, we think of DiMaggio passing the Ultimate Yankee torch directly to Mickey Mantle. But in real life," wrote Stark, "that's not what happened. Joe D. delivered that torch to Berra, who later shoveled it over to Mantle."

Simply put, Yogi Berra, known the world over as one of the most oft-quoted celebrities ever to come out of the United States, was one of the greatest catchers in the history of the game and one of the most successful players in the history of baseball.

Even if Yogi Berra had never been heard from again, his place in baseball history was secure—no matter if the records he established were broken or not. Few men, not even the great Babe Ruth himself, had equaled some of the achievements Berra had forged.

But Berra was not done—not by a long shot.

# ~ Chapter 16 ~

# MANAGING MR. STENGEL'S TEAM

Officially, the New York Yankees released Yogi Berra on October 29, 1963.

Six days earlier, Ralph Houk, the successful Yankees field manager, was tapped by Dan Topping to replace Roy Hamey as the club's general manager. But who would be the new field manager? Unbeknownst to the press, Berra, Houk, and Topping had known the answer for an entire year.

Years later, when Berra was recounting the machinations of how he came to be manager of the Yankees, he said he found out about it a full year in advance. Carmen interrupted and tried to correct him. She claimed, "He didn't know he'd be managing until spring training of 1964, because that's when he told [me] the news."

Berra then corrected her by saying, "I would have told you sooner, but I know how you worry about those things, and I didn't want you to worry an extra year."

"My wife still can't believe I could keep a secret that long. To tell you the truth, I can't either. But I did," Berra said.

Hamey had approached Topping and Houk about leaving the previous winter, and Houk had talked it over with Berra near the same time. Hamey, Weiss's longtime second-in-command, had been suffering ill health, which reached its nadir when he underwent surgery during his tenure as general manager. The secret this triumvirate concealed was the best-kept secret in baseball history, opined several sportswriters of the time.

"I was at the rookie school last year because I was a coach, and the very first day Ralph took me off to a corner," Berra related later.

"How would you like to manage?" asked Houk

"Manage who?" said Berra, confused.

"Here, the Yankees," said Houk.

"Where the hell are you going?" asked Berra.

On September 13, 1963, the secret started to get out. Broadcaster Joe Hasel had discussed the possibility of Houk's and Berra's ascension on Kyle Rote's *Sports Close-Up* radio show on WNEW.

That Berra was a knowledgeable baseball man was without question. The press had been asking him to handicap teams and pennant races for years. And everyone believed he knew a lot about the intracacies of baseball—the hitters, the pitchers, and how to manage a game.

"In his quiet way he can tell you more about the science of baseball than most players have forgotten," said Frankie Frisch on his radio show *Sports Flashes.*

"Yogi is smart and shrewd, a solid baseball man," wrote journalist Arthur Daley. "If Yogi is tapped for the manager's spot, everything will be a lot livelier in the dugout. No matter where Yogi is, he brings his own built-in aura of excitement, color, and conversation with him." Daley also pointed out in another column, "The players respect him as a baseball man."

"If good wishes of his players and fans will have any bearing, Berra will be around" a long time, wrote Joe Trimble for the *Daily News.* "The squat little man with the attractively homely face is one of the most popular ever to have played ball in New York."

But the pressure would be on. Stengel had obviously delivered. And Houk had been no slouch, posting three pennants and two World Series flags.

"His major problem, in the beginning at least, will be the disciplining of men he grew up with. They always kidded this best-natured of men in outrageous fashion, and he enjoyed their banter," wrote Daley. "But what he could accept as a teammate and as a coach, he can take no longer. It will take a strong adjustment by both."

"There had been some skepticism as to whether Berra will be able to impress his authority on Ford and Mantle, two fun-loving pranksters," wrote John Drebinger.

Daley also pointed out that Houk had done a remarkable job in 1963, playing only eight of the 161 games with the full team healthy—Mantle and Maris, among others, had been sidelined during the course of the year.

Shortly before noon on October 24, 1963, at the Savoy Hilton Hotel, Topping announced the appointment of Berra as the next manager of the New York Yankees.

"We're losing a great player and getting a great manager," Topping told the crowd. "The salary is the same as Stengel and Houk started with as managers here."

Berra was kidded about the pay cut. "It wasn't a big cut," Berra responded. The contract was posited to be worth approximately $35,000, which would have been almost $5,000 less than his player/coach contract of the previous year. It was a one-year contract—Berra wasn't sure if he could manage.

"I was a damn fool," Berra admitted 20 years later. "Roy Hamey told me to take a two-year contract, and I said no. I said I wanted a one-year contract. I said I don't know if I can manage. I want to see if I can. I shoulda taken a two-year contract."

Berra revealed that he planned to retain Johnny Sain, Frank Crosetti, and Jim Hegan on his coaching staff. Berra would be given free rein to run the team and make the decisions, and he predicted that the Yankees "are gonna be a terrific team," saying he thought they would be better than the year before.

Berra also announced his retirement as a player. "Managing, I think, is a tough enough job," he said.

"What makes a good manager?" he was asked.

"A good ballclub," responded Berra.

"What will you do when the general manager comes to the clubhouse to second-guess you?"

"I'll throw him out," said Berra with a smile, as Houk laughed in the background.

"Do you believe you can be harsh with the players when the occasion demands?"

Berra answered, "In anything you do, you have to put your foot down somewhere along the line."

When asked if he thought his lack of managerial experience might be an obstacle to the team's success, he told them that he'd been up with the big club for 17 years, "watching games and learning."

Pressed again, he answered defensively, "You can observe a lot by watching."

He continued, saying, "I've worked under a lot of good managers— [Joe] McCarthy, [Bucky] Harris, Stengel, Houk—and I've picked up a little something different from each of them. But I won't pattern myself after anybody. I think everybody has to do things their own way, and that's the way I'll manage."

During the course of the press conference, Berra received a telegram. When asked what it contained, Berra read the telegram from Mickey Mantle and Whitey Ford to the crowd. It congratulated the former backstop on becoming manager and jokingly asked "if you would give us our unconditional release so we can become pro golfers."

"Yogi made a tremendously favorable impression at his coronation ceremony…[and] handled himself with poise and distinction…. No man began a career with more fervent wishes than Lawrence Peter Berra. Such popularity must be deserved," wrote Arthur Daley.

Still there was the worry that Berra was a softie, and as Frisch said, "A good manager is a bit of a louse."

Robert Lipsyte wrote a fascinating piece about Berra the day after his promotion, separating for the readers the difference between the myth and the man. While Yogi was funny—a jokester and buffoon, popular but smart, while still relatively uneducated about life outside baseball—the real Berra was a suspicious slum child who disdained strangers and could talk crudely, especially when he thought someone was putting him on.

"'How the * * * * should I know?' he will answer to a harmless question from a stranger. With a man he trusts, he will sit down and explain his answers," wrote Lipsyte.

Berra was known for his colorful language. In fact, he once exclaimed, "Oh, shit!" during a golf tournament in front of the gallery. It was well known that his language was even more colorful within the confines of the Yankees clubhouse.

Lipsyte wrote, "He has continued to allow people to regard him as an amiable clown because it brings him quick acceptance, despite ample proof, on field and off, that he is intelligent, shrewd, and opportunistic." Lipsyte also pointed out that no one had heard of Yoo-hoo until Berra started promoting it.

On October 25, Yoo-hoo ran large ads in several metropolitan newspapers showing head shots of Berra in his baseball uniform and also dressed in a shirt and tie, with the captions "Manager Yogi Berra, New York Yankees" and "Mr. Lawrence P. Berra, Yoo-hoo Vice-President" respectively.

After the press conference was over, Berra made his way down to the Waldorf-Astoria Hotel to the Topps All-Star Rookie Team ceremonies. In attendance were Rusty Staub and Pete Rose, among others. The master of ceremonies was none other than his old friend Joe Garagiola. As soon as Berra entered the crowded press gathering, people jumped to their feet and gave him a standing ovation. Garagiola then goaded Berra up to the podium to say a few words.

Relaxed and confident, Berra went to the podium, turned, smiled at Garagiola, and asked, "What's new?"

Garagiola told the press, "Yogi was a wise choice, and I'll tell you why. Whatever he chooses to do, he always does well. If he decided to become an astronaut, he'd make John Glenn look as though he was in a slump. That's the kind of guy Yogi is. Even when we were little kids in St. Loo, the quality was there. I was the hot-air merchant. I talked all the time, and Yogi talked hardly at all. But whenever he spoke, he made sense—which is more than anyone could say for me."

In November, Elston Howard was honored with the American League MVP award. In an article praising him, he was quoted as saying that Berra would be an excellent manager and that the Yankees would not miss a beat.

On November 13, Berra held his first press conference as manager, announcing spring-training schedules and naming Jimmy Gleeson as the first-base coach to replace himself. Gleeson had managed in the Yankees' farm system and knew many of their younger players. Much earlier, Berra and Gleeson had met briefly at the New London submarine base, where Gleeson was a chief petty officer.

Berra's first season as manager hit a hiccup when Sain and Houk couldn't come to terms, and it was decided that Ford would serve as a player/coach for the 1964 season. Whitey would be the pitching coach—it was the first time anyone had ever asked a big-time starting pitcher to also serve as a field coach. For these double duties, Ford was handsomely rewarded with a $60,000 contract.

"I picked Whitey because he was just about the smartest pitcher I ever saw, and I know he can handle the young players," Berra told the press corps.

Ford and his wife, Joan, had just come back from a dinner in New Hampshire when Berra called him at his home in Lake Success, New York. "I was so surprised when he brought it up I didn't know what to say, so I handed the phone over to Joan and told her to talk to Yogi for a few minutes while I tried to clear my head," Ford said. "Then I got back on the phone and told him I'd like to think it over and that I'd let him know after sleeping on it. I wanted to be sure I could do two jobs. The mental angle, I mean… pitching every fourth day myself and worrying about the other pitchers the rest of the time. I decided I can do it."

However, this was probably the most questionable move that Berra made during the campaign, and the writers were quick to jump on it.

Asked if he would take himself out of a game, Ford told the crowd, "No, Yogi will still do that. He's done it for years. When he was catching and started looking toward the bench and shaking his head, I knew I was on my way."

In retrospect, the departure of Sain and the addition of Ford spoke volumes about Houk and Berra and their unfamiliarity with their new roles. To the fans and sportswriters of the times, it must have seemed like the inmates were running the asylum. Houk's dismissal of Sain's potential contributions demonstrated a degree of arrogance, and Berra's choice, with the benefit of hindsight, shouts of naiveté and inexperience.

Later in the season, a player who wished to remain unidentified told a reporter, "They took away from us the best manager in baseball. They took away the best pitching coach, Johnny Sain; the best batting coach, Wally Moses…. How do they expect us to win?"

Some surmised that Berra (and Houk) thought the move might make Ford into a more honest citizen, that coaching might force him to grow up.

The writers' suspicions about Mantle and Ford's mischief-making and its effect on the team would be well documented. In the end, unfortunately for Berra, the writers' lack of confidence proved to be well founded.

"Yogi had named Ford his pitching coach, and we were the team's senior citizens, but what the heck, we still broke a few curfews," said Mantle.

There were lots of other changes happening as well. The Yankees did not draw well in 1963, and so, for the 1964 schedule, they added more night games. The Yankees were one of the last holdouts for day games, while many other teams had already shifted the bulk of their games to night starts. Many of the Yankees' road games would be farther across the country, and many of those games would be played at night. Much more of their travel would be done by plane.

Also, the rag-tag, fledgling New York Mets, headed up by George Weiss and Casey Stengel, had drawn more than 1 million in attendance in 1963, while the Yankees had drawn 1,308,920—not a very sizable gap considering one was setting a new standard in futility and the other was a dynasty like few other franchises in sports history.

The Yankees were beginning a new era.

\*   \*   \*

In late January, it was announced that Joe DiMaggio would be returning as a spring-training coach in Florida with the team. Each year DiMaggio had been lengthening the amount of time he spent with the club in springtime, and he found hanging out with the players and coaches exhilarating. Berra, who had endured DiMaggio's icy stare and tirades, also remembered being taken to dinner by the majestic Yankees slugger when Berra was just a rookie. It was something DiMaggio often did in an effort to acclimate younger players to the big leagues.

Berra told the press before the trip south that he would not make the camp too hard. He wanted to take it easy on his veteran players. "I'm leaving Mickey entirely on his own. I don't have to play him full games at all when we start the exhibitions. Mantle was hurt in an exhibition last year.... And I'd like to give the infielders a rest, too," he said.

In the meantime, Berra kept moving on other fronts. In January he was honored at the Catholic Youth Organization's Club of Champions and presented with the Sportsman of the Year Award. And in early February, Garagiola, Berra, and Stan Musial mugged on stage at the New York chapter of the Baseball Writers Association of America dinner. Berra, Stengel, and Houk each took separate turns with speeches.

In late January, Ross Products, a general merchandise importer, announced the Yogi Berra Pitching Trainer. The three-foot-tall inflatable catcher, made from vinyl, was made "in Yogi's likeness and with his familiar No. 8 on the back and with 'Yogi Berra' inscribed on the mitt." The new item would be featured in stores across the country and would retail for $5.00.

*    *    *

As camp approached, the Yankees were heavy favorites to return to the Fall Classic. Several writers said that the Yankees had all the weapons, and with the return to even a modicum of health, unlike the year before, Berra should have a successful first campaign.

The *New York Daily News* ran a cartoon of Berra with the caption, "A cartoonist's dream! With that mug of yours, I hope y' stick aroun' forever."

When asked how the team would fare with Berra at the helm, Mantle joked, "I think we can win in spite of it."

Said Berra to one of the reporters the day before camp opened, "It's a nice job. All you gotta do is win."

In front of everyone, Berra acted with confidence and certainty, like he had been in charge for a long time. But he later admitted it was all a front. "I was too excited to sleep the night before. I had butterflies in my stomach. It was just like the beginning of the World Series or Opening Day of the season. You have the jitters until the first pitch is thrown," he said.

In his inaugural address to the team—usually done behind closed doors, but held by Berra while his troops sat down on the grass of center field at Miller Huggins Field—he listed a series of "don'ts" to his players. That was when he announced the biggest bomb of training camp—the institution of a curfew. Many of the older players complained to the press right away.

But there was no mistaking it: Berra was determined to take control of the squad lest they get too wild. And besides, being a recent player, he knew the shenanigans that went on during Stengel's and Houk's watch.

Berra also insisted on calisthenics. Nobody—not players, coaches, executives, or writers—could ever remember the Yankees experimenting with calisthenics in spring training, including DiMaggio. The camp was run with military precision. Not even the occasionally tempestuous Houk had run such a tight camp.

"Most orderly first day of training camp I ever saw," Houk admiringly told the press.

Indeed, the camp ran smoothly, but the rookie manager and his friend the rookie coach did take some time learning the ropes.

One day in March, Ford burst into the clubhouse, angry and frustrated. "I'm embarrassed, Yog. One of the kids said to me, 'Am I pitching today?' All I could do was mumble and tell him I'd let him know later on because I suddenly realized I couldn't remember who he was," said the flustered Ford. "Worse than that, he was sitting against the wall, and I couldn't peek at the number on his back. Whatcha do in a case like that?"

"Do what I done the other day," nodded Berra. "You get him up on his feet and stall until you get a peek at his number. Then you compare it against the names on your list. That's what I done with Jimmy somebody-or-other. You know the guy I mean—No. 84."

In the preseason, Berra caught up with Hank Bauer, now the manager of the Baltimore Orioles. The two had a friendly chat, after which Bauer told the press, "He's in a terrible spot. If he finishes second, they'll say he had a bad year. But if I finish second, I'm a hero."

This was true. If Berra captured a World Series flag, most would dismiss the achievement, saying that anyone could do it—it was the Yankees organization, after all. And if he finished with anything less, it would be a disaster. It was a no-win situation from the get-go, but Berra knew what he was taking on.

That season, the Yanks' only holdout was the previous year's standout, Jim Bouton. Houk and Berra knew they had to sign the right-hander, but he proved a difficult negotiator, much like Berra himself had been in previous years. In fact, Bouton's holdout angered Berra more than it did Houk, who seemed to take it all in stride.

Berra tried to appear in control at all times. When the Yankees went on a four-game losing streak during spring training, he told the press, "Sure, we're not hitting, so what? Sooner or later you know you're going to see them bust loose, so what's the worry?"

Berra had only one run-in with his players that spring. Roger Maris had tried to show up Berra after being pulled from a spring-training game. Afterward, in the clubhouse, Berra, furious, backed Maris up against the wall, asserting his authority. Maris was a model citizen as a player, and he and Berra never had any more problems after that. Indeed, through the years, Berra always claimed that Maris was among his favorite players.

The press had a field day photographing and following Berra. His stewardship of Major League Baseball's most elite team was fascinating to watch.

Leonard Koppett posited that the Yankees had hired Berra not only because he was knowledgeable, but also because Stengel and the Mets were stealing the headlines of the sports pages, taking some of the thunder away from the lordly Yankees. While management poo-pooed this notion, many sportswriters were in step with Koppett's line of thinking.

Historian David Halberstam wrote years later, "The truth is that the Yankees had made a serious miscalculation if they hired Berra because he was good with the media. Rather, the media was good with him—inventing a cuddly, wise, witty figure who did not, in fact, exist."

Stengel, of course, was complimentary toward Berra. In Koppett's article he was quoted as saying, "He's an intelligent man who may not be brilliant in school, but look how many fine, educated young fellows you've got who still can't find home plate or hit a curveball or remember the signs."

"Berra always applied himself and tended to his business," continued Stengel. "Berra studied, too, and he's made a lot of money and a good place in life, and why wouldn't he just go on and be successful doing it again in doing a new job?"

Like everyone else, Koppett questioned Berra's ability to control men he grew up with but was sure the Yankees system would help support Berra. Unfortunately, this premise proved false in relatively short order.

\*     \*     \*

On Opening Day 1964, CBS radio took out full-page newspaper ads heralding the start of a new season and a new manager. Yoo-hoo took out full-page ads with a doctored photo of Berra dressed as Yankees manager, shaking hands with a likeness of himself as the well-dressed sales executive, with well wishes for a great season from all his friends at Yoo-hoo. Unfortunately, they had to wait. The first two attempts at Opening Day were rained out.

The night before his eventual debut, his children all kissed him good-night and wished him luck. The next morning they left for school before he awoke. Carmen decided to sleep in. Berra shaved, had some eggs, and drove across the George Washington Bridge to the stadium. He arrived a few minutes before 10:00 AM.

The Yankees started the season off with a loss. Berra tried to appear as if he were not affected, telling the press, "No, I don't feel too badly…just as long as it doesn't happen too often."

Despite a standout performance by Ford, the Yankees lost 4–3 to the Red Sox after Ford's wild pitch in the eleventh helped decide the game.

In April the team went 4–4. And in May the team sputtered and stalled, finishing 17–12 for a 21–16 record heading into June.

Sometime early on, the Yankees held High School Sports Editors Day, and a young Marty Appel, future publicist for the Yankees, was a budding high school journalist.

"I asked the first question of Yogi," said Appel. "I asked what the managers talk about at home plate; I saw that he and Bill Rigney had been laughing when they exchanged lineups the night before."

The answer was classic Berra—as Appel recalls, "He said, 'We just shoot the breeze.'"

In April the team was not hitting, possibly because of all the rain delays both New York clubs had to suffer through.

It was in this period that the true nature of the club started to show, and in retrospect, a generational gap was revealed.

"Writers were prompted to compare [the Yankees] to United States Steel and IBM. The air of efficient, heartless, totalitarianism became so thick that the favorite inside joke was 'Big Brother is watchin'," wrote Koppett, no doubt a reference to the last days of Weiss and his detectives trailing players around town, looking for dirt. "In such an environment, flakes were carefully weeded out," wrote Koppett. But Bouton and Joe Pepitone (as well as Phil Linz and Stan Williams) were allowed to stay in this new world order, despite the players' various eccentricities.

The season was about to get more out of control. The young kids were looking to emulate, naturally, the likes of Mantle and Ford, the team's hard-drinking and hard-playing (on and off the field) stars. "That club would have been a test for anybody," Mantle admitted years later.

When Berra had come up, the most withering looks didn't come from the manager, but from older, more mature players who had been hardened by the Depression and the war. Lou Gehrig had schooled DiMaggio and Crosetti. In turn, they rubbed off on Tommy Henrich, Charlie Keller, Vic Raschi, Allie Reynolds, Hank Bauer, and others who policed the ranks themselves. The team leaders felt it was their duty to keep the lower rank-and-file in line. Stengel had a relatively light touch with the team regarding curfews and the like, and he had a "don't ask, don't tell" mentality. But he also knew he had a corps of dedicated players who counted on their World Series money.

On Berra's watch, where were the veterans who were supposed to keep the younger guys in line? Mantle? Ford? Their lifestyle choices were the stuff of comic legend. While they were fun teammates, by the time the leadership torch had been passed to them, they had not grown up enough to take on the mantle of responsibility within the team.

And the younger players, like Bouton and Pepitone, were brash. Pepitone followed Mantle prank for prank, beer for beer. Once, after a game, Pepitone filled Mantle's whirlpool with washing-machine detergent. The aching Mantle slipped into the hot, waiting pool, turned on the motor, and was suddenly awash in a sea of bubbles. While Mantle loved to play tricks, he could sometimes lose it when he was the butt of them, and he chased Pepitone around the clubhouse in a froth (literally and figuratively).

While pranks and late nights out have been part of professional sports lore for decades, gone was the icy, disapproving stare of a Gehrig, a DiMaggio, or a Keller. The younger guys were emulating the older guys, and the older guys were still carrying on like children.

The elder statesmen were gone. The U.S. Steel mentality was gone. If Mantle and Ford were staring at anyone, it was usually a bevy of young ladies at a bar or restaurant. They weren't telling anyone not to put their World Series money at risk. It had been that attitude of self-preservation that had kept the Yankees above so many other clubs. The needs of the players, who had to have the World Series shares, who expected that money, had been one of the backbones of the organization.

Berra was managing a good ballclub, but it was not the Yankees organization he had been brought up in. The same attitudes that were present when he was a rookie were not there to support him once he became the manager.

And perhaps more important, the players never accepted their friend being made manager. In short order, Berra's tenure had the players longing for their old manager, Houk.

"Unfortunately for Yogi," wrote baseball historian Peter Golenbock, "right from the start the players found him neither personable nor humorous, and they seemed to resent his presence as manager, preferring Houk instead... and though the season was barely underway, the players were already criticizing Yogi behind his back for leaving in his starting pitchers for too long. This backbiting continued throughout the season, and many of the players were complaining privately to Houk about Yogi's leadership, his strategy, and his faults."

Many of the players who complained were veterans, although no one has ever precisely identified Mantle or Ford. Many begged Houk to come back as the field manager.

"The general manager listened patiently—too patiently—to what they had to say, but there was little he could do, for a while," according to Golenbock. But Golenbock was not wrong to place part of the burden on Houk. Houk could have been stern with his players, telling them that this was the way it was. He could have backed Berra more, according to some sources. But he seemed to be hedging his bets, as if he never had full confidence in Berra's ability to do the job.

"I don't believe anyone could have done a better job of managing that year than Yogi. It wasn't easy because we had to contend with the presence in the front office of Houk, to whom authority came naturally. The players were fond of Berra, but they didn't fear him," Mantle related 30 years later.

Berra was cautious with his starting staff, and would have his relief pitchers warming up at the first sign of trouble. But he also kept leaving his starting pitchers in longer than he did when he was a catcher. The result was the relievers felt dissatisfied because on some days they would get up and sit down multiple times per game.

"We're going to win the pennant despite Yogi," became a running joke among the relief staff.

At one point Houk asked the dissatisfied Tony Kubek, who had been benched by Berra, if the club was getting away from Berra. Kubek answered in the affirmative.

The Yankees bounced back in June and found themselves, on June 22, in first place. But the next day was a low point. Kubek told Berra he was hurt and couldn't play. As a result, Berra decided he would realign his infield against the second place Orioles and his old friend, Hank Bauer. Berra decided to move Clete Boyer, his hard-hitting third baseman, to short, and he put Phil Linz in at third. The Yankees took a 7–2 lead. In the top of the eighth, Berra pinch hit for Rollie Sheldon, who, up to that point, had been pitching well. The pinch-hitter grounded out, helping to kill an inning. In the bottom of the inning, Berra called in Pete Mikkelsen to relieve. Mikkelsen was a ground-ball pitcher—the problem was that, according to many, Linz, though playing hard, was out of position or misplayed several balls. The Orioles climbed back into the game and won it 9–8.

The players were beside themselves. If Boyer had been at third, they would have won the game.

"The bullpen members were bitching the loudest," wrote Golenbock, "though few noticed that the statistics showed the bullpen to have a 20–7 record with 15 saves at this point."

Pepitone said after the game, "If I was manager, I'd rather see Boyer at third."

Pepitone was a wild man who was loud, outspoken, and loved to act up on the baseball diamond. He drew press no matter what city they played in.

Years later Pepitone said, "I liked Yogi as a manager. He got me to play in 160 ballgames. I used to come up to him and say, 'I don't feel good today.' He'd say, 'You're playing.' I'd say, 'Yogi, I'm sick.' He'd say, 'You're playing.' And he'd turn around and walk away.... He made me play, and I admired him." Pepitone had his best year ever under Berra, knocking in 100 runs.

"He had a perfect disposition for a player or a friend, but not for a manager. He should never have been put in that position. He was not able to be mean, and the players, at least during his first time with the Yankees, did not put out for him. He did not have enough meetings, and he did not know how to motivate. I went back for an Old-Timers' game, and it was obvious to me what the problem was," said his old friend Allie Reynolds.

The next month was an up-and-down affair, but by August 6, the Yankees were back in first place.

In an interview with Norm Miller from the *New York Daily News,* Berra that handling pitchers was the toughest part of being a manager.

"He's been booed on occasion, nearly always for staying one batter too long with a faltering pitcher," wrote Miller.

Berra said that the booing he had been hearing didn't bother him. "We've always been booed on the road. As a player, it made me bear down harder," he said. The problem for Berra was that the booing was coming at home.

And then the wheels fell off again.

For the entire month of August, the Yankees played uninspired ball, the kind that most managers can't cover up. The team was failing him. And with each loss, the backbiting became worse.

"The guys were constantly talking behind Yogi's back," Bouton said years later. "It was really terrible."

Complaints ranged from "Yogi has no tact," to "Yogi never gives you a pat on the back," to "Did you hear what Yogi said in the team meeting yesterday?"

Bobby Richardson and Kubek were the two most vocal dissenters, but much of the team followed willingly, especially the younger players, including Blanchard, Boyer, and Ralph Terry—all the guys who hated Stengel and loved Houk.

Comparing the managers, Bouton pointed out that Houk was a "master psychologist" who knew when to give a pat on the back and when to give a kick in the ass. "He had it all figured out," according to Bouton.

"I think [Berra] thought the team wanted to win as badly as he did. He was wrong. Some of them didn't play hard for him," Jerry Coleman said years later.

The little flare-ups that had plagued the team throughout the summer exploded into an out-of-control wildfire in August aboard the Yankees' bus as they traveled to Chicago's O'Hare Airport. The Yankees had just been swept by the White Sox in a four-game series at Comiskey Park, losing the last game 5–0. New York was mired in third place, four and a half games behind Chicago.

The bus was caught in rush-hour traffic, and the passengers' anger was festering. Berra and the coaches were up front. In the back, Pepitone, Mantle, Ford, Maris, Richardson, and Linz were all grouped together.

Bored and uncomfortable, Linz pulled out a harmonica and some sheet music and decided to play a tune to pass the time and lighten up the mood.

"What are you doing with that thing?" asked Pepitone.

"I'm going to play it," said Linz.

"You gotta be shitting me," said Pepitone.

"F*ck it!" responded Linz. He then proceeded to play "Mary Had a Little Lamb."

"I think Frankie Crosetti put Yogi on that track. I mean, Frankie heard the 'Mary Had a Little Lamb' coming from the back of the bus before Yogi did and said, 'Are you going to take that?'" Jerry Coleman said. "When you lose three games to the White Sox by one run, you don't play the mouth organ on the bus."

Annoyed and angry with his players, the press, and everything else that seemed to be falling down around him, Berra shouted angrily to the back of the bus, "Whoever's playing that thing, shove it up your ass!"

There are differing versions of what happened next. One version, told by Golenbock, had Linz responding to Berra, "Bullshit, man, I can play if I want to."

And another story, told by Mantle, had Linz asking, "What did he say?" and Mantle responding, "He said, 'Play louder.'"

In either case, Linz resumed the annoying children's tune. There had been bad blood between Linz and Berra because of misunderstandings earlier in the year. When the spotty harmonica sound screeched again, Berra came rushing to the back of the bus.

"You'd think you won the pennant instead of having lost four straight. I thought I told you to shove that thing up your ass!" said Berra.

It was obvious to all that Berra's control over the club was at stake. Linz tried to offer up the harmonica, but Berra swiped at it, knocking it flying from Linz's hands. The harmonica struck Pepitone on the leg, cutting his trousers, and the first baseman fell to the floor in mock injury, clutching his leg.

"I need a medic. I need a medic," howled Pepitone in mock agony. "I'll sue. My knee. My knee."

"Why are you getting on me?" Linz hollered back at Berra at one point. "I give 100 percent on the field. I try to win. I should be able to do what I want off the field."

Berra later admitted that Linz was the least of his problems that season.

But in the heat of the moment, Berra shouted at Linz, "I'll take care of you!"

Apparently, after Linz's confrontation with Berra, Crosetti then came back and also had a heated exchange with Linz. Crosetti, ever the quiet man behind the scenes, told reporters it was the worst he had seen in his 33 years in the league.

After that, Mantle picked up the harmonica and said to Ford, who was sitting across from him, "It looks like I'll be managing this club pretty soon. You can be my third-base coach. And here's what we'll do," said Mantle. "One toot, that's a bunt. Two toots, that's a hit-and-run."

The incident was the headline of almost every major newspaper across the country. The Yankees were cracking, according to some reports, and other reports had Houk flying into Boston, where the Yankees were headed, with Berra's job "in jeopardy."

"I called Houk in New York last night to tell him what would be in the papers so he wouldn't be caught by surprise," Berra told the press in Boston the next day. "He told me to do anything I felt right and that he'd back me. That's all there was to it."

Houk, who was en route to Fenway to see the series as previously scheduled, told reporters he had no intention of talking to either Linz or Berra about the incident. But there was no denying that the incident had apparently sealed Berra's fate.

Linz was fined $200. Pictures the next day showing the two sitting next to each other with smiles on their faces did little to quell the controversy.

One radio station in Boston begged fans to unofficially make it harmonica night at Fenway for the Yankees' game against the Red Sox. At the Mayor's Trophy game, against the Mets at Shea Stadium, both Linz and Berra received huge ovations when they appeared, and the Mets players threw harmonicas onto the field.

When the Yankees dropped the first two at Fenway, many in the press announced them officially dead. A 69–52 record left them six games behind the fast-paced Orioles with 41 games to play. Everyone figured them finished. But the Yankees then took the last two to split the series. The Bombers ended August with a 6–2 run. And then in September, the Yankees suddenly woke up—Berra went from a buffoon in the papers to a genius as the Yankees reeled off 22 wins against just six losses.

"It will be told over and over for years to come how the 'dead' Yankees were revived and the 1964 pennant won because the manager, Yogi Berra, got mad at Phil Linz's harmonica playing on a bus," wrote Leonard Koppett.

It now seemed that the harmonica incident had snapped the team out of its funk. Many players saw it as a wake-up call and took their standing in the league as a matter of pride.

"In our eyes, that was the first time Yogi showed all of us his leadership qualities," Mantle admitted years later. "From then on the players had more respect for Berra. They had seen his temper and believed he had drawn a line."

Mantle also wrote, "It was the turning of the tide. From then on we played great."

"I thought Yogi did a helluva job," said Ford years later. In another interview he added, "Yogi actually held the club together.... This incident proved he could be tough when he had to. He showed the rest of the team he wasn't one to back off."

As Koppett tried to remind readers, the swoon the Yankees suffered was mainly because of injuries, most notably to a monthlong resting of Ford, and that the turnaround came on the back of a young pitcher, Mel Stottlemyre, the return of the oft-injured Mantle (who had also been sidelined), and the acquisition of pitcher Pedro Ramos from the Cleveland Indians. Ramos, incidentally, was the first Cuban Yankee.

"The way Mantle forced himself seemed to make all the other players more determined, perhaps a little ashamed of themselves; the way he hit restored everyone's confidence and relaxed the other hitters," Koppett wrote.

\*     \*     \*

In the middle of their August swoon, even more news had popped up. Topping and Webb had sold controlling interest in the New York Yankees to CBS television.

"Topping and Webb had already taken tremendous profits since purchasing the club with Larry MacPhail in 1945 for $2.8 million. Two years later, they bought out MacPhail for $2 million, got that back and more when they sold Yankee Stadium and the land under it for $6.5 million in 1953. All the rest was gravy," reported *Time* magazine on August 21, 1964. "Then why sell? Easy. The gravy was getting thinner. Last year's attendance (1,308,920) was the lowest since World War II and may be heading lower this year."

According to *Time* magazine, "Yogi Berra grinned at the news."

"Gee," said the manager. "Nobody asked me to buy the club. Mickey and I would have bought it."

Some cynical writers suggested that Walter Cronkite manage the Yankees and Berra deliver the news broadcast.

One of the other frequently recounted stories from that summer occurred during a Kansas City game. In the eighth inning, Kansas City was hanging desperately to a one-run lead. The Yankees needed the series badly. Berra, nervous and pacing the dugout, called the bullpen—or so he thought.

The phone actually rang in the kitchen of a small food stand somewhere else in the stadium. "Warm up Stafford. Warm up Stafford," said Berra anxiously.

"All I got to warm up here is hamburgers," said a short-order chef. "You got the wrong number."

On September 17, the Yankees were back in first place.

"Well, we worked awfully hard to make it up to here, and we'll keep on working just as hard to stay," Berra told the press. "We've been playing good ball now, but you got to remember that this is the longest they've all been healthy and in the lineup together."

Berra praised Mantle, Maris, and Kubek for their recent play in helping lift the club. "Before, we weren't getting the hits when we needed them. Now, if one guy makes an out, another one comes through," he said.

On October 3, 1964, the Yankees clinched the American League pennant on the second-to-last day of the season with an 8–3 victory over the Cleveland Indians. Berra was lauded in the press.

"Berra, in Bubbly Bath, Heaves Sigh, Taps Ford," said the headline in the *New York Daily News.* The paper ran photos of Berra doused in champagne. *The New York Times* ran the headline, "Berra Vindicated as Tactician after Bumpy Road to the Pennant."

According to one paper, "His technical baseball judgment was invariably sound. In handling his men, he displayed three great negative virtues prized by baseball players: he didn't second-guess in private, he didn't criticize in public, and he didn't panic when things looked bad."

At one point in the season, Berra had reportedly told his players, "The world ain't come to an end yet."

Ramos was on the mound for the victory over Cleveland, and when the final out was recorded, the Yankees, led by Berra, charged out of the dugout and mobbed Ramos at the center of the diamond.

"Yogi was the center of the celebration in the champagne-splattered dressing room," reported Joe Trimble. "Berra was bathed in the bubbly, most of it poured over his balding pate by Phil Linz, the harmonica rascal who inadvertently helped turn the tide in August."

Berra's name stood beside Miller Huggins, Joe McCarthy, Harris, Stengel, and Houk as Yankee managers who had won a pennant. It was the Yankees' 29th pennant.

"Frankly, I thought we were out of it," Mantle told the press. "Back in August when we lost those four in Chicago and everything was going bad, I gave up on it all. But then we all started playing better—I don't know why —and it all came out fine…. But for me, this one has been the most exciting one of all by far. And I've been here since '51."

"It may not show outside, but it's in here," Berra said, pointing to his chest. "I mean, I been through winning before, but this being my first year and all—well, it's just good, that's all."

Macy's department stores ran a full-page ad in numerous area metropolitan newspapers, featuring a photo of an 8-ball and a tag line in big, bold letters: "You made it. We always knew you would. Because you can't keep Yogi Berra and a team like the Yanks behind the 8-ball. Congratulations to the New York Yankees and a sigh of relief from Macy's and all of New York."

\*    \*    \*

The race in the National League had been even more dramatic than the one in the American League. It was eventually won by the St. Louis Cardinals, led by manager Johnny Keane. Keane and his bunch had also won the pennant on the last day of the season, and also after being declared dead earlier in the year.

Around the middle of the season, the Cardinals and August "Augie" Busch had created a problem. Keane had been a good company man, but with a recent slide crippling the club, Busch had refused to renew Keane's contract and instead had offered a contract to Leo Durocher. This was supposed to be a secret, but it was the worst kept secret in baseball—unlike the Yankees' plans from the year before.

Busch then rescinded the offer to Durocher and offered the angered Keane (who had kept his silence) a new contract. Keane told Busch they would settle it after the Series. These conversations would have a profound affect on Berra.

Despite all of New York coming out to congratulate its newest hero, Berra was already a dead man walking. Houk, perhaps knowledgeable about Busch's double-dealings, had already reached out to Keane. The two sides had talked. Keane, before the World Series even started, knew that if he so chose, he could be the next skipper of the New York Yankees. Houk and Topping had convinced the CBS brass that Berra had to go.

For all the trumpeting of Houk's character, his toughness, and his honesty, his year as general manager working with Berra was, in retrospect, not emblematic of the man he was purported to be. In fact, he proved to be a bad general manager, a man who had risen beyond his capabilities and who proved to be both untrustworthy and somewhat less than honest.

For one thing, Berra had insisted that Stottlemyre be brought up in 1964. Houk, for his part, was trying to salt Stottlemyre away for another year, hoping to bring him up in 1965. He had resisted Berra's entreaties to rush the young, tough pitcher, but with the collapse of the bullpen and the sidelining of Ford, both the situation and Berra forced Houk's hand. Stottlemyre proved to be among the biggest difference-makers that season.

Also, Houk was never honest with Berra. Nor was he tough with the players. In fact, in the next two years, he would entertain and coddle a steady stream of disgruntled players who would insist on his return to the dugout. He would listen to them as they stroked his ego instead of tuning them out and insisting they perform. No one could have imagined going behind McCarthy's, Harris's, or Stengel's back in such an audacious manner. Houk himself would not have tolerated the rate at which the players were backbiting when he was manager. And even fewer could imagine longtime Yankees general manager George Weiss coddling such a corps of whiny stars.

"Houk never kicked those guys out of his office," Bouton pointed out. "He never said, 'Mind your own business, and get the hell out of here.'"

"Houk didn't think Yogi was a good manager. Houk never backed Yogi up. Also, Yogi had not been Houk's choice," Bouton said years later. This had been true—without telling Berra, Topping and Houk promoted Houk and Berra together without Houk's input.

"Houk wanted to get rid of Yogi so he could get his own man in there," said Bouton.

In Houk's defense, the team, as in the previous year, had been besieged by injuries to its major stars, and although no one knew it at the time, Ford's best years were already behind him.

In the meantime, Topping and Webb were more concerned with how they were being perceived by Bill Paley and CBS executives. And they were preoccupied, as any businessmen might be, by the details of a sale involving millions of dollars. In selling controlling interest in the team to CBS, Topping and Webb suddenly found themselves in a revolving series of boardroom maneuvers, and they were rankled by the restrictions placed on them now as employees, missing the freedom they'd had as independent owners.

"CBS now had the Yankees, and Topping was working for them and also trying to hold on to a job for his son," wrote Red Barber.

Berra was not well served by the triumvirate of whining players, preoccupied owners, and the unsupportive Houk. None of them were out to get the well-liked manager, but Berra happened to be caught in a vortex that would continue to chew up managers for the next 14 years, including Houk himself.

It must also be pointed out that Berra was too soft on his players for too long, allowing things to drift to the nadir it had reached with Linz. The storm was partly his own making. Had he cost his team a few games as a rookie manager? Probably. Was he shaky in the beginning? Absolutely. And his nice guy, look-the-other-way attitude certainly hurt him.

But Berra had guided his team back to the World Series, and fans and media alike were still fascinated by him. Robert Lipsyte had covered the Yankees during Berra's career, and at a party in 1964, he met fellow writer David Halberstam, who had just won the Pulitzer Prize for his reporting on Vietnam. For his part, the young Lipsyte desperately wanted to ask Halberstam about Madame Nhu, wife of the chief of secret police in South Vietnam and a woman who, after suggesting that Halberstam be set on fire, said, "I will gladly supply the fluid and the match."

But before Lipsyte could ask the award-winning writer about his harrowing time covering the war, Halberstam, a rabid baseball fan, eagerly asked, "So, what's Yogi Berra really like?"

\* \* \*

It was exciting for Berra to be playing the St. Louis Cardinals in the 1964 World Series. Berra would be going home. Friends. Family. The Hill. And to make the Series even more exciting, Garagiola was announcing on NBC with Phil Rizzuto. Jerry Coleman was also announcing the games. There was no question Berra had friends in the press box.

"It will be good to go home," Berra told the sportswriters.

"In 1964, I was broadcasting the World Series between the Cardinals and the Yankees. During the second game in St. Louis, I remember looking down at the dugout, and it really hit me: Yogi was managing the Yankees in the World Series and I was broadcasting it for NBC," wrote Garagiola years later. "That we could be the same two kids who spent so many nights sitting underneath the lamppost barely seemed possible."

Ford would pitch Game 1. Stottlemyre would pitch Game 2. Kubek was unavailable for the Series, having injured his wrist in the last two weeks of the season. Linz would have to step up in his place.

"Stottlemyre will pitch the second game, no matter what," Berra told the press. "He's a rookie, but he beat Chicago and Baltimore the first two times he pitched, so why can't he pitch in the World Series?"

Ford threw five shaky innings before he was relieved in Game 1. "Suddenly, I didn't have the strength to grab the ball," Ford wrote later. "My arm lost all of its strength. Just like that I couldn't even throw a warm-up pitch." It later proved to be circulatory problems, but the winningest pitcher in World Series history was suddenly finished.

The Cards took the first game 9–5. But Stottlemyre held his own against Bob Gibson, and the Yankees took the second game 8–3 in the newly christened Busch Stadium, with Linz chipping in a home run. The Yankees had stolen one on the road.

Game 3 was a tight affair back in New York. It matched Bouton against Curt Simmons. Simmons eventually tired in the ninth, and reliever Barney Schultz served up, in his own words, "a knuckler that didn't knuckle," which Mantle tattooed into the third deck to take the game.

In Game 4, Roger Craig faced off against Al Downing. Bobby Richardson threw a double-play ball into right field for an error, loading up the bases for Ken Boyer, who made the Yankees pay with a grand slam, and the Cards took the game 4–3. The Series was now tied 2–2.

Announcer Vin Scully once said of Game 5 pitcher Bob Gibson, who worked notoriously fast, "He pitches as if he's double parked." Gibson pitched well enough in 10 innings to win the game 5–2 on the back of a Tim McCarver three-run home run.

The Yankees had a tough task ahead of them—they now had to go to St. Louis and take two to win the Series.

Berra and Houk decided that they would keep the team in New York an extra day, instead of flying out a day in advance. "It was more comfortable this way. We've seen that park now for two games, so it won't make much difference working out there another day. It's a short flight. This way the fellows got another evening at home on Monday," Berra told a skeptical press.

Back in Busch Stadium, Berra tabbed Bouton again for Game 6. Mantle, Maris, and Pepitone all hammered homers, and the Yankees won 8–3.

The stage was now set. Could the Yankees take the final game and the Series? Game 7 would match Gibson versus the inexperienced Stottlemyre. Berra had little choice in the matter—with Ford out, it came down to Stottlemyre or Downing, and Berra chose Stottlemyre.

The first three innings it was a mano a mano affair between the fast-working Gibson and the tall, gangly Stottlemyre. But the Redbirds broke through in the fourth inning for three runs.

"Uncharacteristic Yankee miscues led to the game's first runs in the fourth inning. New York botched a sure double play, allowing the Cards to plate their first run, and St. Louis followed up with a double steal on a botched hit-and-run, with catcher Tim McCarver sliding home past Elston Howard," read one recounting of the events.

Stottlemyre eventually gave way to Downing, when Berra made a switch for a pinch-hitter, trying to get some runs. But once the Cardinals had the lead, they never relinquished it. The Cardinals took the World Series in seven games.

Trimble thundered, "The Yankees 'threw' the World Series today when they lapsed afield again…. The horrible heaves wiped out the effects of a three-run homer by Mantle."

"These were two pretty evenly matched teams," Berra told the press. "It seemed to me that every break they got they capitalized on, and every time we made an error, they scored."

Berra praised Gibson's performance, saying, "Gibson had pretty good stamina, especially after going 10 innings on Monday."

Berra had done a good job, much of it with smoke and mirrors. Ford was washed out. And Mantle, though his bat was strong, proved a liability.

"In that Series with the Cards, he was short of pitchers and had to pitch Stottlemyre on two days' rest. That seldom works," said former Yankees announcer Jerry Coleman.

"The sore-legged Mantle was a defensive liability in center field, and all Series long the Cardinals took advantage of his limited range and poor throwing by taking extra bases," wrote baseball historian Eric Enders.

"Sure it hurts. How can't it? The World Series can be real nerve-wracking, very emotional. It's unlike anything else you feel as a player, coach, or manager. When you're so close to winning, to see victory slip away—it's a terrible emptiness," Berra wrote more than four decades later.

"Baseball men compared what he had done in New York to what Gene Mauch had done in Philadelphia [where the Phillies had blown a large September lead] and concluded that Berra's lighter touch and willingness to let players find their own way was the superior job," wrote historian Halberstam. "Particularly for a team that had suffered so many injuries."

In the clubhouse, Berra said to Mantle, "Take care of those legs. We want you healthy at spring training."

"Sure, Yog. I'll see you there," said Mantle, thinking nothing of it.

On the flight back, Berra was enthusiastic nonetheless. He had won the pennant and had come within one game of winning the World Series.

Berra asked Richardson and Richardson's wife, Betsy, if they thought he should ask for a two-year extension.

"Why not?" asked Betsy. "If it hadn't been for Bobby, you'd have won the Series."

Berra then approached Ford. "Will you be my coach again next year?" Berra asked him.

"Sure, Yog," said Ford. "Thanks."

*    *    *

On October 16, 1964, the day after the World Series loss, Berra was playing golf with Eddie Lopat and Joe Collins at the Ridgewood Golf Course in New Jersey. Later he was called to a meeting, where he was fired.

"I will never forget the first time he got fired," Coleman said. "I was walking up Fifth Avenue, and I ran into him. I wasn't watching where I was going, nor was he, and we bumped."

"Did you get your two years?" asked Coleman. Coleman was going into the Yankees' offices on Fifth Avenue, and Berra was coming out.

"I got fired," Berra responded.

"Three words, but he looked like he had just lost his family," Coleman recalled.

The New York press knew of all the backbiting, but with the winning of the pennant and taking the World Series to seven games, many thought the Yankees and the Cardinals were announcing contract extensions. As it turned out, Machiavelli couldn't have scripted it any better.

At the St. Louis news conference, Johnny Keane shocked the baseball world when he told Busch he would not re-up for the 1965 season. He was officially resigning. At the Yankees conference, without Berra present, the Yankees announced Berra's firing.

"It was strange that year," Berra said. "I never heard from Houk."

"I remember it as being a totally frustrating year," Carmen related. "We had always been such great friends with Ralph and Betty Houk, but once Yogi became the manager and Ralph the general manager, Ralph no longer was Yogi's friend. Yogi suddenly was working under someone who wasn't available and wasn't communicating with him. He was kind of left out there hanging alone. But Yogi didn't feel badly about being fired because he didn't feel that badly about the job he did. He didn't think there was a good reason to fire him."

The St. Louis conference happened first, so at the Yankees' conference, when they announced that Berra had been fired, the press questioned if Keane was in the running. Houk said he didn't know that Keane had resigned. It was a lie—Houk and Keane were already in negotiations.

Berra was offered a job within the Yankees organization as a "special field consultant," though nobody knew what that meant, even the folks offering the job. It was essentially a payoff. He wasn't kicked upstairs, wagged the reporters, "he was kicked sideways."

Berra's comment to the press was, "I don't mind. I'll be spending the year at home. Where can you get a job like this? I don't have to sign in or punch a clock. And the pay is good," quipped the heartbroken manager.

It was a nonbinding offer, so that if another team approached him, he was free to accept, the 39-year-old Berra made sure to tell reporters.

Keane flew to New York straight from his resignation party, and he and Houk hammered out the agreement, then let things simmer for a day or two.

Stan Issacs, who had a column in *Newsday*, wrote of Houk after Keane's hiring, that he was giving him an award: "It is for the number one charlatan, mountebank, boob, quack, fop, fraud, and ass of the sporting panorama."

Many reporters questioned whether Houk could be accused of tampering, since it appeared he had approached an employee of another baseball franchise while they were under contract. While it would seem that they were indeed right, no hard evidence could be found to support it.

"In retrospect, he [Berra] couldn't win," wrote Koppett in *The New York Times*. "Whatever went wrong would be his fault in the minds of his players. If a man didn't hustle, didn't stay in shape, didn't find his own way out of a slump, it was Berra's fault for not making him do it; if anything turned out right, the players believed, it was because they were good enough to overcome the handicaps put in their path."

"The Yankees brass felt Berra had lost disciplinary control of the ballplayers, if he ever had it. When he took the job, he had been warned of the inherent weakness involved: trying to clamp down on players he had been a teammate of, a buddy of," wrote sportswriter Dick Young.

"Yogi Berra wasn't fired by the Yankees brass," wrote Trimble in the *Daily News*. "His own players, both the good boys and the playboys, pulled the rug out from under him. It was one of the most bizarre byplays in baseball history."

Richardson and Kubek told the brass flatly they would not return under Berra.

And Howard told the press, "The man can't control these guys."

"Swimming-pool high jinks at night in Hollywood and vivid parties in Chicago and its suburbs, plus individual rule-breaking led to a *la dolce vita* clique on one hand and a group of serious-minded athletes on the other," observed Trimble.

Trimble continued, "Actually, the winning of the pennant embarrassed the front office, in the sense that it made firing the loveable Yogi more difficult. In sum, the players burned the candle at both ends, and Yogi wound up getting seared."

"Firing Berra was a terrible stroke of public relations," wrote Golenbock.

"I thought Yogi got screwed," said Ford years later. "You know, everybody counted us out of the pennant race after we blew the series with the White Sox in late August. But we played like crazy in September and made it. Yogi was a good baseball man. He deserved to stay."

In another interview, Ford said, "The dumbest thing the Yankees ever did was fire Yogi Berra."

"I still can't believe it," Mantle said more than 30 years later. "No matter what anyone else said, I enjoyed playing for him. And I know he deserved a whole lot better than he got."

The Yankees' offices were flooded with mail, and all the letters were very much against the firing. There were countless "Letters to the Editors" in almost every newspaper in the area. But the one that stood out was from Donald Stanton, of Great Neck, Long Island, who wrote, "Inasmuch as many of the Yankee ballplayers were injured frequently during the season, I think that Mr. Berra did an exceptional job of leading the club to the American League pennant. The firing of Berra was a great mistake, and I hope and think the Yankees will pay the consequences in the coming years."

Stanton had no idea of how right he would be. Keane accepted the job and was fired in a year and a half. Houk returned and fared no better, and the Yankees went into an 11-year downward spiral.

"It's a good bet," Berra remembered, "that Del Webb, one of the co-owners of the Yankees, was in on my getting fired. I do know that when Webb died, he told the doctor who was with him that when he saw me, he should tell me that he made an error.... He was a good doctor. He said I should take an aspirin a day. He told me that in 1952. Some of them are just saying it now."

That was as close to an apology as Berra ever got from the three men who prematurely ended his first managing career with the Yankees.

"After a few days passed, I couldn't resist," admitted Ford. "I called Yogi at home. 'You still giving me that job, Yog?'"

# ~ Chapter 17 ~

# THE NEW YORK METROPOLITANS

Joe Garagiola has said, "Ballplayers always say, 'I'd rather be lucky than good.' Yogi is both."

If there was such a thing as luck or good fortune, Berra seemed to have it in spades, though he might not have known it at the time. What nobody knew for sure then was that the Yankees were about to descend into baseball oblivion, and the Mets were about to ascend to the top of the sport. No man would have any luck turning around the Yankees while they were still owned by CBS. And the Mets were about to go from Gotham's underdogs to its shining stars. Berra would have a front seat. Sometimes getting fired is a good thing.

On October 30, 1964, headlines blared across sports sections: "Berra Gets Bid from Mets" read one. "Berra Considers Job with Mets after Talking with Weiss" screamed another.

"Yogi Berra a Met? What could be more wonderful?" read the first line of Joe Trimble's article for the *New York Daily News*.

"I talked with Yogi on the phone," Mets general manager George Weiss said. "He is going to Pinehurst [North Carolina] on a golfing vacation and will think things over. I contacted him after a mutual friend said he would be interested."

The funny thing about the early Mets is that they were more show than baseball. And that show was being run by two ex-Yankee masterminds—Weiss and Casey Stengel. Most Mets fans were baseball lovers whose original teams, the Dodgers and Giants, had left for the West Coast. The Mets seemed to attract anyone who didn't want to root for the Yankees. Ex-Yankees, it seemed, were welcomed—as long as they were colorful.

The baseball world was so shocked by the Yankee firing, and fans were in such outrage, that Ford Frick, the baseball commissioner, called Ralph Houk to make sure the Yankees would honor their commitment to Berra and that he would be free to go, no strings attached. While Frick put on a good face in public and said he asked Houk, in fact he told Houk how things would be. Frick's office, too, had received dozens of letters regarding the bungled public-relations disaster brought about by Berra's abrupt dismissal.

Many in the press felt "the reuniting of Berra and Stengel would be virtually certain to give the Mets a one-two punch at the box office."

The more Berra delayed, the more the papers wrote columns about what he might do, drawing more and more attention in the press to the already popular Mets. Reports were filed here and there. Had there been a Berra sighting? Berra flew home from Pinehurst, and after staying home one night, he was flying to Chicago. This stimulated more rumors and interest.

Had he committed to the Yankees? The Mets? Someone else?

"Not that I know of," Berra responded when one reporter asked him if he had signed anything.

In truth, Berra had talked to a great number of people and had received a number of offers. Al Lopez, manager of the Chicago White Sox, had called him. Gil Hodges of the Washington Senators had also extended an offer to join his bench as a coach. And Red Schoendienst, who had taken over the Cardinals from Keane, was looking for a coach in St. Louis.

But on November 17, Berra became a New York Met. For the first time in 20 years, he would wear a uniform other than that of the New York Yankees. He signed a two-year contract worth $40,000 per year. He was tagged to be a player/coach.

Not only would he collect a salary from the Mets, but he also received a $25,000 payout from the Yankees for services rendered. It was a small, pitiful gambit by the Yankees to mollify public opinion after dumping their much-loved former pilot.

The Mets made a great show of Berra's hiring, thumbing their proverbial noses at their crosstown rivals. Berra was chauffeur-driven in Weiss's Cadillac by Weiss himself. Few other coaches ever received a press conference. He mugged for photographers on the dais as Donald Grant, the Mets' chairman of the board, helped him with his coat.

The press conference was a zoo. Reporters packed the conference room. They tried to teleconference in Stengel, who was in California, but as was typical of the Mets organization at that time, Stengel was cut off three times. They finally decided to forgo the Old Professor's participation. Reporters joked that the Yankees were trying to tamper with the line. The crowd laughed. No matter, because Berra was the show.

Reporters wanted Berra's side of the story. He tried taking the high road whenever possible. He insisted he wanted to manage again some day. It was assumed by many that when he took the job he was being groomed to manage when Stengel left, or sometime thereafter.

"Right after the World Series, when I wasn't rehired, it was a blow," Berra said of Yankees firing. "But all clubs make changes, and they wanted to make a change, so I understood that."

One can only imagine Berra pacing the fairways of Pinehurst, continuing to question the decision and trying to grasp how a manager who had come that close to winning a World Series could be fired. There is no doubt he must have been replaying the year's events over and over in his mind. His body may have been in Pinehurst, but his heart undoubtedly must have been in the cement-and-cinderblock hallways of Yankees Stadium.

Berra commented, "After a while, a lot of people told me, 'Why don't you go with the Mets?'—writers and so forth—and so I called Casey in California. I had other offers too—I won't mention the clubs—to be a coach and a player, but I wanted to stay in New York because I consider that my hometown now."

"Do you feel you took a scupping from the Yankees?" shouted one reporter.

"No, I don't feel that way. I have no regrets. I was very happy with the Yankees," he replied.

When asked about possibly returning as a player, Berra responded, "I'll go to spring training and get in shape."

In one article, Dick Young cited Berra's last year as a player/coach with the Yankees, when he hit .293 with eight home runs. "If he can approximate that with the Mets, he would win the Rambler awarded annually to their best player," he wrote.

"The main thing was that I didn't want to give up being in uniform, in contact with all the ballplayers and with you writers, instead of off in the stands at some other game," Berra continued, discussing his decision. "My wife, Carmen, and my boys felt the same way, that I belong down on the field. Right now I'm only going to be a coach, but if I do want to manage again, I'm under a good man in Casey. I learned a lot from him in 10 years, and I can learn a lot more."

A couple of weeks later, Houk, out to defend his decision and the Yankees' organization, appeared on WABC-TV with Howard Cosell, Leonard Koppett of *The New York Times,* Dick Young of the *New York Daily News,* and Joseph Reichler of the Associated Press. Houk was eviscerated. Cosell labeled the episode of the show, "The Cold, Cold Yankees." Stated one report, "Houk looked like he had been through an ordeal, rather than the usual TV interview picnic and, if anything, confirmed rather than refuted the program's title."

A few weeks later, Mel Allen was let go and Garagiola was signed by the Yankees to be the lead broadcaster in the game's most well-known and important job—home broadcaster for the New York Yankees. With Stengel and Berra gone, the Yankees lacked color. The Bombers brass thought Garagiola could help infuse the booth with a looser style that might prove more entertaining. Whether anyone liked to admit it or not, this would influence Yankees broadcasts for the next 40 years. From then on, the Yankees announcers were always more conversational than, say, the Mets announcers, who reported the game. Later, when Phil Rizzuto ascended to the booth, he would take this chattering style to a whole new level.

*    *    *

Spring training with his new team went quietly for Berra. By March 2, 1965, Berra was in Mets camp working out the catchers, while Stengel spun yarns for the Florida faithful. Berra then managed against Warren Spahn in an intrateam game, losing 1–0. Stengel had scripted the game decisions, so not much needed to be done.

The Mets opened the spring-training season with—what else?—a loss. In the fifth inning, Stengel dramatically stepped outside the dugout and waved his arms to first-base coach Berra. Berra went up to the plate as a pinch-hitter. He swung wildly at two pitches, took two balls, and then flailed at a third.

Spahn and Berra were teamed up in a battery in mid-March against the world champion St. Louis Cardinals. It might have proved almost too embarrassing for Berra, but he and Spahn kept St. Louis honest while losing 4–3. These were largely promotional stunts the Mets pulled, hoping to find one magic season left in some old veteran's body or at least to put a few fannies in the seats—as Berra and Spahn were still big names.

"It felt strange to be up there," said Berra. When asked what the toughest thing a catcher his age had to do was, he responded, "Bend down."

A game between the Mets and Yankees was predictably the emotional highlight of the spring-training season. As Berra took the field, Keane, Houk, and Stengel all stayed in their respective dugouts, while the rest of the Yankees team came over and hugged their former teammate. There was great applause. And this was before batting practice. His former teammates razzed him about his glove, and chats about friends and family ensued behind the batting cage. Spahn joined in on the act, and he, too, was warmly greeted by the Yankees players.

Asked why he had not spoken with Keane, Berra responded, "What do you want me to do, go over and punch him in the nose?"

While coaching first base, as usual, Berra chatted nonstop with Joe Pepitone and everyone else. At the plate, he continued to struggle with his bat. When the Mets trimmed their squad, he was not activated, but he remained a coach. He had gone 0-for-6 in Florida.

Still, Berra remained popular with the press, and when polled for his opinions on the upcoming season, he was unabashedly a Yankees rooter, telling anyone who would listen that the Orioles would not challenge and that the Yankees were still the class of the American League. He picked them to go all the way and hoped for them to win the pennant. He said he would always root for them, as long as they were in the other league. He remained a Yankee at heart.

On Opening Day at Shea Stadium, the only time Yogi Berra received applause was when he lifted a piece of torn banner from the field of play, a far cry from his days as a beloved Yankee.

By May 1, 1965, Berra was again an activated player and was inserted into the lineup to pinch hit in Cincinnati against the Reds. It was the eighth inning, with two out and a man on. This was where Berra, in his heyday, excelled. But the 40-year-old Berra grounded weakly to first.

In 1965, in a two-week period, Berra played in four games. He got up to bat nine times and reached safely twice, for a batting average of .222. He scored one run and had three strikeouts. On May 11, 1965, he retired again, this time for good.

"Yogi, even here, had one night of glory. A week ago, he caught Al Jackson against the Phils. He got his only two hits. He scored the winning run. Yogi knew it was an illusion," wrote Dick Young.

Berra had caught the whole game, and many were impressed. One newsman called his performance "brilliant."

Might he make a comeback?

"I'm an old man," Berra said, smiling.

"It's hard for me to see the ball," he said later. It was official. His career as a player was over. He only needed to wait for the call from Cooperstown.

Meanwhile, across town with the Yankees, the team was already having trouble by mid-May, and some of Berra's strategies and decisions from the previous season were being hailed as the right moves. Berra had reduced Mickey Mantle's role, resting the oft-injured star as much as possible to keep him healthy, and he had insisted that Mantle play first base whenever possible. But Keane was insistent that Mantle go back to the outfield. As a result, Mantle was already breaking down, and Keane was rethinking Mantle's role. Tony Kubek, who had complained bitterly when Berra had benched him when he was not healthy, was now healthy and playing poorly. Clete Boyer, whom Berra had benched for Phil Linz, was also dreadful. And Stan Williams, whom Berra had rejected out of hand, was dropped by Keane as well in spring training.

On July 25, Stengel was unable to manage the team, as he had broken his hip in a fall and had to be taken to the hospital. Berra suffered a personal defeat when Stengel nominated Wes Westrum to be the interim manager. But the whispers behind the throne were that the Mets' inner circle did not want Berra to take an interim spot because it might take away from his eventual promotion to manager. But this would prove not to be the case.

Another emotional moment for Berra came on July 31, 1965, when he returned to Yankee Stadium for an Old-Timers' game.

"When Yogi Berra was introduced, the thunderous applause had inescapable overtones because just a few minutes before, Johnny Keane, the present Yankee manager, had endured a distinct portion of boos among the cheers for him," said one report. "Evidently these were people whose baseball emotion was committed to a glorious Yankee past. Apparently the dismissal of Yogi still rankles, and the collapse of the current Yankee team is pushing Keane inexorably into a scapegoat role."

By the end of August it was apparent that Stengel could not physically continue as manager, and that his "Amazin' Mets" would have to move on without him. Westrum remained interim manager for the rest of the season. Stengel, in his farewell, put in a plug for Berra, saying, "Mr. Berra did a good job as Yankees manager last year. Anyone which wins a pennant had to do a good job."

Westrum had never managed in the pros, while Berra had taken a team to a World Series. This made Westrum anxious anytime he was with the famous and accomplished Berra the rest of the season.

The newspaper columns were filled with musings on who the rightful manager should be—Berra, Westrum, or maybe Eddie Stanky. Even Leo Durocher was mentioned in passing. Many thought that Berra would have been Stengel's choice, but apparently the Old Professor remained mute on the subject.

Westrum was announced the winner of the Mets managing sweepstakes on November 18, 1965. Weiss cleaned the coaching staff out, except for Berra, who was the only other staff member to remain. Westrum and Weiss picked a new staff, and Westrum was given a one-year contract. The press was puzzled by the move. And Stanky left to be the manager of the White Sox.

The press figured that Berra would run out his contract and consider his options. In the meantime, the Mets used Berra for publicity, making sure he showed up at important signings and events, using his star power to front the fledgling organization.

In reality, Westrum was hired because they felt he was a lame duck from the start. To bring Berra in with no real players in sight would have been a waste. So Westrum was the sacrificial body on the pyre that was the smoldering Mets team. In essence, Westrum was expendable. In the New York sports world, Berra was not.

Berra was still doing promotions and advertising. In May 1965, Baird Chemical Industries hired Berra to pitch its new chemical, sorbitol—a sugar substitute often used in diet foods, diet drinks, and sugar-free chewing gum. Baird paid Berra $1,000 just to stand near large, branded chemical drums. Said a company spokesman, who confessed the chemical giant was trying to humanize itself, "After all, Yogi Berra is almost a byword for dependability."

\*    \*    \*

During spring training in 1966, Berra was always the first coach out on the field. At 11:00 AM sharp he would yell, "Hitters!" He was an everyday coach now. He stayed in shape during the season largely by pitching batting practice. Berra was the man in charge of running the camp and he ran it by stopwatch, as he had his Yankees camp. Every batter got 30 swings. He rotated squads of catchers. He consulted his watch regularly, running his players through their drills.

"[Ken] Boyer, [Eddie] Bressoud, infielders, take three swings each!" he shouted.

Berra joked with the press, saying it was the first time in Florida in 20 year where he didn't have to run.

The Mets lacked an everyday catcher. He told the press, "A baseball team without a number one catcher is like a football team without a quarterback." He also complained that his golf game was suffering that spring training.

In April, Westrum was ailing with the flu, and Berra took over for a brief period. On April 29, Berra notched his first National League win, managing the Mets to a 5–2, come-from-behind win against the Pirates.

According to several reports, "Yogi's success hastened Westrum's recovery, and Wes accompanied the team on its futile bus ride to the ballpark this afternoon" to what was eventually a rainout.

By May 7, Keane was gone, and Houk had resumed control of the faltering Yankees club. In many recountings by sportswriters, Berra received vindication again for his turn at the helm.

In January 1967, he was given the William J. Slocum Memorial Award by the New York chapter of the Baseball Writers Association for "long and meritorious service to baseball." Previous winners had included Tom Yawkey, Al Lopez, Weiss, Stan Musial, Horace Stoneham, Stengel, Frick, and other giants of the game. The dinner was a who's who of baseball, as usual. Throughout the evening, many Yankees jokes and stories were told. Houk and Stengel were lampooned, among others.

On May 31, 1967, Ford retired, and he and Berra played on the Old-Timers team together at Yankee Stadium that summer. The Yankees' old-timers beat the Mets' old-timers 12–8. In July, Berra was reunited with Linz when the Mets made a trade for him with the Phillies. Several promotional pictures were shot of Linz and Berra, now in their Mets uniforms, posing as Berra covered his ear and Linz blew into a harmonica.

Later that month, by a fluke of substitution, an ejection, and injury, the Mets were without a catcher in the seventh inning in a game against Los Angeles. The 42-year-old Berra walked up to first-base umpire Ed Sudol and pleaded, "Let me catch for two innings."

"No chance," replied the shocked Sudol. "It takes 24 hours to get activated by the commissioner. If you do that, though, you can catch all nine innings."

In the bar of the Hilton Hotel in Los Angeles in late July 1967, Westrum and Berra were sitting down when a fan came up and asked Berra for an autograph for his son.

The man then asked Berra as he handed back the autograph, "Is the guy next to you anybody?" Westrum fumed.

At 40½ games back, Westrum knew his time had come, and he quit.

Again, Berra's part-time stewardship was seen as a possible "kiss of death," according to Donald Grant. Salty Parker was designated as interim manager.

"The selection of Parker raised some eyebrows since Berra already has had experience as a manager," wrote sportswriter and author Joseph Durso. "The Mets conceded that they were avoiding any designation for Yogi now precisely because he was a candidate for the manager's chair."

"His elevation now," said Bing Devine, the man who had succeeded Weiss as general manager, "might take on undo significance."

But in October 1967, Berra was passed over again for the permanent manager spot in favor of Gil Hodges. Hodges was 10 times the baseball man Westrum was, with all due respect, but local writers were at a loss as to why the Mets would go out to get Hodges when Berra sat waiting in the bullpen.

Was there a prejudice against Berra somewhere in the organization? Neither Weiss nor Devine, who both had opportunities to promote him, ever did. Maybe they thought he needed seasoning. Maybe they thought he was incompetent. Regardless of the reasoning, Berra would have to wait quietly for his chance again. Berra was waiting for his chance to manage—but he wanted it to be in New York, and he was willing to wait, banking on the fact that someday someone would come knocking.

Hodges hired all new coaches, but he didn't have a choice where Berra was concerned. Berra was on his staff whether he liked it or not. Luckily, Hodges liked and respected Berra. The two had been friendly during their playing days.

Berra was told by Devine publicly, "The board of directors loves you and wants you to stay with the Mets as long as your health permits."

This situation prompted a long, penetrating, and insightful column in *The New York Times* about Berra titled "Nobody's Fool." In it, Robert Lipsyte painted a picture of Berra sitting idly by, watching other men take his job, and wondering aloud why he was being sidelined. What was in it for Grant? What was in it for Berra?

Lipsyte posited that Grant made the deal to bring Hodges back to New York in an effort to bring back a little Dodgers/Giants glory. In Lipsyte's article, Grant was a Machiavellian character—if he could buy off Berra and bring in Hodges, then he could add more image to the team and not have to worry about suffering the ignominy of firing Berra.

Per Lipsyte, "Berra was a splendid ballplayer in his youth, albeit foulmouthed, suspicious, and sometimes nasty." But the journalist intimated that Berra had become hostage to his image. The media had "spun a cotton-candy legend about a dumb and loveable child-man. The legend grew and was sustained and had nothing to do with the Berra who grew older, more confident, who matured and mellowed."

"At 42, Berra is often pleasant, patient, and concerned with ways to make money for his family. He had enough pride, at the end of the 1964 season, to leave the Yankee organization rather than being demoted from manager," wrote Lipsyte. But Berra didn't have enough pride to leave in 1965 when the Mets passed him over. And he didn't leave again this time.

"I'm very satisfied. If I left, y'know, it woulda cost me money to move to another city, and I saved that," Berra said.

What was Berra's endgame? What was Grant's endgame? Berra had been a shrewd and tough negotiator during his contract negotiations. Berra told Lipsyte, "I probably would have said no anyway if something came along. What the hell, I'm still young, right?"

Berra was waiting for a New York job. And if Grant was willing to pay enough to keep him, then he would bide his time. He would sit through other men's press conferences, and he would wait. An unemployed jester is nobody's fool, and Yogi Berra was nobody's fool.

Grant and Berra had both made their deals with the devil—and each other.

\*     \*     \*

Meanwhile, the circus air of Mets camp quickly dissipated, and Hodges started the toughest Mets camp in history. Where Stengel had loaded the team with celebrities and played master of ceremonies and clown, and Westrum had little skill to keep it going, Hodges desperately wanted to win. The change happened overnight. He was soft-spoken, quiet, friendly, but absolute in his authority. It was to be his way, the work was going to be hard, and they were going to accomplish something. The players were exhausted but happy for the change.

In the spring, the Mets brought in a young pitcher named Nolan Ryan.

"He throws harder than Allie Reynolds or Sandy Koufax. His fastball rises like Vic Raschi's. When he pitched against the St. Louis Cardinals this spring, he was faster than anybody," Berra said in one *New York Times* article.

Over the years, Ryan and Berra would remain friendly, with Ryan quipping about his old coach, "If Yogi had gone to college, they would have made him talk clearer, but not better."

Hodges took a corps of players that season—including Eddie Kranepool, Ken Boswell, Cleon Jones, Ron Swoboda, Jerry Koosman, Gary Gentry, Tom Seaver, Tug McGraw, Buddy Harrelson, and Jerry Grote—and cast them into one of the brightest spotlights in the major leagues.

In 1968, the Mets finished with 73 wins—a single-season record for victories in the club's history. By that time, there was already a new handful of colorful stories about Berra. The most famous occurred when Swoboda, mired in a hitting slump, tried to change his stance to be more like that of Frank Robinson. Swoboda was trying to crowd the plate, and Berra scoffed, "If you can't copy him, don't imitate him."

Baseball was changing, but for Berra, the more things changed, the more they stayed the same. Joe DiMaggio was still coaching in spring training, but now, in 1968 and 1969, he was doing it for the Oakland Athletics, not the New York Yankees.

And Bobby Hofman, Berra and Garagiola's childhood friend, the nephew of Circus Solly Hofman and a career utility infielder, continued to show versatility later by doubling as a coach and traveling secretary for budget-minded Charles O. Finley and the Oakland A's. He held that job from 1969 to 1970 and in a second stint in 1974–78.

George Selkirk, Berra's old manager in the minors, was a minor league coordinator for the A's and Orioles. In 1962 he became the Senators' general manager and later added the title of vice president. He returned to the Yankees as a scout in 1970.

The Mets would go on to have a phenomenal year in 1969, and Berra was a part of it.

"There weren't too many days that went by when something he did or said didn't have us laughing," wrote Art Shamsky, an outfielder on that team.

Shamsky recalled that Berra threw batting practice. "Except his batting practice was awful. It was slower than slow. I recall one time complaining about it. He told me, 'Go complain to a coach.'"

*   *   *

To say it was an improbable year would be an understatement. They caught the Cubs, who suffered one of the greatest collapses in baseball history, and surprised everyone by beating the Braves in the playoffs. Against all odds, the Mets went to the World Series.

"Now I've done it all. I've played, managed, and now will coach in a World Series. I've done it all. That is all, isn't it?" Berra told the press.

After dropping the opener to the powerful Baltimore Orioles, the Mets won the World Series by taking the next four straight. Yogi Berra was in the big show yet again. He took part in every game.

"I never saw any team play the way this team played," Berra told the press. The celebration went on and on. Berra was on a winner again.

Only one newspaper wrote a column about Berra that fall. A good question might be why anyone might write about a first-base coach five years removed from his last managing job on the eve of the most surprising run in baseball history. But Berra was always a story.

"No Yankee triumph had ever been sweeter," wrote Leonard Koppett of Berra's pennant-winning night back in 1964. "He was aware he might not ever have a chance at another one. But neither Yogi nor anyone could imagine at that moment that five years later he'd be standing in the first-base coaching box at Shea Stadium, part of the Mets and of a triumph incomparably greater.... And I can't help remembering that the Yankees haven't won anything since."

Neither would the Mets. Not in 1970 or 1971. The Mets played well, but not well enough.

*   *   *

In West Palm Beach on April 2, 1972, coming back from playing 18 holes of golf, Rube Walker, Eddie Yost, Joe Pignatano, and Hodges were walking toward their hotel. It was Easter Sunday. Suddenly, Hodges collapsed. He had suffered a massive heart attack. It was surmised he never knew what hit him; he was likely dead before his body even hit the ground. Hodges was only two days shy of his 48th birthday. His death shocked the baseball world and threw the Mets organization into a wild spin.

Hodges's funeral was on Opening Day of the baseball season, which happened to be postponed due to a players' strike. The Mets organization was supposed to be in Pittsburgh. Instead, it was in rainy, cold, gray New York for the funeral. The famous and the fans crowded the sidewalks. All of New York baseball turned out for Hodges.

Many of the Dodgers greats and former teammates were there, including Don Newcombe, Jackie Robinson, Pee Wee Reese, Carl Erskine, Carl Furillo, and Sandy Koufax, to name a few. Mets and Yankees players and executives also came to pay their respects.

"Gil's coaches sat near the front—Rube Walker, Joe Pignatano, Eddie Yost, and Yogi Berra. Perhaps all of them shared Yogi's knowledge that he had been selected to move into Gil's office," wrote columnist Red Smith.

As the mourners left, Smith pointed out, large gangs of Little Leaguers, wearing the team's colors, crowded the church doors, oohing and ahhing as the players walked by. "Little cheers kept going up, unexpected at a funeral, but somehow good to hear," concluded Smith.

Berra happened to be in Miami when Grant called to ask him to come and visit him in his winter home in Hobe Sound, Florida, abut 40 miles north of Palm Beach. Berra made the drive, and the two men talked.

On April 6, 1972, six and a half years after leaving the Yankees, Berra was back as a manager. Because of the circumstances of his ascension, the mood could not have been more somber at the press conference called to announce his stewardship, and his elation could not have been more tempered.

Carmen told her husband that she thought the job would be a giant headache. And Garagiola reminded him that there was only one sure thing about becoming a manager, and that was being fired.

Still, publicly, Carmen was encouraging. Berra had played his waiting game with Grant and the other New York executives. He had earned the right to do it one more time and show them his previous success with the Yankees had not been a fluke.

Of the promotion, Berra spoke only briefly and quietly, in even tones. "Naturally, I am honored that I was chosen for the job by Mrs. [Joan] Payson and Mr. Grant, but, of course, not at the way the job became open. We left a great man today, and I only hope I can fill his shoes. Gil brought this club along perfectly in spring training, and I think we have a winner," he said.

Berra told the press that he had never been promised the Mets job at any time during his career with the team, but added, "Naturally, I thought about it when that happened to Gil."

Berra signed a two-year deal.

Journalist Arthur Daley was appalled at Grant and the Mets hierarchy. How could they attend a funeral in the morning and schedule a press conference in the afternoon? The headline to Daley's piece, "What Was the Hurry?" was a scathing indictment of the Mets organization and baseball, and it was Daley at his best.

He wrote, "It was a sad day that belonged in its entirety to the memory of the man who had won the admiration and affection of Met fans, Met players, and Met hierarchy. That's what gave the business-as-usual announcements of the news conference a lack of sensitivity that seemed shameful."

Daley went on to point out that the news conference announcing Berra's ascension could have been held a day later and could have been covered without some of the heaviness. The conference seemed to take away from Hodges's memory and was, in Daley's opinion, "tactless."

To say almost everyone had doubts about the new manager was an understatement.

"Yogi was in charge, but every manager has his own mind," Koosman said later. "The same guy wasn't making decisions anymore. And yet, no matter who the manager was, every player was trying to live up to what Gil expected of you. It didn't make any difference who the manager was, whether it was Yogi or someone else. Those would have been big shoes to fill."

"How qualified is Yogi to succeed a man who had preeminent qualifications? It's a good question although it doesn't have a ready answer. One thing that is certain is that Berra is now far better qualified than when he was lifted from the ranks to become Yankees manager for the 1964 season," wrote Daley.

The Mets players had been around Berra for some time but were not sure what to expect of him as the man in charge.

"The Berra legend was already a quarter century in the making, and it came with a full complement of malaprops and apocryphal stories. But those who knew him knew that much of the Yogi Berra legend was the product of newspapermen," wrote baseball historian Donald Honig.

But many of the players came around to Berra.

"Yogi is a very shrewd man, an excellent baseball man," Buddy Harrelson once said. "Someone might laugh at the way he talks, but we don't."

Linz told the press around that time, "I think the Mets will win the pennant with Yogi. He is a good strategist and an excellent judge of pitchers, and he does not panic."

"Yogi was always a very positive person and easygoing. It just took a lot to make Yogi mad. Yogi was a player's manager," said Koosman.

The first thing that really made some kind of difference, good or bad, was the addition of the big-hitting Rusty Staub, who joined the Mets after being traded from the Montreal Expos for three top prospects. Whitey Herzog, the head of the farm system, had felt that the trade for Staub was too costly, but Hodges and Grant liked proven veterans rather than youth.

They also brought up a promising young pitcher named Jon Matlack, of whom Hodges had thought highly. So did Berra. And Matlack rewarded Berra's faith in him with a 15–10 record and a National League Rookie of the Year award.

"Yogi had been a coach on the staff, and when we came back, he was the manager," Matlack said later. "Yogi was good people. Yogi was more of an even-keeled guy than anybody I've ever seen. He was the type of manager who said, 'Here are the bats and balls, guys, here's the lineup. Go do your stuff.'"

Matlack also remembered a funny incident from the years when Berra was managing. They got off the plane, and Berra had to make a stop at the men's room. He told Matlack to make sure the bus didn't leave without him.

"When he got to the bus, his pants were soaking wet. Everyone was sort of laughing and said, 'Hey, Yog, what happened?'"

"You won't believe what happened to me," Berra exclaimed.

"Apparently, he had gone into the restroom and was standing there going to the bathroom, and somebody came in next to him and was going to the bathroom as well, and he looked over at Yogi and realized who he was, and he turned around toward him and said, 'Hey, you're Yogi Berra,' and he peed all over Yogi's leg!" recalled Matlack.

Berra and the Mets won their first game of the season after the strike ended, and as Berra was sitting in his office after the game, a call came through. It was Stengel.

"Hiya, Casey. It was easy, just like you said. Yes, they did a good job today. What's that? You saw it on TV in Glendale? And the boys looked terrific to you? Right. And tell Jim Fregosi he did a fine job at third, and the coaches were tremendous too? I got it—thanks, Case."

The reporters said he was grinning from ear to ear. And then Berra said, "He still doesn't let you get in a word."

The Mets went 14–7 by May 12, 1972. They were off to a solid start.

On May 4, 1972, Berra received news he did not want to hear. His brother John, who lived in Nutley, New Jersey, and who had managed a bowling alley for Berra, died after a battle with cancer. It was not a sudden loss, but it was not easy to take. It was another of his immediate family who had passed on in recent years. John's health had weighed on Berra's mind. Now, sadly, that burden was over.

\* \* \*

The other new addition to the Mets was Willie Mays. His return to New York was the story of the summer. The Mets had stolen a page from the floundering Yankees' playbook yet again by completing a trade with the San Francisco Giants.

On May 11, 1972, Mays said returning to New York was like "coming back to paradise."

The Mets had long-range plans for Mays and discussed them openly. "He can be helpful to us, and we visualize him doing the same thing Yogi did," said Grant. "We're hopeful Willie will help this year and maybe even next.

We've assured him of his baseball future, and I personally hope he is here the rest of his life."

Mays, smartly, turned and said to the press, "That's Yogi's department, man. I'm here as a player now and ready to go to work any way Yogi wants to use me."

Berra spoke up, saying that Mays would "help me in two positions—first base and outfield."

"Yogi and I can get together, and I know I can help this club. You know, the Mets are a very good ballclub, and they're not going to have me playing just because I'm Willie Mays," the slugger said.

Mays admitted he hadn't gotten back into playing shape yet, but he thought he could do it quickly enough, adding, "But, as I said, it's all up to Yogi. I know I can help this ballclub."

Years later Mays said when he knew that Berra was going to be his manager, it was another reminder of his first years in New York. He was genuinely excited.

If Staub and Mays could stay healthy for the year, the Mets could be a force to be reckoned with. And that's pretty much how it went. Mays started off hot, and Staub was also doing well, batting over .300. Combined with a young and aggressive pitching staff, the Mets were potent.

"It was a storybook moment," New York sports editor Ken Samelson said. "In one of [Mays's] first games, he hits a home run to win a game against the Giants. And then the Mets got hot after that for a while."

Shortly after Mays's arrival, the Mets went on an 11-game tear. "They had the best record in the league for a while. *Sports Illustrated* put Willie on the cover: 'The A-Mays-ing Mets.' It was like he had brought them magic," said Samelson.

In May the Mets went 21–7, pushing their record to 30–11, and they led the division by five games. And then the bottom fell out. Staub was injured in the beginning of June, and then a rash of injuries decimated the team like a bad virus. Boswell, Agee, Jones, Fregosi, and even Mays were all dealt injuries, crippling the team's chances.

They finished 12–15 in June and 11–15 in July. And despite a great rallying of the troops in September and early October, it was too late. They finished third behind the Pittsburgh Pirates and the Chicago Cubs.

Additionally, the Berra/Mays relationship began to sour. In July the Mets made a West Coast trip, and they were scheduled to play the Giants at Candlestick Park.

The Mets arrived in San Francisco's airport. "Walking through the airport, distracted by thoughts of playing there again, I walked right into a pillar and nearly knocked myself out," Mays said later.

Berra announced Mays would not play that night, and attendance dropped to about 18,000.

"I went to Yogi before the game. He didn't want me to play, but I told him, 'Yogi, I think I have to play. I think a lot of people are going to pay their money to come out, especially to see me play. If you pay $4.50 to see a person play and he doesn't, I think they're going to be pretty mad.'"

Berra acquiesced.

Mays said it was a weird feeling going into the visitors' locker room. The fans cheered Mays on. And after grounding out and flying out, he hit a center-field shot in his third at-bat that cleared the fence. The fans went crazy with applause.

Conversely, Mays became upset at another point because he felt Berra was playing him too often. Mays, like other aging stars, was used to being able to say when he would and wouldn't play. Berra, after his experience in being too kind to aging stars in 1964, was tough on Mays, insisting he would play when Berra told him to play.

"Yogi had been criticized in 1964 for losing control of his Yankee ball club, and he adamantly refused to let Mays dictate anything," wrote Peter Golenbock.

By September, Mays was openly criticizing Berra for playing him too much and complaining that it was affecting his stats.

"I know he and Yogi had a tough time as far as the lineup went, and a lot of times Willie didn't want to come to the ballpark at all," pitcher Tug McGraw recalled years later.

But Mays's stats tell another story. Mays played in only 69 games for the Mets in 1972 and 66 games in 1973. Both were, by Mays's standards, abysmal years. But he had, without a doubt, been a help to the team. In 1972 Mays was 41 years old. He was a proud superstar, one of the greatest ever to play the game. And one must also think that his inability to perform at the level he had been accustomed to for so many years must have provided a tremendous amount of frustration during these final years of his career.

Despite their differences, Mays would help Berra win games and give pointers to the younger players on whom he made a great impression.

\*    \*    \*

On January 19, 1972, Sandy Koufax, Early Wynn, and Yogi Berra were among those elected to the National Baseball Hall of Fame. A year earlier Berra had been the top vote-getter, but had fallen short by 28 votes. Other inductees were Lefty Gomez, Buck Leonard, Josh Gibson, Ross Youngs, and William Harridge.

Berra said, "I thought maybe I'd make it this year. Even Joe DiMaggio didn't make it his first year. But whenever you make it, it's a great thrill. I got four or five phone calls from friends this morning, and I had to tell them I didn't know anything yet, even though I did."

"It is great to make it, whether it takes one, two, three, or four years. It doesn't matter. Every ballplayer hopes to make it. This is the greatest honor of my life," Berra told the press.

As Koufax and Berra appeared on a stage together, a reporter asked Berra if he ever faced Koufax during a game outside of spring training.

"The year the Dodgers beat us four straight in the World Series [1963], I was the on-deck hitter when he got the final out of the fourth game," Berra said.

How would Koufax have pitched to Berra?

Koufax answered, "Very carefully. Yogi didn't want you to throw strikes."

The induction ceremony was scheduled for August. But in July, there was another ceremony in Berra's honor.

On July 22, 1972, Bill Dickey's and Yogi Berra's No. 8s were officially retired at Yankee Stadium. It was the 26th Old-Timers' Day at the venerable stadium. The Yankees faithful applauded as the numbers were retired. Dickey, still tall, slender, and well-built, was dressed in a Yankees uniform. In attendance was Larry Berra Jr., standing in for his father, whose Mets were on a West Coast swing.

Dickey thanked the fans for being the greatest in the world. And then a prerecorded message by Berra boomed over the loudspeaker. He thanked the fans and Dickey for their support over the years. And he mentioned his absence because of being "with my Mets," which drew a short burst of boos.

Lawrence Peter Berra was inducted into the National Baseball Hall of Fame on August 7, 1972.

Of course, there is a famous story about Carmen and Berra driving to Cooperstown. They got lost, and when Carmen complained, Berra responded, "We're lost, but we're making good time."

Carmen had written his speech for him. He had read and reread the speech. "I have to put on my glasses," he told the crowd as he searched his pockets. Then he addressed the crowd.

"I guess the first thing I ought to say is that I thank everybody for making this day necessary," recalling his gaffe of 1947. The crowd laughed uproariously. He then began to read Carmen's speech.

"I want to thank Bill Dickey for polishing me up as a catcher. I want to thank George Weiss for giving me my first New York contract. I want to thank Casey Stengel, who had the confidence to play me every day. I want to thank my wife, Carmen, the perfect baseball wife," said Berra.

He read on, thanking more people. "My only regrets are that my parents are not here to enjoy this moment with me, that my brother John is not here, and that Gil Hodges is not here. I hope they are proud of me today."

Carmen, Larry, Dale, and Tim were in the audience. Joe Garagiola, as was to be expected, was there, and was seen wiping tears from his eyes as his friend spoke. Phil Rizzuto and Bill Dickey were also there. Berra's voice cracked.

"I want to thank baseball," he said lastly. "It has given me more than I hoped for. When I am finished, I hope I have given it something back."

There was much applause.

A week later, George Weiss, the architect of so many Yankees championship teams, died on August 14th, 1972, at his home in Greenwich, Connecticut. He had won 19 pennants with the Yankees. He was 78 years old.

\*    \*    \*

In the meantime, Berra did have a personal life in 1972. Carmen had been photographed in numerous articles during this period. Blonde, slender, and well-kept, she was considered by other baseball wives and tony Montclair, New Jersey, residents to be the cutting edge of chic. She was a very attractive woman and compared extremely well with women almost half her age.

Baseball wives were used by Mets team publicists for promotions, and one of the more popular events was using the women as models to show spring and fall fashion collections. Carmen was beautiful, and she walked around in swanky outfits with the best of them. She was as smart as she was stunning. She was often her husband's most important sounding board. He didn't do everything she said, but he always discussed things with her to see what her thoughts were. At publicity events where she was on her husband's arm, people often remarked how lucky Berra truly was.

Their sons were as handsome as their mother was beautiful. All grew to be quite tall and lanky, more like Berra's brothers than their father. Larry in particular was quite athletic. During his high school days, he was a star baseball player for the Montclair team. He was 6'1" and 195 pounds and played—what else?—catcher. As an 18-year-old senior in 1968, Larry batted .304 for his team. He received real praise from his coaches.

"He is very tough to strike out," his coach told the press.

"Of course he's a good player," a proud Carmen told reporters. "We hadn't planned a baseball career for him, but that's what he wants so much. I wish him luck."

Colleges and pro scouts were becoming interested in the young Berra. He set the school record for RBIs, ended up on the All-State team, and went on to attend Montclair State College. At the age of 22, Larry was a promising catcher in his own right in the Mets' minor league farm system. However, a serious knee injury required surgery—devastating to a catcher—essentially putting an end to his career before it began.

Berra had numerous good friends and was sometimes able to dazzle his son. Once, when Larry was trying to get tickets to a Frank Sinatra concert, Berra told him, "I'll call Frank."

Larry replied, "I've been your son for 21 years, and I didn't even know you knew Frank Sinatra."

Timothy Thomas "Tim" Berra, about 5'11" and 195 pounds, also excelled in sports. Berra confided that Tim was an excellent baseball player with great potential, but Timmy thought baseball was "boring." Instead of following in his father's baseball footsteps, Tim blazed a new path for himself. Tim was very good at football and was the star halfback at Montclair High School.

Tim attended the University of Massachusetts, where he became a star receiver, and he graduated in 1973. Naturally, his father was a devoted fan. "Yogi always knew everything about the kids' upcoming opponents," Phil Pepe related, including their high school and college statistics.

Larry and Tim's youngest brother, Dale, says, "I remember wandering around the [Yankees] locker room. I'd see Mickey Mantle shaving, Tony Kubek getting dressed.... I decided that was the kind of life I wanted to lead. The ballplayers were grown men, and at the same time they were kids. They were young at heart."

Local newspaper writers also noted that of all Berra's sons, Dale seemed to have the most promise. He was the most natural athlete, lettering in three sports for three years straight.

"I tried," Carmen told the press, "to get the boys to take piano lessons to broaden their horizons, but they became athletes despite me."

"People think I tutored my sons into being ballplayers—no way. I barely played with them because I wasn't there that much," Berra said many years later. "When I'd come home and they'd ask to play, I'd tell them that's what they had brothers for. And Larry, Tim, and Dale used to play all the time with their friends or make up games themselves, no parental interference."

Discussing how often he was away from his kids, Berra pointed out in a different interview that his sons usually came home around 3:30 PM, which was just about the time he usually left for the ballpark, as night games had become more and more popular. And that was when he wasn't on the road.

"In the eyes of his three sons, Yogi is a soft touch who instructs them in the care and feeding of pet turtles and leaves the hard facts of life, like spankings and dirty-neck inspections, to their mother," wrote James Stewart-Gordon in *Rotarian* magazine in May 1959.

"Yogi did not change diapers when the boys were infants, and he had a difficult time being a disciplinarian of the family," added writer Phil Pepe years later.

"That was my job," said Carmen. "You know how easygoing Yogi is, but if he ever got angry, the boys knew enough to behave. Yogi has been the greatest influence on the boys. They idolize their father. They always had a great time together. When the boys were little, Yogi would play touch football with them, or you'd see him on the living room floor, wrestling with them."

"She is a woman who has had the qualities to be father and mother to her children during her husband's absences. Her job has been more difficult than she admits," Pepe added.

Growing up, the Berra boys often played with and against the sons of Frank Tripucka. Tripucka was the backup quarterback on Frank Leahy's unbeaten Notre Dame squads in 1946 and 1947 and was the starter in 1948. Tripucka was named an All-American, and the Philadelphia Eagles drafted him with their number one pick but traded him to the Detroit Lions before the 1949 season began. He started with the Lions in 1949 and then played the next three seasons with the Chicago Cardinals.

The Berras of Montclair and the Tripuckas of Bloomfield had made northern New Jersey their own personal sandlot. The two families visited each other during the holidays, and their towns were traditional sporting rivals. Tim Berra and Mark Tripucka played against each other in high school, but were teammates at University of Massachusetts. In fact, Tim was Mark's roommate.

The Tripuckas and the Berras often drove up to Amherst together, sharing the ride and the company, to watch their sons' games in the fall in Massachusetts. Frank's wife, Randy, and Carmen became good friends, too.

"The only thing Yogi can't get me to go to are those crazy Mets games," Tripucka told the press.

*    *    *

One of the first things that needed to be addressed during the spring of 1973 was center field. Mays was nearly 42 years old, and his best years were well past him. The problem was that the Mets did not have a decent, everyday alternative.

The front-office folks wanted Berra to switch Cleon Jones from left field to center and insert John Milner in left. But Berra had seen Stengel try that much earlier and remembered the disastrous results.

"An underrated evaluator of talent, Berra gave little thought to the front office's recommendation of a realigned outfield," wrote sportswriter Bruce Markusen. Instead, Berra played Mays and Don Hahn in center, kept Staub in right (with his accurate and powerful throwing arm), and Jones in left. Milner played first.

In 1972 Mets general manager Bob Scheffing hired Phil Cavarretta to be the first batting instructor in Mets franchise history. Some players balked, but the move showed that the Mets organization was no longer just trying to put on a good show. The 1969 World Series had put a hunger in the entire organization to achieve again. It was a positive sign of progress.

Of course, the press always had to poke fun at Berra. One cruel instance was when Berra took a liking to a kid named George Theodore. At the time of final cuts, Theodore was batting only .182, and many were surprised to see his name still on the roster. Not only was he not hitting, but he was also a skinny beanpole of a boy at 6'4", 190 pounds, with slumped shoulders and big glasses. He had been nicknamed the Stork. One insensitive writer penned it was no wonder Berra liked him: "Any picture Yogi takes with Theodore, Yogi has to look like a matinee idol."

And of course, Berra still had to address the problems that celebrity brought on. "My coaches used to get mad at me," he said. "We'd go into a bar, and we couldn't sit down and chat. They didn't want to go with me anymore."

In February, the Mets renewed pitcher Tug McGraw with a $75,000 contract, a record for a reliever, and raised Seaver's salary to $140,000. Fregosi and Jones were reclamation projects. And Staub was a holdout. But they had traded for a solid player in second baseman Felix Milan.

But the big news was Mays. Mays came to camp and went out for the first day of spring training wearing tape braces on both knees. Mays told the media that he wanted to come back and play for the Mets in 1973, but only "if I can do it my way." He had shown up a day late for spring training as if to emphasize his point.

"I appreciate that Willie isn't 18 years old—he's 42. But you can't have two sets of rules. I'll have to talk with him tomorrow and see what he can do," Berra told the press.

In truth, Mays had been another of Grant's attempts to link the Mets with the glory years of the Giants and Dodgers, but Mays was not the spark plug Berra wanted. Berra needed more players who could hit and catch regularly. His lineup was filled with a mishmash of raw talent and flakes. Mays had been a superstar for a generation. There was no doubt the young kids on the team looked up to him. Many of the players from that club liked Mays and said they learned a lot from him. Seaver was particularly impressed by him. Mays insisted, for example, on sitting in on pitching meetings before games, asking for a rundown of strategies on each batter. Mays would accordingly adjust his position in center field for each batter.

That spring, as the rest of the team stretched, he arrived late, walked over to the applauding fans in the stands, shook a few hands, and then walked over to the batting cage.

"They're still here," Mays said to reporters, pointing to his taped knees. "I wanted to come down and see if I can play."

To Mays's credit, he knew his situation could start a controversy, and he was open about it. "I don't want to hurt the club. Yogi has ways of guys doing things, and I don't want to break any rules. When I came to the Mets, I didn't know the system the way I did with the Giants for 20 years. I have a tendency to hold back a little in cases like that. I had to try and fit in with the people who were there—I couldn't talk too much…. This year I might talk up more," said Mays.

That Mays could still help the club was not in doubt, though it was, by his standards, an awful year. Mays told the press he was older and had his own set way of doing things, and if allowed to manage his workload, he might be more productive. He complained of having to take too much batting practice, which he did not like.

"I'll explain to Yogi what I like to do, and if he doesn't like it, we'll have to go someplace else," said Mays. Mays was not being vindictive—he understood what he was asking for, and he understood why some managers might not stand for it. He was willing to talk about being a coach, but he felt he could still contribute to the club in the upcoming season. He told the press he wanted to work it out with Berra.

"I made a mistake," Mays told the press in spring training after he took off for two days to San Francisco without telling Berra, meriting a $500 fine and headlines on sports pages around the country. In his autobiography, Mays asserted that, with an off day coming up, he went home to be with his wife, who was sick. Admittedly, he said, he should have told Berra. But on the return, his flights were canceled or delayed, and he ended up missing a day. Mays had tested Berra, and Berra had drawn a line.

Asked if he had consulted with anyone else in the organization, Berra fired back, "I didn't ask anybody's advice. To me, a man's family comes first. But he should tell me he needs to go home…. This morning, I got here at 8:30, and Willie was already in the locker room. He's always early anyway."

Mays, for his part, took it well, and said in public, "He made his point, and he was right. I made a mistake, and I should have told him. Mostly my wife's lonesome, but she'll join me next week."

General manager Bob Scheffing told reporters that he "was satisfied that Yogi took action that was appropriate."

"I don't hear any grumbling from the other players," McGraw added to the press. "They don't resent him; they appreciate him."

With the gaping hole in center field and the front office set on keeping Mays, Berra had to make do. While the press was wary of Berra losing control of his club, many realized that Mays would indeed require separate rules, and that was going to be another cross for Berra to bear. They were two legends of the game, both national figures, and both had pride and a point to make. Mays wanted to play another year in New York; Berra wanted to reestablish himself and take a pennant. Tempers sometimes got hot between the two, but they were able to put their differences aside long enough for an unforgettable year.

Most writers noted that the Mets had a ton of holes in their lineup and a lot of youth, but it would not take a great record to win the division. The Mets started out hot in April going 12–8, playing .600 ball. A nice start to be sure, but the next month was a disaster, and the team finished 9–14 in May. June was no better, with an 11–17 finish. Berra was in trouble.

That spring training, there had been the threat of a walkout, and Marvin Miller, head of the Major League Baseball Players Association, had again led a brief strike. Many of the players had come in heavier than their normal playing weight, and with little spring training, could not work off the extra pounds. Some thought this added to Berra's problems.

"Gil had a strict weigh-in.... We had to be at weight, and if you weren't, it cost you a hundred dollars a pound a day," Koosman said later. "After Yogi took over, that went by the wayside, because Yogi wasn't as strict as Gil, and some guys took advantage of that. Some guys got too heavy. Under Yogi, we just didn't have the discipline that a strict hand can dictate."

"Some of us were getting down on Yogi for the things he did. Then more injuries came, our luck kept getting worse, and the guys started griping a bit," McGraw admitted years later.

Berra had fallen on hard times. Injuries and poor play had plagued the Mets. Matlack, Staub, Harrelson, Jones, Milner, and catcher Jerry Grote had all missed time. Matlack's injury was especially scary, when he was knocked out by a line drive. Berra was the first to reach the pitcher, who was flattened out on the mound. For the first time in his career, Berra heard boos when he attempted to walk onto the field.

Speculation started to swirl through the New York press. Would Billy Martin be brought in to take Berra's job? That speculation made the rounds for a while but was ultimately unfounded. It got to the point where Grant had to issue a public statement: "We have no intention of dropping Berra as the Met manager.... You can't blame him for all the injuries the team has suffered." However, Grant added the caveat, "No, we have no intention of firing Berra unless the public demands it."

The truth of the matter was, Grant wanted to fire Berra.

"Grant adamantly wanted to fire Berra but was afraid of the fan backlash," McGraw said.

"Grant could not get Scheffing to go along with him. In fact, insiders later revealed that when Grant asked Scheffing to drop Yogi, the general manager refused," said sportswriter Jack Lang.

"If you want to fire Yogi, you do it. I won't," Scheffing told Grant.

How safe was Berra's job? No one knew. The *New York Post* asked readers: "Who's to blame? M. Donald Grant, chairman of the board; Bob Scheffing, general manager; Yogi Berra, manager; all of them; none of them?"

Thankfully enough for Berra, the balloting came back: Scheffing 1,448, Grant 1,207, and Berra 611. Only 15 percent of the people thought he was to blame. But that didn't make it any easier for him.

"What's the difference between Gil Hodges and Yogi Berra?" McGraw said, retelling a mean joke that was going around then. "And some joker could always get a laugh by answering 'six innings.'" (In the third inning, Gil was thinking about what he was going to do in the ninth; in the sixth, Yogi was thinking about what he should have done in the third.)

It is well known that Berra and Cleon Jones were not the best of friends. But Jones had been a clutch player for the Mets, and Berra needed his bat. Sportswriter Dick Young pointed to a little-known meeting as one of the pivotal moments of the 1973 season. Berra was frustrated with Jones. He took plays off and looked too casual out on the field. Players also complained. In his San Diego hotel room, Jones complained of tired feet. Berra went to meet with Jones. He made a heartfelt plea.

"The team needs you. I need you," said Berra. Then, half-jokingly, he said, "What are you trying to do, get me fired?"

The plea worked, and Jones rebounded the rest of the year.

By August 15, the season seemed lost to most folks, with the Mets still seven and a half games out of first place.

"There's lots of time yet," Berra told the press. "We can still do it. Look at all the other clubs on top. They're stumbling around like they don't want to win. All we have to do is put a few good games together."

"Yogi kept telling everyone to be patient, that a hot streak was coming. Few took him seriously," wrote Golenbock.

"Everybody in the division has had some kind of winning streak except us. We're due for one. And when we do, just watch us go," Berra insisted.

It was during this time that he said, "You're never out of it until you're out of it," and "It's not over until it's over."

This pair of similar quotes eventually morphed into "It ain't over till it's over." But Berra says he was actually quoting Rocky or Clint Courtney and, to this day, is surprised some reporter hasn't found the original quote. While "It ain't over..." has become the most-used version of the saying and possibly his most famous expression, the exact phrase could not be found in any articles that season. That line did not become the catchphrase it is today until 1974 or 1975, when he was quoted as saying, "It ain't over until it's over." To this day, however, both coach Joe Pignatano and writer Phil Pepe maintain that Berra did indeed utter these famous words in reference to the team's improbable run during the 1973 season.

This quote is the best example of how the writers, even through the 1970s, were constantly packaging Yogi Berra for the public by writing lines or rewriting lines as they saw fit to create what became known as Berraisms. On the one hand, they created a character that didn't exist; on the other, he cashed in on it.

"The Mets were bouncing all over the standings that year, it was true," Berra wrote in his book, *Yogi: It Ain't Over*. In truth, though, Berra was frustrated and down. He thought he could put a winning stretch together, but he hadn't had his Opening Day lineup for more than a dozen or so games the whole year. Injuries were killing them, and morale was hard to keep up. It was a strain on him, but it came with the territory.

It was around this time that McGraw contends he first said, "Ya gotta believe," striking a muscle-popping pose after a pep talk Chairman Grant had delivered in the Mets clubhouse.

Several teammates say they thought he was mocking Grant, but McGraw honestly was repeating a powerful phrase he had come up with to try to encourage himself on the mound. It had been a trying year for McGraw, who did not notch his first win until August 22.

Berra started McGraw in Atlanta in an attempt to get the sagging pitcher's spirits up. Despite McGraw giving up seven runs in six innings, the Mets won the game. McGraw started again, this time against Montreal, and this time he gave up only one run. After that, Berra returned McGraw to the bullpen. By the end of August, a *New York Post* headline read: "Old McGraw New Stopper."

"These were savvy managerial moves that would prove most beneficial to the Mets in 1973," wrote baseball historian Peter Golenbock.

*The Berras (clockwise):*
*Yogi, Carmen, Tim,*
*Larry, and Dale.*

*The Berra boys get a taste of their father's football skills.*

*New Yankees manager Yogi Berra and his mentor Casey Stengel in 1964.* (Photo courtesy of AP/Wide World Photos)

*In 1964, Berra managed the Yankees back to the World Series. New York lost the Series in seven games, and Berra was fired shortly after.*

*Yogi was reunited with former Yankees general manager George Weiss when Berra joined the Mets as a coach in 1964.* (Photo courtesy of AP/Wide World Photos)

*Berra took over as Mets manager in 1972 and led his team to the Fall Classic a year later, this time with the help of pitcher Tom Seaver (left).*

*Manager Billy Martin (left) convinced Berra to join him in the Bronx Zoo in 1976.*
(Photo courtesy of AP/Wide World Photos)

*Yankees owner George Steinbrenner hired Berra to manage the team in 1984; he lasted less than two seasons.* (Photo courtesy of AP/Wide World Photos)

*Berra spent the last seasons of his coaching career with the Houston Astros.*

*Fellow Hall of Famers and lifelong friends Phil Rizzuto and Yogi Berra returned to Newark for opening night at Riverfront Stadium in 1999. Rizzuto passed away in 2007.* (Photo courtesy of AP/Wide World Photos)

*After being fired in 1985 by George Steinbrenner, Berra refused to return to Yankee Stadium for 14 years. He finally ended his self-imposed exile when he threw out the first pitch in New York's 1999 home opener.* (Photo courtesy of AP/Wide World Photos)

*The boys from the Hill: Joe Garagiola and Yogi Berra.* (Photo courtesy of AP/Wide World Photos)

*Always one of the game's great ambassadors, Berra continues to attend events like the annual Baseball Hall of Fame induction ceremony.*

*Yogi Berra waves to an appreciative crowd before a spring-training game in 2000.*

August 5, 1973, was Banner Day at Shea Stadium, and the *Post* ran a sampling of the best and worst spotted in the stands:

> *The Mets Stink. So Does This Banner*
> *Seems Like Old Times*
> *NL Cellar (Summer Home of Y. Berra)*
> *The Mets Are Victims of the Energy Shortage; Out of Gas in*
> *1973*

In late August, McGraw remembered, the fans and press were being pretty brutal. "Yogi Berra never took a course in child psychology, that's for sure, but I remember one thing he did that wasn't too dumb," McGraw recalled. "He got hold of a clipping that said the Mets were horseshit and we were just going through the motions, and he came around to each player and held it up and said, 'See, you're going through the motions.' You think Yogi just wanted to get us riled up. But I think it went deeper than that…. Yogi wanted us to realize that he didn't feel that way."

In late August, on the back of a first-game grand slam by Staub, the Mets took a three-game series against the Padres. Suddenly, the Mets had gained two games on the struggling—but division leading—St. Louis Cardinals.

"It's beginning to feel like 1969!" Koosman yelled in the clubhouse after the sweep.

"That's what I've been telling you! We can do it!" Berra told his players.

"We're going to be the first team that was last in August to win the pennant!" yelled McGraw.

By September 12, they were two and a half games out. On September 20, Mays announced this would be his last year in baseball. On September 21, in front of 55,000 people, the Mets reached .500 and took over first place in the National League East.

Suddenly Berra was the sage old man. His office was crammed with reporters, and he doled out his feelings on the division and the pennant. It was too close to call. Even the fifth-place Chicago Cubs were only two and a half out. It would be a wild ride right to the end.

The *New York Post* ran a headline saying, "Time Is Running Out on the Mets." When asked if time indeed was running out, Berra replied, "Yeah, it's running out, but you're still not out of it until it's automatic."

Pepe wrote, "It's 1969 all over again…it's unbelievable."

On September 25, 1973, the Mets held Willie Mays Night at Shea Stadium. It was an emotional night for him. He had played through pain and injury that year. Through it all, he had remained classy about his differences with Berra. And Mays remained uncritical of Berra's managing, as well.

"You never heard anything from Willie about Yogi," McGraw said later.

After the game, Mays assumed he would leave the team. But owner Joan Payson said, "You can't go home now, Willie."

"So I stayed with the guys, not wanting to force myself on Yogi," Mays wrote later.

With some incredible management of a very tired pitching staff and some timely hitting, the New York Mets won the National League East by defeating the Cubs in Chicago on October 1, 1973.

McGraw was everywhere shouting, "Ya gotta believe!" And everyone was shouting with him.

"The butterflies are gone now. I'm glad it's over," Berra told the press.

Asked if he felt vindicated, Berra replied, "I just like baseball. I'm happy how it turned out. Yes, I guess I do—I haven't thought about it much. I just do my best. I know the fans got on me, but they gotta pick on someone, and it's always the manager."

"We had a crazy finish," Mays remembered.

The Mets were going to the National League Championship Series. Unfortunately for the Yankees, they had finished terribly, and Houk had resigned under new owner George Steinbrenner, who'd bought the team from CBS after it had run the once-proud franchise into the ground.

At one point, *New York Times* sportswriter Dave Anderson asked Yogi, "Have you heard from the front office?" regarding Berra's next contract with the Mets.

"Nothin'," responded Berra.

"You'll probably win it and then get fired anyway," joked Anderson.

"Don't laugh. It happened before," said the Mets manager.

\*   \*   \*

The opponent in the NLCS would be the incredible Cincinnati Reds, a powerful team starring Pete Rose, Johnny Bench, and a slew of other clutch performers. The Reds were heavily favored—no one expected the Mets to win, but the Mets faithful were hopeful.

Berra chose Seaver to start the series, and he lost a tight, close game at Riverfront Stadium in Cincinnati 2–1. The team was down after the loss, but Berra didn't lose his poise. He told the press and his team, "That's only one loss. What the hell, we still got to lose two more. They didn't get so many hits or runs, either."

Matlack pitched the second, allowing only two hits in another pitchers' duel, but the Mets exploded with four runs in the ninth and took the game 5–0, evening the series 1–1.

Back in Shea Stadium for Game 3, the Mets erupted with nine runs in the first four innings and were on their way to a rout. The Reds were frustrated. In the fifth inning Rose chugged toward second, trying to break up a double play. He was unsuccessful, but he barreled into Bud Harrelson while trying to do so.

It was a violent confrontation, and soon the two were fighting on the infield. Both teams' benches cleared as all the players raced onto the diamond. It was pandemonium. Eventually order was restored, but Rose was pelted by debris from the stands when he next tried to take his position in the field. The Reds' manager, Sparky Anderson, pulled his team from the diamond until Mets players convinced the crowd to let the game continue unimpeded.

In Game 4 of the NLCS, the Reds struck back, winning 2–1 on a twelfth-inning home run by Rose. In that game, Staub hit the wall in the outfield chasing a fly ball. The next day he came to the park early, but he was in no shape to play.

"We've come back from injuries before," Berra said when Staub told him he wouldn't be able to play. "All season we've been catching bad breaks, so why should the playoffs be any different?"

"He smiled. Weakly. You could tell he was faking it," sportswriter Dave Hirshey remembered.

In the fifth game at Shea Stadium, Berra inserted Mays to pinch hit. Mays delivered with a single and the Mets, behind Seaver, won the game 7–2. The Mets had won the series in one of the biggest upsets in sports that year. It seemed like the entire crowd poured onto the field when it was over.

*   *   *

Yogi Berra and the Mets were going to the World Series. At the time, they were the team with the worst record in the history of baseball to appear in a World Series. Also, Berra was only the second manager in the history of baseball to manage at least one team to the World Series from both leagues—the other was Joe McCarthy. Since then, only Alvin Dark, Dick Williams, Jim Leyland, Tony La Russa, and Sparky Anderson have equaled that feat (although some would say the latter two exceeded it because they won in both leagues).

The Mets would be facing the defending world champion Oakland A's. The opposing club was stocked with incredible players, including Catfish Hunter, Vida Blue, Reggie Jackson, and many others.

Matlack pitched against Ken Holtzman in the opener, and in a very tight, closely called game, the A's prevailed 2–1. Given that the A's were another amazing powerhouse of a club, the Mets proved to themselves that they belonged.

In the second game in Oakland, the A's led 3–1 after two innings, but the Mets came back to take a 6–4 lead into the ninth. Berra put Mays in for defensive purposes, hoping to close out the win. But Mays failed to catch a fly ball, and the play let the A's tie the game 6–6.

In the twelfth, Mays came up to bat with Harrelson on third and McGraw on first. With a chance to redeem himself, Mays was determined and thought he'd use his experience to help him.

As he stepped into the batter's box, Mays said to catcher Ray Fosse, "Gee, you know, Ray, it's tough to see the ball with that background. I hope he doesn't throw me any fastballs. I don't want to get hurt."

"I waited for [Rollie] Fingers's fastball," said the wily old Mays. Sure enough it came, and Mays smacked it up the middle. The Mets' offense erupted for four runs in the twelfth inning for a come-from-behind 10–7 victory in Game 2.

Game 3 was at Shea Stadium, and the A's stole one back on the road, winning it 3–2 in 11 innings. But the Mets took Games 4 and 5 for an improbable 3–2 Series lead.

It was at this point that Berra may have made a controversial, if not fatal, mistake. Berra elected to go with Seaver in Game 6, hoping to close out the Series right then and there by matching his ace against Catfish Hunter. Seaver was going on short rest, but Berra was trying to avoid having to play a Game 7 in a hostile park. He and Rube Walker took a good, long look at Seaver. Seaver told them he could do it.

Seaver gave up one run each in the first and third innings, but he pitched extremely well. Another run in the eighth sealed the loss, as the Mets' offense seemed to vanish in the face of Hunter's pitching.

Holtzman pitched Game 7 against Matlack. Matlack gave up four runs in the third, and that would be enough as Holzman, too, seemed to mesmerize the Mets hitters. The A's took the game, 5–2, and the Series.

In retrospect, the choice of Seaver meant little, as his three runs allowed would not have stood up in either contest. The A's pitching made the difference in the final two games.

Berra had done a masterful job guiding his team past two of the most vaunted baseball teams of the era, the Oakland A's (the last team to win three straight championships) and the Big Red Machine of Cincinnati. His undermanned, oft-injured club had shocked the baseball world and almost took it all. But the real stunner was that Gene Mauch took his third Manager of the Year award for the National League by piloting the Montreal Expos into third place in the National League East.

Discussing his friend Berra after the Series, Garagiola told the press, "When the Yankees fired him, that hurt him. So he takes another job managing. I told him he was nuts, managers get fired. But he wanted to show everybody he could manage. He has."

On October 24, Pepe wrote, "Back in July, it was a cinch the Mets would have a press conference this week to name their manager for 1974. It was less a cinch the man's name would be Yogi Berra."

The news that week out of Yankee Stadium was that they were looking for a manager.

"Judging by Berra's success with the Mets this year, the Yankees had one of the best managers then [1964], too," wrote Joe Durso in the *Times*. "Now, ironically, the Yankees must challenge Berra's sudden charisma."

It was sweet vindication for Berra.

Berra signed a three-year deal with the Mets worth an estimated $75,000 per year. He was playing golf at the White Beeches Country Club when the signing was announced.

"Now I'm finally going to relax…and I'm finally going to get to see Timmy play football this Saturday. We're not going to Europe or anything like that. Carmen says she's gotta stay home now and take care of our 17-year-old baby [Dale]," he said.

*    *    *

Sometime in 1974, during spring training, Carmen and Berra held a banquet at the St. Petersburg Yacht Club in Florida for the team and press. It was an off-the-record night, where players and writers could cut loose with no recriminations.

Berra and Carmen were at the head of a large table. Coaches and their wives sat near the middle, and the sportswriters and their wives were seated at the other end. A well-dressed, well-kept, middle-aged woman approached Berra and shoved one of the restaurant's menus in front of him.

"Sign this," she demanded. Berra was almost always accommodating, but this rude woman had put him off. He told her he would sign it after he had his dinner. She groused and left the table in a huff. After a round of drinks, the woman returned and shoved the menu in his face again. Berra repeated his first answer to her. After she left, the appetizers were served. Then the woman returned, louder, more drunk, and more obnoxious.

"Please, Yogi, sign it for her," said Carmen, obviously annoyed at the woman.

The woman thrust the menu in his face again. "Sign it to my son, Donnie, with best regards and congratulations from your best pal, Yogi Berra," she demanded. Berra refused.

"You won't? Then to hell with you!" she shouted.

Writer Maury Allen recalled, "The woman then took the huge menu and began tearing it up and throwing several pieces in front of Berra as the coaches ushered her away. Being famous and recognizable, as Yogi is, may not always be the most pleasant life experience."

The 1974 season didn't go much better for Berra than the banquet had. The Mets were again affected by injuries, and Berra's relationship with Jones worsened. The team played .400 ball for the first three months of the season, then rallied to play .550 ball in July before settling for a dismal 71–91 record at the end of the season. Fans were disappointed. It did not go well.

\*     \*     \*

Spring training in 1975 began with a distraction, when Jones was found in the back of a van with a 21-year-old woman who was not Mrs. Jones. The former superstar told St. Petersburg police his name was C. Joseph Jones. The real problem was that the woman was in possession of drugs, and the two were arrested. The Mets front office leveled a fine at the truculent star and made him issue an apology at a press conference.

On July 18, Berra "inserted Jones into a game as a pinch-hitter. After the at-bat, Berra told Jones to stay in the game and take his position in the field. Jones refused, instead walking away from his manager," wrote baseball writer Bruce Markusen. This was the final straw. Some tried to say Berra was racially biased against Jones, but those charges were unfounded. Jones had become sullen and difficult. Berra refused to let Jones back on the team, regardless of the apology, and insisted that Jones had to go.

Grant disagreed. First, he did not like being dictated to by his manager, and second, he liked Jones because he was the star of the Miracle Mets of 1969, always a good showpiece. But Jones's production and attitude were not what they once were.

Berra stood firm and told Grant, "It's him or me."

On July 27, the Mets released Jones.

"I wish Cleon all the luck in the world. I think he wasted a lot of his talent, and I believe I bent over backward to try and help him," Berra told the press. "It's not a matter of black and white. It's a matter of I wouldn't be able to face any of my players if I took him back. Like I said, I covered for Jonesy a lot. July 18th was the icing on the cake."

But Berra's 1975 edition of the New York Mets fared no better than the 1974 team, arriving at a record of 54–48 by the end of July, playing .529 ball. Seaver was going upstairs behind Berra's back to management to complain. After a five-game losing streak, the front office had had enough.

Berra was fired after the Mets were shut out in both games of a doubleheader against Montreal. M. Donald Grant said, "It's been a decision that's been going through our heads for some time…. It had nothing to do with falling attendance, dissension on the team, the recent problem we had over Cleon Jones, or the Yankees' change of manager [Billy Martin had been hired the previous weekend]. Nothing had anything to do with it but the performance of the team…."

Berra was not surprised by the firing. The Mets had been playing only mediocre baseball. And his problems with Jones had worsened things, as had his strained relationship with Seaver.

Berra, as usual, was classy in dismissal. He was home when he finally got the call after having been out much of the day—avoiding the inevitable.

He came in the next day to make sure the photographers got a photo of his handshake with one of his coaches, Roy McMillan, who was taking his job. He asked that writers be good to McMillan, and he wished his replacement the best of luck. Berra also insisted on saying good-bye to his players. He shook hands with many of them—some of whom cost him his job.

Most writers felt that Berra had been set up as the patsy, the fall guy. With the Yankees moving into Shea Stadium as cotenants while the city refurbished Yankee Stadium, Catfish Hunter's signing, and the sizeable attendance decrease for the Mets, many felt Grant was looking for someone to blame, someone on whom he could take out his frustrations. When Berra put his foot down over Jones, he essentially lit the fuse to the keg of gunpowder Grant had placed under his chair. Grant had hoped to bring in Martin as manager, but Martin chose to take over the Yankees.

"It's a shame a good baseball man is fired because of recalcitrant ballplayers," Mauch said of the firing.

While Yogi was saying his good-byes, Carmen called the manager's office and spoke with McMillan. "It's your wife," McMillan told Berra. The phone had rung so many times at their home that Carmen was leaving. She wanted to know when he would return to deal with the calls.

"I tried my best, so I know I did all right," Berra told reporters. "My only regret is that although I won two pennants in four tries, I didn't win the World Series.... That's the only thing I didn't do in baseball.

"Will I spend time mowing the lawn? Naw. It's too big. I got two acres and a 15-room house," he chortled. "Carm, she's relieved it's over with. I love baseball and I love New York."

"He's a heck of guy," said Joe Torre, the Mets' third baseman.

"It was obvious that things were being wasted," said Matlack. Matlack indicted the players' talents as well as Berra's. He felt they weren't living up to their potential.

As if to make people feel better, Berra told players and staff alike, "Don't worry about me. I'll be around."

# ~ Chapter 18 ~

# LIVING IN THE BRONX ZOO

In the meantime, Berra and Carmen went with the Tripuckas to watch football that fall. Timmy had an incredible season in 1973 at the University of Massachusetts. He had returns of 93, 97, and 63 yards and several other long runs as a kickoff and punt returner. Carmen and Berra were proud parents, showing up for as many of Tim's games as they could.

Tim Berra was drafted by the Baltimore Colts in the 17th and final round of the National Football League draft in January 1974. He was the 421st player taken overall.

Tim played for the Baltimore Colts the entire 1974 season, running back punts and kickoffs. He gained 373 yards through 16 games, averaging 7.1 yards per return on punts and 19.9 yards per kickoff return. He had two fumbles. He was waived by the Colts in September 1975 and did not play again. He was picked up by the New York Giants in 1976, but was placed on injured reserve before the season started.

On September 29, 1975, Casey Stengel passed away. Many former Yankees, including Berra, mourned his passing. The Old Professor was buried at Forest Lawn Memorial Park in Glendale, California. In November a memorial service was held in his honor at St. Patrick's Cathedral. Berra was photographed with Terence Cardinal Cooke, the singer Robert Merrill, baseball commissioner Bowie Kuhn, and other celebrities. Donald Grant was there, and he gave the eulogy.

In early October, another member of the Mets organization died—owner Joan Whitney Payson. Berra attended her funeral, along with the entire Mets organization.

*    *    *

That Berra might end up as a new Yankees coach with Billy Martin as a manager was not a shock to the baseball world. It seemed like a natural fit. Even as Berra was leaving the Mets, he was being asked if he had heard from his old team yet. He had not. But Grant and Payson had always known he would probably go back.

Berra told reporters he would consider going back to the Yankees, but he had not been asked to. Basically, the reporters were soliciting the job for him. In fact, he said he'd listen to anybody.

It was clear from news reports that Steinbrenner and Martin were talking about it.

Carmen was against the whole thing—she wanted her husband back from baseball. Carmen told the press she wanted her husband "to take a year off and relax, but he never has listened to me."

Years later Martin said, "I love the guy, but he was not meant to be a manager. I don't think he can be. He is a great coach—he knows more baseball than almost anybody—but he is not mean enough. You have to be mean to manage these guys.… He is not. Never will be. Yogi has always been underrated. They don't know."

There were a thousand reasons Martin wanted Berra on the team. Martin had loved Stengel, and the one thing Stengel always said was that Berra was his good-luck charm. And Martin wanted his old friend around. He wanted a good baseball mind. He wanted another man from the glory days to connect the new team to the past tradition (Ellie Howard was one of the few holdovers from the previous staff that Martin took over). He wanted someone with encyclopedic baseball knowledge.

Yogi Berra was the first new coach he hired for the 1976 season. Martin called him not long after the whole debacle with the Mets.

"I called Yogi on the phone. I told him, 'I know it's hard for you to come back here to the Yankees, but I'd really like to have you with me. You'd be working closely with me, and I really think that would be great,'" Martin said. "I told him he'd be on the bench with me, and help me handle substitutions, and I told him he'd be my ambassador to the guys on the bench."

Martin added, "The guys will tell you when they're mad at me, and I'll take care of it."

"Yeah, I'd like to," said Berra.

Berra's assent, Martin said, "really made me happy. Yogi's a rare breed."

Of Berra's and Martin's relationship, writer Phil Pepe said, "Billy would always cry on Yogi's shoulder. That's who Billy turned to in those days."

Berra's exile from the Yankees had lasted 10 years. He was brought back into the fold officially on December 5, 1975, although the two sides had come to an understanding much earlier.

Asked at the news conference if he was still angry, Berra demurred, saying, "After all, it's a whole new regime since I was there before."

"Yogi is coming back," said Gabe Paul, the Yankees president.

"Yogi who?" asked someone in the crowd.

"I didn't think we needed a second name," laughed Paul.

During the conference, it was said that one of Berra's strongest traits was his ability to communicate. But journalist Dave Anderson pointed out that Berra had been fired from both clubs because the franchises said he couldn't communicate with his players. It was a facetious point. But Martin still felt the need to say that Berra was a fine communicator and would act as a fine buffer between him and the players.

The crowd joked that Berra would now save 15–20 minutes in commuting time and 75¢ in tolls.

Ever mindful of money, Berra shook his head. "It's a buck fifty going over the Triborough Bridge."

"For the next few years, Berra, along with his old teammate Elston Howard, provided the Yankees with some quiet comfort and a sense of the team's remarkable tradition," wrote the great baseball writer Roger Kahn.

But Martin almost got fired in the first weeks of training camp, and Berra did indeed have to play communicator.

Steinbrenner was furious because Martin wouldn't ride on the bus to and from games with his players. Instead, Martin and his coaches rode separately.

"I want to talk to you," Steinbrenner fumed at Martin. Steinbrenner was screaming, "You told me you were going to take the bus!"

Martin felt sure Steinbrenner was actually angry about losing to the Mets in a spring-training game. Either way, he assured him he never intended to ride with the players—that way, he and the coaches could talk openly about the players without fear of being overheard.

"I don't care. Get Yogi in here. I want to get this straight!" the owner bellowed.

When Berra arrived, Steinbrenner, obviously hot, asked, "Yogi, when you managed, did you ride in the bus?"

"No," said Berra.

"You didn't ride in the bus?" asked the incredulous Steinbrenner.

"No, I liked to ride in the car with my coaches so we could talk, just like Billy does," said Berra.

Berra liked working with the players, especially with catcher Thurman Munson. "I'd like to see him throw the ball better. I keep telling him to stand up when he throws, not to throw sidearm from a crouch like he does sometimes. That's when he throws wild. I tell him, 'You're not going to get anybody that way anyway, so stand up and throw.' He's a helluva player."

When spring came and the baseball season started, there was a photo in the *New York Daily News* of Berra, Martin, and Howard all smiling in the newly renovated Yankee Stadium. The Yankees' PR staff knew what it was doing.

While everyone else was oohing and ahhing over the new stadium, Berra looked at the grounds and noted that the infield and the outfield sloped. "They must have graded this field in a rowboat," Berra said to the press, surely much to the publicity man's horror.

On Opening Day many Yankees old-timers returned, and the Yankees christened the new stadium with a win. All was right with the world.

That year the Yankees won the American League East and took the American League Championship Series 3–2 from Kansas City in dramatic fashion, with Chris Chambliss hitting a ninth-inning, game-winning home run that was the Shot Heard 'Round the World for a younger generation. Unfortunately, the Yankees met the Cincinnati Reds in the World Series.

Incredibly, it was Berra's 18th World Series: 14 as a player, one as Yankees manager, one as a Mets coach, one as Mets manager, and now one as a

Yankees coach. Players and fans alike asked him for his autograph. Berra was as popular as ever.

Catfish Hunter, who three years earlier had pitched against Berra's Mets in the World Series and was now with the Yankees, chuckled, "Yogi's in the World Series any way it goes."

When asked to compare this Yankees team to previous squads, Berra remarked, "This club is looser than those clubs were. We had some loose guys—Mantle and Ford—but on this team almost everybody is an agitator. Everybody is on everybody else."

In the end, the Yankees were overmatched in the Series. The Reds had too many offensive and defensive weapons and swept the Yankees 4–0. Still, it had been a successful year, and Berra had been a part of it. Things were happening in the Bronx again.

After the season, Martin extended contract offers to all the coaches. All said they would re-up, but it was clear Berra—along with fellow coaches Bob Lemon and Howard—were manager material. Berra was asked if he had been contacted by anyone for that job.

"No one has contacted me about anything, and I haven't gone after anything," Berra told the press. "There's a lot of time yet. You always listen. That doesn't mean you'll take it. But I'll never go ask for anything."

\*    \*    \*

The next year, 1977, started off with the passing of famous saloon keeper Toots Shor. Shor had been an institution in New York for decades. In the 1940s, '50s, and '60s, Shor's restaurants were filled with a strange mélange of celebrities—famous athletes, movie stars, politicians, millionaires, sportswriters, journalists, and playwrights. Shor knew everyone in New York.

At one point, Shor had supposedly introduced the Nobel Prize–winning writer Ernest Hemingway to Berra.

"Yogi, this is Ernest Hemingway. He's a writer," said Shor.

Berra shook the man's hand. "What paper you with, Ernie?" Berra supposedly said.

No record of the actual meeting took place, but Shor and the writers loved to recount it.

Shor's had been a haven for the baseball players of the era, as well as the stars of football's New York Giants. All of the sporting world showed up for Shor's wake. It was the end of an era.

Meanwhile, Steinbrenner signed Reggie Jackson, believing he was the player the Yankees needed to reclaim their World Series crown.

The year was a topsy-turvy one. Jackson and Martin both seemed to be struggling with the power dynamic their personalities had created. The feisty manager seemed constantly at odds with the loud, brash, superstar Jackson. Both needed each other, but they mixed like oil and water. Martin's temper could boil over in seconds, and Jackson's bravado could transform into boorish and selfish behavior the next.

On June 18, 1977, in a nationally televised game in Boston, Jackson jogged up to a ball hit to right field before he nonchalantly picked it up and tossed it back in. The Yankees were losing 7–4, and Jackson had let Jim Rice hustle to second base instead of charging the ball to cut off Rice's advancement.

In the dugout, Martin was furious about Jackson's apparent lack of effort. He called Jackson in and sent out a replacement. Jackson trotted defiantly to the dugout and confronted Martin on the steps of the dugout.

"You show me up, and I'll show you up," Martin screamed at Jackson.

"What did I do? What did I do?" Jackson shot back, his hands in the air. "How could you do this to me on national television?"

Martin turned his back on Jackson.

"You're not a man," Jackson yelled out.

According to Martin, it was then that Jackson said, "Don't you dare ever show me up again, you motherf*cker!"

Martin shot back, "I won't take that from anyone."

Martin said later, "I went right after him, and Elston Howard tried to stop me, and I threw him out of the way, but I couldn't get past Yogi. Yogi has those iron hands, and he grabbed me by the crotch and pulled me back. I swear if Yogi hadn't stopped me, I would have beat the hell out of him. It's a good thing [Yogi] grabbed me."

Martin continued, saying, "Reggie's big, but I wasn't afraid of him. He was lucky Yogi was there."

For his part, Jackson said, "Yogi still had Billy in a bear hug, which was lucky for Billy."

The following day, there were several meetings as Gabe Paul and Steinbrenner weighed Martin's future. Was he losing control of his team? Was he just too hot-tempered? Either way, the Yankees were now news for the wrong reason across the nation, as that flare-up became the most notorious moment in baseball that season. The tape of that incident has been played countless times in the years since.

Though he was still miffed, Jackson asked Steinbrenner not to fire Martin. Paul met with the players and coaches. Many of the players fought for Martin.

In the meantime, Martin was showing the press all the black-and-blue marks he had received from the incident. Martin blamed Berra for man-handling him. "That damned Yogi, picking on a 160-pound guy," he said.

Berra had never really understood his own strength. It had been a running joke on the Yankees for decades that you did not want Berra poking you in the chest with his gnarled, hardened fingers.

Jackson was suspended for five games that season, and the Yankees won all five without him. Martin felt vindicated. But Jackson was there for a reason, and he had a terrific season, along with many other Yankees including Munson, Graig Nettles, and Chris Chambliss.

It was a turbulent year, but at one point, Berra told the press it wasn't as bad as they were making it out to be. "I didn't see nobody punch anybody yet," he said.

*   *   *

Despite the internal turmoil, the Yankees won the American League East, then again dispatched the Kansas City Royals in the American League Championship Series. In the World Series, New York met their old nemesis, the Dodgers. In Game 6, Jackson hit three home runs on three consecutive pitches to lead his team to another world championship. It was just like old times.

Berra enjoyed yet another ticker-tape parade down the Canyon of Heroes in downtown New York.

\* \* \*

A week or two later, Dave Bristol, the manager of the Atlanta Braves, was released, and a day after that, Berra told the media he would be interested in the job. He also said he had not been contacted by the Braves organization, and he never was. But clearly Berra still yearned to be a manager.

Never one to let things slow down, in January 1978, Berra, with his son Tim and a group of investors, opened Yogi Berra's Racquetball Hall of Fame Club in Fairfield, New Jersey, on Route 46. It was a state-of-the-art facility. And racquetball, which had been big in the West, was now catching on in the East.

"We're going to get them all back into prime baseball condition on our racquetball courts," Carmen said of current and former Yankees living in the area, including Martin, Roy White, Chambliss, Mickey Rivers, and others.

Whitey Ford remembered a story about Berra's racquetball club. President Gerald Ford and Berra were playing golf one day in the same foursome.

"Yogi mentioned to the president that he owned this racquetball club in New Jersey," Ford related.

"Do you play racquetball, Mr. President?" Berra asked.

"Yes, I have on occasion," replied the president.

Berra then pulled a card out of his wallet and handed it to him.

"Here, Mr. President," said Berra. "Just in case you're ever in New Jersey and you want to play racquetball."

The card entitled the bearer to play free at Berra's club.

Ford said, "On the other side of the card was stamped, 'Good Tuesdays Only.'"

Berra was also still a vice president at Yoo-hoo. In fact, as late as 1985, a large picture of Berra that read "Me-He for Yoo-hoo" could be found in right-center at the field in Ft. Lauderdale.

The Berras were now ensconced in Montclair, New Jersey. Carmen was a Republican fund-raiser in the county. Berra played golf at most of the surrounding country clubs as either a member or a guest. Some clubs he did not like because he felt they had excluded him when he was younger. It seemed to him he was a fine guest for the members to parade through the clubhouse, but when it came time to join, they were a little less welcoming. But by now, Berra and the family were a star attraction in Montclair—an institution. And he looked, in many respects, like many other businessmen of the period. He was still trim, but his forehead belied his years as his hairline began to recede. He was almost always photographed with glasses now. He was more businessman than baseball icon.

Berra's prime passion in this period of his life was his golf game.

"He was glad it rained on the Yankees' victory parade because he said, 'If I had to be in this parade on a nice day instead of at the golf course, I'd be very mad,'" confided Carmen.

While golf was a treasured distraction, and he still enjoyed watching winter sports and attending New Jersey Devils hockey games, baseball still held a grip on him.

"Right now I'm happy, but soon I'll be ready to go to spring training," he said.

*     *     *

The Yankees defense of their championship got off to a rocky start in 1978. New York entered May at 10–9, then tore through the month with 19 wins and eight losses. But they cooled in June and July, playing just .500 ball.

The combustible relationship between Steinbrenner and Martin finally exploded that summer, and the manager was either fired or resigned, depending on who is telling the story. Bob Lemon, not Berra, was named to replace Martin.

For Berra there was another sad note early that summer—John C. "Johnny" Schulte, the man who had signed Berra to the Yankees contract with the infamous $500 bonus, had died. He was 82 years old.

Dugout controversies aside, the Yankees rallied from 14 games behind the torrid Boston Red Sox, tied the race on the last day of the season, and forced a one-game playoff, which they won.

Next, the Yankees met the Dodgers in a rematch of the 1977 World Series, and the Bronx Bombers were triumphant again, taking the Series 4–2.

Berra had collected yet another championship.

\*    \*    \*

The revolving door that became the Yankees' manager spot during the Bronx Zoo era spun again in 1979, as Steinbrenner rehired Billy Martin during the season, only to fire him for a second time in October. The one constant during this time was Berra's presence as bench coach. He was one of the coaches who helped retain a semblance of steadiness through all the posturing of Steinbrenner and the various managers he hired.

"As a coach, sometimes serving at first base, sometimes in the dugout, he has enjoyed a job that was beneficial to him and the Yankees. It kept him in baseball in a highly secure position, and it gave the Yankees the benefit of his vast baseball knowledge and his even more widespread popularity," wrote sportswriter Murray Chass.

What many knew but didn't write about was that Berra had been offered the manager job several times by Steinbrenner, but had refused. Carmen was adamant that she did not want her husband to manage the New York Yankees again. His previous managing jobs had taken a toll on him. She did not like the negative press almost all managers receive; as a coach, he had none of the pressure and all of the fun of still being involved in baseball. But the idea of managing one more time gnawed at Berra.

\*    \*    \*

On July 15, 1980, Berra was once again a topic of discussion after future Hall of Fame catcher Johnny Bench broke Berra's home-run record for a catcher with his 314th dinger. Berra sent Bench a telegram that read: "Congratulations! I knew the record would stand until it was broken."

Bench eventually retired at the end of 1983 and was voted into the Hall of Fame in 1989.

"There has been a tendency to rate Berra the second-best hitting catcher of the modern era—behind Johnny Bench," Phil Rizzuto once wrote. "I have always found this comparison puzzling. Berra leads Bench in batting average by nearly 20 points, as well as in RBIs and total runs scored, despite the fact that Yogi had fewer at-bats. Bench leads only in total home runs.... As for Yogi's overall contribution to his team, Yogi's teams outperformed Bench's."

Without any disrespect to Bench, who is one of the top two or three catchers of all time, Rizzuto is right. Plus, Berra caught three no-hitters in his career, Bench one. Berra has three MVPs and Bench two. Both were excellent players. But modern sportswriters are quick to call Bench the best ever, which is difficult to justify when looking at both numbers and accomplishments. Berra and Dickey certainly rate as high (if not higher) when the entirety of their careers is taken into account.

\*    \*    \*

On December 14, 1980, Elston Howard died. Berra was devastated. "Yogi and Elston Howard were always together. They were inseparable," recalled writer Phil Pepe. "Every morning on the road, there was Yogi and Ellie having breakfast together in the hotel restaurant. It was like a standing arrangement."

Berra was sent to the AA minor leagues to scout their farm system during the strike-marred season of 1981. When play resumed, the Yankees returned yet again to the World Series, but this time they fell to the Dodgers, losing 4–2.

# ~ Chapter 19 ~

# MANAGING
# MR. STEINBRENNER'S YANKEES

Improbably, Billy Martin was back at the helm of the Yankees for the 1983 season. Predictably, by June his future with the team was in doubt yet again. The names of the usual suspects—Jeff Torborg, Don Zimmer, and Yogi Berra—were already starting to be mentioned as replacements.

In that same season, Bowie Kuhn decided he would not seek another term as commissioner. Sportswriter George Vecsey wrote a column wherein he invented humorous answers for a number of people who might have applied for the job. In answer to, "What would I do if I was commissioner?" he wrote for Berra: "I would appoint my wife, Carmen, and my childhood friend, Joe Garagiola, as my assistants. Since Joe invented all my funny lines, he'd be great doing public relations for baseball. And since Carmen advised me on our investments and has warned me to not even think of being the Yankee manager again, she'd be a great financial adviser to baseball."

The Yankees ended up 91–71 in 1983, in third place behind the Orioles and Tigers. Martin was fired, and on December 16, 1983, Berra was appointed manager of the New York Yankees for the second time in his career.

Berra's face filled the entire front page of the *New York Daily News,* with a giant headline that read, "Hello, Yogi!" That Berra would be offered the job if Martin and Steinbrenner could not patch up their differences had been established since early December.

Sportswriter Dave Anderson wrote, "Asked if he had been offered the job by George Steinbrenner during a Thursday night conversation in West Orange, New Jersey, at a Boy Scout dinner, Yogi Berra added to his linguistic lore by saying, 'Well, a little bit.' Yogi Berra went on to say that the principal owner 'said I was the number one choice. He asked if I'd be interested, and I said I'd have to think about it.'"

It was a little late in the season to be hiring managers. The truth was that Steinbrenner had been trying to woo Los Angeles Dodgers manager Tommy Lasorda to New York. But the Dodgers organization made Lasorda a huge offer instead and persuaded the charismatic manager to remain in Los Angeles.

When asked at the press conference why he had not accepted Steinbrenner's earlier entreaties, Berra told the press, "My age had something to do with it. I've achieved just about everything a man can achieve. I've won the Most Valuable Player award, I've made the Hall of Fame, and I've won two pennants as a manager. But I've never won a championship. I felt that this club was capable of winning one. In the past, George talked to me about the job. I really didn't know the players that well. But I think I know these guys real well, and I think they can win."

Asked if he was concerned with the possibility of Steinbrenner's meddling, Berra responded, "I don't care what he does. That don't bother me. I don't get mad. I always believe four heads are better than one."

"I'll argue with George about things probably, and then I'll find out," Berra conceded to the press when asked how he would deal with Steinbrenner when he was upset. "Why did I accept two years? I want to retire after that. I just hope George takes care of me, too."

Since he had named Martin manager in 1975, Steinbrenner had made nine changes at the manager's spot. Berra was the fifth man to enter this revolving door.

The players responded positively to the switch. Yankees catcher Rick Cerone told the press, "How can you not bust your butt for Yogi?"

Don Baylor, who'd had a few confrontations with Martin, felt badly the manager had been fired. But when asked about Berra, he said, "'I can't wait to play for him.... It's getting to play every day for a Hall of Famer, and a Yankee Hall of Famer at that. Yogi played in [14] World Series, and I'm looking for my first Series ring."

Willie Randolph said, "Yogi has helped us all over the years. I want to give something back to the man. It makes a difference when you can say I'm going to go out and give something for that man. Sometimes you think you're doing that anyway, but you're not. And Yogi can be tough when he wants to. Everybody says 'good old Yogi,' but just try that nonchalant stuff, and he'll put you in your place."

Even Tom Seaver, now with the White Sox, chimed in. "From what I know of the Yankees, I think he's the perfect manager for that club. He doesn't put too many harnesses on. He doesn't overmanage. He puts the players on the field who he thinks are the best players. He also doesn't come apart under pressure. That could help in his dealings with his owner. You don't see him get upset unless it's with a player who gives something less than his best effort," the pitcher said.

Other players, like Goose Gossage and Steve Kemp, remained reserved or skeptical, tiring of the Yankees-manager merry-go-round.

One intrepid newspaper reporter even found Phil Linz for a comment. "He's a good guy," said Linz, by then owner of a restaurant in Manhattan, "but I thought Billy was excellent, too, though I never played for him. Kids still come into my East Side restaurant and say, 'My father remembers you and your harmonica.'"

"When they ask me to play it," he added, "I tell them to come back on a slow night."

Noted newspaper columnist William Safire wrote, "Yogi Berra, upon appointment to his second term as manager of the New York Yankees, flashed his familiar, lopsided grin and waggled a finger at his friends in the press: 'You guys ain't gonna get too much from me.'"

Clyde King told the press he had been grateful for Berra's help during the two-month-long period King served as the Yankees' manager in 1982. "He's far more alert than people realize he is. The things he brought up to me in the dugout, the things he noticed in the clubhouse...." he said.

Berra was asked after Christmas what the best present he received was. "I guess the manager's job was the best present," said Berra. But Berra was also proud of what he gave. "I got my wife some Gucci stuff and put money in it…. Let her buy what she needs," he said.

But amid the celebration of the new job, on February 24, 1984, Berra lost another old friend when Albert V. Olivieri died. The inventor of Yoo-hoo had been living in Hollywood, Florida, and was 70 years old.

When spring came, "Yogi's Back!" was the title of the *Sports Illustrated* season preview issue in April 1984. The photo showed Yogi in pinstripes, wearing the familiar No. 8, looking over a baseball field.

The ascension to manager had always been a point of contention in the Berra household, but after Carmen had a chance to reflect on the change, she told the press, "I didn't want him to take the manager's job. I didn't think it was a good idea. I said, 'You've done everything in baseball; why do you want to manage now?' He said, 'I haven't won a World Series.' After he took the job, I changed my mind. Now that he has it, I'm glad. If that's what he wants to do, that's fine with me. At this stage in his life, it would be good if he could win that World Series."

"I could have had other jobs," Berra said. "I could have had Atlanta, Texas—I didn't want to go. New York's my home. I made a lot of friends here. People have been nice to me. I never asked to be manager here. I could've put in for it like some do, but I never did. This is a challenge. I won a pennant in each league. The only thing I never won was a World Series. The kids told me to do it. They said: 'Dad, what do you have to lose? You'll only be in baseball a few more years. You'll probably want to retire or something. Do it now while you got the chance.'"

And Berra knew what the job would be like. He went into it with his eyes wide open. "I know what I'm stepping into," he admitted.

"I probably wish I would have gone further," Berra said of his efforts to be taken more seriously. "I speak funny. There are some words you're going to hear from me probably when you come in after a game. You may get some Berraisms. I don't really think I'm saying that until I read them. But my kids get on me. They say: 'There you go, Dad. There's another one.' Every time I say something, if I say something wrong, they'll jump on me."

\*    \*    \*

In 1984, spring training was not as smooth as some had hoped it would be. Berra decided to play Ken Griffey in center and place Don Mattingly at first. Griffey, the aging star from the Big Red Machine, had wanted to play first base to save his legs. Like Willie Mays years earlier, Griffey needed rest. But Mattingly was a tremendous weapon, and Berra wanted him as a steadying presence at first. Then aging star third baseman Graig Nettles balked at the threat of platooning at third base and demanded to be traded. Pitcher Dave Righetti was moved to a relief role in the bullpen. Lou Piniella talked of retirement. It was an uneasy time as many of the Yankees who had been a part of the teams from 1976 to 1981 were now getting older.

Eventually, Nettles was traded to the Padres. It was not a popular trade with the players—Righetti, for one, was openly bitter about Nettles's departure. However, moving Righetti to the bullpen proved to be a great replacement for the departed Goose Gossage, and Righetti proved to be an excellent closer. During the course of the year, Berra heard from the sportswriters over and over every time a starter failed how a Righetti start would have gotten a win. In fact, it wasn't until the beginning of the 1985 season that the writers admitted that "Rags," as Righetti was affectionately known, was an excellent reliever.

"Isn't it time all those who criticized Yogi Berra for putting Dave Righetti in the bullpen admit that the Yankee manager was right?" asked Phil Pepe in the *Daily News*. "Righetti, who had frequent arm problems as a starter, has been sound as a reliever."

But it wasn't long before the stress of being the manager of the New York Yankees began to take its toll on Berra.

"In his office off the Yankee clubhouse, the 58-year-old manager had [lit] a cigarette, taken a puff, and slipped it into the slot of a glass ashtray. He leaned back in his chair, apparently unperturbed by the loss or by being a manager again after having been a Yankee coach for eight seasons. But the cigarette betrayed him," wrote Dave Anderson. "For about two years Yogi Berra hadn't smoked much. But now he's smoking often. Being a manager can do that to your nerves, especially being a Yankee manager for George Steinbrenner."

This was what Carmen had worried about. This is what managing did to Berra, to any man. It took years off his life.

Like any other team Berra ever managed, the Yankees suffered a slow start while Berra played with all the possible parts. Further impeding their momentum, April was a soggy month with a number of rainouts.

By the end of June, the Yankees were 33–41, and things were getting ugly. But in July and August, they played well over .600 ball and won 38 games while only dropping 21. They ended the season 87–75. But the real problem was that Sparky Anderson's Detroit Tigers had gone on a tear, eventually winning the pennant and the World Series handily. The truth was that few other teams had a shot against the red-hot Tigers.

*    *    *

By February 1985, speculation began to circulate that Steinbrenner was ready to fire Berra. Stories filled with names of possible replacements ran rampant. This was what it meant to be a Steinbrenner manager. But on February 20, 1985, Steinbrenner declared Berra's job was safe for the upcoming season.

"Yogi will be the manager this year, period," Steinbrenner told the press. "I said the same thing last year, and I stuck to my word. A bad start will not affect Yogi's status, either. In the past I have put a lot of pressure on my managers to win at certain times. That will not be the case this spring."

Steinbrenner was trying hard to turn a new leaf. "I'm not going to worry if we lose a game to Boston or to the Mets [in spring training]. We've got some players we want to take a look at, and that's what's going to get done," he promised.

"We had our meeting here," Berra told the press, "and it went very well. He told me not to worry about spring training. Just worry about the season. That doesn't mean I'm not gonna win as many games as I can down here. This helps, though. It lets me manage with a clear mind."

However, many sportswriters were quick to remind Berra that Steinbrenner had told Bob Lemon the same thing in 1982, then fired him two weeks later.

*    *    *

Dale Berra, Carmen and Berra's youngest son, developed into a very good ballplayer. He signed with the Pittsburgh Pirates in 1975. Dale was a highly sought draft pick that year, being drafted 20th in the first round. That was the year that Berra had been fired by the Mets in July, which freed up his time considerably.

"That was the summer Dale had signed with the Pirates, and he was playing in upstate New York," Carmen recalled. "So we simply got in our car and followed Dale around. We had a lot of fun. That probably softened the blow [of being fired], following Dale around."

His best years in Pittsburgh were 1982—batting .263 with 10 home runs and 61 RBIs—and 1983—batting .251 with 10 home runs and 52 RBIs. After committing 30 errors in three different seasons, Dale's career fielding percentage was .956. As a result, his nicknames were "BooBoo" (a reference to the secondary character on the Yogi Bear cartoons) and "Stonehands."

On December 20, 1984, Dale Berra, Jay Buhner, and Alfonso Pulido of the Pittsburgh Pirates were traded to the New York Yankees for Steve Kemp, Tim Foli, and cash. It was only the second time a father would manage his son in the history of the major leagues. It was major news in the sports world.

"I don't think there will be any problem; the only problem will be in the minds of other people," Carmen told the press. "You have to know the individuals involved. You have to know that with Yogi, the most important thing is the team. Winning comes first, and he's not going to favor Dale at the expense of the team just because [Dale is] his son.... And you have to know Dale. He idolizes his father. He is not going to do anything to jeopardize Yogi's job."

"I'm not going to call him Skip. I'll call him what I've always called him—Dad. Who am I kidding? Everyone knows he's my father," Dale told reporters.

"If he does his job, he plays. If not, he sits," Berra told *People* magazine.

"I'm elated," Dale told the press. "It's a dream come true. This is the first time my dad has seen me play on the pro level."

"Yeah, I finally get to see my son play," Berra chuckled. When asked what he thought of Dale as a player, Berra replied that his son was an "adequate" infielder.

But Carmen was a proud mama and a cautious wife. She knew the precarious position the manager of the Yankees was always in. She told the press, "I know this: if Yogi is fired and Dale is still there, he'll play as hard for the next manager as he does for his father."

Dale showed everyone he was a chip off the old block when he said, "Our similarities are different."

During this period in his life, Berra was spending more time with his sons, especially at family gatherings. "When dinner is over, they might play *Trivial Pursuit* or watch home movies or talk about sports. All sports," wrote Pepe of the *Daily News*.

The Yankees did not start the season well. They started off 6–7 after losing two out of three to the Boston Red Sox. On the day after, April 26, many of the beat writers were surprised to find Berra still behind the manager's desk.

"All I know is that I'm still here," Berra told them.

"The phrase 'for now,' although unspoken, hovered over the room," wrote sportswriter Paul Needell.

"Everyone is saying if he doesn't win tonight, he's out tonight. That's not the case," Steinbrenner assured the writers and Berra.

"No question the guys are playing uptight," designated hitter Don Baylor added. "They're trying to do more than they're capable of. And it's all for the manager. It would be different if there was a manager here who nobody respected or gave a damn about. Losing is hurting us, but nobody in this room is hurting more than Yogi. And we realize that."

But several more losses made a liar out of Steinbrenner, and Berra was fired on April 28, 1985. The capper for Steinbrenner had been a three-game sweep by the Chicago White Sox. The Yankees were only 16 games into the season. Berra was replaced by—of all people— Billy Martin.

Baylor and Mattingly were both bitter about the move. Baylor threw a trash can across the clubhouse. Mattingly had tears in his eyes. Dave Winfield and Griffey were also upset, but mostly at Rickey Henderson, who greeted the news of working with Martin with glee.

With a smile, Berra said, "What do you guys need?" to the reporters gathered around him. "All you need is a headline. This is three times for me. That's the way this game is. My contract doesn't say I have to do anything if I am fired, so I'm going to go home and play golf."

As was his custom, Berra went around the clubhouse, shaking hands with all the players and other personnel.

"This is the hardest thing for me to take," pitcher John Montefusco said. "Yogi was a friend to everyone, but it wasn't Yogi's fault. Nothing surprises me anymore."

At first, Dale refused to talk to the press. Then he said, "That's the way this game is today."

Later, he said, "He took it with real class, like the real man that he is.... He told me not to feel bad for him—that his time is passed now, but the future is all mine. I feel awful, but I also feel proud watching him go around the clubhouse shaking hands with every player and seeing how they reacted."

Clyde King, the Yankees' general manager, rode on the team flight to Dallas that Sunday night. He told sportswriter Bill Madden, "The whole thing didn't really hit me until I sat down here next to this seat where Yogi always was."

The next day, Mike Lupica interviewed Berra at home.

"What's the use of getting angry? I did the best I can, and the players did, too," Berra said.

He had gone home and then went to the Montclair Country Club to hit a bucket of golf balls. On his way home, a car stopped on the street and a man got out and shouted, "We're still with you, Yogi!"

Berra told Lupica that he'd spoken to Steinbrenner, saying, "It wasn't nothing much. Just a phone call."

Berra also told Lupica he had called Martin, reporting, "I told him we got a helluva team, and we're gonna snap out of it."

Lupica talked about the three bleacher seats from Yankee Stadium that Berra still had from the old stadium, before the renovation in the mid-1970s. And he talked about how far away that old stadium and Berra were from baseball today.

The Berra clan was preparing for the first communion of granddaughter Lindsay, while Berra played with Larry III, gently tossing him a softball. Wrote Lupica, "After 42 years, Yogi had a day off."

"I don't get mad easy, and even when I do, I don't stay mad," Berra said. "I got mad in 1984. We had a meeting in the owner's office. We had too many meetings, I thought."

Years later, Berra told of a 1984 meeting with Steinbrenner that ended in an argument. It involved a pack of cigarettes.

"The 24 guys I wanted to be on the team were not the same guys who the owner wanted on the team. It wasn't just one guy.... It was four or five guys who the owner wanted and the coaches and I didn't.... We talked a lot, and I said something like, 'If you want that team, can I say that this is your team if we lose?'... I knew that the coaches and I knew more about judging baseball ability than anyone else in the room," Berra related.

"Anyway, this meeting got so bad that I called the owner some bad names and threw a pack of cigarettes at him.... One of the coaches said I threw the pack down on his desk and it bounced up and hit him. I don't know. I know I threw them, and I know I was hot," Berra said.

"Nobody ever talks to me that way," Steinbrenner supposedly responded.

"He was mad, I was mad.... I wondered if the thrown pack of cigarettes came back my way the next year. What I mean is, the next year, 1985, I managed 16 games, and it was over. I was never told why I was fired," remembered Berra.

Allegedly, Berra said it was his team to manage and he would start who he wanted to start. Tempers flared, especially with the volatile Steinbrenner. So incensed was Steinbrenner that he questioned Berra's abilities and charged nepotism in the case of Berra starting his own son over some of the other players. By some accounts, Steinbrenner even brought up Dale's involvement with the shameful cocaine scandal that was brewing.

In the 1980s cocaine use was up substantially. And baseball players were no different than the rest of society. However, they had more money and were higher-profile users than most. Dealing drugs and drug abuse reached epidemic proportions in a number of clubhouses. Ex-Pirate John Milner had admitted to buying $200 worth of cocaine in the bathroom stalls beneath Three Rivers Stadium.

Several Pittsburgh Pirates, including Dale Berra, Lee Lacy, Lee Mazzilli, Milner, Dave Parker, Rod Scurry, and other notable major league players—Willie Aikens, Vida Blue, Enos Cabell, Keith Hernandez, Jeffrey Leonard, Tim Raines, and Lonnie Smith—were called before a Pittsburgh grand jury in the fall of 1985. Their testimony led to the drug trials, which made national headlines in September 1985. It was the most notorious baseball-related scandal since the Black Sox of 1919.

In order to play baseball during the 1986 season, Dale eventually had to donate 10 percent of his salary to charity, by order of the commissioner's office. He was released by the New York Yankees on July 27, 1986.

\*    \*    \*

In the summer of 1985, Berra went to Fargo, North Dakota, to play golf in the Roger Maris Celebrity Benefit Golf Tournament, established after the former Yankees great was diagnosed with lymphoma. At some point during the tournament, Berra expressed some doubt about North Dakota's claim that it was indeed one of the nation's leading potato-growing states.

"You don't have enough potatoes to fill my front yard," he supposedly said. Berra doesn't personally recall saying it.

The Red River Valley Potato Growers Association decided to use the publicity to its advantage. "The association announced in December they were loading an 18-wheel tractor trailer with their potatoes, 23 tons worth, and heading the truck for Berra's home in Montclair, New Jersey," it said.

Berra's response, when he heard about the stunt, was, "Boy, I only asked for a bag full."

But the growers' association intended them ultimately for a charity cause. The trailer had on its side, in big letters, "The Red River Valley & Yogi Go to Bat for the Needy."

When asked how many ways they had eaten the potatoes, Berra told *People* magazine, "French fries, home fries, scalloped, and mashed; my wife just yelled at me—tomorrow we're going to have mashed."

\* \* \*

Three days after being fired by the Yankees in 1985, Berra appeared at the Shea Stadium Director's Room, where he and Carmen dined with Houston Astros owner Dr. John J. McMullen. The three then watched the game from Mets owner Nelson Doubleday's private luxury box. They posed for pictures, and no one told the press anything—although the message was clear to see.

McMullen had indeed offered Berra the opportunity to manage the Houston Astros. Berra turned him down.

Eventually, after the Yankees missed the postseason that fall, the Yankees replaced Martin with Lou Piniella. King approached Berra and asked him to be Piniella's bench coach. Berra refused that, too.

But on November 5, 1985, the Astros called their second major news conference that week, after earlier announcing the hiring of rookie manager Hal Lanier. The team announced that Berra was coming to Texas to be the bench coach for Lanier and the Astros. Berra was 60 years old.

Asked about refusing the manager's job, Berra responded, "John's too good a friend, and I want it to remain that way."

Berra was on his way to a weeklong cruise with Carmen. He arrived in Houston in midmonth and was welcomed by Lanier.

"He'll be a big asset to our club," Lanier told the press. "Yogi has been exposed to every facet of the game. He has coached first and third base as well as managed."

To fans of the Texas club, Berra brought instant authenticity to a floundering franchise. To New Yorkers, used to seeing Berra in the pinstripes and grays of the local teams, both with their interlocking *NY* insignias, Berra seemed an unnatural sight in the rainbow-colored Houston Astros uniforms of that period, with the star of Texas emblazoned on the front. Berra was an instant sensation in Houston.

\* \* \*

That fall, Maris's cancer spread, and it looked as if he would not be able to beat it.

Berra said, "I was down in Houston when he was real sick, and I wanted to see him, but they wouldn't let me. They said he was too bad off. I was really upset about that. We had a lot of great players on the Yankees, and Roger was one of them. Give me nine Roger Marises each year, and I'll take my chances."

"He left the hospital in tears," wrote sportswriter Maury Allen.

"It tore me up not to be able see him that one last time. They told me he was too sick," Berra said.

Maris died on December 14, 1985.

*    *    *

Berra liked the Dome because it was very predictable and there were no rainouts. He got to go home when they played the Mets and Phillies, and being in the National League, he was traveling to play the Cardinals in St. Louis. He was now able to visit friends and family regularly once again.

"We play the Mets in May," he said early in 1986, "and Carm is going to stay home and then come down when we go back to Houston. We got a nice place right near the Galleria shopping center, but I hope she doesn't spend all her time shopping."

The Berra magic was back in 1986. Houston got off to a hot 15–6 start, and to top it off, the Astros signed Dale as a free agent on July 26, 1986, briefly reuniting father and son. He would be released October 3, 1987, and retired from professional baseball.

A host of star ballplayers, including Nolan Ryan and Mike Scott, led the team to its first Western Division title in franchise history. And there was Berra, fired one year, in postseason play the next with another team. *The New York Times,* the *New York Daily News,* and the *New York Post* all did stories on the subject. Each was fascinated by whether Berra's luck would hold out and land him in another World Series.

"Would anyone bet against him making it 22 this year?" asked Pepe in the *Daily News.* "The man has the Midas touch. He got into the bowling business before the boom and sold before the crash. He lent his name to the Yoo-hoo chocolate drink company and wound up with a vice-presidency. Whatever he touches becomes gold."

The Astros went to the 1986 National League Championship Series versus Berra's old team, the New York Mets. The Mets were too strong for the Astros, but no one doubted the Berra mystique. The sixth game of that series, a 16-inning, drama-filled affair, is one of the most memorable NLCS moments in baseball history.

Berra served as coach for three more years, finally calling it quits in 1989. While he was in Houston, Berra was keen to follow the fortunes of the New York franchises—he was always a Gotham kid at heart. He even gave new Yankees manager Lou Piniella some advice via the sportswriters: "Don't lose two games in a row."

But he would not step foot back in Yankee Stadium, he said, as long as Steinbrenner was there.

Berra's resolve was tested on August 22, 1988, when he and Bill Dickey were honored with plaques to be hung in Monument Park at Yankee Stadium. Berra's plaque calls him "A legendary Yankee" and cites his most famous quote, "It ain't over till it's over." However, the honor was not enough to shake Berra's conviction that Steinbrenner had broken their personal agreement; Berra would not set foot in the stadium for another decade.

The Astros of 1987, '88, and '89 had never lived up to the promise of 1986. Lanier was fired at the end of the 1989 season. Berra decided it was time to go—for good.

"I felt in spring training that this might be it," Berra said, referring to his retirement from coaching on September 25, 1989. "I figured after 42 years it was time to try something else. I've got seven grandkids, and I want to see more of them. I want a chance to travel more before I die. If we want to make a trip to Europe, we might just do it…. I couldn't ask for anything else from my career. This had nothing to do with anything that happened during the season. I had said I would take it one year at a time."

He was 64 years old, and he had nothing to do the next day. He was seen playing golf not long afterward.

# ~ Chapter 20 ~

# YOGI BERRA, INCORPORATED

In 1989 Berra and Tom Horton, a small-press business publisher who had known Berra for some years, authored a book titled *Yogi: It Ain't Over*. The book got mediocre reviews, but fans bought it in droves. It was a huge success, a *New York Times* best seller, and the most up-to-date history of Berra's life at that time. It was a hit, and Berra was as popular as ever.

Berra and Carmen sat down with their friend, radio personality Arlene Francis, at the famed restaurant Sardi's in New York for an interview about the book.

"What's your book about, Yogi?" Arlene asked.

"I don't know, I haven't read it," Berra answered.

Berra seemed to have problems answering the questions. In reality, Berra hated interviews and tended toward yes and no answers. He was so uncomfortable that during one commercial break, Francis asked Berra, "Yogi, have you read this?"

"No, why should I? I was there!" replied Berra.

It was a headline in *USA Today* the next day. Berra's thinking was that he spent countless days with the writer, and he trusted Horton. If he hadn't, Horton wouldn't have gotten the job. Berra actually said he would prefer to read something else, remarking, "I would rather read about a new Ping driver, or who was going to coach third base for the Yankees next year."

"Hardly anybody would quarrel...that Winston Churchill has been replaced by Yogi Berra as the...favorite source of quotations," reported *The New Yorker* magazine in 1991.

But amid all the good in Berra's life, he also dealt with sadness. An old friend and the hero of the Brooklyn Dodgers' 1955 World Series team, Sandy Amoros, was suffering from pneumonia and was in serious condition. Sandy Amoros Day was declared in Brooklyn, and Berra appeared at a parade in order to raise money for his friend's medical expenses. Amoros died shortly after, on June 27, 1992.

\*   \*   \*

In April 1993, it was déjà vu all over again for Yoo-hoo and Berra. While he was in the middle of his boycott of George Steinbrenner and Yankee Stadium, Berra was in the midst of making up with another old stand-by—Yoo-hoo.

Berra had been feuding with the Yoo-hoo company about the same time he started his acrimonious separation from the Yankees. The Olivieri family, creators of the drink, had been solicitous of Berra's opinions in the past, but later owners were less interested in what Berra thought.

"The new ones wanted to change everything," Berra said. "They weren't like the originals.... They didn't try to bring me in at all."

"We sold our stock. We had no company contact. That was the end of it," Carmen added.

And Berra felt that the drink's flavor had changed as well. "It didn't taste right," he said. "It was too dark. They cut down the quality."

In fact, the formula had been changed.

"One year, the formula changed 26 times," said Eugene Kreuscher, president of the soft-drink division of Austin, Nichols and Company, which acquired Yoo-hoo in 1988.

"But Mr. Berra did not know that the original formula was restored about a dozen years ago—or so Yoo-hoo says—and that the company has recovered from some lean years," wrote Richard Sandomir of *The New York Times* in April 1993.

Berra felt the company had skimped on the chocolate and other ingredients in an effort to save money and create better profit margins. The National Advertising Division of the Council of Better Business Bureaus had even found the Yoo-hoo company guilty of faulty advertising in 1984, which further tarnished the brand's name.

"Now we use the best cocoa from Denmark," Kreuscher said.

In January 1993, Brandon Steiner, the head of a company that matches stars to advertisers, "asked Yogi to be part of a Yoo-hoo promotion featuring 20 greats in a baseball card and memorabilia sweepstakes." Both sides admitted that Berra said no several times, complaining that the drink didn't taste like it used to.

"It hit a nerve," Steiner said.

"Mr. Berra slowly relented. He wanted to know details about Austin, Nichols and Lifestyle Marketing, the firm that created the summer promotion. He was not eager to come in to save a company if it might be dying," reported Sandomir.

"The management they've got now is good. The drink is just about back to normal," Berra told Sandomir.

Berra shunned the idea of full-blown spokesmanhood. But his was the featured card in the promotion, and he recorded a radio commercial and made personal appearances.

Berra was entertaining a comeback with Yoo-hoo, but any work he did for the company would have to fit into his schedule, which at this time included Hardee's commercials and his Pringles potato chips endorsement. By the end of the 20th century, the Yoo-hoo brand was bought by Cadbury Schweppes Americas Beverages and is now targeted toward teenagers interested in skateboarding and rock music. But, with the success of the promotion in the midst of the baseball memorabilia mania, Berra had at least kissed and made up with the chocolate-drink company.

Then, Berra received yet another blow when he lost another friend. Former Los Angeles Dodgers pitcher Don Drysdale died on July 3, 1993.

Berra said, "Going to the memorial service for Don Drysdale was very hard for me. He was a hard pitcher to face, and I am lucky I didn't have to do it very often. We shared a room during a golf tournament in Florida, and he let me use his car. It was a brand-new Ford station wagon in 1957, I think, and I lost the keys."

*     *     *

In 1993 Berra's sons, Larry, Tim, and Dale, and Tim's wife, Betsy, formed LTD Enterprises. According to business reporter Patricia Winters Lauro, their intention was "to market their father's career after they realized that Mr. Berra was inundated with about 100 letters a week, most of them seeking his autograph. As sports memorabilia grew in popularity, the sons decided they were better suited than agents to protect and promote their father's image. LTD now runs a thriving mail-order business and has a Yogi site on the World Wide Web, complete with a Yogi store, a whole range of memorabilia, and Yogi links to favorite sports sites."

"I couldn't sell widgets, but I can sell Yogi Berra—it's so easy," said Dale.

For once, Berra was far behind the curve here. Mickey Mantle, Joe DiMaggio, and a host of famous players had been working the card-show circuit for years, living off their fame by signing autographs for money. Having not made the millions playing ball that players today make, it was a good source of revenue for them after their playing days were over. And many adult fans did not mind paying the fees that the famous players from bygone eras were charging.

DiMaggio and Mantle had formed corporations long before Berra's, but Berra's sons had the benefit of having a product like "Yogi Berra" to sell. It was a small step beyond what most other athletes had done, though to be sure, DiMaggio had been way ahead of him.

The Berra family collected the stories and yarns, apocryphal or not, that the sportswriters had been spinning for years, and packaged them to sell the idea of Berra as much as the man himself.

Always a popular endorser, Berra now advertised a wide array of products, and his penchant for reviewing films for friends and family—as he was still an avid movie-watcher—turned into a part-time, short-lived gig as a movie reviewer.

LTD Enterprises capitalized on Berra's fame and the goodwill of his legions of fans and used it to their advantage. It was smart business, done in a way few other ballplayers had done before. Richard Ben Cramer, in his biography *Joe DiMaggio,* described the harried slugger selling signed baseballs for $400 and bemoaning Berra's image branding, sneering, "How about that cunning resin model of Yankee Stadium housed in a clear, plastic dome and mounted on a handsome wood-grain base with a genuine replication of Yogi Berra's genuine signature?"

Still, LTD's many successes were yet to come. Along with endorsements and baseball card show appearances, Berra, like his friend Mantle—one of his few contemporaries who was as wildly popular—would soon embark on an incredible and unlikely literary career.

\*    \*    \*

In 1993 Cora and Phil Rizzuto celebrated their 50th wedding anniversary at Yankee Stadium. George Steinbrenner himself honored the couple at home plate. However, Berra was not present at this event, and it pained his old friend and former roommate Rizzuto.

"I had hoped Yogi would come to the affair at the stadium, but he didn't. I respect him for his convictions. He won't go back to Yankee Stadium as long as George owns the team. End of subject," said Rizzuto.

"Rizzuto's been going to Yankee Stadium for 53 years. And he is still trying to find a way to beat the toll on the George Washington Bridge," Berra said of his old friend Scooter.

On November 12, 1993, another old friend, Bill Dickey, died at the Rose Care Nursing Center in Little Rock, Arkansas. He was 86 years old. He had retired there in 1977 as a securities representative for a Little Rock brokerage firm.

But on February 25, 1994, Berra was a part of some great news. He called his friend Rizzuto to tell him that the Scooter had made it into the Hall of Fame.

"Did Yogi call collect?" was Rizzuto's first reaction from his Hillside, New Jersey, home.

"My number has been in Yogi's phone book so long it still has letters, like Butterfield 8, or Susquehanna 5000. Yogi's number used to be Pilgrim 8. Yogi knew I would be home," Rizzuto said.

Rizzuto's acceptance speech was one of the most memorable induction speeches ever delivered. It rambled endlessly, but was funny and endearing all the while. His fans and friends seemed to eat it up. Halfway through his own speech, he stopped and said, "This is going nowhere. You see how I do this? I get sidetracked, then I don't know where I was going. See, I did it again! Oh, listen, anytime you want to leave, go ahead."

Berra and Johnny Bench, who were on the stage with Rizzuto at the time, both stood up and walked off the stage. The crowd went wild with laughter and applause, and the two returned.

In 1995 Berra made numerous appearances, most notably the Yankees Legends collector's memorabilia show at the Taj Mahal in Atlantic City, New Jersey, along with DiMaggio, Don Larsen, Rizzuto, Reggie Jackson, and Mantle. Tickets were both expensive and hard to come by. People complained of the prices, but the crowd was immense nonetheless.

On August 13, 1995, Mantle died after a long battle with liver problems. Mantle's hard living had caught up with him, and his death was a blow for many Yankees of that era. Regardless of his wild lifestyle, Mantle had endeared himself to many, and especially to his teammates.

On May 16, 1996, Berra and Carmen drove to Continental Airlines Arena to attend the Montclair State University graduation ceremonies where Berra would receive an honorary doctorate from son Dale's alma mater. He and actor Bruce Willis were being honored. Carmen, Larry, Tim, and Dale were all in attendance, with their spouses and seven children.

"I don't know yet whether people should call me Dr. Yogi or Dr. Lawrence.... I'm going to call Bobby Brown and tell him I'm a doctor, too," said Berra, who was now 71 years old.

Berra admitted that he was suffering from stage fright before he gave his speech. During the address, Berra told the audience, "I didn't really say everything I said."

He then bestowed some advice on the students, repeating some of his most oft-quoted lines, like "It ain't over till it's over," "when you come to a fork in the road, take it," and many others.

The latter was a reference to the directions Berra would give people coming to his house for the first time. He lived on a circular street, so it didn't matter if visitors took a left or a right—either direction would bring guests around to his house.

Of the Berraisms, he said, "I wish I could say them when I wanted to because I would have made a fortune by now."

The pairing of Willis and Berra was not so odd, as they had been neighbors on Highland Avenue in Montclair. "[Bruce] was a perfect neighbor. He never said a word," joked Berra.

Berra had been keeping up a high profile in Montclair. He was very giving with his time, performing readings at the local library for little children and helping out at local fund-raisers.

On June 28, 1998, Frank Scott, Berra's agent and old friend—and baseball's first player agent—died. It was the loss of yet another good friend for Berra and Carmen.

In 1998 Berra also ventured back into the literary world, publishing *The Yogi Book: I Didn't Really Say Everything I Said.* This was a series of quotations that had been attributed to Berra over the years. He took credit for as many sayings as possible. Since they had already been attributed to him, few saw any harm in him putting them in a book. Filled with pictures from throughout his career and published just in time for Father's Day, the book was a smash success.

And Berra publicized it with all the vigor he had put into his baseball career.

It was the first of three smash-hit books for Berra. It was a classic LTD Enterprises venture—simple, enjoyable, and filled with all the things people loved about the Yogi Berra the writers had created.

## ~ Chapter 21 ~

# THE LEGACY OF YOGI BERRA

On May 1, 1997, an event was held over an open, bulldozed patch of land at one end of Montclair State University. It was the dedication ceremony for the construction of Yogi Berra Stadium, set to open a year later. During the school year it would be the home of the Montclair baseball team. In the summer it would be the home of the New Jersey Jackals of the Northern League.

Berra threw a ceremonial first pitch to christen the stadium. It was not lost on any of the reporters that Berra had yet to attend a function at Yankee Stadium since being fired by Steinbrenner in 1985. When asked if Steinbrenner would be welcomed at Berra's stadium, he said, "I don't know about that. I guess it's up to him if he wants to come."

Steinbrenner's name had come up because he had been mentioned as a possible donator to the facility. But organizers, knowing of Berra's feud with the Yankees owner, dropped the idea. At the time, Steinbrenner had been trying to talk the city into giving him a new stadium, and he was threatening to move to New Jersey if he didn't get it. Mayor Rudy Giuliani was pitching the idea of a west side stadium, but with little luck. It seemed like Steinbrenner's flirtation with New Jersey was at an end, and the reporters pointed out that Berra ended up with the stadium deal in New Jersey, not Steinbrenner.

"During my career I played in many stadiums with famous names.... Now I have my name on a stadium, too. It makes me very proud," Berra said.

At its capacity, the new stadium would hold more than 7,000 patrons. Berra said he liked the intimate environment.

The stadium was part of a larger complex, which included softball fields and an ice rink, as well as a home for the Yogi Berra Museum. The complex was funded with monies from Floyd Hall Enterprises, Montclair State, and the New Jersey Educational Facilities Authority. And old Yankees publicist Marty Appel was Berra's publicist for the new complex.

The museum is currently the home of various artifacts, including the mitt with which Berra caught the only perfect game in World Series history, several autographed and game-used items, three World Series championship trophies, and all 10 of Berra's championship rings.

Berra is very involved with the project to this day, and he frequents the museum for signings, discussions, and other events. It is Berra's intention to teach children important values such as sportsmanship and dedication, both on and off the baseball diamond.

The museum was finally dedicated in late October 1998. Ted Williams, wheelchair-bound, attended the dedication ceremonies. He told the crowd that Berra was among the fiercest of competitors. Williams said that Berra would greet him wearing his rings, not wanting Williams to forget what he had earned.

"Every finger on his hand had a World Series ring," Williams said. "He'd wave and say, 'Hi, Ted. How ya doing?'"

Whitey Ford, Ralph Branca, and Larry Doby were also in attendance.

According to the Yogi Berra Museum, "Yogi Berra's dignity and unshakable principles were never more evident than during his 14-year refusal to return to Yankee Stadium after his ignominious firing as manager by George Steinbrenner 16 games into the 1985 season. However, Berra accepted the Yankee owner's heartfelt apology to him and his wife, Carmen, in a private meeting in January 1999, at the Yogi Berra Museum and Learning Center, a reconciliation that paved the way for his celebrated return to the Yankee family."

In truth, Berra had not forgiven Steinbrenner for having an underling fire him over the phone and for allegedly making undue remarks about Dale. Suzyn Waldman, the highly regarded radio broadcaster, had brokered the peace. Steinbrenner made the gesture of coming to Berra's museum in a show of respect.

"Hello, Yogi," Steinbrenner said cautiously when he arrived.

"You're 10 minutes late," Berra quipped as he greeted the Yankees owner.

"I know I made a mistake by not letting you go personally. It's the worst mistake I ever made in baseball," Steinbrenner said.

"If I could get Yogi to come back," said Steinbrenner, warming to the occasion, "I'd bring him over with a rickshaw across the George Washington Bridge."

Writer Alan Levy pointed out, "Note that Steinbrenner did not apologize for the decision to fire Berra. But humbly acknowledging that his manner of doing it was inappropriate and unnecessarily painful made the apology effective."

Steinbrenner also came bearing gifts. Within the museum one can find a riveting exhibit of the original bronze plaques of Yankees greats DiMaggio and Mantle, which had been on the Yankee Stadium center-field wall until its renovation in 1974–75. These were donated by Steinbrenner when he arrived in 1999. He also promised his old employee a Yogi Berra Day at Yankee Stadium later in the 1999 season.

"With the year 2000 coming, everyone is thinking about the future, about peace, about making things right," Carmen told the press.

"Along those lines," Harvey Araton wrote in *The New York Times,* "Steinbrenner admitted that the death of Mickey Mantle in 1995 and the near loss of Joe DiMaggio last month made him feel a sense of urgency in making amends."

"There was a missing piece," he said, alluding to the recent record-setting, 125-victory Yankees season, and it was Berra.

"He's got to forgive me and come back," Steinbrenner told Carmen in a private moment. Steinbrenner was hoping to persuade Berra to return and help raise the team's championship banner on Opening Day the next spring to make 1998 complete.

Steinbrenner toured the museum with Berra. At one point he said he never really realized how important a part of the Yankees dynasty Berra had been.

Berra told the press, "It's over." He had accepted the Boss's apology and claimed he might show up at Yankee Stadium the next season for the first time in 14 years.

"I told him, 'You've got to do what you've got to do,'" Dale Berra said. "But 14 years is long enough, the most you can get out of it."

After his 14-year feud, Berra had gained a whole new measure of respect. People used words like *dignity, character,* and *principled* when they talked about Berra now. He had gained some extra measure of respect from the writers and especially from the fans. He was the anti-Steinbrenner Yankee. He had become a Yankees player who Mets fans loved. By standing up to Steinbrenner, he had ascended, somehow, into another realm of über-legend.

Berra's estrangement from Yankee Stadium and Steinbrenner had not dampened his love of the team. He followed both New York teams ardently, the Yankees more so than the Mets. He and Joe Torre had been friends for years. And after the 1996 and 1998 world championships, Berra called Torre with his congratulations.

In 1996 Berra and Torre had spoken before the World Series, Berra trying to offer advice to his younger friend. Torre admitted that though Berra and Reggie Jackson had warned him about the tremendously powerful emotional experience, Torre was not fully prepared when his name was introduced before the first game.

Berra had also called Torre after the Yankees won their first game in the 1998 Series.

"He just congratulated me—'Good luck, kid,'" Torre said. "That really makes me feel good. When we got our rings last year, I tried to put pressure on him to come out here and give me my ring, but he wouldn't come. He felt good that I thought of him that way…. I've done it a number of times, inviting him. I've invited him to spring training, but he tends to ignore me."

On March 1, 1999, Berra showed up at Legends Field in Florida for the Yankees' spring training.

"Yogi Berra visited Legends Field today, and the first thing Joe Torre did was place a Yankees cap on the Yankees legend's head," wrote sportswriter Jack Curry.

"I haven't worn a baseball cap in a long time," Berra said.

"I thought he was getting cheated by this whole thing," Torre said. "There's a lot of things he enjoys that he didn't get the chance to do."

Yankees center fielder Bernie Williams, who had been in the organization since 1985, had never met Berra and asked if he could meet the Hall of Famer. "Berra showed Williams and Derek Jeter the special ring the Yankees received for winning five straight World Series titles from 1949 to 1953, and the two players acted like 12-year-olds," reported Curry.

"You guys can do it if you stay together," Berra told them.

"I'm not going anywhere," said Williams, who signed a seven-year, $87.5 million deal the previous November.

Berra looked at Jeter and said, "I don't know about you."

Williams quickly countered by saying, "He'll be here, too."

\*   \*   \*

On March 8, 1999, DiMaggio died, losing his fight with lung cancer. Again, another link to the great years of Yankees domination had passed. Many now felt that Berra was the greatest living Yankee. And they were right. Berra had been the link between DiMaggio and Mantle. Berra is one of the greatest catchers in the history of the game and one of only a handful of men to have brought clubs from both leagues to the World Series.

Several writers noted how much smaller Berra is than most of today's players. Yet many of his home runs had taken place when the outfield of Yankee Stadium was even bigger than the newer, scaled-down green spaces of the renovated stadium.

In another sign that the frost between Berra and the Yankees had thawed, on April 5, 1999, it was announced that the 1998 world championship trophy would go to the Yogi Berra Museum for temporary display. Then, on April 9, 1999, Berra finally walked back onto the field at Yankee Stadium to a standing ovation. Before his introduction was finished, more than 56,000 fans went wild as the 73-year-old Hall of Famer waved to the crowd. Pitcher David Cone greeted him on the mound. Berra threw the first pitch out to catcher Joe Girardi to open the season and then enjoyed the game from the comforts of Steinbrenner's luxury box.

Berra was back where he belonged. He was back in the stadium where he was once one of the most maligned, most beloved, and yet most feared players in professional baseball.

"I was a little nervous out there," he said. "It was like any Opening Day. I don't care how long you've played. You're always a little nervous."

An awed Cone said, "To see Yogi walk out there and get the ovation he got after all these years was tremendous. It was one of the loudest ovations I've heard at Yankee Stadium."

"It felt great after 14 years," said Berra, who predicted a Chili Davis grand slam from the television booth.

"I was always a Yankees fan," said the Yankees' old catcher. "I always watched them on TV. I think they have a good team this year. I think they can win it again."

Fellow Hall of Famers Ford and Rizzuto raised the 1998 championship flag, but Berra was the marquee attraction.

"I've been asking him for 14 years [about returning]," Ford said. "I don't care what you think of Steinbrenner. The people really miss you."

On June 26, Berra sat in the Mets' dugout with the players and coaches while waiting to be announced. He was there to throw out the first pitch of the summer Subway Series between the Mets and Yankees.

Like the Yankee players the month before, Mets players started approaching Berra.

"They kept coming over to where Yogi sat next to the bat rack, carrying pens and new baseballs, politely asking him to sign. Todd Pratt, a backup catcher, came over, introduced himself, shyly handed Yogi a ball. So did Alberto Castillo, another Mets catcher. Like kids. Like kids in Mets caps from high up in the bleachers," wrote Mike Lupica. "Yogi is a bridge to more memories than anyone."

"Mike Piazza...came over in full catcher's equipment to shake Yogi Berra's hand. He seemed to be twice Berra's size. Somehow though...Piazza seemed to be the one who was looking up, at a ballplayer out of New York's baseball past, one of the giants of the past," wrote Lupica.

Someone told Berra it was time to throw the first pitch.

"I'm gonna have to cheat like hell to get this ball to home plate," laughed the nervous Berra.

As Steinbrenner had promised, July 18, 1999, was Yogi Berra Day at Yankee Stadium. Don Mattingly, Whitey Ford, Rizzuto, Bill White, and Don Larsen were all there to honor No. 8. The New York Yankees gave Berra a trip to Italy, and Torre presented Berra with a 1998 world championship ring.

Then Larsen took the mound. Berra settled in behind home plate. The two turned back the clock to 1956 and Larsen's perfect World Series game.

"Larsen threw to Yogi, and we all cheered. Little did we know how ironic that little replay would become," wrote Lou DiLullo, publisher of Yankeetradition.com, who was there that day.

The stars were truly aligned that day because Cone, with Berra and Larsen in the stands, pitched a perfect game. It was one of the most memorable days in modern Yankees history.

"We re-created our game before the game," Berra said. "He did it in the real. I'm glad we were both here for this."

The Berra magic was at work again. And Berra was never more popular.

\*    \*    \*

Over the years, Berra had appeared in dozens of commercials for products like Miller Lite, Pepsi-Cola, and Jockey underwear. In May 1999, he appeared in a funny television commercial for Nike about baseball, and he also appeared in a local commercial for Hilltop Nissan, a New Jersey auto dealer. In addition, PBS was making a documentary about him, and he was publishing books.

During the filming of the PBS special, Berra and a film crew made big news in St. Louis, setting up camp there for three days while they filmed Berra walking the old streets.

"They filmed Berra, 74, and [Bob] Costas walking in the neighborhood and chatting with some of Berra's boyhood friends—Mickey Garagiola, Lou Baroli, and Charley Riva. One of his best friends—former St. Louis Cardinals catcher Joe Garagiola—couldn't arrange his schedule to be in St. Louis for the filming. But Carmen Berra, his wife, and Bonnie Morse, his sister-in-law," provided some touching moments, reported the *St. Louis Post-Dispatch*.

The film also featured his sister, Josie Sandowski, who still lived in their childhood home, now with her husband.

Berra and his merchandising were so popular that *The New York Times* business section devoted a large story to him. LTD was now thriving.

"Marketers say the legendary Yankee is topical for a host of reasons, ranging from the renewed popularity of baseball to the Yankees' winning ways to the need for heroes. Also, his well-publicized rapprochement with the Yankees owner, George Steinbrenner, which came after years of bad blood, was more than just cathartic. It helped put Mr. Berra back in the spotlight," wrote business writer Patricia Winters Lauro.

"There has always been an interest in Yogi Berra because he has a strong and colorful personality," said Nova Lanktree, president of Lanktree Sports Celebrity Network in Chicago, who had worked with Berra in the past. "He just has those charismatic qualities that transcend time. Even the younger people get him."

"The business is nothing more than the Berra family taking care of its own," Dale said, referring to LTD Enterprises.

There was no question that the Yogi Berra Museum was also raising Berra's profile in the media. The museum was now becoming a hot spot and would only continue to do so. Not only was it a smaller version of Cooperstown in some ways, but it also became a great venue for small events like book signings and baseball collection exhibitions.

The year 1999 saw the end of an era in the Berra household. The 40-lane bowling alley that had opened to huge fanfare as Berra-Rizzuto Lanes in 1959, more recently known as Astro Bowl, had closed. While the family had not owned it for some time, the news created a twinge of sadness.

Toward the end of 1999, Berra appeared at number 40 on *The Sporting News'* list of the 100 greatest baseball players, and fan balloting elected him to the Major League Baseball All-Century team.

In May 2000, rumors abounded of Ford having a recurrence of cancer. Concerned that his friend might be ill, Berra called him for an update.

"You dead yet?" Berra said.

"I'm still here," Ford assured him.

But on November 5, 2000, Barbara Ellen Short, Carmen's mother, died. Affectionately known by her more than 17 grandchildren as Momo, she was one month short of her 94th birthday. The Berras went back to Missouri to mourn with the many relatives from both sides of their families.

*     *     *

In 2001 Berra published another new book, *When You Come to a Fork in the Road, Take It!* It was a collection of Berraisms and other insights, and it, too, was a best seller.

In June of that year, Berra did a series of signings in and around the St. Louis area. The *St. Louis Post-Dispatch* responded with major coverage: current photos, schedules, classic photos, and images of book covers. St. Louisans were celebrating the return of a native son.

By 2000 Berra was now a regular at Yankees spring training. He could be seen chatting with Torre, Williams, and Jeter. Yankees fans could see the passing of the torch from one championship generation to another in the same way that DiMaggio had lent his aura to the teams of the 1970s as the grand old man of the franchise.

Berra usually eschewed such a moniker, deferring to Ford or Rizzuto. But in fact, DiMaggio had not handed the ball off to anyone but Berra, who held the spot until Mantle grew into it. Berra was an incontrovertible link in the chain of great Yankees. The Yankees lineage went from Babe Ruth to Lou Gehrig to DiMaggio to Berra to Mantle to Thurman Munson and Graig Nettles and Reggie Jackson to Williams and Jeter.

By 2000 it was acknowledged that Berra had in fact become the face of the Yankees, a sort of goodwill ambassador for the team. He became an image of the classiness the franchise wanted to emphasize, instead of Steinbrenner's legacy of managerial changes. He was a symbol of all that was best and glorious about the Yankees. And for his part, he embraced it—if for no other reason than he wanted to be around the game. He enjoyed the camaraderie that the clubhouse and dugout afforded. It was not unusual to see him waddling across the field in Tampa or in the Bronx, coming down the painted cinderblock stairs within the stadium's bowels, always chatting with the players and coaches.

And at playoff and World Series games, Berra was preeminent among the famous Yankees the organization trotted out for these televised games, along with Jackson and Rizzuto, among others.

"Do you know who Paul O'Neill reminds me of? Mantle. Oh, Mickey would break the water cooler, he got so mad, but he just wanted to win," Berra once said.

"You know, a lot of guys say, 'You're a bad-ball hitter,'" Berra related. "I said, 'No, the ball looked good to me. I swung at it.' I could leave a pitch alone the first time like that. The next time, I hit at it, and I do something with it."

"I have fun with Jeter. You know, sometimes he strikes out on that ball up here," Berra continued.

"What'd you swing at that ball for?" Berra asked Jeter.

"It looks good," Jeter said. "You used to swing at it."

"Yeah, but I hit it. You don't," razzed Berra.

Berra loved to tease Jeter, asking the probable Hall of Fame shortstop why he only had three World Series rings.

And he loved to call relief pitcher Mariano Rivera "Skinny."

He was a popular presence at the 2000 and 2001 World Series.

New York Mets catcher Piazza talked about how long the postseason already was when he played for the Mets, whose Subway Series against the Yankees ended on October 26.

"I remember when we were in the World Series in 2000 talking to Yogi Berra, and he said that their World Series were usually over October 7 or 6," Piazza said.

In 2001 the Yankees faced the Oakland A's in the American League Divisional Series. Torre's team had dropped the first two games at home, 5–3 and 2–0. The Yankees would have to go to Oakland and take two on the West Coast to earn a trip home for a chance to win the series. Few people thought the Yankees would be able to force a fifth game.

"Torre was packing for the cross-country flight to Oakland and happened to see an old blue hat Yogi Berra had given him a few years ago. The hat, from Yogi's museum, says 'It Ain't Over Till It's Over' across the front," wrote Chris Colston for *USA Today Baseball Weekly.* "Torre grabbed it and had his equipment manager sew a FDNY or NYPD patch on the right side. Torre wore it to the workout-day press conference on Friday and the pregame conference."

"It's not the most attractive thing, but neither is my hairline," Torre said. "So it's sort of a push."

The Yankees swept the last three games of the series and advanced, then won the pennant against the Seattle Mariners before falling to the Arizona Diamondbacks in seven games in the World Series. Still, Torre had invoked Berra's famous slogan and good luck in an effort to rally his team, and it had responded.

"Joe started wearing the cap during the playoffs, when the Yankees were losing to the Oakland A's. Then the Yankees rallied, beat the A's and the Seattle Mariners, and won some unbelievable games in the World Series. With Mariano Rivera pitching the last inning of the final game, most people thought victory was automatic. All the final result did was prove something I said a long time ago: in baseball, you don't know nothing," Berra opined in the op-ed section of *The New York Times*.

Berra went to other players' museums to promote the Yankees anywhere and everywhere. He went to an event at the Babe Ruth Museum in Baltimore to promote an exhibit of American and Japanese baseball history. And Major League Baseball also took advantage of his services and visage.

With all the events and obligations Berra had, it is perhaps fitting to note that Berra was not always punctual. Business guru Harvey Mackay claimed in one of his columns that Berra had a habit of being late for appointments, writing, "Usually, he was about a half-hour late. One time he showed up only 15 minutes behind schedule. Proudly he proclaimed, 'This is the earliest I've ever been late.' But do you think Yogi was ever late for a ballgame?"

Despite his business and public relations duties, however, Berra was first and foremost keen on his old team. He'd consider each season's group and assess their dynamic. For instance, when the Yankees acquired pitcher Mike Mussina, Berra said, "Do you know what I told Mike Mussina the other day? I said, 'You just joined a really good group. They're like the guys I played with. They don't fight. They just want to win.'"

\*   \*   \*

In July 2002, Berra's friend Ted Williams passed away.

"This is a sad day for baseball, a sad day for anybody who knew Ted. Nobody was more loyal, generous, courageous, more respected than Ted. He sacrificed his life and career for his country. But he became what he always wanted to be: the greatest hitter ever," Berra told the press.

In 2003, Berra and Dave Kaplan published *Ten Rings*. As with his others, this book was both a critical and a financial success. In it Berra recounted numerous stories from his life in baseball, centered around the 10 World Series the Yankees won during his career as a player.

In June of that year, Elizabeth Avenue, birthplace of Yogi Berra, Joe Garagiola, and Jack Buck, was renamed Hall of Fame Place. The players' children showed up, with families in tow, for the dedication ceremonies. Granite plaques were installed in front of each of their homes, commemorating their passage through St. Louis. Former members of the boys' old childhood team, the Stags A.C., sat in the front row. "I'd like to thank my sister Josie for making this day necessary," Berra joked on stage. She and the crowd howled with laughter.

Although the Yankees lost the World Series 4–2 to the Florida Marlins that fall, October brought a one-man play to Broadway starring Ben Gazzara. It was called *Nobody Don't Like Yogi* and was written by Tom Lysaght.

The play is set on the afternoon of the Old-Timers' game in 1999, when Berra returns to Yankee Stadium after staying away for 14 years. Gazzara, as Berra, visits the old manager's office and recalls many highlights from his career, ranging from his St. Louis childhood to managing the Yankees (both times).

The show was a critical and monetary success.

"At 73, Mr. Gazzara actually looks a little like Mr. Berra, who is now 78. Wearing a jacket and tie and wire-rim glasses, he affects quite well Mr. Berra's gruff vocal tones, and he plays the role with great aplomb, gently embodying the soft-spoken legend that Mr. Lysaght has chosen to outline here," wrote Bruce Weber for *The New York Times* theater review.

Gazzara had a similar background to Berra's. "I'm the son of Sicilian immigrants," he said, "and grew up on 29th Street between First and Second Avenues, the Bellevue district. I never spoke a word of English—only Sicilian—to my parents, in their whole lives."

"There is a Yogi Berra Museum in Montclair, New Jersey, and it is to there, a year ago, that Gazzara and playwright Lysaght journeyed to try to win Berra's approval of the project," wrote theater journalist Jerry Tallmer.

"The Berras had received the play, and somebody in the family had read it and had had some questions as to whether they should endorse it because of [Berra's son] Dale's problems as a young guy that are mentioned in the play," Tallmer reported.

"Tom and I got dressed to the nines, and the first thing I see when we walked into the museum is a bottle of vodka on a table. I laughed and had some vodka and cranberry juice, and Yogi started asking me about my childhood. I told him I was a Yankee fan before I was born, and that I dreamed and lived and died for Joe DiMaggio. I used to sit out in the bleachers at the stadium—that's when the outfielders would throw their gloves on the grass between innings in those days—and I could see Joe D. up close when he came to pick up his glove," Gazzara recalled.

"Yogi brought out photographs—of him jumping all over Don Larsen after the perfect game, of Jackie Robinson stealing home on a slide that Yogi still believes was an out—and I thought to myself, 'Ahh, we got him,'" Gazzara said.

But just then Carmen entered and told Gazzara and Lysaght that she was concerned about how the Dale situation was handled. She stated that she preferred that the play not go forward.

"Let's not press this; let's just be gentlemen and go home," said Lysaght.

"When Mrs. Berra said that, Yogi let out an embarrassed laugh," Gazzara confided. "I felt his sweetness and his tenderness. He hugged me so hard, I thought my ribs would crack. It would have been nice to get the Berra family in on the production, but as I've also said, it speaks to Yogi's honor that he is not participating."

*   *   *

A year later, Carmen threw out the first pitch to help dedicate the new softball stadium at Montclair State University. It was one of the few softball-only stadiums in the country.

On May 12, 2005, Yogi Berra turned 80 years old. Yogi and Carmen planned to spend the day at home. Larry (who still lives nearby in Hillsdale), Tim, Dale, and the now 10 grandchildren would come visit them. And Berra got a phone call from Garagiola, who said Berra always returns the favor on his birthday each February.

Garagiola said, "He'll call me and leave a message on my answering machine, singing, 'Happy Birthday to you, happy birthday to you, you're catching up to me, happy birthday to you. From Yogi Berra.' He tells me who it was, like I thought it was Pavarotti or Bocelli singing to me."

Garagiola was now living in Scottsdale, Arizona, and, much like Berra, he was one of his small town's most famous residents. His son, Joe Jr., was general manager of the Arizona Diamondbacks. "I keep busy. I'm filling in weekends on Diamondbacks telecasts when the regular broadcasters go up to the Fox Network for *Game of the Week,* and I still do spots occasionally on *Today,*" he said.

In 2005 Berra filed a $10 million lawsuit against Turner Broadcasting System because, without permission, the company used Berra's name in an ad for the hit television series, *Sex and the City.* The word *Yogasm* appeared with a list of possible meanings, one of which was "sex with Yogi Berra." It was the front-page story of the *New York Post.*

*   *   *

Montclair's Fourth of July parade in 2005 was highlighted by the participation of grand marshals Yogi and Carmen Berra.

"It doesn't rain on Yogi's parade," said Carmen of the day's pleasant weather.

The Berras' participation meant a lot to parade organizers. Many people from the surrounding towns drove in to get a glimpse of the famous ballplayer and his wife.

"This wouldn't be Montclair without the Berra family," said CNBC anchor Tyler Matheson, a town resident since 1988 and parade emcee.

After the parade, the mayor led the crowd in singing "Happy Birthday" to Berra in honor of his recent birthday. The organizers had planned on offering an ice cream cake, and when they asked Berra what his favorite flavor was, he told them "frozen yogurt."

He was as popular as ever. His face was all over television, including starring opposite a duck in an AFLAC insurance commercial. "He deals with it every day of his life," Carmen said of his popularity. "I'm so accustomed to it. The women are worse than the men—all ages. It's amazing."

"He still works out at the Richard J. Codey Arena at South Mountain in West Orange, still gets his morning cup of joe at his favorite coffee shop in Verona, still savors a single vodka on the rocks every night. He still plays cards Wednesday nights at Montclair Country Club and golfs there every chance he gets," wrote journalist Christopher Hahn.

Both he and Carmen still frequent Pals Cabin in West Orange, New Jersey, where they used to dine regularly with former Houston Astros and New Jersey Devils owner John McMullen and his wife, Jackie.

"He's a very broad individual, unlike the public perception," McMullen once said of his longtime friend Berra. "You'll never find him saying a bad word about anybody. I would have to say I consider him one of the best friends I have."

\*    \*    \*

In September 2006, Rizzuto started to get around less and less. The Scooter, who was then 89 years old, and his wife, Cora, couldn't make it to Yankee Stadium for Old-Timers' Day.

Although his mobility might have lessened, his opinions did not.

"Derek Jeter should win the MVP award," Rizzuto, the last Yankee shortstop to capture MVP honors, told the *New York Post*'s Kevin Kernan.

Rizzuto continued, "I've always loved the way he plays, he just glides.... Being around him and the way he handles himself with people—everything is perfect."

Yogi and Carmen Berra went to visit their old friend several times. Either Rizzuto's wife, Cora (whom Rizzuto still lovingly referred to as his bride), or one of the Scooter's children was there every day.

"Derek [Jeter] just broke my father's record for games played as a Yankee shortstop," said Rizzuto's eldest daughter, Patricia. "If it had to be somebody, we're glad it was Derek."

In 2007, Rizzuto's health began to fail again, and this time he could not will himself beyond his body's betrayal. Berra visited his ailing friend every Wednesday at his home in Hillside, New Jersey. Later, as Rizzuto's health further deteriorated, he was moved to a nursing home in West Orange, where he and Berrra would play bingo until the Scooter fell asleep.

The last visits were particularly hard for Berra.

"It was pretty bad the last month or so. He had pneumonia," Berra said. "He was gradually going down. You could tell. He wasn't awake much of the time."

Rizzuto eventually passed away on August 13, 2007, at the age of 89.

"Phil was a gem, one of the greatest people I ever knew, a dear friend, and a great teammate," Berra said. "He was a heck of a player, too. When I first came up to the Yankees, he was like a big—actually small—brother to me.... He's meant an awful lot to baseball and the Yankees, and has left us with a lot of wonderful memories."

\*    \*    \*

In October 2006, Yankees blogger and journalist Peter Abraham reported that "nine beat writers and WFAN's Sweeny Murti just had a 15-minute, private interview with Joe Torre in his office. Yogi Berra and Frank Torre were there when we arrived."

As usual, especially when there were big series in town, like the Red Sox or the playoffs, Torre always made sure to invite Berra, as well as his other usual good-luck charms, comedian Billy Crystal and composer Marvin Hamlisch, both huge Yankees fans.

In May 2007, with the season seemingly falling apart, Torre, as superstitious as any baseball or sports manager, brought in all his good-luck charms again. As the Red Sox had just come down to New York for an early-season meeting with the Yankees, Berra took his time hanging around Torre's office. He also took time to visit both benches.

"Yogi Berra was in the clubhouse before the game to visit [Boston manager Terry] Francona, whom he has known for many years. He even autographed baseballs for many players," wrote John Altavilla of the *Hartford Courant.*

"Yogi always stops in to say hello to us," Francona said. "From my point of view, something like that is truly awesome."

Berra watched the game with Crystal and Hamlisch in Steinbrenner's luxury box.

But the highlight of May placed Yogi Berra squarely where it had all begun. Berra had been invited back to St. Louis, a place that he had visited less and less over the years and whose familiar sights seemed to be fewer and fewer. And yet, there were still people he knew in the old neighborhood.

As Garagiola had once said, "I've lived a lot of places since leaving St. Louis, but I still call it home. Home is where you grew up."

Berra had been asked by Saint Louis University to address the 2007 graduating class and to receive an honorary doctorate. On May 19, 2007, Yogi Berra stepped up to the platform to address the crowd in the city on whose streets he had played as a boy in the neighborhood known as the Hill. It was the university's 189th commencement. A few years earlier, Berra had also received an honorary doctorate from Roger Williams College, which friends overheard him referring to as "Roger Maris College."

"The crowd of about 10,000 inside the Scottrade Center gave Berra a standing ovation before he gave his commencement address," wrote Kim Bell for the *St. Louis Post-Dispatch.*

Julius Hunter, the university's vice-president for community relations, played the straight man, asking Berra questions to set up his one-liners.

> *Hunter: Since you've been back, have you been to the Hill?*
> *Berra: Nobody goes there anymore. It's too crowded.*

The crowd rippled with laughter at the obvious set-ups and applauded with each famous line uttered by the iconic octogenarian.

As part of his actual speech, Berra told the graduates, "If I went back to the dugout and beat myself up, I would have been down in the minors in no time. There will be days when you wish you were back in class at SLU. Life gets tough, so be tougher. Stand up. Take your lumps. And before too long, you'll understand what it takes to be a winner."

"The university presented Berra with an honorary doctor of laws degree for his exemplary athletic accomplishments, his charitable contributions to young people and their education, and for his 'incomparable contribution to humor and philosophy,'" reported Bell.

Carmen sat proudly near him. Donning a professorial cap and gown, Lorenzo Pietro Berra, son of two Italian immigrants and better known now as Yogi Berra, had indeed come a long way in the world.

# AFTERWORD

In April of 2009, Yogi Berra threw out the first pitch from the pitcher's mound of the new Yankees Stadium. He was the Yankees' oldest living legend.

"I've got the dirt," Berra told sportswriter Joe Lapointe. He told Lapointe he had soil samples from the base paths and the pitching mound from the old Yankee Stadium. Not the ballpark of his glory days, but from the refurbished stadium that the Yankees called home from 1976 to 2008. Yogi was seeking a larger prize. "I told them I'd like to have the home plate," Berra said. "They said, 'Well, maybe.'" He wanted it for the Yogi Berra Museum & Learning Center.

Lapointe reasoned that Berra was one of the major icons of New York City baseball in the 20th century, writing that Yogi was "the living embodiment of America's most famous professional sports team, an approachable and unpretentious Hall of Famer who represents a proud franchise not always associated with such qualities. An icon of New York baseball's past and present, Berra appeared at the closing ceremonies last season for Yankee Stadium and Shea Stadium, and he is on display in the new stadiums, too. There he is on the video board in Citi Field's rotunda, reaching to tag Jackie Robinson in the 1955 World Series as Robinson stole home. There he is in a big photo in the new Yankee Stadium, embracing Don Larsen after Larsen's perfect game in the 1956 Series. And there he is in the new Stadium's museum, in statue form, catching a pitch from Larsen."

For more than a decade, from 1999 to the present, Yogi has been the unofficial mascot/celebrity of Yankees spring training, and an entirely new generation of Yankees have circled him and embraced him. Today's young stars hang on his words, hoping for a nod from the antediluvian slugger.

Like the clockwork of the galaxy, Berra's schedule was immutable. According to sportswriter Harvey Araton, "He checks into the same hotel in the vicinity of George M. Steinbrenner Field and requests the same room. He plans his days methodically—wake up at 6:00 AM, breakfast at 6:30, depart for the complex by 7:00—and steps outside to be greeted by the same driver he has had for the past dozen years."

His driver was none other than former Yankees great Ron Guidry, known affectionately by the players as Gator.

"It's like I'm the valet," Guidry told Araton. "Actually, I am the valet."

In fact, Guidry had gone so far as to wear a custom-made cap at Yankees spring training, with an embroidered inscription that read, "Driving Mr. Yogi," a spoof of the hit movie starring Morgan Freeman and Jessica Tandy, *Driving Miss Daisy*. Araton eventually went on to write a book of the same name about the decade-plus friendship between Guidry and Berra. They were inseparable at Yankees spring training.

"He's a good guy. We hang out together in spring training," said Yogi in his usual deadpan manner.

Gator befriended Yogi when Berra returned from his self-imposed exile from the Yankees at Steinbrenner's request.

"There was really nobody else that he had to sit and talk with, to be around after the day at the ballpark," Guidry said. "So I just told him, 'I'll pick you up, we'll go out to supper,' and that's how it started. It wasn't like I planned it. It just developed."

They dressed in the locker room together, they sat in the clubhouse together, and ate dinner or went to the movies together. Guidry was required to make a large feast of fried frog legs.

"He calls me at home this year to remind me about the frog legs—'Did you get 'em yet?'" Guidry said. "I said, 'Yogi, it's freaking January, calm down.'"

Guidry held out hope that once in a while he would be able to choose a restaurant other than one of the five preapproved Berra favorites.

"See, I really love the old man, but because of what we share—which is something very special—I can treat him more as a friend and I can say, 'Get your butt in my truck or you're staying,'" Guidry told Araton. "He likes that kind of camaraderie, wants to be treated like everybody else, but because of who he is, that's not how everybody around here treats him.

"So I'll say, 'Yogi, tonight we're going to Fleming's, then to Lee Roy Selmon's tomorrow, and then the night after that you stay in your damn room, have a ham sandwich or whatever, because the world doesn't revolve around you and I'm taking a night off.'"

And it was Guidry who helped bridge the gap between the Hall of Fame old-timer and today's stars. The two would sit in the clubhouse watching the game, and talk about strategy or pick out tell-tale signs. Eventually, Yogi would notice something about a pitcher or a hitter. Once, Yogi saw that Nick Swisher was striking out consistently on breaking balls. It seemed that opposing pitchers had developed a book on Swisher. Yogi mentioned to Guidry that Swisher should position himself more toward the front of the batter's box to attack the pitch sooner.

Guidry told Berra to talk to Swisher himself, but Berra demurred. After another unsuccessful at-bat, Guidry got up and said to Swisher, "He wants to talk to you," motioning toward Berra. Berra passed along his observation. Next time up, Swisher smashed a double and later scored, and then insisted on sitting next to Berra again after he came into the dugout.

Berra was often seen walking around the clubhouse, stopping to say hello to Jorge Posada or Derek Jeter or Mariano Rivera, always with a smile. Yogi also offered advice to catcher Francisco Cervelli: set up his target, his glove, a little earlier.

"That's going to cut my movement," Cervelli said. "I've got a lot of energy. So, I have to save that energy and get a little quieter behind the plate. If I can get better, I want to make those adjustments. He knows what he's talking about. He said, 'Every time I watch you, I like what I see.' He's the man, bro."

Pitcher Joba Chamberlain was also fond of Berra. When Chamberlain was arrested on drunk drinking charges in Nebraska in 2010, a police tape recorded him discussing Berra with the trooper.

"He might not be as tall as the front of your car," Chamberlain said of Berra. When Chamberlain's words were circulated by the thesmokinggun.com, he quickly called Berra to apologize. Berra took it in stride.

"Oh, that was funny," Berra told Lapointe. "I said, 'You know I'm your buddy.' I called him 'Shorty.'"

Chamberlain is 6'2".

He and Berra frequently talked during spring training, when Berra dressed daily in full uniform along with other former Yankees.

"But that's the thing—for Yogi, spring training is his last hold on baseball," Guidry added. "When he walks through that door in the clubhouse, sits at the locker, puts on his uniform, talks to everybody, jokes around, watches batting practice, goes back in, has something to eat, and then he and I will go on the bench and watch the game, believe me, I know how much he really looks forward to it."

In July of 2010, Yogi Berra suffered a fall at his home in New Jersey; on his way to his car before a haircut appointment, he tripped and fell, suffering injuries that required a two-week stay in the hospital. The accident caused him to miss Old-Timers' Day at Yankee Stadium for the first time since he and George Steinbrenner had made amends. Yogi's mishap had coincided with the passing of the longtime, controversial Yankees owner. In that time, much of their relationship was rehashed.

The fall was a small trip but left major repercussions for the then-84-year-old icon. After recovering, his step was a little slower, his speech a little quieter, his energy a little lower. By his own admission he was no longer able to drive.

The following year, after much consternation, Yogi's wife, Carmen, allowed him to attend spring training. Guidry had campaigned heavily with Carmen to allow Berra to attend his annual pilgrimage.

"I know Carmen feels he's going to be fine and occupied because I'm around," Guidry told Araton. "But this year may be harder than the rest because of what happened. I'm just going to have to watch a little more closely to see what he can do."

"He's got a whole different body than when he played," Carmen said in a telephone interview with the press just a year earlier. "His legs are half the size. He had big calves, big thighs."

All went well until March 10, 2011, when *The New York Times* reported that Berra had been taken to a hospital after falling backward in the Yankees clubhouse at Bright House Field. According to the article, "Berra did not hit his head and was transported in an ambulance to Morton Plant Hospital for precautionary reasons, the team said. Berra, 85, stumbled after his sneaker caught in the carpet as he went to get a cup of soup. Berra was alert and has spoken with his wife, Carmen. The Yankees said Berra was released from the hospital about 4:00 PM."

On May 12, 2012, the Yankees invited Berra to Yankees Stadium to celebrate his 87th birthday. The organization treated Yogi and his family to a large cake. Yogi got a slice as well as an earful from a ballpark of the pinstripe faithful, belting out a lusty rendition of "Happy Birthday."

But in 2013 Berra did not attend spring training. The *New York Daily News* headlines blared Berra's absence, and other metropolitan papers followed suit. Of course, Berra hadn't made it to the 2012 Yankees playoffs games either.

"He's fine," Dave Kaplan, director of the Yogi Berra Museum & Learning Center, told the Associated Press. "Travel is tough, so he won't be there this year. He plans to be at the Stadium this season."

And appear he did. In July of 2013, at Yankees' Old Timers Day, 88-year-old Yogi Berra and Whitey Ford (then 84) were the last Yankees to be announced. They had not appeared down on the floor of the Stadium. They had been kept out of sight. An oversized golf cart burst from beyond the center-field wall, and the crowd erupted.

That fall, Yogi's beloved St. Louis Cardinals made it to the World Series. He could not make it. He did not visit the Hill. He did not see all his old friends. Gone were the days of Joe Medwick and the other old-time Cardinals. However, granddaughter Lindsay Berra, the daughter of Yogi's oldest son, Larry, did make it. Lindsay had worked at *ESPN The Magazine* for more than 13 years. In January of 2013 she started reporting for MLB.com.

According to *St. Louis Post-Dispatch* columnist Joe Holleman, Lindsay "went to dinner at Atlas in the Central West End with the family of her great-aunt Bonnie Morse of Clayton, which includes Steve Mahfood, former director of the Missouri Department of Natural Resources. (Bonnie's sister, Carmen, has been married to Yogi for almost 65 years.)."

"The last time (before this series) I was in St. Louis was when I was covering hockey for ESPN and I came in for a Blues game," Berra told Holleman. "That time, I spent it with the Berra side."

Lindsay said she was raised, obviously, as a Yankee fan.

"But Grandpa always rooted for the Cardinals," Lindsay said. "You know it broke his heart they didn't draft him and took Joe (Garagiola) instead."

Some dreams die hard, even for an icon.

# Sources

## Introduction

"The subject of said discussion…" Erskine, Carl with Burton Rocks. *What I Learned from Jackie Robinson*. New York: McGraw-Hill, 2005.

"This is Ebbets Field…" Erskine, Carl with Burton Rocks. *What I Learned from Jackie Robinson*. New York: McGraw-Hill, 2005.

"When I left that discussion…" Erskine, Carl with Burton Rocks. *What I Learned from Jackie Robinson*. New York: McGraw-Hill, 2005.

"Yogi came up and…" Erskine, Carl with Burton Rocks. *What I Learned from Jackie Robinson*. New York: McGraw-Hill, 2005.

"The knockdown was up…" Erskine, Carl with Burton Rocks. *What I Learned from Jackie Robinson*. New York: McGraw-Hill, 2005.

"When I next saw the…" Erskine, Carl with Burton Rocks. *What I Learned from Jackie Robinson*. New York: McGraw-Hill, 2005.

"Lawdie Berra grew up…" Garagiola, Joe. *It's Anybody's Ballgame*. New York: Jove Books, 1989.

"Yogi is not…" Lipsyte, Robert. "The Man and the Myth." *The New York Times,* October 25, 1963.

"How the * * * *…" Lipsyte, Robert. "The Man and the Myth." *The New York Times,* October 25, 1963.

"Those who liked Yogi…" Koppett, Leonard. "A Legend of the Game." *The New York Times,* October 2, 1973.

"It's the part…" Garagiola, Joe. *It's Anybody's Ballgame*. New York: Jove Books, 1989.

## Chapter 1

"Ellis Island was originally…" National Park Service. "Ellis Island History," Statue of Liberty–Ellis Island Foundation, Inc., http://www.statueofliberty.org.

"Served as the New York…" National Park Service. "Ellis Island History," Statue of Liberty–Ellis Island Foundation, Inc., http://www.statueofliberty.org.

"Annie Moore, a…" National Park Service. "Ellis Island History," Statue of Liberty–Ellis Island Foundation, Inc., http://www.statueofliberty.org.

"First-and-second…" National Park Service. "Ellis Island History," Statue of Liberty–Ellis Island Foundation, Inc., http://www.statueofliberty.org.

"Pietro Berra first saw…" The Statue of Liberty–Ellis Island Foundation, Inc., Pietro Berra Manifest.

"After he worked…" Berra, Yogi and Tom Horton. *Yogi: It Ain't Over.* New York: McGraw-Hill, 1989.

"Hill guineas…" Berra, Yogi and Ed Fitzgerald. *Yogi: The Autobiography of a Professional Baseball Player.* New York: Doubleday, 1961.

"An early settlement…" Fox, Tim. *Where We Live: A Guide to St. Louis Communities.* St. Louis: Missouri Historical Society Press, 1995.

"The area came to…" Fox, Tim, *Where We Live: A Guide to St. Louis Communities.* St. Louis: Missouri Historical Society Press, 1995.

"There weren't any…" Berra, Yogi and Ed Fitzgerald. *Yogi: The Autobiography of a Professional Baseball Player.* New York: Doubleday, 1961.

"Pietro ruled his little…" Schoor, Gene. *The Story of Yogi Berra.* New York: Doubleday, 1976.

"Few women on the block…" Garagiola, Joe. *Baseball Is a Funny Game.* New York: Bantam Books, 1980.

"Maybe a new pair of…" Dorr, Dave. "Whatever Happened to…Mickey Garagiola?" *St. Louis Post-Dispatch,* July 23, 1998.

"Dinner was always…" Berra, Yogi and Ed Fitzgerald. *Yogi: The Autobiography of a Professional Baseball Player.* New York: Doubleday, 1961.

"I used to like…" Berra, Yogi and Ed Fitzgerald. *Yogi: The Autobiography of a Professional Baseball Player.* New York: Doubleday, 1961.

"What did I do?" Berra, Yogi and Ed Fitzgerald. *Yogi: The Autobiography of a Professional Baseball Player.* New York: Doubleday, 1961.

*"Andiamo due pane!"* Garagiola, Joe. *Baseball Is a Funny Game.* New York: Bantam Books, 1980.

"You know the…" Volland, Victor. "Family Bakery on the Hill Still Home." *St. Louis Post-Dispatch,* October 7, 1999.

"Papa saw the paper…" Garagiola, Joe. *Baseball Is a Funny Game.* New York: Bantam Books, 1980.

"I would sleep in…" Berra, Yogi and Ed Fitzgerald. *Yogi: The Autobiography of a Professional Baseball Player.* New York: Doubleday, 1961.

"They were all…" Dorr, Dave. "Whatever Happened to…Mickey Garagiola?" *St. Louis Post-Dispatch,* July 23, 1998.

"Sandlot baseball is…" Billhartz, Cynthia. "Sandlot's Sad Lot." *St. Louis Post-Dispatch,* September 12, 2001.

"Never had to…" Billhartz, Cynthia. "Sandlot's Sad Lot." *St. Louis Post-Dispatch,* September 12, 2001.

"You have to…" Billhartz, Cynthia. "Sandlot's Sad Lot." *St. Louis Post-Dispatch,* September 12, 2001.

"With hand-me-down…" Schoor, Gene. *The Story of Yogi Berra.* New York: Doubleday, 1976.

"Everybody chipped in…" Garagiola, Joe. *Baseball Is a Funny Game.* New York: Bantam Books, 1980.

"We played with…" Billhartz, Cynthia. "Sandlot's Sad Lot." *St. Louis Post-Dispatch,* September 12, 2001.

"I must have…" Berra, Yogi and Ed Fitzgerald. *Yogi: The Autobiography of a Professional Baseball Player.* New York: Doubleday, 1961.

"Yogi made our…" Garagiola, Joe. *It's Anybody's Ballgame.* New York: Jove Books, 1989.

"All of us Stags…" Berra, Yogi and Ed Fitzgerald. *Yogi: The Autobiography of a Professional Baseball Player.* New York: Doubleday, 1961.

"Yogi was the…" Garagiola, Joe. *It's Anybody's Ballgame.* New York: Jove Books, 1989.

"When I heard that…" Berra, Yogi and Ed Fitzgerald. *Yogi: The Autobiography of a Professional Baseball Player.* New York: Doubleday, 1961.

"The kids whose pops…" Garagiola, Joe. *Baseball Is a Funny Game.* New York: Bantam Books, 1980.

"He'd get the…" Garagiola, Joe. *It's Anybody's Ballgame.* New York: Jove Books, 1989.

"I used to worship…" Berra, Yogi and Ed Fitzgerald. *Yogi: The Autobiography of a Professional Baseball Player.* New York: Doubleday, 1961.

"My brother Tony…" Berra, Yogi. Interview, "Lawrence Peter 'Yogi' Berra," Academy of Achievement, recorded June 1, 2005, New York City, http://www.achievement.org/autodoc/page/ber0int-2 (accessed February 20, 2007).

## Chapter 2

"Entertained ambassadors, royalty…" Sack, Marianne Peri. "Historical Review," Italian Club of St. Louis, http://www.italystl.com/italianclub (accessed February 20, 2007).

"I enjoyed it…" Berra, Yogi and Ed Fitzgerald. *Yogi: The Autobiography of a Professional Baseball Player.* New York: Doubleday, 1961.

"You'll never hit…" Garagiola, Joe. *It's Anybody's Ballgame.* New York: Jove Books, 1989.

"I played a lot…" Berra, Yogi. Interview, "Lawrence Peter 'Yogi' Berra," Academy of Achievement, recorded June 1, 2005, New York City, http://www. achievement.org/autodoc/page/ber0int-2 (accessed February 20, 2007).

"I could tell…" Berra, Yogi and Ed Fitzgerald. *Yogi: The Autobiography of a Professional Baseball Player.* New York: Doubleday, 1961.

"Now we look…" Schoor, Gene. *The Story of Yogi Berra.* New York: Doubleday, 1976.

"Joey and I were…" Berra, Yogi and Ed Fitzgerald. *Yogi: The Autobiography of a Professional Baseball Player.* New York: Doubleday, 1961.

"I was a lousy…" Berra, Yogi and Dave Kaplan. *When You Come to a Fork in the Road, Take It!* New York: Hyperion, 2001.

"It's sometimes better…" Schoor, Gene. *The Story of Yogi Berra.* New York: Doubleday, 1976.

"I realize now…" Berra, Yogi and Dave Kaplan. *When You Come to a Fork in the Road, Take It!* New York: Hyperion, 2001.

"Work in a shoe…" Berra, Yogi. Interview, "Lawrence Peter 'Yogi' Berra," Academy of Achievement, recorded June 1, 2005, New York City, http://www.achievement.org/autodoc/page/ber0int-2 (accessed February 20, 2007).

"Where were you…" Schoor, Gene. *The Story of Yogi Berra.* New York: Doubleday, 1976.

"I want to be a…" Schoor, Gene. *The Story of Yogi Berra.* New York: Doubleday, 1976.

"'Baseball,' answered young…" Schoor, Gene. *The Story of Yogi Berra.* New York: Doubleday, 1976.

"I'd rather pitch…" Mungo, Van. "Joe Medwick," National Baseball Hall of Fame, http://www.baseballhalloffame.org/hofers/detailjsp?playerId=118904 (accessed February 20, 2007).

"You know who…" Garagiola, Joe. *It's Anybody's Ballgame.* New York: Jove Books, 1989.

"As kids, we…" Berra, Yogi and Dave Kaplan. *What Time Is It? You Mean Now?* New York: Simon & Schuster, 2002.

"When a guy…" Garagiola, Joe. *It's Anybody's Ballgame.* New York: Jove Books, 1989.

"One day at a movie…" Garagiola, Joe. *It's Anybody's Ballgame.* New York: Jove Books, 1989.

"We're all movie…" Roswell, Gene. *The Yogi Berra Story.* New York: Julian Messner, Inc., 1958.

"From the moment…" Garagiola, Joe. *It's Anybody's Ballgame.* New York: Jove Books, 1989.

"You look just…" Berra, Yogi and Ed Fitzgerald. *Yogi: The Autobiography of a Professional Baseball Player.* New York: Doubleday, 1961.

## Chapter 3

"The kid can hit…" Roswell, Gene. *The Yogi Berra Story.* New York: Julian Messner, Inc., 1958.

"By the time we…" Garagiola, Joe. *It's Anybody's Ballgame.* New York: Jove Books, 1989.

"I don't want to…" Roswell, Gene. *The Yogi Berra Story.* New York: Julian Messner, Inc., 1958.

"Don't worry, kid…" Roswell, Gene. *The Yogi Berra Story.* New York: Julian Messner, Inc., 1958.

"What about a…" Roswell, Gene. *The Yogi Berra Story.* New York: Julian Messner, Inc., 1958.

"'Mr. Berra,' said…" Roswell, Gene. *The Yogi Berra Story.* New York: Julian Messner, Inc., 1958.

"The boy is too…" Berra, Yogi and Ed Fitzgerald. *Yogi: The Autobiography of a Professional Baseball Player.* New York: Doubleday, 1961.

"I couldn't understand…" Berra, Yogi and Ed Fitzgerald. *Yogi: The Autobiography of a Professional Baseball Player.* New York: Doubleday, 1961.

"All this kid wants…" Berra, Yogi and Ed Fitzgerald. *Yogi: The Autobiography of a Professional Baseball Player.* New York: Doubleday, 1961.

"I've often thought…" Garagiola, Joe. *It's Anybody's Ballgame.* New York: Jove Books, 1989.

"Lots of noses got…" Schoor, Gene. *The Story of Yogi Berra.* New York: Doubleday, 1976.

"Money was a serious…" Berra, Yogi and Ed Fitzgerald. *Yogi: The Autobiography of a Professional Baseball Player.* New York: Doubleday, 1961.

"I borrowed money…" Schoor, Gene. *The Story of Yogi Berra.* New York: Doubleday, 1976.

"How much time…" Schoor, Gene. *The Story of Yogi Berra.* New York: Doubleday, 1976.

## Chapter 4

"Landing craft support…" Berra, Yogi. Interview by Keith Olbermann, *Countdown with Keith Olbermann,* MSNBC-TV, June 7, 2004.

"I don't think…" Berra, Yogi and Ed Fitzgerald. *Yogi: The Autobiography of a Professional Baseball Player.* New York: Doubleday, 1961.

"Being a young guy…" Berra, Yogi. Interview by Keith Olbermann, *Countdown with Keith Olbermann,* MSNBC-TV, June 7, 2004.

"I wanted to see…" Berra, Yogi. Interview by Keith Olbermann, *Countdown with Keith Olbermann,* MSNBC-TV, June 7, 2004.

"We had a lead…" Berra, Yogi. Interview by Keith Olbermann, *Countdown with Keith Olbermann,* MSNBC-TV, June 7, 2004.

"We had orders…" Berra, Yogi. Interview by Keith Olbermann, *Countdown with Keith Olbermann,* MSNBC-TV, June 7, 2004.

"If it hits, let…" Schoor, Gene. *The Story of Yogi Berra.* New York: Doubleday, 1976.

"The only thing…" Berra, Yogi and Ed Fitzgerald. *Yogi: The Autobiography of a Professional Baseball Player.* New York: Doubleday, 1961.

"One minute it…" Schoor, Gene. *The Story of Yogi Berra.* New York: Doubleday, 1976.

"It's all right with…" Schoor, Gene. *The Story of Yogi Berra.* New York: Doubleday, 1976.

"I hear there's…" Schoor, Gene. *The Story of Yogi Berra.* New York: Doubleday, 1976.

"We came back…" Berra, Yogi. Interview by Keith Olbermann, *Countdown with Keith Olbermann,* MSNBC-TV, June 7, 2004.

"Of that terrible…" Berra, Yogi. Interview by Keith Olbermann, *Countdown with Keith Olbermann,* MSNBC-TV, June 7, 2004.

"You're a ballplayer?" Schoor, Gene. *The Story of Yogi Berra.* New York: Doubleday, 1976.

"That was a wild…" Schoor, Gene. *The Story of Yogi Berra.* New York: Doubleday, 1976.

"You're pretty fixed…" Roswell, Gene. *The Yogi Berra Story.* New York: Julian Messner, Inc., 1958.

"That kid catcher?" Schoor, Gene. *The Story of Yogi Berra.* New York: Doubleday, 1976.

"Truth be told…" Daley, Arthur. "Nature Boy." *The New York Times,* March 20, 1949.

"I'm Yogi Berra…" Schoor, Gene. *The Story of Yogi Berra.* New York: Doubleday, 1976.

"So I waited…" Daley, Arthur. "Nature Boy." *The New York Times,* March 20, 1949.

"Maybe I didn't…" Schoor, Gene. *The Story of Yogi Berra.* New York: Doubleday, 1976.

## Chapter 5

"Get him a room…" Roswell, Gene. *The Yogi Berra Story.* New York: Julian Messner, Inc., 1958.

"George 'Twinkletoes' Selkirk…" Bedingfield, Gary. "George Selkirk," Baseball-Library.com, http://www.baseballlibrary.com/baseballlibrary/ballplayers/S/Selkirk_George.stm (accessed February 20, 2007).

"Selkirk had been…" Bedingfield, Gary. "George Selkirk," BaseballLibrary.com, http://www.baseballlibrary.com/baseballlibrary/ballplayers/S/Selkirk_George.stm (accessed February 20, 2007).

"During the 1930s…" Weiss, Bill and Marshall Wright. "1941 Newark Bears," MinorLeagueBaseball.com, http://web.minorleaguebaseball.com/milk/history/top100.jsp?idx-86 (accessed February 20, 2007).

"Following the 1931 season…" Weiss, Bill and Marshall Wright. "1941 Newark Bears," MinorLeagueBaseball.com, http://web.minorleaguebaseball.com/milk/history/top100.jsp?idx-86 (accessed February 20, 2007).

"I was an old clubhouse…" Berra, Yogi and Ed Fitzgerald. *Yogi: The Autobiography of a Professional Baseball Player.* New York: Doubleday, 1961.

"Come on, put out the light…" Berra, Yogi and Ed Fitzgerald. *Yogi: The Autobiography of a Professional Baseball Player.* New York: Doubleday, 1961.

"Yogi doesn't forget…" Rizzuto, Phil and Tom Horton. *The October Twelve.* New York: Forge Books, 1994.

"The world needs…" Rizzuto, Phil and Tom Horton. *The October Twelve.* New York: Forge Books, 1994.

"It will always be…" Garagiola, Joe. *It's Anybody's Ballgame.* New York: Jove Books, 1989.

"The Bears came…" Associated Press. "Bears in Playoffs, Conquer Chiefs, 5–4." *The New York Times,* September 9, 1946.

"When Gore called Tatum…" Associated Press. "Montreal Ousts Newark." *The New York Times,* September 18, 1946.

"Either way, I…" Berra, Yogi and Ed Fitzgerald. *Yogi: The Autobiography of a Professional Baseball Player.* New York: Doubleday, 1961.

"Already figured in the…" Effrat, Louis. "Yanks Defeat Athletics, 4–3, 7–4." *The New York Times,* September 23, 1946.

"Berra, a 21-year-old…" McCulley, Jim. "Yanks Sweep Twin Bill." *New York Daily News,* September 23, 1946.

"This ain't Newark…" Schoor, Gene. *The Story of Yogi Berra.* New York: Doubleday, 1976.

"And Mel Ott…" Schoor, Gene. *The Story of Yogi Berra.* New York: Doubleday, 1976.

"The work of Bobby…" Effrat, Louis. "Yanks Vanquish Athletics by 9–6." *The New York Times,* September 24, 1946.

"I guess it was Paul…" Ford, Whitey and Phil Pepe. *Slick.* New York: William Morrow, 1987.

"Everybody on Elizabeth…" Berra, Yogi and Ed Fitzgerald. *Yogi: The Autobiography of a Professional Baseball Player.* New York: Doubleday, 1961.

"You better pick them…" Berra, Yogi and Ed Fitzgerald. *Yogi: The Autobiography of a Professional Baseball Player.* New York: Doubleday, 1961.

## Chapter 6

"The Yankees' record…" Garagiola, Joe. *It's Anybody's Ballgame.* New York: Jove Books, 1989.

"He can hit what…" Roswell, Gene. *The Yogi Berra Story.* New York: Julian Messner, Inc., 1958.

"Don't be alarmed…" Daley, Arthur. "Out of the Clouds with the Yankees." *The New York Times,* March 12, 1947.

"Yogi Berra, of course…" Daley, Arthur. "Yank's Pitching, Except One Lapse by Chandler, Encourages Harris." *The New York Times,* March 20, 1947.

"Manager Bucky Harris…" Drebinger, John. "Boston's Three in Ninth Beat Bombers, 5–4." *The New York Times,* March 28, 1947.

"Looks as though something…" Drebinger, John. "Bombers Overcome Hassett Tars, 19–5." *The New York Times,* April 8, 1947.

"He has the biggest…" Schoor, Gene. *The Story of Yogi Berra.* New York: Doubleday, 1976.

"There's no way…" Schoor, Gene. *The Story of Yogi Berra.* New York: Doubleday, 1976.

"Don't let them…" Roswell, Gene. *The Yogi Berra Story.* New York: Julian Messner, Inc., 1958.

"Good hitters usually…" Garagiola, Joe. *It's Anybody's Ballgame.* New York: Jove Books, 1989.

"I know you…" Daley, Arthur. "Short Shots in Sundry Directions." *The New York Times,* June 12, 1947.

"If I hear your…" Cramer, Richard Ben. *Joe DiMaggio: The Hero's Life.* New York: Touchstone, 2000.

"I called for the…" Schoor, Gene. *The Story of Yogi Berra.* New York: Doubleday, 1976.

"Just walk up…" Cramer, Richard Ben. *Joe DiMaggio: The Hero's Life.* New York: Touchstone, 2000.

"He'd get off…" Hahn, Christopher. "It Ain't Over." *New Jersey Monthly,* July 2006.

"The many jokes…" Schoor, Gene. *The Story of Yogi Berra.* New York: Doubleday, 1976.

"Sometimes the writers…" Shapiro, Milton J. *Heroes behind the Mask.* New York: Julian Messner, Inc., 1968.

"Joe Trimble of the…" Berra, Yogi and Ed Fitzgerald. *Yogi: The Autobiography of a Professional Baseball Player.* New York: Doubleday, 1961.

"Charlie Keller had…" Berra, Yogi and Ed Fitzgerald. *Yogi: The Autobiography of a Professional Baseball Player.* New York: Doubleday, 1961.

"Opposing players…" Berra, Yogi and Ed Fitzgerald. *Yogi: The Autobiography of a Professional Baseball Player.* New York: Doubleday, 1961.

"Washington pitcher…" Berra, Yogi and Ed Fitzgerald. *Yogi: The Autobiography of a Professional Baseball Player.* New York: Doubleday, 1961.

"From the dugout…" Berra, Yogi and Ed Fitzgerald. *Yogi: The Autobiography of a Professional Baseball Player.* New York: Doubleday, 1961.

"The sportswriters recognized…" Roswell, Gene. *The Yogi Berra Story.* New York: Julian Messner, Inc., 1958.

"One of nature's…" Daley, Arthur. "Nature Boy." *The New York Times,* March 20, 1949.

"Yogi Berra is…" Daley, Arthur. "At the Baseball Writer's Show." *The New York Times,* February 7, 1949.

"To the sportswriters…" Stewart-Gordon, James. "Yogi Berra the Yankee Nonesuch," *Rotarian* magazine, May 1959.

"Everyone calls him…" Daley, Arthur. "Nature Boy." *The New York Times,* March 20, 1949.

"Once before a…" Roswell, Gene. *The Yogi Berra Story.* New York: Julian Messner, Inc., 1958.

"Yogi, you just…" Roswell, Gene. *The Yogi Berra Story.* New York: Julian Messner, Inc., 1958.

"Yogi was very…" Rizzuto, Phil and Tom Horton. *The October Twelve.* New York: Forge Books, 1994.

"A cuddly, noble savage…" Lipsyte, Robert. "The Man and the Myth." *The New York Times,* October 25, 1963.

"They dubbed Yogi…" Koppett, Leonard. "A Legend of the Game." *The New York Times,* October 2, 1973.

"I just got the…" Roswell, Gene. *The Yogi Berra Story.* New York: Julian Messner, Inc., 1958.

"The embarrassed Yogi…" Daley, Arthur. "Short Shots in Sundry Directions." *The New York Times,* June 12, 1947.

"What happened?" Berra, Yogi and Ed Fitzgerald. *Yogi: The Autobiography of a Professional Baseball Player.* New York: Doubleday, 1961.

"Yogi Berra, the freshman…" Daley, Arthur. "Waiting for the World Series." *The New York Times,* September 30, 1947.

"The suspicion is…" Daley, Arthur. "It Happened in Brooklyn." *The New York Times,* October 4, 1947.

"I should have..." Schoor, Gene. *The Story of Yogi Berra.* New York: Doubleday, 1976.

"Don't bother writing..." Daley, Arthur. "It Happened in Brooklyn." *The New York Times,* October 4, 1947.

"Yogi Berra, playing..." Trimble, Joe. "Yanks Champs! Trim Flock, 5–2." *New York Daily News,* October 7, 1947.

"The Dodgers stole..." Daley, Arthur. "Nature Boy." *The New York Times,* March 20, 1949.

"Berra got a number..." Drebinger, John. "Harris Outlines Plans to Teach." *The New York Times,* March 4, 1948.

"A guy doesn't..." Daley, Arthur. "Nature Boy." *The New York Times,* March 20, 1949.

## Chapter 7

"Later on, when..." Berra, Yogi and Ed Fitzgerald. *Yogi: The Autobiography of a Professional Baseball Player.* New York: Doubleday, 1961.

"Buy the beer..." Berra, Yogi and Ed Fitzgerald. *Yogi: The Autobiography of a Professional Baseball Player.* New York: Doubleday, 1961.

"As Carmen remembers..." Hann, Christopher. "It Ain't Over." *New Jersey Monthly,* July 2006.

"She was the prettiest..." Berra, Yogi and Ed Fitzgerald. *Yogi: The Autobiography of a Professional Baseball Player.* New York: Doubleday, 1961.

"The girls won't..." Schoor, Gene. *The Story of Yogi Berra.* New York: Doubleday, 1976.

"Probably the most..." Garagiola, Joe. *It's Anybody's Ballgame.* New York: Jove Books, 1989.

"Carmen Short didn't..." Houston, Maureen. *The Book on Yogi Berra.* Amarillo, TX: Amarillo Globe News, August 19, 2001.

"Yogi never did..." Schoor, Gene. *The Story of Yogi Berra.* New York: Doubleday, 1976.

"This girl, Yogi..." Garagiola, Joe. *It's Anybody's Ballgame.* New York: Jove Books, 1989.

"There were about..." Daley, Arthur. "When Yogi Was Scared." *The New York Times,* March 14, 1949.

"Yogi and Carmen..." Rizzuto, Phil and Tom Horton. *The October Twelve.* New York: Forge Books, 1994.

"Unlike most baseball..." Stewart-Gordon, James. "Yogi Berra: The Yankee Nonesuch." *Reader's Digest,* May 1959.

"Look, it was you..." Stewart-Gordon, James. "Yogi Berra: The Yankee Nonesuch." *Reader's Digest,* May 1959.

"I used to stick..." Barra, Allan. "Yogi Berra Fields Some Questions." *The Wall Street Journal,* October 28, 2004.

"Please get Frank..." Roswell, Gene. *The Yogi Berra Story.* New York: Julian Messner, Inc., 1958.

## Chapter 8

"Berra, a rugged..." McGowen, Roscoe. "Contracts Signed by Lindell, Berra." *The New York Times,* February 14, 1948.

"Berra was the..." Shapiro, Milton J. *Heroes behind the Mask.* New York: Julian Messner, Inc., 1968.

"Baseball writers are..." Shapiro, Milton J. *Heroes behind the Mask.* New York: Julian Messner, Inc., 1968.

"You know, Marshall..." Drebinger, John. "Yankees' Hurlers in Need of Work." *The New York Times,* March 3, 1948.

"Hey, Rizzuto, why..." Daley, Arthur. "Overheard at St. Pete." *The New York Times,* March 11, 1948.

"The rehabilitation of..." Drebinger, John. "Harris Outlines Plans to Teach." *The New York Times,* March 4, 1948.

"That laxity is going to..." Drebinger, John. "Harris Outlines Plans to Teach." *The New York Times,* March 4, 1948.

"Yogi made quite..." Effrat, Louis. "67,924 See Indians Beat Yanks under Lights." *The New York Times,* June 12, 1948.

"Then came the hoots..." Effrat, Louis. "67,924 See Indians Beat Yanks under Lights." *The New York Times,* June 12, 1948.

"Boys, I'm one..." Garagiola, Joe. *Baseball Is a Funny Game.* New York: Bantam Books, 1980.

"I think you..." Schoor, Gene. *The Story of Yogi Berra.* New York: Doubleday, 1976.

"My most difficult..." Gerlach, Larry R. *The Men in Blue.* New York: Viking Press, 1980.

"Yogi Berra wasn't..." Gerlach, Larry R. *The Men in Blue.* New York: Viking Press, 1980.

"[He] quickly…" Wolf, George D. "Ryne Duren Stats," BaseballLibrary.com, http://www.baseball-almanac.com/players/player.php?p=durenry01 (accessed February 20, 2007).

"He's got four…" "The Long and Short." *The New York Times.* May 1, 1960.

"I'll give you…" Daley, Arthur. "Overheard at St. Pete." *The New York Times,* March 11, 1948.

"Ball!" Berra, Yogi and Ed Fitzgerald. *Yogi: The Autobiography of a Professional Baseball Player.* New York: Doubleday, 1961.

"Yogi Berra was…" Gerlach, Larry R. *The Men in Blue.* New York: Viking Press, 1980.

"Bert Campaneris was…" Gerlach, Larry R. *The Men in Blue.* New York: Viking Press, 1980.

"Yogi was not…" Gerlach, Larry R. *The Men in Blue.* New York: Viking Press, 1980.

"Why don't you…" Daley, Arthur. "Overheard at the Stadium." *The New York Times,* July 1, 1948.

"Nature Boy gave…" Daley, Arthur. "Overheard at the Stadium." *The New York Times,* July 1, 1948.

"The ball just…" Daley, Arthur. "Overheard at the Stadium." *The New York Times,* July 1, 1948.

"Berra could move…" Rizzuto, Phil and Tom Horton. *The October Twelve.* New York: Forge Books, 1994.

"Berra to this day…" Seidel, Michael. *Ted Williams: A Baseball Life.* Lincoln: University of Nebraska Press, 2003.

"Must be an iodine…" Seidel, Michael. *Ted Williams: A Baseball Life.* Lincoln: University of Nebraska Press, 2003.

"You old Dago…" Berra, Yogi. Interview, "Lawrence Peter 'Yogi' Berra," Academy of Achievement, recorded June 1, 2005, New York City, http://www.achievement.org/autodoc/page/ber0int-2 (accessed February 20, 2007).

"Have a good…" Rizzuto, Phil and Tom Horton. *The October Twelve.* New York: Forge Books, 1994.

"As our catcher…" Rizzuto, Phil and Tom Horton. *The October Twelve.* New York: Forge Books, 1994.

"I liked to talk…" Berra, Yogi. Interview, "Lawrence Peter 'Yogi' Berra," Academy of Achievement, recorded June 1, 2005, New York City, http://www.achievement.org/autodoc/page/ber0int-2 (accessed February 20, 2007).

"Watch out for Yogi…" Daley, Arthur. "A Sizzling Afternoon at the Stadium." *The New York Times,* July 5, 1949.

"[Ted] didn't like…" Berra, Yogi. Interview, "Lawrence Peter 'Yogi' Berra," Academy of Achievement, recorded June 1, 2005, New York City, http://www.achievement.org/autodoc/page/ber0int-2 (accessed February 20, 2007).

"Yankees pitcher Tommy…" Halberstam, David. *Summer of '49.* New York: William Morrow and Company, 1989.

"When we played…" Rizzuto, Phil and Tom Horton. *The October Twelve.* New York: Forge Books, 1994.

"In 1948 Yogi Berra…" Halberstam, David. *Summer of '49.* New York: William Morrow and Company, 1989.

"Then why the hell…" Halberstam, David. *Summer of '49.* New York: William Morrow and Company, 1989.

"When Henrich had…" Halberstam, David. *Summer of '49.* New York: William Morrow and Company, 1989.

"Whatsa matter…" Cramer, Richard Ben. *Joe DiMaggio: The Hero's Life.* New York: Touchstone, 2000.

"The most valuable…" Daley, Arthur. "No Electioneering Near the Polls." *The New York, Times,* July 4, 1948.

"Does Berra ever…" Daley, Arthur. "No Electioneering Near the Polls." *The New York, Times,* July 4, 1948.

"'Nuts,' joined…" Daley, Arthur. "No Electioneering Near the Polls." *The New York, Times,* July 4, 1948.

"Yogi Berra has quit catching…" Creamer, Robert. *Stengel: His Life and Times.* New York: Simon & Schuster, 1984.

## Chapter 9

"I had many…" Einstein, Charles, ed. *The Third Fireside Book of Baseball.* New York: Simon and Schuster, 1968.

"I was such…" Einstein, Charles, ed. *The Third Fireside Book of Baseball.* New York: Simon and Schuster, 1968.

"We're ready to…" Schoor, Gene. *The Story of Yogi Berra.* New York: Doubleday, 1976.

"Yogi's holdout…" "Berra of Yankees Granted Salary Increase." *The New York Times.* February 27, 1949.

"Berra's value…" *The New York Times,* "Berra of Yankees Granted Salary Increase," February 27, 1949.

"But Casey liked…" Creamer, Robert. *Stengel: His Life and Times.* New York: Simon & Schuster, 1984.

"Fortunately for Berra…" Halberstam, David. *Summer of '49.* New York: William Morrow and Company, 1989.

"It might be…" Shapiro, Milton J. *Heroes behind the Mask.* New York: Julian Messner, 1968.

"My assistant manager…" Creamer, Robert. *Stengel: His Life and Times.* New York: Simon & Schuster, 1984.

"Normally Stengel…" Creamer, Robert. *Stengel: His Life and Times.* New York: Simon & Schuster, 1984.

"Frank Graham said…" Creamer, Robert. *Stengel: His Life and Times.* New York: Simon & Schuster, 1984.

"Aware, as no one…" Creamer, Robert. *Stengel: His Life and Times.* New York: Simon & Schuster, 1984.

"I liked him…" Rizzuto, Phil and Tom Horton. *The October Twelve.* New York: Forge Books, 1994.

"That's it! You call…" Mantle, Mickey with Herb Gluck. *Mickey: An American Hero.* New York: Jove Paperbacks, 1986.

"When I told…" Berra, Yogi with Dave Kaplan. *Ten Rings.* New York: William Morrow, 2003.

"Get up close…" Schoor, Gene. *The Story of Yogi Berra.* New York: Doubleday, 1976.

"Converting Berra from…" Schoor, Gene. *The Story of Yogi Berra.* New York: Doubleday, 1976.

"We all knew…" Rizzuto, Phil and Tom Horton. *The October Twelve.* New York: Forge Books, 1994.

"Give him two…" Schoor, Gene. *The Story of Yogi Berra.* New York: Doubleday, 1976.

"He taught me…" Berra, Yogi with Dave Kaplan. *Ten Rings.* New York: William Morrow and Company, 2003.

"Berra is why…" Schoor, Gene. *The Story of Yogi Berra.* New York: Doubleday, 1976.

"Hey, Yogi, I…" Daley, Arthur. "Overheard at St. Pete." *The New York Times,* March 20, 1949.

"When I phoned…" Daley, Arthur. "Overheard at St. Pete." *The New York Times,* March 20, 1949.

"X-Rays of Berra's…" Roswell, Gene. *The Yogi Berra Story.* New York: Julian Messner, Inc., 1958.

"How's your wife…" Shapiro, Milton J. *Heroes behind the Mask.* New York: Julian Messner, Inc., 1968.

"Don't stab at…" Halberstam, David. *Summer of '49.* New York: William Morrow and Company, 1989.

"A high outside…" Halberstam, David. *Summer of '49.* New York: William Morrow and Company, 1989.

"They tipped off…" Halberstam, David. *Summer of '49.* New York: William Morrow and Company, 1989.

"Don't turn, Yogi…" Halberstam, David. *Summer of '49.* New York: William Morrow and Company, 1989.

"I played right…" Rizzuto, Phil and Tom Horton. *The October Twelve.* New York: Forge Books, 1994.

"Just catch. I'll pitch." Garagiola, Joe. *Baseball Is a Funny Game.* New York: Bantam Books, 1980.

"Raschi pitched better…" Berra, Yogi and Ed Fitzgerald. *Yogi: The Autobiography of a Professional Baseball Player.* New York: Doubleday, 1961.

"When Lopat was…" Rizzuto, Phil and Tom Horton. *The October Twelve.* New York: Forge Books, 1994.

"No slow balls…" Robinson, Kirk. "Ed Lopat," TheBaseballPage.com, http://www.thebaseballpage.com/players/lopated01.php (accessed February, 20, 2006).

"Counting the screwball…" Rizzuto, Phil and Tom Horton. *The October Twelve.* New York: Forge Books, 1994.

"He's still got…" Roswell, Gene. *The Yogi Berra Story.* New York: Julian Messner, Inc., 1958.

"When he had to go…" Koppett, Leonard. "Stengel Ponders 'The Year of Berra'." *The New York Times,* April 12, 1964.

"It's impossible to…" Berra, Yogi. Interview, "Lawrence Peter 'Yogi' Berra," Academy of Achievement, recorded June 1, 2005, New York City, http://www.achievement.org/autodoc/page/ber0int-2 (accessed February 20, 2007).

"First and foremost…" Larsen, Don with Mark Shaw. *The Perfect Yankee.* Champaign, IL: Sports Publishing LLC, 2006.

"It is just not..." Berra, Yogi and Tom Horton. *Yogi: It Ain't Over*. New York: McGraw-Hill, 1989.

"There was only..." Halberstam, David. *Summer of '49*. New York: William Morrow and Company, 1989.

"Hey, Yogi, what..." Halberstam, David. *Summer of '49*. New York: William Morrow and Company, 1989.

"Silvera, you're catching..." Halberstam, David. *Summer of '49*. New York: William Morrow and Company, 1989.

"Sure he surprised..." Associated Press. "Doby Fined by Boudreau." July 21, 1949.

"By the time..." Halberstam, David. *Summer of '49*. New York: William Morrow and Company, 1989.

"In 1949, my..." Rizzuto, Phil and Tom Horton. *The October Twelve*. New York: Forge Books, 1994.

"Ironically, the Dodgers..." Daley, Arthur. "The Man in the Iron Mask." *The New York Times,* May 21, 1950.

"I know he..." Berra, Yogi with Dave Kaplan. *Ten Rings*. New York: William Morrow, 2003.

"Don't make a..." Berra, Yogi and Ed Fitzgerald. *Yogi: The Autobiography of a Professional Baseball Player.* New York: Doubleday, 1961.

## Chapter 10

"You sent back..." Schoor, Gene. *The Story of Yogi Berra*. New York: Doubleday, 1976.

"Only the unpredictable..." Dawson, James P. "Rizzuto, Reynolds, Porterfield All Fall in Line with Yankees." *The New York Times,* January 24, 1950.

"Yogi apparently is..." McGowen, Roscoe. "27 Yanks in Fold as Silvera Signs." *The New York Times,* February 17, 1950.

"You're not doing..." Schoor, Gene. *The Story of Yogi Berra*. New York: Doubleday, 1976.

"Sure he got..." Drebinger, John. "Berra of Yanks Still a Holdout." *The New York Times,* March 7, 1950.

"However, [Berra] made..." Drebinger, John. "Berra of Yanks Still a Holdout." *The New York Times,* March 7, 1950.

"Casey Goes to..." Trimble, Joe. "Casey Goes to Bat—Gets Raises for Raschi, Yogi." *New York Daily News,* March 8, 1950.

"Weiss admitted that…" Trimble, Joe. "Casey Goes to Bat—Gets Raises for Raschi, Yogi." *New York Daily News,* March 8, 1950.

"General manager George…" Drebinger, John. "Raschi, Berra Sign Contracts with Yankees after Stengel Acts." *The New York Times,* March 8, 1950.

"Sure, his feet…" Drebinger, John. "Raschi, Berra Sign Contracts with Yankees after Stengel Acts." *The New York Times,* March 8, 1950.

"Yes sir…" Roswell, Gene. *The Yogi Berra Story.* New York: Julian Messner, Inc., 1958.

"There are three…" Garagiola, Joe. *It's Anybody's Ballgame.* New York: Jove Books, 1989.

"I could understand…" Ford, Whitey and Phil Pepe. *Slick.* New York: William Morrow and Company, 1987.

"I'd go to the bathroom…" Ford, Whitey and Phil Pepe. *Slick.* New York: William Morrow and Company, 1987.

"When I got…" Ford, Whitey and Mickey Mantle with Joseph Durso. *Whitey and Mickey.* New York: Viking Press, 1977.

"We'd have been…" Roswell, Gene. *The Yogi Berra Story.* New York: Julian Messner, Inc., 1958.

"Wake me up…" Ford, Whitey and Mickey Mantle with Joseph Durso. *Whitey and Mickey.* New York: Viking Press, 1977.

"He's the boss…" Roswell, Gene. *The Yogi Berra Story.* New York: Julian Messner, Inc., 1958.

"We don't hit…" Roswell, Gene. *The Yogi Berra Story.* New York: Julian Messner, Inc., 1958.

"Let's see you…" Roswell, Gene. *The Yogi Berra Story.* New York: Julian Messner, Inc., 1958.

"Casey had Berra…" Creamer, Robert. *Stengel: His Life and Times.* New York: Simon & Schuster, 1984.

"The pudgy receiver…" Drebinger, John. "Berra Leads Drive in Victory by 13–6." *The New York Times,* August 23, 1950.

"I never shook…" Roswell, Gene. *The Yogi Berra Story.* New York: Julian Messner, Inc., 1958.

"But first of all…" Daley, Arthur. "Four Straight." *The New York Times,* October 8, 1950.

"There was the…" Daley, Arthur. Cinema Review, *The New York Times,* December 21, 1950.

"In 1950, Phil…" Baker, Jim. "Gotta Love the Entertainers," ESPN.com, http://proxy.espn.go.com/mlb/columns/story?columnist=baker_jim&id=1703413, January, 13, 2004 (accessed February 27, 2007).

"Part of his…" Talese, Gay. "Diamonds Are a Boy's Best Friend." *The New York Times* magazine, October 1, 1961.

"She excused herself…" Talese, Gay. "Diamonds Are a Boy's Best Friend." *The New York Times* magazine, October 1, 1961.

"Scott understood immediately…" Halberstam, David. *Summer of '49.* New York: William Morrow and Company, 1989.

"There had been…" Litsky, Frank. "Frank Scott, 80, Baseball's First Player Agent." *The New York Times,* June 30, 1998.

"Later baseball clients…" Litsky, Frank. "Frank Scott, 80, Baseball's First Player Agent." *The New York Times,* June 30, 1998.

"Scott knew an…" Litsky, Frank. "Frank Scott, 80, Baseball's First Player Agent." *The New York Times,* June 30, 1998.

"I never guarantee…" Litsky, Frank. "Frank Scott, 80, Baseball's First Player Agent." *The New York Times,* June 30, 1998.

"Far apart…. I'm…" Associated Press. "Berra, Yanks Far Apart." January 28, 1951.

"I think my…" Associated Press, "Berra Asks Yanks for $13,000 Raise." February 1, 1951.

"I can give…" Berra, Yogi and Ed Fitzgerald. *Yogi: The Autobiography of a Professional Baseball Player.* New York: Doubleday, 1961.

"They always told…" Berra, Yogi and Ed Fitzgerald. *Yogi: The Autobiography of a Professional Baseball Player.* New York: Doubleday, 1961.

"You said a…" Berra, Yogi and Ed Fitzgerald. *Yogi: The Autobiography of a Professional Baseball Player.* New York: Doubleday, 1961.

"It means primitive…" Berra, Yogi and Ed Fitzgerald. *Yogi: The Autobiography of a Professional Baseball Player.* New York: Doubleday, 1961.

"How much you…" Berra, Yogi and Ed Fitzgerald. *Yogi: The Autobiography of a Professional Baseball Player.* New York: Doubleday, 1961.

"That is exclusively…" Dawson, James P. "Catcher's Salary Reported $30,000." *The New York Times,* March 1, 1951.

"I got responsibilities…" Keene, Kerry. *1951: When Giants Played the Game.* Champaign, IL: Sports Publishing, LLC, 2001.

## Chapter 11

"Hopalong Berra looks…" Keene, Kerry. *1951: When Giants Played the Game.* Champaign, IL: Sports Publishing, LLC, 2001.

"I noted that…" Carrieri, Joseph R. *Searching for Heroes.* Mineola, NY: Carlyn Publications, 1995.

"I really don't have…" Carrieri, Joseph R. *Searching for Heroes.* Mineola, NY: Carlyn Publications, 1995.

"Let me put it to you…" Carrieri, Joseph R. *Searching for Heroes.* Mineola, NY: Carlyn Publications, 1995.

"Don't forget that…" Daley, Arthur. "Play Ball!" *The New York Times,* April 17, 1951.

"We pitch to…" Keene, Kerry. *1951: When Giants Played the Game.* Champaign, IL: Sports Publishing, LLC, 2001.

"Yogi called for…" Ford, Whitey and Mickey Mantle with Joseph Durso. *Whitey and Mickey.* New York: Viking Press, 1977.

"My husband dropped…" Rizzuto, Phil and Tom Horton. *The October Twelve.* New York: Forge Books, 1994.

"I'm sorry, Wahoo…" Shapiro, Milton J. *Heroes behind the Mask.* New York: Julian Messner, Inc., 1968.

"The pitcher, who…" Trimble, Joe. "Reynolds' No-Hitter Won Twice." *New York Daily News,* September 29, 1951.

"Don't worry, Yogi…" Drebinger, John. "Yanks Clinch Flag." *The New York Times,* September 29, 1951.

"When I got…" Berra, Yogi with Dave Kaplan. *Ten Rings.* New York: William Morrow and Company, 2003.

"Yogi told me…" Ford, Whitey and Mickey Mantle with Joseph Durso. *Whitey and Mickey.* New York: Viking Press, 1977.

"For a moment…" Drebinger, John. "Yanks Clinch Flag." *The New York Times,* September 29, 1951.

"When I die…" Berra, Yogi with Dave Kaplan. *Ten Rings.* New York: William Morrow and Company, 2003.

"That Yogi Berra…" United Press International. "Relied on Sinker, Says Left-Hander." October 5, 1951.

"You've got lots…" Schoor, Gene. *The Story of Yogi Berra.* New York: Doubleday, 1976.

"You're supposed to…" Schoor, Gene. *The Story of Yogi Berra.* New York: Doubleday, 1976.

"Okay, Slick, the…" Berra, Yogi with Dave Kaplan. *Ten Rings.* New York: William Morrow and Company, 2003.

"This squat little…" Schoor, Gene. *The Story of Yogi Berra.* New York: Doubleday, 1976.

"More power to…" Daley, Arthur. "Man with Splinters." *The New York Times,* January 20, 1952.

"Yogi Berra, the…" Trimble, Joe. "Yogi, Garver, Allie 1-2-3 in MVP Vote." *New York Daily News,* November 9, 1951.

"I was afraid…" Trimble, Joe. "Yogi, Garver, Allie 1-2-3 in MVP Vote." *New York Daily News,* November 9, 1951.

"I didn't realize…" Trimble, Joe. "Yogi, Garver, Allie 1-2-3 in MVP Vote." *New York Daily News,* November 9, 1951.

"I thought Allie…" Daley, Arthur. "Yogi and the Award." *The New York Times,* November 14, 1951.

"He ain't, though…" Daley, Arthur. "Yogi and the Award." *The New York Times,* November 14, 1951.

"Every day was busy…" Berra, Yogi with Dave Kaplan. *Ten Rings.* New York: William Morrow and Company, 2003.

"Be careful, Yogi…" Berra, Yogi with Dave Kaplan. *Ten Rings.* New York: William Morrow and Company, 2003.

"I just tell…" Drebinger, John. "Berra and McDougald Sign Yankee Contracts." *The New York Times,* January 24, 1952.

"What he considers…" Drebinger, John. "Berra and McDougald Sign Yankee Contracts." *The New York Times,* January 24, 1952.

"Berra said his…" Keene, Kerry. *1951: When Giants Played the Game.* Champaign, IL: Sports Publishing, LLC, 2001.

"Baseball isn't the…" Advertisement, Display Ad 132—No Title, Doodle Oil Bait Perfume. *The New York Times,* June 1, 1952.

"Who's going to…" Advertisement, Display Ad 35—No Title, My Beer Is Rheingold—The Dry Beer! *The New York Times,* September 12, 1952.

"He insisted on…" Schoor, Gene. *The Scooter: The Phil Rizzuto Story.* New York: Charles Scribner's Sons, 1982.

"Mr. Berra had…" Rizzuto, Phil and Tom Horton. *The October Twelve.* New York: Forge Books, 1994.

"Yogi could be…" Rizzuto, Phil and Tom Horton. *The October Twelve.* New York: Forge Books, 1994.

"There was a…" Roswell, Gene. *The Yogi Berra Story.* New York: Julian Messner, Inc., 1958.

"Casey always batted…" Roswell, Gene. *The Yogi Berra Story.* New York: Julian Messner, Inc., 1958.

"I loved to watch…" Roswell, Gene. *The Yogi Berra Story.* New York: Julian Messner, Inc., 1958.

"I used to…" Roswell, Gene. *The Yogi Berra Story.* New York: Julian Messner, Inc., 1958.

"I didn't like…" Roswell, Gene. *The Yogi Berra Story.* New York: Julian Messner, Inc., 1958.

"You over it…" Roswell, Gene. *The Yogi Berra Story.* New York: Julian Messner, Inc., 1958.

"The other guys…" Roswell, Gene. *The Yogi Berra Story.* New York: Julian Messner, Inc., 1958.

"Yogi Berra's homer…" Mantle, Mickey. "Mantle Belittles His Game-Winning Homer." United Press International, October 7, 1952.

"Tell me the…" "From Force of Habit," Sports of the Times, *The New York Times,* October 8, 1952.

"It was a…" Schoor, Gene. *The Story of Yogi Berra.* New York: Doubleday, 1976.

"Safely crash-landed his…" Baseball Almanac, "Year in Review: 1953 American League," http://www.baseball-almanac.com/yearly/yr1953a.shtml (accessed March 31, 2007).

"Hey, muscles…" Daley, Arthur. "Star among Stars." *The New York Times,* July 15, 1953.

"I'm hip deep…" Daley, Arthur. "All Even." *The New York Times,* October 3, 1953.

"That seemed to…" Trimble, Joe. "Yanks Win Record Fifth." *New York Daily News,* October 6, 1953.

"No, no…" Trimble, Joe. "Yanks Win Record Fifth." *New York Daily News,* October 6, 1953.

"There were eight…" Madden, Bill. *Pride of October.* New York: Warner Books, 2003.

"There was about…" McGowen, Roscoe. "Berra Signs and Becomes Highest-Salaried Catcher in History of Yankees." *The New York Times,* January 23, 1954.

"If anything happened…" Daley, Arthur. "Overheard at the Stadium." *The New York Times,* June 14, 1953.

"In soccer, you…" Daley, Arthur. "Just Listening." *The New York Times,* September 3, 1954.

"We were at…" McGowen, Roscoe. "Berra Signs Yanks' Contract." *The New York Times,* November 4, 1954.

"Berra's powerful and…" Young, Dick. "Yogi Tops Three Indians for MVP Award." *New York Daily News,* December 10, 1954.

"Stengel leans heavily…" Daley, Arthur. "Our Boy, Yogi." *The New York Times,* December 13, 1954.

"Some people told…" Young, Dick. "Yogi Tops Three Indians for MVP Award." *New York Daily News,* December 10, 1954.

"He now gets…" Daley, Arthur. "Overheard in St. Pete." *The New York Times,* March 11, 1955.

"Hey, Yog, you…" Daley, Arthur. "Overheard in St. Pete." *The New York Times,* March 11, 1955.

"I finally get…" Wimbish, Ralph. "Hank Never Thought in Black and White." *New York Post,* February 10, 2007.

"You can say…" TheBaseballPage.com, "Elston Howard," http://www.thebaseballpage.com/players/howarel01.php (accessed April 22, 2007).

"The Yankees played…" Wimbish, Ralph. "Hank Never Thought in Black and White." *New York Post,* February 10, 2007.

"Later that season…" Wimbish, Ralph. "Hank Never Thought in Black and White." *New York Post,* February 10, 2007.

"How ya doing, Yog…" Daley, Arthur. "Waiting for the Stars." *The New York Times,* July 11, 1960.

"The most famous…" Post, Paul and Ed Lucas. "Stealing Home." *Baseball Digest,* August 2002.

"I knew he…" Enders, Eric. *100 Years of the World Series.* New York: Sterling, 2005.

"He was out…" Post, Paul and Ed Lucas. "Stealing Home." *Baseball Digest,* August 2002.

"Umpire Bill Summers…" Editorial, *New York Daily News,* October 1, 1955.

"Went wild…" Ford, Whitey and Phil Pepe. *Slick.* New York: William Morrow and Company, 1987.

"Yogi gets very…" Raimondi, Marc. "Mets Hold Jackie Robinson Night at Shea" SNY.tv.com, http://www.sny.tv/news/article.jsp?ymd=20070422&content_id=1427287&oid=36018&vkey=9 (accessed April 23, 2007).

"Sure, I saw the…" Post, Paul and Ed Lucas. "Stealing Home." *Baseball Digest,* August 2002.

"Yeah, I really do…" Post, Paul and Ed Lucas. "Stealing Home." *Baseball Digest,* August 2002.

"Martin and McDougald…" Trimble, Joe. "Dodgers Champs!" *New York Daily News,* October 5, 1955.

"'I run and run…" Frommer, Harvey. "Dodgers Finally Beat Yanks in World Series, October 4, 1955" Harvey Frommer on Sports, http://www.travel-watch.com/dodgersbeatyanks10-4-55.htm (accessed April 12, 2007).

"He said the incoming…" Mozley, Dana. "Great Catch by Sandy Broke Yankees' Back." *New York Daily News,* October 5, 1955.

"If he wasn't…" Swirsky, Seth. "Sandy Saves the '55 Dodgers" Seth.com, http://www.seth.com/coll_themeballs_11.html (accessed February 15, 2007).

"Maybe it's because…" Young, Dick. "Third MVP for Yanks' Berra." *New York Daily News,* December 4, 1955.

"But Yogi was…" Daley, Arthur. "In Mild Dissent." *The New York Times,* December 6, 1955.

## Chapter 12

"The ballplayers…" Gelb, Arthur. "News and Gossip Gathered on the Rialto." *The New York Times,* April 24, 1955.

"Ice cream snack bar…" Not Attributed, Classified Ad 7—No Title, *The New York Times,* February 20, 1955.

"You won't be…" Daley, Arthur. "Overheard at the Stadium." *The New York Times,* April 14, 1955.

"My dad, Albert Olivieri…" Tucci, Jackie Olivieri. Letter, Yoohooworld.tripod.com, http://yoohooworld.tripod.com/history/history%20letter.htm (April 22, 2007).

"In the 1920s, Natale Olivieri…" Hough, Brian. History, Yoohooworld.tripod.com, http://yoohooworld.tripod.com/history/history.htm (accessed April 22, 2007).

"When I was a…" Tucci, Jackie Olivieri. Letter, Yoohooworld.tripod.com, http://yoohooworld.tripod.com/history/history%20letter.htm (April 22, 2007).

"I had pictures of…" Tucci, Jackie Olivieri. Letter, Yoohooworld.tripod.com, http://yoohooworld.tripod.com/history/history%20letter.htm (April 22, 2007).

"They selling any…" Daley, Arthur. "Intricate Operation." *The New York Times,* May 21, 1959.

"Yogi and Yoo-hoo…" Sandomir, Richard. "For Yoo-Hoo and Yogi, It's Deja Vu All Over Again." *The New York Times,* April 20, 1993.

## Chapter 13

"The biggest ovation…" Associated Press. "Tokyo Children Invade Stadium," October 22, 1955.

"Everybody says a…" Golenbock, Peter. *Dynasty.* Englewood Cliffs, NJ: Prentice-Hall Inc., 1975.

"We're going over…" Schoor, Gene. *The Scooter: The Phil Rizzuto Story.* New York: Charles Scribner's Sons, 1982.

"Red, I'm all…" Barber, Red. *The Broadcasters.* New York: The Dial Press, 1970.

"Jim, sit down…" Barber, Red. *The Broadcasters.* New York: The Dial Press, 1970.

"Rizzuto had never…" Barber, Red. *The Broadcasters.* New York: The Dial Press, 1970.

"I loved it…" Schoor, Gene. *The Scooter: The Phil Rizzuto Story.* New York: Charles Scribner's Sons, 1982.

"Nothing could have…" Larsen, Don with Mark Shaw. *The Perfect Yankee.* Champaign, IL: Sports Publishing LLC, 2006.

"Yogi had sized up…" Larsen, Don with Mark Shaw. *The Perfect Yankee.* Champaign, IL: Sports Publishing LLC, 2006.

"He's very selective…" Larsen, Don with Mark Shaw. *The Perfect Yankee.* Champaign, IL: Sports Publishing LLC, 2006.

"We can't throw…" Larsen, Don with Mark Shaw. *The Perfect Yankee.* Champaign, IL: Sports Publishing LLC, 2006.

"In my opinion…" Larsen, Don with Mark Shaw. *The Perfect Yankee.* Champaign, IL: Sports Publishing LLC, 2006.

"I think he was…" Larsen, Don with Mark Shaw. *The Perfect Yankee.* Champaign, IL: Sports Publishing LLC, 2006.

"He looked cool…" Mozley, Dana. "Larsen, Still Wobbling, Gives Credit to Berra." *New York Daily News,* October 9, 1956.

"The score was…" Houston, Maureen. "The Book on Yogi." Knight-Ridder Newspapers, August 19, 2001.

"The crowd gave…" Trimble, Joe. "History Is Made in Series Classic." *New York Daily News,* October 9, 1956.

"For the first time…" Trimble, Joe. "History Is Made in Series Classic." *New York Daily News,* October 9, 1956.

"A grin broke…" Trimble, Joe. "History Is Made in Series Classic." *New York Daily News,* October 9, 1956.

"Except for the…" Larsen, Don with Mark Shaw. *The Perfect Yankee.* Champaign, IL: Sports Publishing LLC, 2006.

"Again Newk got…" Young, Dick. "Four Yankee Homers Bludgeon Dodgers, 9–0." *New York Daily News,* October 11, 1956.

"Man, that Berra…" Young, Dick. "Four Yankee Homers Bludgeon Dodgers, 9–0." *New York Daily News,* October 11, 1956.

"I warned him…" Young, Dick. "Four Yankee Homers Bludgeon Dodgers, 9–0." *New York Daily News,* October 11, 1956.

"That was a good…" Daley, Arthur. "A Case of Necessity." *The New York Times,* September 18, 1959.

"He was thrilled…" *New York Daily News,* "Yogi's Father Expected It." October 11, 1956.

"One of the three…" *New York Daily News,* "Berra Honored by 'Hill' Friends." October 19, 1956.

"The doctors said…" Berra, Yogi and Dave Kaplan. *When You Come to a Fork in the Road, Take It!* New York: Hyperion, 2001.

"When I saw…" Berra, Yogi and Dave Kaplan. *When You Come to a Fork in the Road, Take It!* New York: Hyperion, 2001.

"Yogi Berra's caddie…" Daley, Arthur. "Yogi's Caddie." *The New York Times,* December 19, 1956.

"I get bigger…" Daley, Arthur. "Yogi's Caddie." *The New York Times,* December 19, 1956.

"Mr. Berra stood at…" *The New York Times,* "Topics of the *Times.*" January 8, 1957.

"I always enjoy…" Daley, Arthur. "Stop, Look, and Listen." *The New York Times,* January 9, 1957.

"Don't be so…" Daley, Arthur. "Stop, Look, and Listen." *The New York Times,* January 9, 1957.

"Let's go to…" Daley, Arthur. "Stop, Look, and Listen." *The New York Times,* January 9, 1957.

"We walk in…" Daley, Arthur. "Stop, Look, and Listen." *The New York Times,* January 9, 1957.

"We start making…" Young, Dick. "Berra Batting .221 for Yanks—300 in the Bowling Lanes." *New York Daily News,* June 10, 1958.

"That's the one…" Young, Dick. "Berra Batting .221 for Yanks—300 in the Bowling Lanes." *New York Daily News,* June 10, 1958.

"But he'll know…" Young, Dick. "Berra Batting .221 for Yanks—300 in the Bowling Lanes." *New York Daily News,* June 10, 1958.

"I've gotten a…" Daley, Arthur. "Overheard in St. Pete." *The New York Times,* March 11, 1957.

"Listen, Casey, before…" Daley, Arthur. "Overheard in St. Pete." *The New York Times,* March 11, 1957.

"I've been around…" Allen, Maury. *Roger Maris: A Man for All Seasons.* New York: Donald I. Fine, Inc., 1986.

"You jungle bunny!…" Golenbock, Peter. *Dynasty.* Englewood Cliffs, NJ: Prentice-Hall Inc., 1975.

"I want to thank…" Golenbock, Peter. *Dynasty.* Englewood Cliffs, NJ: Prentice-Hall Inc., 1975.

"We're here to…" Golenbock, Peter. *Dynasty.* Englewood Cliffs, NJ: Prentice-Hall Inc., 1975.

"Martin and the brother…" Golenbock, Peter. *Dynasty.* Englewood Cliffs, NJ: Prentice-Hall Inc., 1975.

"I know Bauer didn't…" Ford, Whitey and Mickey Mantle with Joseph Durso. *Whitey and Mickey.* New York: Viking Press, 1977.

"We never did find…" Martin, Billy and Peter Golenbock. *Number 1: Billy Martin.* New York: Delacourt Press, 1980.

"The Yankees' reported…" United Press International, "Castoffs at the Cash Box." August 14, 1957.

"Hit him? Why, I…" Phillips, McLandish. "Yankee Is Linked to Fight in Café." *The New York Times,* May 17, 1957.

"I won't pitch Ford…" North, Arthur and David Quirk. "Berra and Ford Benched after AM Brawl." *New York Daily News,* May 17, 1957.

"I love Bauer, Martin…" North, Arthur and David Quirk. "Berra and Ford Benched after AM Brawl." *New York Daily News,* May 17, 1957.

"I think a Copa…" Berra, Yogi with Dave Kaplan. *Ten Rings.* New York: William Morrow and Company, 2003.

"Bronx delicatessen owner…" *Time* magazine, "Old Potato Face." September 11, 1964.

"Do you know…" Araton, Harvey. "Spanning Dynasties with Yogi." *The New York Times,* December 5, 2000.

"Did you lose any teeth?" Berra, Yogi and Ed Fitzgerald. *Yogi: The Autobiography of a Professional Baseball Player.* New York: Doubleday, 1961.

"All my good…" Daley, Arthur. "The Nose Knows." *The New York Times,* July 4, 1957.

"Does your face hurt?" Berra, Yogi and Ed Fitzgerald. *Yogi: The Autobiography of a Professional Baseball Player.* New York: Doubleday, 1961.

"I hope you'll…" *The New York Times,* "Kindly Weatherman." July 10, 1957.

"I saw your mother…" *The New York Times,* "Kindly Weatherman." July 10, 1957.

"If he says so…" Effrat, Louis. "Berra's Handling of Bunning Is Key Factor." *The New York Times,* July 10, 1957.

"Berra, trying hard…" Drebinger, John. "Bombers Bow, 6–4." *The New York Times,* July 14, 1957.

"All I need…" Trimble, Joe. "Yogi Learns Specs Prolong His Career." *New York Daily News,* August 18, 1957.

"I was having…" Berra, Yogi and Kaplan, Dave. *Ten Rings.* New York: William Morrow and Company, 2003.

"I'd have caught…" Daley, Arthur. "Man with a Piano." *The New York Times,* September 6, 1957.

"Me know the…" Daley, Arthur. "As Seen through a Revolving Door." *The New York Times,* October 4, 1957.

"Sure, I had a bad…" Trimble, Joe. "Yanks Sign Berra at $2,500 Cut." *New York Daily News,* January 10, 1958.

"Do I ever take…" Drebinger, John. "Yankees' Howard Due for Busy 1958." *The New York Times,* March 4, 1958.

"You think he…" Associated Press, "Outfield No Lonely Outpost to Yogi." July 22, 1958.

"One day when I…" Shannon, Mike. *Tales from the Dugout.* Chicago: Contemporary Books, 1994.

"Mickey Mantle was…" Shannon, Mike. *Tales from the Dugout.* Chicago: Contemporary Books, 1994.

"I started him off…" Shannon, Mike. *Tales from the Dugout.* Chicago: Contemporary Books, 1994.

"Which came within…" Young, Dick. "Yanks Champs, Crush Braves 6–2." *New York Daily News,* October 10, 1958.

"Yogi Berra sets..." Associated Press, "Strikeout Record Set by Matthews." October 9, 1958.

## Chapter 14

"Yogi's days as..." Drebinger, John. "Yanks Always Well-Fortified behind Plate." *The New York Times,* February 21, 1959.

"Funny thing, every time..." Drebinger, John. "One Old Cat Time Nearer for Yankees." *The New York Times,* February 2, 1959.

"Daddy, you've got..." Berra, Yogi and Ed Fitzgerald. *Yogi: The Autobiography of a Professional Baseball Player.* New York: Doubleday, 1961.

"When Mom had to..." Berra, Yogi and Ed Fitzgerald. *Yogi: The Autobiography of a Professional Baseball Player.* New York: Doubleday, 1961.

"Mom, it's Lawdie..." Berra, Yogi and Ed Fitzgerald. *Yogi: The Autobiography of a Professional Baseball Player.* New York: Doubleday, 1961.

"I just hope..." Daley, Arthur. "A Case of Necessity." *The New York Times,* September 18, 1959.

"Everything up until..." Trimble, Joe. "Yogi 'Chokes' Up Finally—As Fans Give Him 'Day.'" *New York Daily News,* September 20, 1959.

"It's too bad Mom..." Berra, Yogi and Ed Fitzgerald. *Yogi: The Autobiography of a Professional Baseball Player.* New York: Doubleday, 1961.

"In my 10 years..." Trimble, Joe. "Yogi 'Chokes' Up Finally—As Fans Give Him 'Day.'" *New York Daily News,* September 20, 1959.

"You the man who..." Berra, Yogi and Ed Fitzgerald. *Yogi: The Autobiography of a Professional Baseball Player.* New York: Doubleday, 1961.

"To an Ex-American..." Golenbock, Peter. *Dynasty.* Englewood Cliffs, NJ: Prentice-Hall Inc., 1975.

"For the first time..." Berra, Yogi and Ed Fitzgerald. *Yogi: The Autobiography of a Professional Baseball Player.* New York: Doubleday, 1961.

"In Italy, they..." *The New York Times,* "Berra, Home Again, Says Italy." December 20, 1959.

"I was in his..." Berra, Yogi and Tom Horton. *Yogi: It Ain't Over.* New York: McGraw-Hill, 1989.

"Yogi, you play..." Daley, Arthur. "Overheard in St. Pete." *The New York Times,* March 14, 1960.

"There is one..." Daley, Arthur. "Overheard in St. Pete." *The New York Times,* March 14, 1960.

"He failed to distinguish…" Drebinger, John. "Cards Defeat Yanks, 2–0." *The New York Times,* March 20, 1960.

"If all the games…" Berra, Yogi and Ed Fitzgerald. *Yogi: The Autobiography of a Professional Baseball Player.* New York: Doubleday, 1961.

"You don't see…" Berra, Yogi and Ed Fitzgerald. *Yogi: The Autobiography of a Professional Baseball Player.* New York: Doubleday, 1961.

"Where are the soft…" *The New York Times,* "League Is Too Good to Suit Berra." May 1, 1960.

"Now, it's Yogi Berra…" Trimble, Joe. "Yogi Next Left-Field Tenant." *New York Daily News,* April 29, 1960.

"I just wanna…" Daley, Arthur. "Overheard at the Stadium." *The New York Times,* May 31, 1960.

"Hey, Yog, what's…" Berra, Yogi and Ed Fitzgerald. *Yogi: The Autobiography of a Professional Baseball Player.* New York: Doubleday, 1961.

"Was the one mentioned…" Effrat, Louis. "Yanks 7–5 Choice to Capture Title." *The New York Times,* October 4, 1960.

"Berra, it was…" Young, Dick. "Bucs Fear Berra." *New York Daily News,* October 4, 1960.

"If I were the manager…" Effrat, Louis. "Left-Field Choice Bothers Stengel." *The New York Times,* October 8, 1960.

"Yogi, why don't…" Talese, Gay. "Toots Shor Opens Fifty-second Street Tent." *The New York Times,* October 8, 1960.

"You amaze me…" Daley, Arthur. "Escape from Torture." *The New York Times,* October 10, 1960.

"It flew high and…" Young, Dick. "Bucs Win in Ninth on Maz HR, 10–9." *New York Daily News,* October 14, 1960.

"When did I know…" Sheehan, Joseph M. "Wet Towels Fly in Bucs Quarters." *The New York Times,* October 14, 1960.

"We outplayed…" Berra, Yogi with Dave Kaplan. *Ten Rings.* New York: William Morrow and Company, 2003.

"Why aint'cha in…" Daley, Arthur. "The Little Record Breaker." *The New York Times,* October 18, 1960.

"Yogi gives me…" Effrat, Louis. "Author Berra Sings Yankees Pact." *The New York Times,* January 13, 1961.

# Chapter 15

"The enveloping warmth…" Daley, Arthur. "A Venture into Literature." *The New York Times,* February 5, 1961.

"He should have…" Tucker, Howard M. "Berra Makes Pitch to Sell Books." *The New York Times,* February 11, 1961.

"Look, it may be…" Drebinger, John. "Great to Be a Yankee?" *The New York Times,* May 10, 1961.

"I'm going to try…" Trimble, Joe. "Yogi Gets His Wish." *New York Daily News,* June 13, 1961.

"A comparison of…" Trimble, Joe. "Yogi Gets His Wish." *New York Daily News,* June 13, 1961.

"Amiable Yogi worked…" Drebinger, John. "Class Takes Over." *The New York Times,* August 4, 1961.

"This is like stealing…" Schumach, Murray. "Yankee Sluggers Make Film Debuts." *The New York Times,* August 24, 1961.

"This is my last…" Daley, Arthur. "Overheard at the Stadium." *The New York Times,* September 3, 1961.

"Merlyn and I were…" Mantle, Mickey with Herb Gluck. *The Mick: An American Hero.* New York: Jove Books, 1985.

"Merlyn, I wouldn't…" Mantle, Mickey with Herb Gluck. *The Mick: An American Hero.* New York: Jove Books, 1985.

"Why, Mr. Berra…" Daley, Arthur. "Hail the Conquering Hero." *The New York Times,* March 23, 1962.

"The thing was that…" Ford, Whitey and Mickey Mantle with Joseph Durso. *Whitey and Mickey.* New York: Viking Press, 1977.

"Sure enough, Yogi…" Ford, Whitey and Mickey Mantle with Joseph Durso. *Whitey and Mickey.* New York: Viking Press, 1977.

"This was the first…" Berra, Yogi with Dave Kaplan. *Ten Rings.* New York: William Morrow, 2003.

"Once, I struck out…" Ford, Whitey and Mickey Mantle with Joseph Durso. *Whitey and Mickey.* New York: Viking Press, 1977.

"It's a little tougher…" Drebinger, John. "Yankees and Angels Start Baseball Training." *The New York Times,* February 12, 1963.

"Hey, Whitey, let's…" Daley, Athur. "Casey's Little Helper." *The New York Times,* October 25, 1963.

"Aw, he just kept…" *The New York Times,* "Game Toughest for Ex-Yankee." October 3, 1963.

"Yogi Berra was not…" Stark, Jayson. *The Stark Truth.* Chicago: Triumph Books, 2007.

## Chapter 16

"He didn't know…" Garagiola, Joe. *Baseball Is a Funny Game.* New York: Bantam Books, 1980.

"My wife still can't…" Daley, Arthur. "The Peerless Leader." *The New York Times,* March 1, 1964.

"I was at the…" Daley, Arthur. "The Peerless Leader." *The New York Times,* March 1, 1964.

"In his quiet way…" Wollinsky, Russell with Frankie Frisch. "Sports Flashes," BaseballHallofFame.com, http://www.baseballhalloffame.org/library/columns/rw_050224.htm (accessed May 8, 2007).

"If good wishes of…" Trimble, Joe. "Yogi Ends Playing Career, Takes Cut for Pilot's Job." *New York Daily News,* October 15, 1963.

"His major problem…" Daley, Arthur. "The Changing of the Guard." *The New York Times,* October 23, 1964.

"What makes a good…" Trimble, Joe. "Yogi Ends Playing Career, Takes Cut for Pilot's Job." *New York Daily News,* October 15, 1963.

"You can learn…" *The New York Times,* "Quotation of the Day." October 25, 1963.

"I've worked under…" McCulley, Jim. "Yogi Says He's Real Manager." *New York Daily News,* October 25, 1963.

"Yogi made a tremendously…" Daley, Arthur. "Casey's Little Helper." *The New York Times,* October 25, 1964.

"No man began a…" Daley, Arthur. "Casey's Little Helper." *The New York Times,* October 25, 1964.

"'How the * * * * should…" Lipsyte, Robert. "The Man and the Myth." *The New York Times,* October 25, 1963.

"Yogi was a wise…" Daley, Arthur. "Expert Opinion." *The New York Times,* October 30, 1963.

"I was so surprised…" Trimble, Joe. "Yanks Name Ford Pitching Coach in Surprise Switch." *The New York Times,* November 16, 1963.

"No, Yogi will…" Trimble, Joe. "Yanks Name Ford Pitching Coach in Surprise Switch." *The New York Times,* November 16, 1963.

"They took away from…" Koppett, Leonard. "Berra: A Losing Winner." *The New York Times,* October 17, 1964.

"I'm leaving Mickey entirely…" Drebinger, John. "Yogi Lays Down the Law." *The New York Times,* February 18, 1964.

"In Yogi's likeness…" *The New York Times,* "Phone Company Is Up to Date." January 29, 1964.

"It's a nice job…" Daley, Arthur. "Emperor Yogi Takes Over." *The New York Times,* February 17, 1964.

"I was too excited…" Daley, Arthur. "The Peerless Leader." *The New York Times,* March 1, 1964.

"Most orderly first day…" Drebinger, John. "Yogi Lays Down the Law." *The New York Times,* February 18, 1964.

"Sure, we're not hitting…" Drebinger, John. "Rain, Fruitless 100-Mile Trip." *The New York Times,* March 28, 1964.

"The truth is that…" Halberstam, David. *October 1964.* New York: Villard Books, 1994.

"No, I don't feel…" Miller, Norm. "Yogi Shrugs off Opening Day Loss." *New York Daily News*, April 17, 1964.

"I asked the first…" Appel, Marty. *Now Pitching for the Yankees.* Kingston, NY: Total Sports Illustrated, 2001.

"Writer were prompted…" Koppett, Leonard. "Staid Yankees Get Zany Look with Help of Pepitone, Bouton." *The New York Times,* April 26, 1964.

"Unfortunately for Yogi…" Golenbock, Peter. *Dynasty.* Englewood Cliffs, NJ: Prentice-Hall Inc., 1975.

"The general manager…" Golenbock, Peter. *Dynasty.* Englewood Cliffs, NJ: Prentice-Hall Inc., 1975.

"I don't believe…" Mantle, Mickey with Mickey Herskowitz. *All My Octobers.* New York: HarperCollins, 1994.

"We're going to…" Golenbock, Peter. *Dynasty.* Englewood Cliffs, NJ: Prentice-Hall Inc., 1975.

"The bullpen members…" Golenbock, Peter. *Dynasty.* Englewood Cliffs, NJ: Prentice-Hall Inc., 1975.

"If I was manager…" Golenbock, Peter. *Dynasty.* Englewood Cliffs, NJ: Prentice-Hall Inc., 1975.

"He had a perfect…" Berra, Yogi and Tom Horton. *Yogi: It Ain't Over*. New York: McGraw-Hill, 1989.

"He's been booed…" Miller, Norm. "First 14 Weeks Lotsa Fun." *New York Daily News,* July 21, 1964.

"The guys were…" Golenbock, Peter. *Dynasty.* Englewood Cliffs, NJ: Prentice-Hall Inc., 1975.

"I think he thought…" Berra, Yogi and Tom Horton. *Yogi: It Ain't Over*. New York: McGraw-Hill, 1989.

"I think Frankie Crosetti…" Berra, Yogi and Tom Horton. *Yogi: It Ain't Over*. New York: McGraw-Hill, 1989.

"Why are you…" Trimble, Joe. "Discord on Yank Bus." *New York Daily News,* August 21, 1964.

"It looks like…" Mantle, Mickey with Mickey Herskowitz. *All My Octobers*. New York: HarperCollins, 1994.

"It will be told…" Koppett, Leonard. "Myth Traces Yankees' Revival to Linz, a Harmonica Rascal." *The New York Times,* September 25, 1964.

"In our eyes that…" Mantle, Mickey with Herb Gluck. *The Mick: An American Hero*. New York: Jove Books, 1985.

"I thought Yogi…" Ford, Whitey and Mickey Mantle with Joseph Durso. *Whitey and Mickey*. New York: Viking Press, 1977.

"Yogi actually held…" Ford, Whitey and Phil Pepe. *Slick*. New York: William Morrow, 1987.

"The way Mantle…" Koppett, Leonard. "Myth Traces Yankees Revival to Linz, a Harmonica Rascal." *The New York Times,* September 25, 1964.

"Topping and Webb…" *Time* magazine, "The Big Eye League." August 21, 1964.

"Gee…" *Time* magazine, "The Big Eye League." August 21, 1964.

"Warm up Stafford…" Koppett, Leonard. "Digit Dialing." *The New York Times,* September 15, 1964.

"Well, we worked…" *The New York Times,* "Top Credit Given to Kubek, Mantle." September 18, 1964.

"Yogi was the…" Trimble, Joe. "Yanks Rally to Fifth-Straight Pennant." *New York Daily News,* October 4, 1964.

"Frankly, I thought…" *The New York Times,* "Yankees Celebrate Their Toughest, Most Exciting Pennant of All." October 4, 1964.

"It may not…" *The New York Times,* "Yankees Celebrate Their Toughest, Most Exciting Pennant of All." October 4, 1964.

"Houk never kicked…" Golenbock, Peter. *Dynasty.* Englewood Cliffs, NJ: Prentice-Hall Inc., 1975.

"CBS now had…" Barber, Red. *The Broadcasters.* New York: The Dial Press, 1970.

"In 1964, I was…" Garagiola, Joe. *It's Anybody's Ballgame.* New York: Jove Books, 1989.

"It was more…" Koppett, Leonard. "Ford Gives Way to Right-Hander." *The New York Times,* October 14, 1964.

"Uncharacteristic Yankee miscues…" Office of the Commissioner of Major League Baseball, "1964 World Series, Game 7, Gibson & the Cards end the Yankee Dynasty." October 15, 1964.

"The Yankees 'threw'…" Trimble, Joe. "Cards Take It All as Yanks Fold, 7–5." *New York Daily News,* October 16, 1954.

"These were two…" Trimble, Joe. "Cards Take It All as Yanks Fold, 7–5." *New York Daily News,* October 16, 1954.

"In that Series…" Berra, Yogi and Tom Horton. *Yogi: It Ain't Over.* New York: McGraw-Hill, 1989.

"Sure it hurts. How…" Berra, Yogi. "Losing Isn't a Loss." *The New York Times,* November 7, 2001.

"Baseball men compared…" Halberstam, David. *October 1964.* New York: Villard Books, 1994.

"Take care of those…" Mantle, Mickey with Herb Gluck. *The Mick: An American Hero.* New York: Jove Books, 1985.

"Why not?" Halberstam, David. *October 1964.* New York: Villard Books, 1994.

"Will you be…" Ford, Whitey and Mickey Mantle with Joseph Durso. *Whitey and Mickey.* New York: Viking Press, 1977.

"I will never…" Berra, Yogi and Tom Horton. *Yogi: It Ain't Over.* New York: McGraw-Hill, 1989.

"It was strange that…" Chass, Murray. "All Jokes Aside, Berra Is Back on Top." *The New York Times,* February 13, 1984.

"I remember it…" Chass, Murray. "All Jokes Aside, Berra Is Back on Top." *The New York Times,* February 13, 1984.

"I don't mind…" *The New York Times,* "Yogi Gets New Post." October 17, 1964.

"It is for the…" Golenbock, Peter. *Dynasty.* Englewood Cliffs, NJ: Prentice-Hall Inc., 1975.

"In retrospect, he…" Koppett, Leonard. "Berra: A Losing Winner." *The New York Times,* October 17, 1964.

"The Yankees brass…" Young, Dick. "Player/Coach Yogi Shifts to Shea." *New York Daily News,* November 18, 1964.

"Yogi Berra wasn't…" Trimble, Joe. "Bad Guys and Good Guys Put Yogi in the Middle." *New York Daily News,* October 21, 1964.

"Swimming pool…" Trimble, Joe. "Bad Guys and Good Guys Put Yogi in the Middle." *New York Daily News,* October 21, 1964.

"I thought Yogi…" Ford, Whitey and Mickey Mantle with Joseph Durso. *Whitey and Mickey.* New York: Viking Press, 1977.

"It's a good bet…" Anderson, Dave. "When Yogi Threw His Cigarettes." *The New York Times,* March 28, 1989.

"After a few days…" Ford, Whitey and Phil Pepe. *Slick.* New York: William Morrow, 1987.

## Chapter 17

"Ballplayers always say…" Garagiola, Joe. *It's Anybody's Ballgame.* New York: Jove Books, 1989.

"I talked with Yogi…" Trimble, Joe. "Berra Gets Bid From Mets." *New York Daily News,* October 3, 1964.

"The reuniting of Berra…" Strauss, Michael. "Berra Considers Job with Mets after Talking with Weiss." *The New York Times,* October 30, 1964.

"Do you feel you…" Young, Dick. "Player/Coach Yogi Shifts to Shea." *New York Daily News,* November 18, 1964.

"If he can approximate…" Young, Dick. "Player/Coach Yogi Shifts to Shea." *New York Daily News,* November 18, 1964.

"The main thing…" Koppett, Leonard. "Berra Signs Two-Year Contract as Coach with Mets at $35,000 a Season." *The New York Times,* November 18, 1964.

"Houk looked like…" Gould, Jack. "TV: A Sports Interview with Hard-Hitting Candor." *The New York Times,* November 30, 1964.

"Yogi, even here…" Young, Dick. "Yogi Retires as Player." *New York Daily News,* May 12, 1965.

"I'm an old man…" *The New York Times,* "'Old-Man' Berra to Play No More." May 12, 1965.

"Mr. Berra did a…" Daley, Arthur. "End of the Trail." *The New York Times,* August 31, 1965.

"After all, Yogi…" *The New York Times,* "Baird, Like the Mets, Turns to Yogi." May 6, 1965.

"Yogi's success hastened…" *The New York Times*, "Mets Washed Out." May 1, 1966.

"Let me catch…" Durso, Joseph. "Mets' 603rd Loss Is Most Memorable." *The New York Times*, July 29, 1967.

"Is the guy next…" Golenbock, Peter. *Amazin'*. New York: St. Martin's Press, 2002.

"The selection of…" Durso, Joseph. "Westrum Quits as Mets Manager." *The New York Times*, September 22, 1967.

"His elevation now…" Durso, Joseph. "Westrum Quits as Mets Manager." *The New York Times*, September 22, 1967.

"Berra was a splendid…" Lipsyte, Robert. "Nobody's Fool." *The New York Times*, October 19, 1967.

"At 42, Berra is…" Lipsyte, Robert. "Nobody's Fool." *The New York Times*, October 19, 1967.

"I'm very satisfied…" Lipsyte, Robert. "Nobody's Fool." *The New York Times*, October 19, 1967.

"He throws harder than…" *The New York Times*, "Ryan, Met Hurler, Talks Slowly but Fastball Breaks Big Sticks." April 14, 1968.

"There weren't too…" Shamsky, Art with Barry Zeman. *The Magnificent Seasons*. New York: St. Martin's Griffin, 2004.

"Now I've done it…" Shamsky, Art with Barry Zeman. *The Magnificent Seasons*. New York: St. Martin's Griffin, 2004.

"No Yankee triumph…" Koppett, Leonard. "The Year Yogi Won the Pennant." *The New York Times*, December 28, 1969.

"Gil's coaches sat…" Smith, Red. *Strawberries in the Wintertime*. Chicago: Quadrangle, 1974.

"Naturally, I am…" Trimble, Joe. "Berra Signs Two-Year Pact as Mets Manager." *New York Daily News*, April 7, 1972.

"It was a sad day…" Daley, Arthur. "What Was the Hurry?" *The New York Times*, April 9, 1972.

"Yogi was in charge…" Golenbock, Peter. *Amazin'*. New York: St. Martin's Press, 2002.

"The Berra legend was…" Ross, Alan. *Mets Pride*. Nashville: Cumberland House Publishing, 2007.

"Yogi is a very…" Ross, Alan. *Mets Pride*. Nashville: Cumberland House Publishing, 2007.

"I think the Mets…" Ross, Alan. *Mets Pride.* Nashville: Cumberland House Publishing, 2007.

"Yogi was always a…" Ross, Alan. *Mets Pride.* Nashville: Cumberland House Publishing, 2007.

"Yogi had been a…" Golenbock, Peter. *Amazin'.* New York: St. Martin's Press, 2002.

"When he got to…" Golenbock, Peter. *Amazin'.* New York: St. Martin's Press, 2002.

"Hiya, Casey. It was…" *The New York Times,* "Berra Congratulated by Familiar Voice." April 16, 1972.

"Coming back to…" Foley, Red. "Mets Deal Brings Willie 'Back to Paradise.'" *New York Daily News,* May 12, 1972.

"He can be helpful…" Foley, Red. "Mets Deal Brings Willie 'Back to Paradise.'" *New York Daily News,* May 12, 1972.

"It was a storybook…" Golenbock, Peter. *Amazin'.* New York: St. Martin's Press, 2002.

"Yogi had been criticized…" Golenbock, Peter. *Amazin'.* New York: St. Martin's Press, 2002.

"I know he and…" Golenbock, Peter. *Amazin'.* New York: St. Martin's Press, 2002.

"I thought maybe…" Durso, Joseph. "Dodger Pitcher, 36, Youngest to Enter Shrine; Koufax, Berra, Wynn in Hall of Fame." *The New York Times,* January 20, 1972.

"It is great to…" Trimble, Joe. "Sandy, Yogi, and Wynn Run 1-2-3." *New York Daily News,* January 20, 1970.

"I have to put…" Schoor, Gene. *The Story of Yogi Berra.* New York: Doubleday, 1976.

"I want to thank Bill…" Koppett, Leonard. "Yogi in Hall: I Hope I'll Put Something Back." *The New York Times,* August 8, 1972.

"He is very tough to…" Goldaper, Sam. "Yogi Berra's Big Boy, Larry." *The New York Times,* April 30, 1968.

"I'll call Frank…" Hann, Christopher. "It Ain't Over," *New Jersey Monthly,* July 2006.

"I remember wandering…" Friedman, Jack. "As a Father-Son Team, the Berras—Yogi and Dale—Manage to Play Their Roles." *People* magazine, April 8, 1985.

"I tried..." Warners, Ray. "The Berras and the Tripuckas, or the Games Some People Play." *The New York Times,* January 28, 1973.

"People think I..." Berra, Yogi and Dave Kaplan. *What Time Is It? You Mean Now?* New York: Simon & Schuster, 2002.

"In the eyes of..." Stewart-Gordon, James. "Yogi Berra: The Yankee Nonesuch." *Reader's Digest,* May 1959.

"Yogi did not change..." Pepe, Phil. "Dale-Yogi: Will It Be Berrable?" *New York Daily News,* April 7, 1985.

"That was my job..." Pepe, Phil. "Dale-Yogi: Will It Be Berrable?" *New York Daily News,* April 7, 1985.

"The only thing Yogi..." Warners, Ray. "The Berras and the Tripuckas, or the Games Some People Play." *The New York Times,* January 28, 1973.

"An underrated evaluator..." Markusen, Bruce. *Tales from the Mets Dugout.* Champaign, IL: Sports Publishing, LLC, 2007.

"Any picture Yogi takes..." Markusen, Bruce. *Tales from the Mets Dugout.* Champaign, IL: Sports Publishing, LLC, 2007.

"If I can do it..." Durso, Joseph. "Mays Has His Way, and Yogi Has His Way." *The New York Times,* March 2, 1973.

"I appreciate that..." Durso, Joseph. "Mays Has His Way, and Yogi Has His Way." *The New York Times,* March 2, 1973.

"They're still here..." Durso, Joseph. "Mays Has His Way, and Yogi Has His Way." *The New York Times,* March 2, 1973.

"I'll explain to Yogi..." Durso, Joseph. "Mays Has His Way, and Yogi Has His Way." *The New York Times,* March 2, 1973.

"I made a mistake..." Durso, Joseph. "Mays Fined by Berra; Berra Acts Alone Mays is Fined $500 by Berra." *The New York Times,* March 12, 1973.

"I didn't ask anybody's..." Durso, Joseph. "Mays Fined by Berra; Berra Acts Alone Mays is Fined $500 by Berra." *The New York Times,* March 12, 1973.

"I don't hear any..." Durso, Joseph. "Mays Fined by Berra; Berra Acts Alone Mays is Fined $500 by Berra." *The New York Times,* March 12, 1973.

"Gil had a strict weigh-in..." Golenbock, Peter. *Amazin'.* New York: St. Martin's Press, 2002.

"Some of us were..." Golenbock, Peter. *Amazin'.* New York: St. Martin's Press, 2002.

"We have no intention..." Schoor, Gene. *The Story of Yogi Berra.* New York: Doubleday, 1976.

"Grant adamantly wanted…" Golenbock, Peter. *Amazin'.* New York: St. Martin's Press, 2002.

"Grant could not get…" Golenbock, Peter. *Amazin'.* New York: St. Martin's Press, 2002.

"If you want to…" Golenbock, Peter. *Amazin'.* New York: St. Martin's Press, 2002.

"Who's to blame?" Markusen, Bruce. *Tales from the Mets Dugout.* Champaign, IL: Sports Publishing, LLC, 2007.

"What's the difference…" Golenbock, Peter. *Amazin'.* New York: St. Martin's Press, 2002.

"The team needs you…" Markusen, Bruce. *Tales from the Mets Dugout.* Champaign, IL: Sports Publishing, LLC, 2007.

"There's lots of time yet…" Schoor, Gene. *The Story of Yogi Berra.* New York: Doubleday, 1976.

"Yogi kept telling everyone…" Ross, Alan. *Mets Pride.* Nashville: Cumberland House Publishing, 2007.

"The Mets were bouncing…" Berra, Yogi and Tom Horton. *Yogi: It Ain't Over.* New York: McGraw-Hill, 1989.

"These were savvy managerial…" Golenbock, Peter. *Amazin'.* New York: St. Martin's Press, 2002.

"Yogi Berra never took…" McGraw, Tug, with Joseph Durso. *Screwball.* Boston: Houghton Mifflin Company, 1974.

"Yeah, it's running out…" *New York Post,* "Time Is Running Out on the Mets." September 4, 1973.

"It's 1969 all over again…" Pepe, Phil. It's 1969 All Over Again." *New York Post,* September 23, 1973.

"You never heard…" McGraw, Tug, with Joseph Durso. *Screwball.* Boston: Houghton Mifflin Company, 1974.

"You can't go home…" Mays, Willie with Lou Sahadi. *Say Hey.* New York: Simon & Schuster, 1988.

"The butterflies are…" *The New York Times,* "I Never Gave Up, and Neither Did the Players, Says Berra about How the Mets Won the Eastern Title; Happy after Game is Called." October 2, 1973.

"We had a crazy finish…" Mays, Willie with Lou Sahadi. *Say Hey.* New York: Simon & Schuster, 1988.

"'Nothin',' responded Berra…" Anderson, Dave. "Two Managers." *The New York Times,* October 3, 1973.

"That's only one loss…" *The New York Times,* "Loss of Opener Fails to Shake Berra's Poise." October 7, 1973.

"We've come back from…" Hirshey, Dave. "Downcast Rusty Told Yogi: I Can't Swing…I Can't Play." *New York Daily News,* October 11, 1973.

"He smiled. Weakly…" Hirshey, Dave. "Downcast Rusty Told Yogi: I Can't Swing…I Can't Play." *New York Daily News,* October 11, 1973.

"Gee, you know, Ray…" Mays, Willie with Lou Sahadi. *Say Hey.* New York: Simon & Schuster, 1988.

"When the Yankees fired…" *The New York Times,* "What They Are Saying." October 21, 1973.

"Back in July, it was…" Pepe, Phil. "Mets Tell Yogi They Believe Via Three-Year Contract." *New York Daily News,* October 24, 1973.

"Judging by Berra's success…" Durso, Joseph. "The Yanks' Burden: Hire Williams; Dave Anderson Yanks Need Another Pitcher; the Ground Rules." *The New York Times,* October 27, 1973.

"Now I'm finally going…" Durso, Joseph. "Berra Gets Reward: A Three-Year Contract." *The New York Times,* October 24, 1973.

"Sign this…" Allen, Maury. *All Roads Lead to October.* New York: St. Martin's Press, 2000.

"The woman then took…" Allen, Maury. *All Roads Lead to October.* New York: St. Martin's Press, 2000.

"Inserted Jones into a…" Markusen, Bruce. *Tales from the Mets Dugout.* Champaign, IL: Sports Publishing, LLC, 2007.

"I wish Cleon all the…" *New York Daily News,* "Cleon Gets Release." July 26, 1975.

"I tried my best…" Durso, Joseph. "Berra Back with Mets, for a Good-Bye." *The New York Times,* August 8, 1975.

"Will I spend time…" Durso, Joseph. "Berra Back with Mets, for a Good-Bye." *The New York Times,* August 8, 1975.

## Chapter 18

"I love the guy, but…" Berra, Yogi and Tom Horton. *Yogi: It Ain't Over.* New York: McGraw-Hill, 1989.

"I called Yogi on…" Martin, Billy and Peter Golenbock. *Number 1: Billy Martin.* New York: Delacourt Press, 1980.

"Yeah, I'd like to…" Martin, Billy and Peter Golenbock. *Number 1: Billy Martin.* New York: Delacourt Press, 1980.

"Yogi is coming back..." Anderson, Dave. "Yogi Will Communicate Very Well." *The New York Times,* December 6, 1975.

"I want to talk to you..." Martin, Billy and Peter Golenbock. *Number 1: Billy Martin.* New York: Delacourt Press, 1980.

"I don't care. Get..." Martin, Billy and Peter Golenbock. *Number 1: Billy Martin.* New York: Delacourt Press, 1980.

"I'd like to see him..." Anderson, Dave. "Yogi, Coach, and World Series Perennial." *The New York Times,* October 17, 1976.

"Yogi's in the World Series..." Anderson, Dave. "Yogi, Coach, and World Series Perennial." *The New York Times,* October 17, 1976.

"This club is looser..." Anderson, Dave. "Yogi, Coach, and World Series Perennial." *The New York Times,* October 17, 1976.

"No one has contacted..." Chass, Murray. "Martin Unlikely to Shuffle Coaching Staff." *The New York Times,* September 16, 1976.

"You show me up, and..." Allen, Maury. *All Roads Lead to October.* New York: St. Martin's Press, 2000.

"I won't take that..." Martin, Billy and Peter Golenbock. *Number 1: Billy Martin.* New York: Delacourt Press, 1980.

"Reggie's big, but I..." Martin, Billy and Peter Golenbock. *Number 1: Billy Martin.* New York: Delacourt Press, 1980.

"Yogi still had Billy..." Jackson, Reggie and Mike Lupica. *Reggie.* New York: Villard Books, 1984.

"That damned Yogi, picking..." Montgomery, Paul. "Martin Saved in Manager's Job after Yankee Team Conference; Martin Stays in Pilot's Job after Yankee Team Meeting." *The New York Times,* June 21, 1977.

"I didn't see nobody..." Durso, Joseph. "Yanks Win, 5–3, and Take 2-1 Edge in Series." *The New York Times,* October 15, 1977.

"We're going to get..." Wilner, Paul. "Yogi Berra: At Bat in Montclair." *The New York Times,* January 8, 1978.

"He was glad it rained..." Wilner, Paul. "Yogi Berra: At Bat in Montclair." *The New York Times,* January 8, 1978.

"As a coach, sometimes..." Chass, Murray. "All Jokes Aside, Berra Is Back on Top." *The New York Times,* February 13, 1984.

"There has been a..." Rizzuto, Phil and Tom Horton. *The October Twelve.* New York: Forge Books, 1994.

## Chapter 19

"Asked if he had been…" Anderson, Dave. "Berra Number One for Now." *The New York Times,* December 5, 1983.

"My age had something…" Madden, Bill. "Boss' Ax Finally Falls as Yogi Replaces Billy." *New York Daily News,* December 17, 1983.

"I'll argue with…" Madden, Bill. "Boss' Ax Finally Falls as Yogi Replaces Billy." *New York Daily News,* December 17, 1983.

"Yogi has helped us…" Chass, Murray. "All Jokes Aside, Berra Is Back on Top." *The New York Times,* February 13, 1984.

"He's a good guy…" Tuite, James. "Player Reactions Mixed on Martin." *The New York Times,* December 17, 1983.

"I guess the manager's…" Eskenazi, Gerald. "Gifts of This Season Evoke Dreams of Next Season." *The New York Times,* December 26, 1983.

"I didn't want him…" Chass, Murray. "All Jokes Aside, Berra Is Back on Top." *The New York Times,* February 13, 1984.

"Isn't it time all…" Pepe, Phil. "Give Yogi Some Credit." *New York Daily News,* April 21, 1985.

"In his office off…" Anderson, Dave. "Another Cigarette for Yogi Berra." *The New York Times,* April 4, 1984.

"Yogi will be the…" Madden, Bill. "Steinbrenner Says Yogi's Job Is Safe for the 1985 Season." *New York Daily News,* February 21, 1985.

"We had our meeting…" Madden, Bill. "Steinbrenner Says Yogi's Job Is Safe for the 1985 Season." *New York Daily News,* February 21, 1985.

"That was the summer…" Chass, Murray. "All Jokes Aside, Berra Is Back on Top." *The New York Times,* February 13, 1984.

"I don't think there…" Pepe, Phil. "Dale-Yogi: Will It Be Berrable?" *New York Daily News,* April 7, 1985.

"I'm not going…" Pepe, Phil. "Dale-Yogi: Will It Be Berrable?" *New York Daily News,* April 7, 1985.

"I'm elated…" Friedman, Jack. "As a Father-Son Team, the Berras—Yogi and Dale—Manage to Play Their Roles." *People* magazine, April 8, 1985.

"Yeah, I finally…" Friedman, Jack. "As a Father-Son Team, the Berras—Yogi and Dale—Manage to Play Their Roles." *People* magazine, April 8, 1985.

"I know this: if…" Pepe, Phil. "Dale-Yogi: Will It Be Berrable?" *New York Daily News,* April 7, 1985.

"All I know is that…" Nedell, Paul. "Boss Buries Hatchet, Doesn't Hatchet Berra." *New York Daily News,* April 26, 1985.

"The phrase 'for now'…" Nedell, Paul. "Boss Buries Hatchet, Doesn't Hatchet Berra." *New York Daily News,* April 26, 1985.

"No question the…" Nedell, Paul. "Boss Buries Hatchet, Doesn't Hatchet Berra." *New York Daily News,* April 26, 1985.

"The whole thing…" Madden, Bill. "Grim Flight Aboard Air Boss." *New York Daily News,* April 30, 1985.

"What's the use of…" Lupica, Mike. "Yogi Comes Home." *New York Daily News,* April 30, 1985.

"I don't get mad…" Anderson, Dave. "When Yogi Threw His Cigarettes." *The New York Times,* March 28, 1989.

"The 24 guys I wanted…" Anderson, Dave. "When Yogi Threw His Cigarettes." *The New York Times,* March 28, 1989.

"You don't have…" Shannon, Mike. *Tales from the Dugout.* Chicago: Contemporary Books, 1994.

"I was down in Houston…" Allen, Maury. *Roger Maris: A Man for All Seasons.* New York: Donald I. Fine, Inc., 1986.

"Would anyone bet…" Pepe, Phil. "Hey, Hey, Yogi." *New York Daily News,* September 26, 1986.

"I felt in spring training…" *New York Daily News,* "It's Over! Yogi's Hanging 'Em Up." September 26, 1989.

## Chapter 20

"No, why should I?" Rizzuto, Phil and Tom Horton. *The October Twelve.* New York: Forge Books, 1994.

"But Mr. Berra did not…" Sandomir, Richard. "For Yoo-Hoo and Yogi, It's Deja Vu All over Again." *The New York Times,* April 20, 1993.

"Going to the memorial…" Rizzuto, Phil and Tom Horton. *The October Twelve.* New York: Forge Books, 1994.

"To market their father's…" Lauro, Patricia Winters. "One of Baseball's Colorful Figures Finds He Is in Demand Again." *The New York Times,* April 30, 1999.

"How about that cunning…" Cramer, Richard Ben. *Joe DiMaggio: The Hero's Life.* New York: Touchstone, 2000.

"I had hoped Yogi…" Rizzuto, Phil and Tom Horton. *The October Twelve.* New York: Forge Books, 1994.

"Rizzuto's been going…" Rizzuto, Phil and Tom Horton. *The October Twelve.* New York: Forge Books, 1994.

"This is going nowhere..." Shannon, Mike. *Tales from the Dugout.* Chicago: Contemporary Books, 1994.

"I don't know yet..." Bondy, Filip. "Call Him Dr. Yogi." *New York Daily News,* May 17, 1996.

"[Bruce] was a perfect..." Bondy, Filip. "Call Him Dr. Yogi." *New York Daily News,* May 17, 1996.

## Chapter 21

"During my career..." Bondy, Filip. "Call Him Dr. Yogi." *New York Daily News,* May 17, 1996.

"Every finger on his hand..." Araton, Harvey. "On the Other Side of the River, Another Hailing of Champions." *The New York Times,* October 25, 1998.

"Hello, Yogi..." Araton, Harvey. "Yogi and the Boss Complete Makeup Game." *The New York Times,* January 6, 1999.

"Along those lines..." Araton, Harvey. "Yogi and the Boss Complete Makeup Game." *The New York Times,* January 6, 1999.

"He's got to forgive..." Araton, Harvey. "Yogi and the Boss Complete Makeup Game." *The New York Times,* January 6, 1999.

"Berra showed Williams..." Curry, Jack. "Legend Dons Cap at Legends Field." *The New York Times,* March 2, 1999.

"Berra looked at..." Curry, Jack. "Legend Dons Cap at Legends Field." *The New York Times,* March 2, 1999.

"I was a little..." Curry, Jack. "Berra Returns, and Fans Relish It." *The New York Times,* April 6, 1999.

"To see Yogi walk..." Curry, Jack. "Berra Returns, and Fans Relish It." *The New York Times,* April 6, 1999.

"It felt great after..." Curry, Jack. "Berra Returns, and Fans Relish It." *The New York Times,* April 6, 1999.

"I've been asking..." Curry, Jack. "Berra Returns, and Fans Relish It." *The New York Times,* April 6, 1999.

"They kept coming..." Lupica, Mike. "Yogi's from Era of Fan-tastic Baseball." *New York Daily News,* June 28, 1998.

"I'm gonna have to..." Lupica, Mike. "Yogi's from Era of Fan-tastic Baseball." *New York Daily News,* June 28, 1998.

"They filmed Berra, 74..." Olson, Carolyn. "Yogi Berra Comes Home." *St. Louis Post-Dispatch,* August 10, 1999.

"Marketers say the…" Lauro, Patricia Winters. "One of Baseball's Colorful Figures Finds He Is in Demand Again." *The New York Times,* April 30, 1999.

"There has always…" Lauro, Patricia Winters. "One of Baseball's Colorful Figures Finds He Is in Demand Again." *The New York Times,* April 30, 1999.

"Do you know who…" Araton, Harvey. "Spanning Dynasties with Yogi." *The New York Times,* December 5, 2000.

"You know, a lot…" Berra, Yogi. Interview, "Lawrence Peter 'Yogi' Berra," Academy of Achievement, recorded June 1, 2005, New York City, http://www.achievement.org/autodoc/page/ber0int-2 (accessed February 20, 2007).

"What'd you swing…" Berra, Yogi. Interview, "Lawrence Peter 'Yogi' Berra," Academy of Achievement, recorded June 1, 2005, New York City, http://www.achievement.org/autodoc/page/ber0int-2 (accessed February 20, 2007).

"Torre was packing…" Colston, Chris. "Yankees Celebrate Life and Pennant." *USA Today, Baseball Weekly,* October 24, 2001.

"It's not the most…" Colston, Chris. "Yankees Celebrate Life and Pennant." *USA Today, Baseball Weekly,* October 24, 2001.

"Joe started wearing…" Berra, Yogi. "Losing Isn't a Loss." *The New York Times,* November 7, 2001.

"Usually, he was…" Mackay, Harvey. "'Fashionably Late' Has No Place in Business." *Post-Bulletin,* May 23, 2007.

"Do you know what…" Araton, Harvey. "Spanning Dynasties with Yogi." *The New York Times,* December 5, 2000.

"This is a sad day for baseball…" Associated Press, "Death of Ted Williams…. Tributes to Ted Williams," July 5, 2002.

"At 73, Mr. Gazzara actually…" Weber, Bruce. "A Metaphysician for Whom Baseball Is Life and Vice Versa." *The New York Times,* October 31, 2003.

"I'm the son of…" Tallmer, Jerry. "Ben Gazzara, a Diehard Yankee Fan, Plays Yogi." *Downtown Express,* volume 16, issue 25, November 18–24, 2003.

"The Berras had received…" Tallmer, Jerry. "Ben Gazzara, a Diehard Yankee Fan, Plays Yogi." *Downtown Express,* volume 16, issue 25, November 18–24, 2003.

"When Mrs. Berra said…" Tallmer, Jerry. "Ben Gazzara, a Diehard Yankee Fan, Plays Yogi." *Downtown Express,* volume 16, issue 25, November 18–24, 2003.

"He'll call me and…" *Hartford Courant,* "Happy Birthday, Yogi." May 12, 2005.

"It doesn't rain on…" Brubaker, Paul and Mark S. Porter. "The Catcher in the Ride: Carmen and Yogi Berra Lead off Independence Day Celebration." *Montclair Times,* July 6, 2005.

"This wouldn't be Montclair…" Brubaker, Paul and Mark S. Porter. "The Catcher in the Ride: Carmen and Yogi Berra Lead Off Independence Day Celebration." *Montclair Times,* July 6, 2005.

"He deals with it…" Hann, Christopher. "It Ain't Over," *New Jersey Monthly,* July 2006.

"Derek Jeter should…" Kernan, Kevin. "Rizzuto Fights on in Latest Battle." *New York Post,* September 12, 2006.

"Derek just broke my…" Kernan, Kevin. "Rizzuto Fights on in Latest Battle." *New York Post,* September 12, 2006.

"It was pretty bad…" Willis, George. "Fond Farewell." *New York Post,* August 15, 2007.

"Phil was a gem…" Price, Ed. "Phil Rizzuto Dead at 89." *New Jersey Star Ledger,* August 14, 2007.

"Nine beat writers and…" Abraham, Peter. "A Few Minutes with the Skipper." Lohud Yankees Blog, www.lohud.com/blogs/2006_10_01_yankeearchive. html (accessed May 30, 2007).

"Yogi always stops in…" Altavilla, John. "Drew Goes Hitless Again." *Hartford Courant,* May 23, 2007.

"Roger Maris College…" *New York Post,* "The Rumble, Dr. Yogi's Prescription, Tells Grads to 'Stand Up, Take Lumps.'" May 27, 2007.

"The crowd of about…." Bell, Kim. "'Yogi-Isms' Inspire SLU Grads." *St. Louis Post-Dispatch,* May 20, 2007.

"If I went back to…" *New York Post,* "The Rumble, Dr. Yogi's Prescription, Tells Grads to 'Stand Up, Take Lumps.'" May 27, 2007.

"The university presented…." Bell, Kim. "'Yogi-Isms' Inspire SLU Grads." *St. Louis Post-Dispatch,* May 20, 2007.

# INDEX

Aaron, Henry, 136, 192, 197
Abbott, George, 170
Abraham, Peter, 346
Adams, Ace, 49
African American players
    first appearances in All-Star Game, 117
    first player for Yankees, 163
    first player to break color barrier, 77–79
agents, sports, 135–37, 329
Aikens, Willie Mays, 319
All-Star Games/teams, 99, 110, 117, 131, 138, 143, 155, 159, 164, 175, 190–91, 193, 201, 218, 223
Allen, Maury, 293, 321
Allen, Mel, 95, 177, 178, 260
Alston, Walter, 136, 178
Altavilla, John, 347
American Association Blues, 54
American Baseball Academy, 136
American Hockey League, 10
Amoros, Sandy, 166, 324
Anderson, Dave, 288, 299, 310, 313–14
Anderson, Sparky, 289, 314
Annual Baseball Player's Golf Tournament, 158–59
Anselmo, Tony, 48–49
Appel, Marty, 237, 332
Araton, Harvey, 333
Arizona Diamondbacks, 341, 344
Associated Press, 58, 59, 137, 162, 175, 194, 197
Atlanta Braves, 304
Atlanta Crackers, 68
Avila, Bobby, 143–44, 162, 191–92

Babe Ruth Museum, 341
Badenhausen, Carl, 177
Bainbridge Naval Base, 39, 40
Ballantine Beer, 177, 197
Baltimore Colts, 297
Baltimore Orioles, 208, 220, 221, 223, 235, 240, 269
Bank, Aaron, 45
Barber, Red, 80, 177–78, 249
Barnes, Robert H., 48

*Baseball Digest,* 164
Baseball for Italy, Inc., 203–4
Baseball Hall of Fame, 276, 278, 306
baseball memorabilia, 325, 326–27, 328
Baseball Writers Association of America, 158, 234, 265
basketball, 136
Bauer, Hank, 130, 146, 155, 157, 163, 185, 186–89, 193, 195, 205, 223, 235, 238, 240
Baylor, Don, 310–11, 316
BBC Industries of New York City, 216–17
Bednarik, Chuck, 213
*Behind the Plate* (Berra and Ferdenzi), 221
Bell, Kim, 347, 348
bench-jockeying, 71
Bench, Johnny, 289, 306–7, 328
Berardino, Johnny, 76
Berra, Anthony (brother), 4, 9, 10, 16, 18, 22, 85
Berra, Carmen Short (wife), 125, 135, 186, 189, 227, 278, 292, 295, 304
    Bergen County, New Jersey home, 142–43
    children, 122, 144, 280
    and children's sports careers, 279, 315–16
    European vacation, 203–5
    marriage, 85–87
    Montclair, New Jersey home, 205
    and Montclair State University, 344
    mother's death, 338–39
    mother's illness, 133
    and Yogi's accomplishments, 348
    and Yogi's contracts, 139
    and Yogi's honors and awards, 148, 201, 202, 277
    and Yogi's managing career, 253, 270, 298, 306, 309, 312, 314, 316
    and Yogi's popularity, 162, 344–45
Berra, Dale Anthony (son), 171, 182, 213, 277, 279, 315–16, 317, 318, 319, 321, 326, 334, 338, 343
Berra, John (brother), 5, 9, 10, 18, 22, 122, 184, 202, 273
Berra, Lawrence Allen (son), 122, 199, 202, 213, 277, 278–79, 326

403

Berra, Lawrence Peter "Yogi"
  All-Star Games/teams, 99, 110, 131, 138, 143, 155, 159, 175, 190–91, 193, 201, 218, 223
  amateur boxer, 19–20
  Astros coach, 320, 321–22
  autobiography, 215–16
  Baseball Hall of Fame induction, 276, 277
  baseball story book, 221
  birth of, 5
  book signings, 215–16, 339
  books about, 215–16, 221, 286, 323, 329, 339, 342
  borrowing, penchant for, 220–21
  boxing, 19–20
  brother's death, 273
  business ventures, 170–73, 183–84, 209, 216–17, 221, 231
  career statistics, 94, 178, 190, 191, 192, 193, 196, 201, 203, 212, 217, 218, 221, 222, 225–26, 262, 306–7
  as a catcher, 146–47, 217
  charities, 190, 216
  children, 122, 144, 171, 182, 278–80, 315–16, 326–27, 344
  coaching career, 222–24, 298–307, 320, 321–22
  contract negotiations/salaries, 35, 89, 102–3, 125–27, 137–39, 140, 148, 150, 158, 161, 175, 182, 193, 199, 205, 213, 229, 258, 292
  dislike of doubleheaders, 98–99, 117–18
  early childhood, 5–18
  early playing career, 29–37, 49–50
  early years in baseball (childhood), 9, 11–12, 14, 15, 18, 20–21, 22, 23
  education, 17–18, 22–23
  80th birthday, 344
  end of Yankee career, 224–26
  endorsements/advertisements, 135–37, 149–50, 169, 209, 216–17, 264, 324–25, 337–38, 345
  eyeglass episode, 191–92
  famous lines, 199–200, 207, 218, 285–86, 347
  father's death, 220
  film about, 337
  financial security, 135–36, 150
  fired as Mets manager, 294–95
  fired as Yankees manager, 253–56, 316–17
  first full year in Major League Baseball, 78
  first grand-slam home run, 76
  first player to have an agent, 135–37
  first Yankee to re-sign, 193
  football, 12–13, 15
  grandchildren, 344
  and harmonica incident, 242–44, 246, 265
  as highest-paid catcher, 140, 161, 175, 182
  on hitting, 141
  home in Bergen County, New Jersey, 142–43
  home in Montclair, New Jersey, 205, 278–80, 304–5, 344–45
  home in St. Louis, Missouri, 3–18, 76–77, 119, 122–23, 182, 342, 347–48
  home-run record broken, 306
  home-run records, 178, 192, 193, 196, 201, 217

  honorary degrees, 328–29, 347, 348
  honors and awards, 121, 147–48, 158, 161–62, 166–67, 201–2
  illnesses, 76, 78, 81, 83, 109, 207
  injuries, 15, 109, 118–19, 143–44, 153, 189, 192, 194, 220
  in Italy, 203–5
  in Japan, 157–58, 175
  lawsuit against Turner Broadcasting System, 344
  in left field, 207
  legacy of, 331–48
  literary career, 153, 215–16, 221, 286, 323, 327, 329, 339, 342
  love of golf, 158–59, 161, 171, 253, 269, 292, 304–5, 317, 319, 322
  love of sports, 14–15, 18
  managing career, 98, 227–56, 270–95, 297, 309–17
  marriage, 85–87
  Mets manager, 270–95, 297
  mother's death, 200–201
  mother's illness, 133
  movie debut, 218–19
  "Mr. Yoo-hoo," 171–73, 209, 216–17, 324–25, 231, 304
  MVP awards, 121, 147–48, 161–62, 166–67
  naval service, 37, 39–50
  No. 8 retired, 276–77
  off-season jobs, 149–50
  Old-Timers' games at Yankee Stadium, 263, 265, 276–77
  outfield, moves to, 217–18
  parents emigration to America, 3
  personal appearances, 135, 136, 139, 149, 169–70, 183, 190, 216, 328
  play about, 342–43
  as player/coach, 222, 258, 260
  playing career with Mets, 257–95
  playing career with Yankees, 33, 34, 35–37, 49–226
  public speaking, 201–2
  radio shows, 169, 196
  relationship with father, 22–24
  released from Yankees, 227
  remarks about his looks, 71–75
  retirement as player, 229
  retirement from coaching, 322
  retires as catcher, 217
  sandlot baseball games, 11–12, 14, 33
  signal-calling incident, 111–13
  signing bonus issue, 31–32, 33, 35
  soccer, 14, 21–22
  son traded to Yankees, 315–16
  Sportsman of the Year Award, 234
  St. Louis University commencement address, 347–48
  television appearances, 139, 149, 155, 156, 169, 176, 182, 192, 205, 210
  as third baseman, 206
  300 Club (home runs), 201
  thriftiness, 35–36, 71
  toy likeness of, 209, 234

2,000<sup>th</sup> major league game, 221
William J. Slocum Memorial Award, 265
working career, 23–27, 33, 83, 122–23, 138–39, 149–50
World Series, 77–81, 121, 132–33, 154–55, 157, 164–66, 193, 197, 210–13, 219–20, 222, 224, 249–52, 290–91, 300–301, 303–4, 305, 307
Yankees coach, 298–307
Yankees manager, 227–56, 309–17
Yogi Berra Day, 201–2, 337
Yogi Berra, Inc., 323–29
Yogi Berra Night, 76–77
"Yogi" nickname, 27
and Yoo-hoo Beverage Company, 171–73, 209, 216–17, 231, 304
Berra, Michael (brother), 5, 10, 15, 16, 18, 22, 33
Berra, Paulina (mother), 3, 4–5, 6, 8, 13, 16, 24, 25, 33, 35, 39–40, 47, 119, 133, 182, 200–201
Berra, Pietro (father), 3–8, 9, 10, 13–14, 17–18, 22–23, 24, 83, 182, 202–3, 220
Berra, Timothy Thomas "Tim" (son), 202, 213, 222, 277, 279, 280, 297, 304, 326
Berraisms, 90, 149, 202, 286, 329, 339
Bevens, Bill, 79
Billhartz, Cynthia, 11
Black Sox scandal of 1919, 319
Blades, Ray, 65
Blanchard, Johnny, 199, 211, 225, 241
Blue, Vida, 290, 319
Bodie, Gary, 37, 39
Bolger, Ray, 121
Boone, Ray, 144
Boston Braves, 101, 153
Boston Red Sox, 37, 62, 95, 96, 109, 110, 116, 119, 128, 131, 144, 154, 178, 194, 195, 244, 305, 347
Boswell, Ken, 268
Boudreau, Lou, 118
Bouton, Jim, 172, 235–36, 238, 241, 242, 248, 250, 251
bowling, 183–84, 216, 221, 338
boxing, 19–20
Boyer, Clete, 240, 241, 262
Boyer, Ken, 264
Bragan, Bobby, 194
Branca, Ralph, 78, 136, 145, 332
Brecheen, Harry, 223
Bressound, Eddie, 264
Bridwell, Al, 26
Bristol, Dave, 304
Brooklyn Dodgers, 34, 37, 62, 66, 101, 110, 129, 145, 153, 158
  in 1947 World Series, 77–81
  in 1949 World Series, 119–21
  in 1952 World Series, 154–55
  in 1953 World Series, 156–57
  in 1955 World Series, 164–66, 324
  in 1956 World Series, 178–81
Brooklyn Dodgers (football team), 134
*Brooklyn Eagle,* 80
Brosnan, Jim, 215

Brown, Bobby, 56–57, 60, 66, 68, 76, 85, 87, 154, 170
Browne, Leo, 29–30, 33
Buck, Jack, 342
Buhner, Jay, 315
Bunning, Jim, 172, 191, 195–96
Burge, Les, 58, 59
Burgess, Smoky, 210
Burnes, Bob, 30
Busch, August "Augie," 247, 253
Busch Stadium, St. Louis, 250, 251
Buvasi, Buzzie, 158
Byrne, Tommy, 91

Cabell, Enos, 319
Camel Cigarettes, 209
Campanella, Roy, 110, 117, 119, 120–21, 136, 138, 140, 147, 153, 156, 158, 166, 176, 181, 182, 196–97
Campaneris, Bert, 94
Campanis, Al, 58
Caray, Harry, 85
Carey, Andy, 160
Carleton, Tex, 25
Carrieri, Joe, 141
Carter, Gary, 225
Casey, Hugh, 37, 78
Castillo, Alberto, 336
Causino, Joe, 20, 24, 102
Cavarretta, Phil, 281
CBS radio, 237
CBS television, 156, 192, 205
  controlling interest in Yankees, 245, 248, 249, 288
Cerone, Rick, 310
Cerv, Bob, 210–11
Chambliss, Chris, 300, 303, 304
Chandler, Happy, 75
Chandler, Spud, 60, 78, 106
Chapman, Sam, 37
Chass, Murray, 306
Chicago Cardinals, 280
Chicago Cubs, 26–27, 158, 160–61, 274, 287, 288
Chicago White Sox, 178, 190, 196, 242, 258, 263, 311
Cincinnati Reds, 156, 206, 262, 289–90, 301
  in 1961 World Series, 219–20
Cleveland Indians, 9, 18, 37, 91, 110, 114, 118, 144, 155, 160, 178, 185, 189, 245, 246
Clotworthy, Bob, 158
CNBC, 345
Coates, Jim, 72, 206
cocaine use, 318–19
Cocaterra, Bob, 46
Cochrane, Mickey, 120
Coleman, Jerry, 154, 156, 166, 175, 180, 220, 242, 250, 252, 253
Collins, Joe, 159, 169, 253
Colman, Frank, 60
Colston, Chris, 340–41
Columbia Records, 150
Columbia University, 202
Combs, Earle, 95

Cone, David, 335, 336, 337
Continental Baseball League, 205
Cooper, Walker, 99
Copacabana (nightclub), 186–89
Corriden, John "Lollipop," 133
Cosell, Howard, 260
Costas, Bob, 337
County Stadium, Milwaukee, 197
Cousy, Bob, 136
Covington, Wes, 197
Craig, Roger, 250
Cramer, Richard Ben, 71, 326–27
Creamer, Robert, 103–4, 131
Crespi, Frank "Creepy," 15
Crosetti, Frank, 223, 229, 238, 242, 243
Crystal Billy, 346, 347
Cuban players, first player for Yankees, 245
Curry, Jack, 334
Cuyler, Kiki, 68

Daley, Arthur
    on Berra as Mets manager, 271–72
    on Berra as Yankees manager, 228, 230
    on Berra's playing career, 67, 69–70, 73, 74, 76, 78,
        81, 95, 99, 120, 132, 142, 148, 162, 167, 192,
        202, 212–13, 215
Damn Yankees (musical comedy), 169–70
Daniel, Dan, 100, 141
Dark, Alvin, 176
Davis, Sammy, Jr., 185–87
Davis, Spud, 15
Dawson, James P., 125
Dawson, Jim, 35
Day, Doris, 218
Dean, Daffy, 51
Dean, Dizzy, 15, 51
Detroit Lions, 280
Detroit Tigers, 37, 68, 76, 92–93, 97, 110, 130, 132,
    142, 178, 207–8, 222, 314
Devine, Bing, 266
DeWitt, Charlie, 126–27
Dickey, Bill, 57, 61, 66, 104–7, 120, 140, 154, 225,
    276–77, 322, 327
DiLullo, Lou, 337
DiMaggio, Dom, 37
DiMaggio, Joe
    and Berra's adjustment to right field, 70–71
    death of, 335
    first six-figure contract, 109
    hires agent, 136
    injuries, 72, 83, 146
    MVP awards, 166
    Oakland A's coach, 268
    playing career with Yankees, 61, 66, 84, 95, 97, 98,
        104, 117, 142, 166, 202, 226, 238
    revenue from sports memorabilia, 326, 328
    salary, 109, 138, 140, 150
    World Series, 78, 80, 81, 146
    Yankees spring-training coach, 233
Dobson, Joe, 95

Doby, Larry, 117, 118, 136, 160, 162, 190, 332
Dodger Stadium, Los Angeles, 224
Doerr, Bobby, 97, 116, 117
Doubleday, Nelson, 320
Downing, Al, 250, 251
Drebinger, John
    on Berra as Yankees manager, 228
    on Berra's playing career, 68, 127, 131, 158, 199,
        207, 218
Dressen, Charlie, 69
drugs, illegal, 318–19
Drysdale, Don, 69, 201, 325
Dubiel, Walt, 53
Duren, Ryne, 93, 216
Durocher, Leo, 15, 66, 161, 162, 247
Durso, Joseph, 266, 292

Eastern Baseball League, 29
Ebbets Field, Brooklyn, NY, 79, 117, 165, 178, 181
Edmonds (baseball team), 20–21, 22
Edwards, Bruce, 120
Effrat, Louis, 60, 61, 92, 189–90, 210
Ellis Island, immigration station on, 1–2, 3
endorsements/advertisements, 135–37, 149–50, 169,
    209, 216–17, 264, 324–27, 337–38, 345
Ennis, Del, 132
Erskine, Carl, 270
ESPN, 134, 225
Europe, baseball in, 203–4
Evers, Johnny, 26

Farrar, Margaret, 138
Farrell, Jackie, 149
Fear Strikes Out (Piersall), 195
Feeney, Chub, 161
Feller, Bob, 136, 150
Fenway Park, Boston, 119, 154
Ferdenzi, Til, 221
Ferrick, Tom, 115
Fingers, Rollie, 290
Finley, Charles O., 268
Fitzgerald, Ed, 215
Flaherty, John, 207
Flores, Jesse, 60
Florida Marlins, 342
Foli, Tim, 315
football, 12–13, 15, 136, 297
Ford, Edward Charles "Whitey," 61–62, 179, 186, 187,
    209, 332
    and Berra as manager, 230, 244, 255, 256
    and Berra's return to Yankee Stadium, 336, 337
    hires agent, 135, 136
    illness, 338
    injuries, 245
    as player/coach, 232–33, 235, 237, 250, 252
    playing career with Yankees, 115, 129, 130, 144,
        147, 155, 164, 165
    practical jokes, 36, 220–21
    retires as player, 265
    World Series, 164, 165

Ford, Gerald, 304
Fosse, Ray, 290
Fox, Nellie, 157, 175
Fox, Tim, 4, 9
Foxx, Jimmie, 166
Francis, Arlene, 323
Francona, Terry, 347
Franks, Herman, 59
Frawley, William, 121
Fregosi, Jim, 273, 274, 281
Frey, Lonny, 86
Frick, Ford, 201, 218, 258
Friend, Bob, 210
Frisch, Frankie, 15, 51, 228, 230
Frommer, Harvey, 166
Furillo, Carl, 78, 157, 270

Gambaro, Lino, 8
Gambaro, Stefano and Anna, 8
Garagiola, Adele, 10
Garagiola, Angelina, 5, 58
Garagiola, Audrie Rose, 85, 122
Garagiola, Giovanni, 4, 5, 7, 14, 58
Garagiola, Joe, 139–40, 190, 191, 206, 211, 257, 270,
    277, 291, 342, 347
  Berra as "the last of the playing umpires," 91
  on Berra's boxing career, 19, 20
  Berra's enagagement and wedding, 85–86
  on Berra's hitting ability, 69
  on Berra's sensitivity, 84, 74
  on Berra's "Yogi" nickname, 27
  broadcasting career, 161, 162–63, 200, 250, 260,
    344
  with Cardinals, 30–31, 32–33, 50, 51, 57–58,
    62–63, 68, 83–84, 108, 129, 142
  with Cubs, 160–61
  early childhood, 8, 9, 10, 11, 12, 13, 14–15, 16,
    17, 19, 20, 21
  early playing career, 29–31, 34
  early years in baseball (childhood), 9, 11, 12, 13,
    20–21, 22, 23–24, 26
  with Giants, 161
  injuries, 15
  interest in broadcasting, 129
  Joe Garagiola Night, 57–58, 76
  marriage, 122
  personal appearances, 231, 234
  with Pirates, 160
Garagiola, Mickey, 6, 7, 10, 58, 122
Garagnani, Julius "Biggie," 84
Garcia, Mike, 157
Garroway, Dave, 149
Garver, Ned, 148
Gaynor, Sydney, 119
Gazzara, Ben, 342–43
Gehrig, Lou, 104, 105, 109, 181, 238
Gelb, Arthur, 169–70
Geller, Max A., 216, 217
Gentry, Gary, 268
Gernert, Dick, 192

Gibson, Bob, 250, 251, 252
Gibson, Josh, 276
Gifford, Frank, 136, 213
Gilliam, Jim, 179
Gimbels (department store), 209
Gionfriddo, Al, 79, 80
Girardi, Joe, 335
Giuliani, Rudy, 331
Gleason, Jackie, 211
Gleeson, James "Gee Gee," 48, 49, 231
Glenn, Joe, 48
Golenbock, Peter, 187, 239, 240, 242, 255, 285, 286
golf, 158–59, 161, 171, 253, 269, 292, 304–5, 317,
    319, 322
Gomez, Lefty, 105, 276
Gore, Artie, 59
Gossage, Goose, 311, 313
Graham, Frank, 103
Grange, Red, 135
Grant, Cary, 218
Grant, M. Donald, 259, 266–67, 271, 282, 284, 286,
    293, 294
Great Depression, 6, 7, 17
Griffey, Ken, 313, 316
Gross, Milton, 147
Grote, Jerry, 268, 284
Groton, Connecticut, 47–48
Groton Raiders, 48–49

Hahn, Christopher, 84, 345
Hahn, Don, 281
Halberstam, David
  on Berra as manager, 236, 249, 252
  on Berra's playing career, 97–98, 102, 103, 111,
    112, 113, 116, 117, 119, 135
Hallahan, Bill, 15
Hamey, Roy, 138–39, 227, 229
Hamlisch, Marvin, 346, 347
Harrelson, Bud, 268, 272, 284, 289, 290
Harridge, William, 276
Harris, Bucky, 66, 67, 68, 69–70, 72, 73, 74, 78, 79,
    80, 81, 89, 90–91, 98, 100, 103, 178
Harris, Mickey, 95
*Hartford Courant,* 347
Hartnett, Gabby, 178
Hasel, Joe, 228
Hatten, Joe, 78
Hawks (sports club), 11, 15
Heath, Jeff, 76
Hegan, Jim, 119, 229
Hemingway, Ernest, 301–2
Henderson, Rickey, 316
Henrich, Tommy, 61, 66, 78, 80, 90, 95, 98, 100,
    113–14, 238
Hermanski, Gene, 81
Hernandez, Keith, 319
Herzog, Whitey, 128, 272
Heusser, Ed, 25
Hirshberg, Al, 195
Hirshey, Dave, 289

hockey, 10, 84, 148, 305
Hodges, Gil, 136, 149, 156, 179, 208, 258
    death of, 269–70
    difference between Berra and, 285
    Mets manager, 266–67, 268
Hofman, Bobby, 26, 27, 108, 268
Hofman, Circus Solly, 26
Holcombe, Ken, 59
Holmes, J.G. Tom, 43
Holtzman, Ken, 290, 291
Honig, Donald, 272
Honochick, Jim, 222
Hope, Bob, 121
Hornsby, Rogers, 51
Horton, Tom, 323
Houk, Ralph, 66, 95, 102, 180, 213, 219, 225, 258
    and Berra as Yankees manager, 227–28, 232, 234,
        235, 239, 240, 242, 243–44, 247–48, 249,
        251
    and Yankees firing of Berra, 253, 258, 260
    as Yankees manager, 255, 261, 265, 288
Houston Astros, 320, 321–22
Houston, Maureen, 84, 180
Howard, Elston, 163, 176, 182–83, 186–87, 194,
    197, 199, 206, 207, 210, 211, 225, 231, 298, 300,
    301, 307
Hubbard, Cal, 91–92
Huggins, Miller, 109, 290
Hunter, Catfish, 290, 291, 294, 301
Hunter, Julius, 347
Hurley, Ed, 143
Hutchinson, Freddie, 37

immigration, New York Harbor, 1–3
International League, 50, 53, 55, 58, 66
Irvin, Monte, 145
Issacs, Stan, 179, 254
Italian immigrants, 3–6, 21
Italy, baseball in, 203–4

Jackson, Reggie, 290, 302–3, 328, 334
Japan, 157–58, 175
Jensen, Jackie, 157
Jeter, Derek, 335, 340, 345, 346
Joe DiMaggio: A Hero's Life (Cramer), 71, 326–27
John XXIII, Pope, 204
Johnson, Billy, 78, 98
Johnson, Earl, 95, 131
Jones, Cleon, 268, 274, 281, 284, 285, 293–94
Jones, Edwin, 187, 189
Jorgensen, Johnny, 58
Juelich, Jack, 15

Kahn, Roger, 138
Kain, Shaky, 36
Kaline, Al, 166, 219
Kansas City Athletics, 190, 205, 224, 245, 300
Kansas City Blues, 48
Kansas City Royals, 303
Kaplan, Dave, 342

Karpel, Herb, 59
Keane, Johnny, 247–48, 253–54, 255, 261, 263, 265
Keene, Kerry, 141, 150
Keller, Charlie, 60, 66, 72, 74, 97, 98, 99, 238
Kellert, Frank, 165
Kemp, Steve, 311, 315
Kernan, Kevin, 345
Kiernan, Walter, 169
Kiner, Ralph, 150
King, Clyde, 311, 317, 320
Kinnamon, Bill, 94
KMOX radio, 51
Konstanty, Jim, 132
Koosman, Jerry, 268, 271, 272, 284, 287
Koppett, Leonard, on Berra's playing career, 74, 236,
    237–38, 244, 245, 254, 260, 269
Korean War, 155–56
Koslo, Dave, 146
Koufax, Sandy, 224, 270, 276
Kranepool, Eddie, 268
Kreuscher, Eugene, 324, 325
Krichell, Paul, 49–50, 61
Kubek, Tony, 240, 241, 250, 254, 262
Kucks, Johnny, 186, 187
Kuhn, Bowie, 309

La Lorraine (steamer ship), 2–3
La Russa, Tony, 290
Laclede-Christy Clay Products Company, St. Louis, 4, 7
Lacy, Lee, 319
Landis, Kenesaw Mountain, 25
Lang, Jack, 284
Lanier, Hal, 320, 322
Lanktree, Nova, 338
Lardner, Ring, 72
Larsen, Don, 115, 152, 179–81, 205, 225, 328, 337
Lasorda, Tommy, 310
Lauro, Patricia Winters, 136, 326, 338
Leahy, Frank, 280
Lemon, Bob, 157, 162, 301, 305, 314
Leonard, Buck, 276
Leonard, Jeffrey, 319
Lepcio, Ted, 189
Levy, Alan, 333
Lindell, Johnny, 74, 80, 97, 98, 99
Linz, Phil, 238, 240, 242–43, 244, 246, 249, 250, 262,
    265, 272, 311
Lipsky, Robert, 74, 208–9, 230–31, 249, 266–67
Litsky, Frank, 135
Little Creek, Virginia, 40, 47
Lollar, Sherman, 66, 79, 95, 194, 225
Lombardi, Vince, 136
Lopat All-Stars, 157–58
Lopat, Eddie, 97–98, 112, 114, 115, 118, 157, 183,
    253
Lopez, Al, 120, 258
Los Angeles Angels, 224
Los Angeles Dodgers, 224, 303, 310
LTD Enterprises, 326–27, 329, 338
Lucas, Ed, 164, 165

Lupica, Mike, 181, 317–18, 336
Lysaght, Tom, 342, 343

Mack, Connie, 81, 196
Mack, Jimmy, 55
MacPhail, Larry, 34, 49, 50, 57, 61, 66, 245
Macy's (department store), 215–16, 247
Madden, Bill, 317
Maglie, Sal, 178, 192
*Magnificent Yankees, The* (Meany), 153
Maguire, Jack, 129
Major League Baseball
    Berra's first full year in, 78
    Berra's 2,000th major league game, 221
Major League Baseball All-Century team, 338
Major League Baseball in Europe, 204
Manager of the Year award, 291
managers, baseball
    Berra as Mets manager, 270–95, 297
    Berra as Yankees manager, 227–56
    first to win World Series with two teams, 81
Mantle, Mickey, 146, 175, 186, 187, 224, 226
    on Berra and Stengel, 104
    and Berra as manager, 230, 234, 239–40, 242, 243,
        244, 255
    death of, 328
    drinking exploits, 179, 219
    endorsements, 136, 137, 170
    hires agent, 135, 136
    injuries, 233, 245, 262
    MVP award, 182
    personal appearances, 210
    playing career with Yankees, 142, 152, 154, 155,
        157, 159, 160, 190, 194, 196, 208–9, 210,
        217, 222, 224, 238, 247, 250, 251, 252
    practical jokes, 36, 221, 238
    revenue from sports memorabilia, 326, 328
    and Ruth's home-run record, 218
    and Timmy Berra, 222
    World Series, 155
Mapes, Cliff, 116
Marciano, Rocky, 169
Mariani, Frank, 19
Maris, Roger, 136, 205, 209, 218, 236, 242, 251,
    320–21
Markusen, Bruce, 281, 293
Marshall, Clarence, 90
Marshall, Willard, 99
Martin, Alfred Manuel "Billy," 141, 181, 183–84, 284
    and Copacabana incident, 186–89
    playing career with Yankees, 104, 128, 155, 157,
        166
    traded to Kansas City A's, 190
    Yankees manager, 294, 298–300, 301, 302–3, 305,
        306, 309, 316, 317, 320
Martin, Pepper, 65
Martin, Stu, 15
Matheson, Tyler, 345
Matlack, Jon, 272, 284, 289, 290, 291, 295
Matthews, Wid, 160

Mattingly, Don, 313, 316, 337
Mauch, Gene, 291, 294
Mauch, Gus, 118
Mayor's Trophy, 99
Mays, Willie, 136, 162, 273–74, 275–76, 280, 281–83,
    287, 288, 290
Mazeroski, Bill, 212
Mazzilli, Lee, 319
McCarthy, Joe, 53, 131
McCarver, Tim, 251
McCulley, Jim, 60
McDougald, Gil, 149, 155, 166, 185, 194–95
McGowen, Roscoe, 89, 126
McGraw, John, 101
McGraw, Tug, 268, 281, 283, 284, 285, 286, 287,
    288, 290
McGuire, Jack, Jr., 27, 32
McKinley, Bill, 92–93
McMillan, Roy, 294, 295
McMullen, John J., 320, 345
McQuinn, George, 100
Meany, Tom, 120, 153
Medwick, Joe "Ducky," 15, 25–26, 51, 70, 86
Merkle, Fred, 26–27
Mexican League, 120
Meyer, Billy, 55
Mikkelsen, Pete, 240
Miksis, Eddie, 80
Milan, Felix, 281
Miller, Marvin, 284
Miller, Norm, 241
Milner, John, 281, 284, 318
Milwaukee Braves, 192–93, 197
Milwaukee Brewers, 102
Minoso, Minnie, 162
Mize, Johnny, 51, 99, 117, 132, 155
Modowar, John, 216
Montclair, New Jersey, Berra's home in, 205, 278–80,
    304–5, 344–45
Montclair State College, 278
Montclair State University, 328–29
    softball stadium, 344
    Yogi Berra Museum, 332, 335, 338
    Yogi Berra Stadium, 331–32
Montefusco, John, 317
Montreal Expos, 272, 286, 291
Montreal Royals, 58–59
Moore, Johnny, 59
Moore, Terry, 15, 51
Most Valuable Player (MVP) awards, 81, 121, 146,
    147–48, 161–62, 166–67, 182, 231
Mozley, Dana, 166, 180
Munger, Red, 108
Mungo, Van, 25
Munson, Thurman, 300, 303
Murrow, Edward R., 156
Murtaugh, Danny, 210, 212
Murti, Sweeny, 346
Musial, Stan, 51, 84, 117, 122, 159–60, 164, 166, 182,
    185, 190–91, 201, 234

Mussina, Mike, 341
Mustaikis, Alex, 59
*My Favorite Summer 1956* (Mantle), 179

Nashua Dodgers, 120
National Baseball Hall of Fame, 276, 278, 306
NBC television, 149, 169, 176, 250
Needell, Paul, 316
Negro Leagues, 120
Nettles, Graig, 303, 313
New England League, 120
New Jersey Devils, 305
New Jersey Jackals, 331
*New York Daily News*
    on Berra as Astros coach, 321
    on Berra as Yankees coach, 300
    on Berra as Yankees manager, 228, 234, 241, 246,
        254, 309, 313
    on Berra's playing career with Mets, 257, 266
    on Berra's playing career with Yankees, 60, 72,
        127, 145, 147, 157, 162, 164, 166, 180, 188,
        210, 218
New York Football Giants, 148, 155, 216, 297, 302
New York Giants (baseball), 26–27, 49, 101, 108, 117,
    129, 145, 161
    in 1951 World Series, 145–46
*New York Herald-Tribune,* 73
New York Mets, 101, 165, 220, 233, 244, 322, 336
    Berra as manager, 270–95, 297
    Berra as player/coach, 257–95
    Berra fired as manager, 294–95
    death of manager Hodges, 269–70
    injuries, 274, 284, 289, 293
    1965 season, 260–63
    1966 season, 264–65
    1967 season, 266–68
    1968 season, 268
    1969 season, 268–69
    1970–71 seasons, 269
    1972 season, 269–76
    1973 season, 280–92
    in 1973 World Series, 290–91
    1974 season, 291–93
    1975 season, 293–95
*New York Post,* 286, 287, 288, 344, 345
New York Rangers, 148
*New York Times,* 342
    on Berra as Mets manager, 288
    on Berra as Yankees manager, 246, 254
    on Berra's playing career, 60, 67, 73, 76, 90, 103,
        105, 136, 138, 142, 158, 169, 172, 188, 189,
        211
*New York Times Book Review,* 215
*New York World Telegram,* 100, 120
New York Yankees, 49
    Berra as coach, 298–307
    Berra as face of the, 339–41
    Berra as manager, 227–56, 309–17
    Berra as player/coach, 222–24, 260
    Berra fired as manager, 253–56, 316–17

Berra released from Yankees, 227
Berra's playing career with, 33, 34, 35–37, 49–226
Berra's son traded to, 315–16
CBS television and controlling interest in, 245,
    248, 249, 288
Copacabana incident, 186–89
exhibition games, 66–67, 208
first African American player, 163–64
first Cuban player, 245
harmonica incident, 242–44, 246, 265
minor league team of, 50, 51, 53–59
Most Valuable Player (MVP) awards, 81, 121, 146,
    147–48, 161–62, 166–67
musical comedy about, 169–70
night games, 65–66
in 1942 World Series, 33
1947 season, 65–81
in 1947 World Series, 77–81
1948 season, 89–100
1949 season, 105–23
in 1949 World Series, 119–21
1950 season, 125–37
in 1950 World Series, 132–33
1951 season, 137–47
in 1951 World Series, 145–46
1952 season, 152–55
in 1952 World Series, 154–55
1953 season, 155–57
in 1953 World Series, 156–57
1954 season, 158–60, 161–62
1955 season, 163–67
in 1955 World Series, 164–66
1956 season, 175–82
in 1956 World Series, 178–81
1957 season, 185–93
1958 season, 193–97
1959 season, 199–203
1960 season, 205–13
in 1960 World Series, 210–13
1961 season, 217–20
1962 season, 220–22
in 1962 World Series, 222
1963 season, 222–24, 227–31, 233
in 1963 World Series, 224
1964 season, 232–56
in 1964 World Series, 249–52
1965 season, 261, 262
1976 season, 298–301
1977 season, 301–5
in 1977 World Series, 303–4
1978–79 seasons, 305–6
1980 season, 306–7
1983 season, 309
1984 season, 313–14
1985 season, 314
*New Yorker, The* magazine, 323
Newark Athletic Club, 158
Newark Bears, 50, 51, 53–59
Newcombe, Don, 69, 117, 119, 120, 181, 270
*Newsday,* 179, 254

Newsom, Bobo, 78
Niarhos, Gus, 66, 89, 95, 98, 102, 103, 109, 157
no-hitters, 145, 148
*Nobody Don't Look Like Yogi* (play), 342–43
Noren, Irv, 160
Norfolk Air Station (baseball team), 37
Norfolk Tars, 33, 68
Norfolk, Virginia, 34–37, 40
Northern League, 331

Oakland Athletics, 268, 290–91, 340
Oakland Oaks, 102
Olbermann, Keith, 43, 47
Olivieri, Albert V., 216, 312
Olivieri, Natale, 171
O'Neill, Paul, 182, 340
O'Neill, Steve, 68, 119
Orsatti, Ernie, 15
Ott, Mel, 49, 57
Owen, Marv, 25

Pacific Coast League, 49, 102
Padgett, Don, 37
Page, Joe, 78, 121
Paley, Bill, 249
Paparella, Joe, 116–17
Parker, Dave, 319
Parker, Salty, 266
Patterson, Red, 130, 148
Paul, Gabe, 299, 303
Payson, Joan Whitney, 271, 288, 297
*People* magazine, 315, 319
Pepe, Phil, 149, 280, 286, 288, 291, 299, 307, 313, 321
Pepitone, Joe, 238, 240–41, 242, 243, 251, 261
perfect game, Larsen's, 179–81, 225, 332
Pesky, Johnny, 116, 117
Philadelphia Athletics, 60, 144, 154, 160
Philadelphia Phillies, 132–33, 265
Phillips, Jack, 59, 109
Piazza, Mike, 336, 340
Piedmont League, 33
Piersall, Jimmy, 195
Pignatano, Joe, 269, 270, 286
Pinelli, Babe, 180
Piniella, Lou, 313, 320, 322
Pittsburgh Pirates, 15, 60, 101, 160, 274, 315
    in 1960 World Series, 210–13
    drug use among, 318–19
Pius XII, Pope, 46
Player of the Year Award, 158
Podres, Johnny, 165, 166
Post, Paul, 164, 165
Povich, Shirley, 137
Pratt, Todd, 336
Price, Walter, 11
Pucci, Ben, 10
Pulido, Alfonso, 315
Pyle, C.C. "Cash–and–Carry," 135

Rackley, Marv, 58
racquetball, 304
radio shows, 196–97, 228
Raines, Larry, 189
Raines, Tim, 319
Ramos, Pedro, 245, 246
Randolph, Willie, 165, 311
Raschi, Vic, 59, 60, 61, 66, 78, 110–11, 112, 113, 114, 116, 126, 127, 132, 143, 144, 159, 238
*Reader's Digest,* 73, 87
Red River Valley Potato Growers Association, 319
Reese, Pee Wee, 78, 79, 119, 179, 181, 197, 219, 270
Reichler, Joseph, 260
Reiser, Pete, 78, 86
Rennie, Rud, 73
Reynolds, Allie, 66, 78, 98, 110–12, 113–14, 115, 144, 145, 147, 148, 156–57, 238
Reynolds, Carl, 105
Reynolds, Quinton, 67
Rheingold Beer, 151
Rice, Grantland, 161
Rice, Jim, 302
Richards, Paul, 210
Richardson, Bobby, 87, 205, 210, 241, 242, 250, 252, 254
Rickey, Branch, 30, 31–32, 34, 55, 142, 205
Righetti, Dave, 313
Rigney, Bill, 237
Rivera, Mariano, 340, 341
Riverfront Stadium, Cincinnati, 289
Rivers, Mickey, 304
Rizzuto, Cora, 345, 346
Rizzuto, Patricia, 346
Rizzuto, Philip Francis, 37, 61, 66, 67, 99, 129, 154, 155, 165, 170, 277
    as advisor to Berra, 149, 150, 170
    baseball academy, 147
    Baseball Hall of Fame induction, 327–28
    on Berra and signal-calling incident, 112–13
    on Berra's career statistics, 306–7
    and Berra's career with Yankees, 90, 95, 96, 97, 225
    on Berra's sensitivity, 74
    broadcasting career, 177–78, 183, 250, 260
    business ventures, 183–84, 221
    charities, 216
    death of, 345–46
    50th wedding anniversary, 327
    friendship between Berra and, 122, 133–34, 143, 150, 151–52
    MVP award, 149
    released from Yankees, 176–77
    salary, 138
    World Series, 78, 79
Rizzuto-Berra Lanes (bowling), 184, 221, 338
R.J.R. Nabisco, 197
Roberts, Robin, 157, 169
Robertson, Oscar, 136
Robinson, Aaron, 66, 225
Robinson, Eddie, 37

Robinson, Jackie, 58, 77–78, 117, 119, 129, 147, 155, 164–65, 169, 179, 181, 197, 270
Roger Williams College, 347
Rookie of the Year award, 272
Rosar, Buddy, 60
Rose, Pete, 231, 289
Roswell, Gene, 20, 73, 74, 106, 152, 216
Rote, Kyle, 228
Ruggeri's Restaurant, St. Louis, 10, 122–23, 138–39, 200
Ruppert, Jacob, 54–55
Ruth, Babe, 54, 75, 99, 100, 104, 109, 218, 226, 341
Ryan, Nolan, 268, 321
Ryba, Mike, 72

Safire, William, 311
Sain, Johnny, 229, 232
St. Louis Browns, 10, 37, 76, 99–100, 118, 119, 126–27, 148, 154
St. Louis Cardinals, 50–51, 55, 65, 78, 247, 261, 287
    Garagiola with, 30–31, 32–33, 50, 51, 57–58, 62–63, 68, 83–84, 108, 129, 142
    Gashouse Gang, 25, 51
    Knothole Gang, 15
    in 1964 World Series, 249–52
St. Louis Flyers, 10, 84
St. Louis Globe-Democrat, 16, 25, 30
St. Louis, Missouri, Berra home in, 3–18, 76–77, 119, 122–23, 182, 342, 347–48
St. Louis Post-Dispatch, 11, 16, 25, 337, 339, 347
St. Louis University, 15, 17, 347–48

Samelson, Ken, 274
San Diego Padres, 287, 313
San Francisco Giants, 222, 275
sandlot baseball, 11–12, 14, 33
Sandomir, Richard, 324, 325
Sandowski, Josephine Berra (sister), 182, 200, 337, 342
Saturday Evening Post, 137
Sauer, Hank, 158
Scarborough, Ray, 73
Schalk, Ray, 225
Schoendienst, Red, 51, 258
Schoor, Gene, 6, 11, 46, 71, 85, 151
Schulte, John C. "Johnny," 33, 305
Schultz, Barney, 250
Score, Herb, 185
Scott, Frank, 87, 134–37, 329
Scott, Mike, 321
Scripps-Howard News Service, 131
Scully, Vin, 251
Scurry, Rod, 319
Seattle Mariners, 341
Seaver, Tom, 268, 281, 282, 289, 290, 291, 294, 311
Seidel, Michael, 95–96
Selkirk, George "Twinkletoes," 53–54, 56, 58, 59, 268
Seminick, Andy, 132
Sex and the City (TV series), 344
Shamsky, Art, 268–69
Shapiro, Milton, 71, 89–90, 103

Shaughnessy, Frank, 59
Shea, Frank, 67, 99, 122
Shea, Spec, 78
Shea Stadium, Queens, NY, 244, 262, 287, 288, 289, 290, 291, 294
Sheffing, Bob, 281, 283, 284
Sheldon, Rollie, 240
Shor, Toots, 158, 177, 183, 211, 301–2
Short, Barbara Ellen (mother-in-law), 338–39
Short, Bill, 206
Siebern, Norm, 195
sign stealing, 195–96
signal calling, 111–13
Silvera, Charlie, 66, 95, 102, 118, 119–20, 157, 169, 180, 182–83, 225
Simmons, Curt, 157, 250
Sinatra, Frank, 278–79
Skowron, Moose, 72, 160, 191, 209, 216, 217, 224
Slaughter, Enos, 51, 157, 177, 196
Slocum, Frank, 212
Smith, Al, 166
Smith, Lonnie, 319
Smith, Red, 138, 206, 270
Snider, Duke, 119, 136, 157, 159–60, 179, 208
Soar, Hank, 92, 159
soccer, 14, 21–22, 204
Spahn, Warren, 261
Sporting News, The, 138, 201
Sports Illustrated, 169, 215, 274, 312
sports memorabilia, 325, 326–27, 328
Sportsman of the Year Award, 234
Sportsman's Park, St. Louis, 30, 57–58, 62, 99, 127
sportswriters, 89–90, 99, 103–4, 125, 128
Stags A.C. (baseball team), 11, 12, 15–16, 17, 20–22, 342
Stanky, Eddie, 80, 263
Stanton, Donald, 255
Stark, Jayson, 225–26
Starr, Dick, 118
Statue of Liberty, 3
Statue of Liberty–Ellis Island Foundation, Inc., 2
Staub, Rusty, 231, 272, 274, 281, 284, 287, 289
Steinbrenner, George, 288, 298, 299–300, 302, 303, 305, 306, 310, 314, 316, 318, 322, 331, 332–34, 338
Steiner, Brandon, 325
Stengel, Charles Dillon "Casey," 16–17, 98, 228, 273
    death of, 297
    Mets manager, 220, 233, 234, 236, 257, 260–61, 263
    Yankees fire, 213
    Yankees 1949 season, 101–2, 103–4, 105, 106, 107, 109, 111, 112, 115, 117–19, 121
    Yankees 1950 season, 127, 128, 130–31, 134
    Yankees 1951 season, 143
    Yankees 1952 season, 153
    Yankees 1954 season, 160
    Yankees 1955 season, 163, 170
    Yankees 1956 season, 175–76, 176
    Yankees 1957 season, 185, 188, 190

Yankees 1958 season, 194, 196, 197
Yankees 1959 season, 199, 202, 203
Yankees 1960 season, 205, 206, 207, 210–11
Stephens, Junior, 116
Stevens, Marvin A., 67
Stewart-Gordon, James, 279
Stirnweiss, George, 80, 99, 122
Stottlemyre, Mel, 245, 248, 250, 251
Sturdivant, Tom, 176
Sudol, Ed, 265
Sukey, Bill, 36
Sullivan, Ed, 139, 216
Sullivan, Frank, 164
*Summer of '49* (Halberstam), 98, 111
Summers, Bill, 93, 159, 164–65
Sutherland, Jock, 134
Swoboda, Ron, 268

Talese, Gay, 134, 136, 137
Tallmer, Jerry, 343
Tatum, Tom, 59
Tebbetts, Birdie, 96, 110, 118, 131, 140, 156
television, Berra's appearances on, 139, 149, 155, 156,
    169, 176, 182, 192, 205, 210
*Ten Rings* (Berra), 148, 182, 342
Terry, Ralph, 212, 241
*That Touch of Mink* (movie), 218–19
Theodore, George, 281
Thomson, Bobby, 99, 145
Tiger Stadium, Detroit, 207–8
*Time* magazine, 188, 189, 245
Tittle, Y.A., 136
Toots Shor's (restaurant), 158, 177, 183, 211, 301–2
Topping, Dan, 102, 134, 140, 188, 202, 203, 213, 227,
    229, 245, 248, 249
Torborg, Jeff, 309
Torre, Frank, 192
Torre, Joe, 295, 334, 337, 340–41, 346–47
Triandos, Gus, 194
Trimble, Joe
    on Berra as Yankees manager, 228, 246, 251, 254,
        255
    on Berra with Mets, 257
    on Berra's playing career, 72, 127, 145, 147, 148,
        153, 157, 166, 180, 191–92, 218
Tripucka, Frank, 280
Tripucka, Mark, 280
Tripucka, Randy, 280
Trout, Dizzy, 142
Tucci, Anthony, 172
Tucci, Jackie Olivieri, 171, 172
Turley, Bob, 179, 195–96
Turner Broadcasting System, 344

umpires, 91–94
United Press International (UPI), 146, 175, 188
*USA Today,* 323
*USA Today Baseball Weekly,* 340–41

Vecsey, George, 309

Veeck, Bill, 102
Volpe, Ray, 48

WABC radio, 169
WABC–TV, 260
Wagner, Robert, 176
Walker, Dixie, 78
Walker, Rube, 269, 270, 291
*Wall Street Journal,* 172
Walsh, Dee, 30
warning track, 54
Warren, Earl, 211
Washington Elite Giants, 120
Washington Senators, 81, 105, 132, 154, 164, 170,
    194, 258
Webb, Del, 102, 141, 147, 245, 249, 255–56
Weber, Bruce, 342
Weiss, Bill, 54–55
Weiss, George M., 83, 104, 107, 134, 194, 203, 233
    Berra's contract negotiations with, 33, 35, 89,
        102–3, 125–27, 137–38, 140, 148, 150, 158,
        161, 175, 182, 193, 199, 205
    death of, 277
    as Mets general manager, 257, 258–59
    player trades, 190, 205
    releases Rizzuto from Yankees, 176–77
    spying on players, 238
Werber, Bill, 105
Westrum, Wes, 263–64, 265–66
*When You Come to a Fork in the Road, Take It!* (Berra),
    339
White, Bill, 337
White, Roy, 304
White, Sam, 191–92
Wilks, Ted, 108
William J. Slocum Memorial Award, 265
Williams, Bernie, 335
Williams, Joe, 131
Williams, Stan, 238, 262
Williams, Ted, 62, 95–97, 116, 144, 145, 155–56, 202,
    206–7, 332, 342
Willis, Bruce, 328, 329
Wimbish, Ralph, 163
Winfield, Dave, 316
WINS radio, 196–97
wives, baseball, 278
WNEW radio, 228
Wolf, George D., 93
Woodling, Gene, 106, 119, 155, 208
Woods, Jim, 177
Works Progress Administration (WPA), 30
World Series
    historic firsts of 1947 game, 78
    Larsen's perfect game in 1956 World Series, 179–81
    1934, Cardinals vs. Tigers, 25
    1936, Yankees vs. Giants, 105
    1939, Yankees vs. Reds, 105
    1942, Cardinals vs. Yankees, 33
    1946, Cardinals vs. Red Sox, 62
    1947, Yankees vs. Brooklyn Dodgers, 77–81, 196

1949, Yankees vs. Brooklyn Dodgers, 119–21
1950, Yankees vs. Phillies, 132–33
1951, Yankees vs. Giants, 145–46
1952, Yankees vs. Brooklyn Dodgers, 154–55
1953, Yankees vs. Brooklyn Dodgers, 156–57
1954, Giants vs. Indians, 161
1955, Yankees vs. Brooklyn Dodgers, 164–66
1956, Yankees vs. Brooklyn Dodgers, 178–81
1957, Yankees vs. Milwaukee Braves, 192–93
1958, Yankees vs. Milwaukee Braves, 197
1960, Yankees vs. Pirates, 210–13
1961, Yankees vs. Reds, 219–20
1962, Yankees vs. San Francisco Giants, 222
1963, Yankees vs. Los Angeles Dodgers, 224
1964, Cardinals vs. Yankees, 249–52
1973, Mets vs. Oakland A's, 290–91
1976, Yankees vs. Reds, 301
1977, Yankees vs. Los Angeles Dodgers, 303–4
1978, Yankees vs. Los Angeles Dodgers, 305
1981, Yankees vs. Los Angeles Dodgers, 307
1984, Padres vs. Tigers, 314
1999, Yankees vs. Atlanta Braves, 182
2003, Yankees vs. Marlins, 342
World War I, 5
World War II, 34, 39–47, 133, 134
WPIX television, 201, 205
Wright, Marshall, 54–55
Wynn, Early, 276

Yankee Stadium, 61, 76, 79, 87, 99–100, 109, 165–66, 179
    Berra returns to, 335–37
    Berra's refusal to return to, 331, 332–34
    Old-Timers' games at, 196, 263, 265, 276–77
    renovated, 300, 335
    sale of, 245
    Yankees co-tenancy at Shea Stadium, 294
    Yogi Berra Day at, 201–2, 337
Yankeetradition.com, 337
Yatkeman, Butch, 30
Yawkey, Tom, 95, 128
Yogi: It Ain't Over (Berra), 286, 323
Yogi: The Autobiography of a Professional Baseball Player (Berra and Fitzgerald), 215–16
Yogi Bear (cartoon character), 223
Yogi Berra Day, 201–2, 337
Yogi Berra Museum, 332, 335, 338
Yogi Berra Night, 76–77
Yogi Berra Pitching Trainer (toy), 209, 234
Yogi Berra Stadium, 331–32
Yogi Berra Story, The (Roswell), 216
Yogi Berra (Trimble), 153
Yogi Berra's Racquetball Hall of Fame Club, 304
Yogi Book: I Didn't Really Say Everything I Said, The (Berra), 329
Yoo-hoo Beverage Company, 171–73, 209, 216–17, 231, 304, 312, 324–25
Yost, Eddie, 269, 270
Young, Dick
    on Berra as Mets manager, 285
    on Berra's playing career, 162, 167, 181, 184, 197, 210, 212, 260, 262
Youngs, Ross, 276

Zarilla, Al, 116
Zimmer, Don, 309